Jane Drakard

A MALAY FRONTIER:
UNITY AND DUALITY IN
A SUMATRAN KINGDOM

SOUTHEAST ASIA PROGRAM PUBLICATIONS
Southeast Asia Program
Cornell University
Ithaca, New York
1990

Cornell Southeast Asia Program Publications
640 Stewart Avenue, Ithaca, NY 14850-3857

Studies on Southeast Asia No. 7

ISBN 0-87727-706-0

To Barbara Alford

CONTENTS

ILLUSTRATIONS

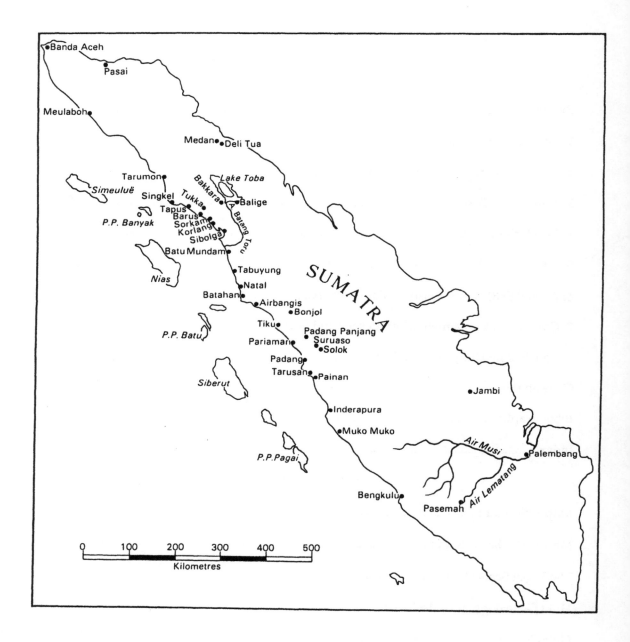

Map 1. Sumatra

PREFACE

A number of recent works on Malay history and culture have developed a theme of cultural unity and structural similarities in the area which is often described as "the Malay world." These studies have contributed to an increased awareness, among historians, of indigenous political categories and motivation. There remains, however, a need to test and refine these categories in local situations which are remote from the major centers of Malay political history. The usefulness of models of, for example, governmental patterns, or *kerajaan*, should not obscure the existence of tensions and variation within Malay culture. The study of local variation may serve to expand our appreciation of a diversity of political experience and to sharpen our perceptions of Malay political behavior.

In particular, it is important to examine Malay cultural and political forms at the point where they interact with other cultures. The study of kingdoms on the fringes of the archipelago may allow an examination of local culture in frontier situations where it comes under stress. Did Malays always absorb outsiders into their cultural and political life, or was the "Malay world" itself capable of adaptation and variation? By concentrating on these issues we may develop our understanding of the applicability and explanatory power of the term "Malay world."

In the following study Malay perceptions of authority and government are explored by means of a comparative reading of two texts from a region on the western frontier of the archipelago. The region in question is Barus on the northwest coast of Sumatra. Barus, it will appear, provides an opportunity to examine issues of authority and political organization in a situation where "Malay world" expectations were tested and challenged. The geographical and historical circumstances of this kingdom provoked issues which were not resolved along the lines of the conventional Malay *kerajaan* and which are explored and seemingly debated in the literature of Barus.

Although Barus was an important early center for resin exports which was visited by foreign merchants over a lengthy period, it lies far from the traditional heartland of Malay civilization. To reach the northwest coast of Sumatra from Melaka or the Riau Lingga archipelago is a lengthy journey by sea, and overland the region is separated from east Sumatra, from the Minangkabau highlands, and from Sumatra's northern tip by difficult and sometimes impenetrable mountains. Between the narrow coastal stretch which was inhabited by Malays and others and was visited by foreign merchants, and the difficult hill country which bordered the coast, and which was inhabited by Batak clans, an essential relationship existed. Interaction between coast and interior has long been recognized as an important feature in Sumatran history, but it is one which has been, as yet, little explored in detail. An examination of relations between hill and coast in Barus experience contributes to our understanding of this interaction. What I shall focus on, above all, is the consequence of this hill-coastal relationship for the character of Malay political culture in Barus.

Of particular importance in Barus was the presence over a lengthy period of two royal families, originating from Batak and Malay antecedents respectively. From time to time this resulted in two kings ruling over what was considered to be a single kingdom. While such an arrangement is not unknown in Malay polities it is certainly not conventional, and the history and literature of Barus opens a window onto what was clearly a tense situation. Within Barus, dual kingship provoked a type of questioning and testing of the nature of political authority and the arrangement of government which is not usually apparent in the better known Malay kingdoms or royal chronicles.

An intertextual approach is central to the methodology employed here. Principally the study focusses upon a close reading of two Malay texts, the royal chronicles of Hilir and Hulu Barus. These, in turn, have been read in the light of other Malay works from Sumatra and the Peninsula. The Malay texts have also been examined against the background of European sources on Barus history which focus upon the central issues of duality and of interaction between Bataks and Malays and between hill and coast. In this way it is hoped to uncover the structures and conceptual framework of two divergent approaches to royal authority and to relate these, in turn, to the wider context of Malay political forms. In its entirety, the study aims to demonstrate the flexibility and creativity of Malay political theorizing and the options available for variation and adaptation within the "Malay world."

The diverse nature of the sources available for a study of dual kingship in Barus raises historiographical problems which should be discussed at the outset. This applies particularly to the use of material from different periods of Barus's past. The Malay texts which are read and discussed in Chapters Three to Eight date from the nineteenth century and, while they refer in large part to an earlier period, they cannot be taken as direct evidence of anything but nineteenth century perceptions. From the mid-seventeenth century onward, however, Dutch sources are available which offer their own perspective on coastal/hinterland relations in Barus and on the tension provoked by the issue of dual kingship. Clearly, without this external view we would know less about the way in which events were seen to unfold in Barus from the seventeenth to the nineteenth century. Contemporary foreign accounts, therefore, provide an intertext against which the Malay sources may be read and which offer a context for understanding them. This does not mean that they hold any absolute objective status as past records, or that their role lies in providing a check on a local historiographical tradition. The Malay and Dutch sources which are read here have not been used to establish a narrative account of what happened in Barus between the seventeenth and nineteenth centuries. Rather, they are each treated as perceptions of the past, in a study where the local, Malay, response is of primary interest.

In Chapters One and Two external records are used to establish a picture of the Barus polity as it appears in European sources. In both chapters the reader will acquire information and insights which will inform the subsequent reading of the Malay texts. Chapter Three introduces the two Malay chronicles, and in Chapters Four to Seven the texts are subjected to close comparative scrutiny. For this purpose, I have chosen an episodic format, in which the narratives are compared episode by episode and conclusions about their structure and content are discussed at the end of each episodic slice. This is inevitably a lengthy process, but one which has the advantage of separating consideration of the chronicles themselves from extraneous, referential, information relating to the non-local, European, intertext. Chapter Eight reconsiders European and Malay sources for Barus and reviews the Barus chronicles in the light of Malay works from other centers and of the political culture of other parts of "the Malay world."

*   *   *

The study is a revised version of an MA thesis which was originally presented in the Department of History at Monash University. There are many people who deserve thanks for their contributions to both the original and the revised form. Among those who helped me in Barus and Sibolga are Nasrul Zahiruddin, Rusdin Tanjung, Teti Rohani Saleh, Dharmeni, Irma and Ina Pasaribu and their family, Bapak Dhamanhuri Sinaga, Chasmir Tanjung, Zainal Arafin Pasaribu, and the Ikatan Keluarga Besar Pesisir Tapanuli Tengah "Fansuri" in Jakarta.

In the course of my research I received assistance and advice from representatives of a number of institutions. In Indonesia I am grateful for the help I received from Dr Hasan Ambary of the Pusat Penelitian Arkeologi Nasional, from Daeng Malewa in Sibolga, and from the staff of the Arsip Negara and the Museum Nasional. In the Netherlands I received assistance from the staff of the Algemeen Rijksarchief, the Oriental Manuscripts collection of the Leiden University Library, and the Koninklijk Instituut voor de Tropen. My research was carried out on a Monash University Graduate Scholarship, and travel to Holland and Indonesia was made possible by a grant from the Centre of Southeast Asian Studies at Monash University.

I am indebted to the late Lode Brakel who first suggested that I study Barus and to the following who helped in a variety of ways: David Chandler, Nuriahan Mat Daud, Tony Day, Kate Howell, Teuku Iskandar, Russell Jones, Margaret Kartomi, Ruurdje Laarhoven, Ian Mabbett, Jamie Mackie, Campbell Macknight, Pierre-Yves Manguin, Hirosue Masashi, Virginia Matheson, Tony Reid, Merle Ricklefs, the late Cyril Skinner, Helen Soemardjo, Nuriah Taslim, and Paul Tickell. Anthony Milner and O.W. Wolters read and commented extensively on drafts of the thesis. Their encouragement has been important to me.

John Legge has had more to do with Barus than he might at first have expected; my debt to him cannot be reckoned.

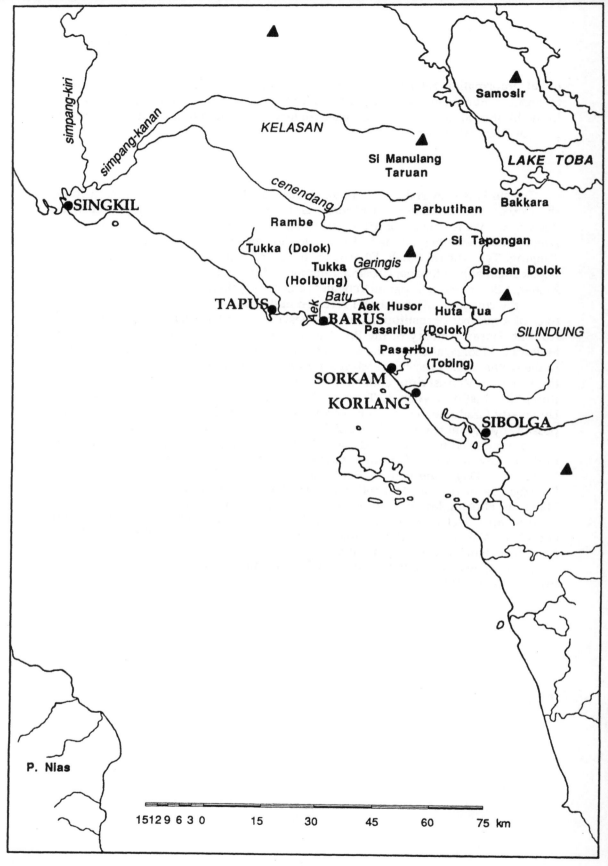

Map 2. The Barus Region

1

INTRODUCTION:
A MALAY FRONTIER

This study is concerned with traditional authority and ideas of government in one little known part of the Malay archipelago. For a period of some two hundred years two royal families coexisted in Barus, a small kingdom on the coast of northwest Sumatra. Designated Hilir (downstream) and Hulu (upstream), the two families remained in an uneasy state hovering between conflict and truce in which they ruled the kingdom, together, in rotation, or in a state where one family managed to eclipse the other for a period. It is necessary at the outset to appreciate the fact that the distinction between Hulu and Hilir rulers in Barus was not simply a case of two rulers located in geographically distinct parts of one kingdom, as was the case in some Malay polities. Rather, the existence of "Hulu" and "Hilir" rulers in Barus was a reflection of more subtle and complex distinctions between different ethnic groups, geographical domains, and styles of political authority. For most of the period with which we are concerned, the two rulers lived in settlements which were but a kilometer or so apart and close to the sea, and both exercised authority in the interior. To understand this situation it will be necessary to consider the ecological, ethnic, and economic situation of Barus as it is revealed in the available sources.

The royal chronicles of Hulu and Hilir Barus together offer a nineteenth century perspective on mutual relations between the families, on the way in which each presented claims to royal authority, and on the nature of that authority itself. In addition to these local presentations of the past, there exists a range of secondary and contemporary sources which help us to understand the particular situation in Barus and to appreciate the context in which the chronicles were written and received. This chapter will concentrate on those external sources, in order to provide a setting within which to explore the issue of duality and to consider the manner in which this is presented in the Malay texts.

BARUS: ITS HISTORY AND GEOGRAPHY

Modern Barus lies against the narrow coastal stretch which skirts west Sumatra from north to south. At various points on the coast the central Sumatran spine of mountains (Bukit Barisan) reaches close towards the sea, for instance at Sibolga where the traveler experiences a steep descent from the hills around the Toba plateau. But at Barus, some ten kilometers depth of flat land lies between hills and beach.

Barus sits between Sibolga, to the southeast, and the remote fishing village of Singkel to the northwest. Now a small and isolated town, it can be approached by car, either along the mainly unsurfaced coastal road from Sibolga which frequently crosses on wooden planks, or peters out at, numerous small watercourses, or by a longer, inland, route. This trip of some sixty kilometers can take up to four hours. From Sorkam onwards one begins to enter the Barus region, but in the past Sorkam was part of the kingdom of Barus which stretched as far down the coast as Natal.

Barus consists of two principal *kampung*, both lying on the Batu Garigis river.[1] These are the upstream (Mudik) and downstream (Hilir) settlements, and, although the modern commercial and administrative center of Barus is now located downstream at the river mouth, in the past Kampung Mudik was of considerable importance in Barus affairs. The Hilir *kampung* is part trading and part fishing settlement. On the shore one finds the fishing community, with boats, tackle, and dried fish spread along the beach where, occasionally, one may also come across coins, Arab and Dutch, which serve as reminders of Barus's past. Standing on the shore and looking away from the southward coastal sweep of curved beach, the island of Morsala can be seen lying off the Bay of Tapanuli, and to the right is a long, thin, palm-covered promontory called Kepala Ujung or Ujung Tanah. Further still, and out of view, lies Nias.

The lie of the land is vital to understanding the past of Barus. Behind the flat and the cultivated lowlands stretch forested hills, which produce the camphor and benzoin resins for which Barus became known among traders in early times. Behind these again is the high plateau which forms the center of the Toba Batak lands. The hinterland of Barus forms a natural path to the southerly part of the Toba highlands. Modern roads now connect the interior more certainly with Sibolga, but in the past, when the journey was made by foot down the gloomy forested gorges and steep inclines, the Barus route to and from the highlands was most important. Behind Barus, in the valleys of Rambe and Tukka, the various hinterland paths converge and lead the traveler down gradually to the foothills which border the Barus flat.

Barus has received little scholarly attention, but when it is mentioned in histories of Indonesia it is often in connection with its prominence as a camphor and benzoin port.[2] It has also been noted that the port of Barus, with its hinterland links, was a likely avenue for contact between the isolated Batak interior and the outside world and may, in early times, have provided a channel for Indian influence on Batak languages and thought.[3] Scholarly work has concentrated on the period before the sev-

---

[1] Also known as the Aek Siraha, and, in earlier times as the Aek Si Buluan. See J. W. Stemfoort and J. J. Siethoff, *Atlas van Nederlandsch Oost-Indie* (Batavia: Department van Kolonien, 1897–1904).

[2] See, for instance, L. van Vuuren, "De Handel van Baroes Als Oudste Haven op Sumatra's Westkust, verklaard en voor de Toekomst Beschouwd," *TAG*, 25, 6 (1908): 1389–1402; N. J. Krom, *Hindoe-Javaansche Geschiedenis* (The Hague: Nijhoff, 1931), pp. 157, 204, 212, and passim; and O. W. Wolters, *Early Indonesian Commerce* (Ithaca and London: Cornell University Press, 1967). Barus is also frequently associated with the mystic poet Hamzah Fansuri; see L. F. Brakel, "Hamza Pansuri. Notes on: Yoga practices, Lahir dan Zahir, The 'Taxallos', Punning, A Difficult passage in the Kitab al-Muntahi, Hamza's likely place of birth, and Hamza's Imagery," *Journal of the Malaysian Branch of the Royal Asiatic Society* (hereafter *JMBRAS*) 52, 1 (1979): 89–92.

[3] For instance, Lance Castles, "Statelessness and Stateforming Tendencies among the Batak before Colonial Rule," in *Pre-Colonial State Systems in Southeast Asia*, ed. Anthony Reid and Lance Castles (Kuala Lumpur: Malaysian Branch of the Royal Asiatic Society, 1975), p. 67; and J. Tideman, *Hindoe-Invloed de in Noordelijk Batakland* (Amsterdam: Bataksche Instituut, 1936), pp. 8–9. On Indian influence in the Bataklands and the possible role of the Lobo Tua settlement at Barus, see also E. Edwards McKinnon, "New Light on the Indianization of the Karo Batak," in

enteenth century. It has been suggested that, because of the geographical and climatic specificity of the resin-producing trees, this area was probably always an important source of camphor and benzoin.[4] But scholars have disagreed about this and, in the present state of fossil and botanical research, informed speculation is all that is possible.[5] What is evident is a long association between the place name Barus and the name for camphor in Chinese and Malay sources. In Malay, camphor is known as *Kapur Barus* and, since 1897, when the toponym P'o-lu-shih was identified by Kern as a transcription of Barus, scholars have linked the Indonesian country which was known as P'o-lu in Chinese records, and was mentioned from the sixth to the ninth centuries as a source of camphor (P'o-lu perfume), with Barus in northwest Sumatra.[6] Doubt, however, has been cast over the actual location of Barus, or P'o-lu, in this early period. O. W. Wolters has questioned the identification of P'o-lu with Barus in Tapanuli and has suggested that the name Barus may have referred, at that time, to a region encompassing much of the north of Sumatra including the north east and west coasts of the island.[7] Wolters concluded that the first certain identification of the place name Barus with its modern west coast location occurs in the sixteenth century *Suma Oriental* of Tomé Pires.[8]

Whether or not the port which was known to the Chinese as P'o-lu was located on the west coast of Sumatra in the seventh to ninth centuries AD, there is evidence that Barus, as we now know it, was a trading center visited by foreign merchants in

---

Cultures and Societies of North Sumatra, ed. Rainer Carle (Berlin/Hamburg: Reimer, 1987), pp. 81–110.

[4]A number of studies suggest that geographical and climatic conditions make the hills behind Singkel, Barus, and Sibolga particularly suitable for the growth of productive camphor trees and benzoin bushes. For instance, van Vuuren, "De Handel van Baroes," pp. 1394–1401; P. van Zon, "Korte Mededeelingen omtrent den Kamferboom," *Tectona* 3 (1915): 220–24; J. Kreemer, "De Winning van Kamferhout, Kamferolie en Kamfer in het Singkelsche," *TAG* 33 (1916): 880–87; H. Loos, "Iets over Benzoe in Tapanoelie," *Teysmannia* 32 (1921): 398–408. A much older study is that of W. H. de Vriese, *De Kamferboom van Sumatra* (Leiden: de Breuk, 1851). In the nineteenth and twentieth centuries, van Vuuren and other administrators in northwest Sumatra attempted to improve their particular regions by transplanting camphor and benzoin trees with a view to plantation culture. The trees were, however, found not to be productive in areas other than those in which they grew naturally. Van Vuuren, "De Handel van Baroes," and Loos, "Iets over Benzoe."

In the past, resins and oil extracted from these plants were used variously as fumigants, medicine, and perfumes, and it is only in recent times that they have been replaced by chemical substitutes. For his numerous references to this trade, see Wolters, *Early Indonesian Commerce*, under "Camphor" and "Benzoin" in the Index. Also van Vuuren, "De Handel van Baroes," pp. 1390–91.

[5]F. L. Dunn, for instance, suggests that Wolters and others have overemphasized the importance of Sumatra as a source of resins; F. G. Dunn, *Rain Forest Collectors and Traders: A Study of Resource Utilization in Modern and Ancient Malaya* (Kuala Lumpur: Malaysian Branch of the Royal Asiatic Society, 1975).

[6]H. Kern, *Verspreide Geschriften Onder Zijn Toesicht Verzameld* (The Hague: Nijhoff, 1917) vol. 6, p. 216; P. Pelliot, "Deux itinéraires de Chine en Inde à la fin du VIIIe siècle," *BEFEO* 4 (1904): 340; G. Ferrand, "Le K'ouen-louen et les Anciennes Navigations Interocéaniques dans le Mers du Sud," *JA* (July–August 1919), pp. 53–57; and Krom, *Hindoe-Javaansche Geschiedenis*, pp. 115 and 120. See also Wolters, *Early Indonesian Commerce*, p.185 and Ch. 12, n. 77.

[7]Wolters, *Early Indonesian Commerce*, Ch. 12, especially pp. 187–96.

[8]Ibid, pp. 180–81. See also Fatimi, "In Quest of Kalah," *JSEAH* 1, 2 (1960): 101, n. 31 for an earlier and less thoroughly argued version of the suggestion that P'o-lu (Barus) covered a large area.

search of resins from at least the tenth century. This is indicated in Arab sources, where the region is referred to by its other name, that of Fansur. This dual nomenclature is a puzzling feature of early Barus history.[9] It has never been questioned that the Fansur of Arab seamen refers to Barus on the west coast, and the name is usually thought to have been derived from that of a small settlement in the region of modern Barus known as Pansur or Pancur.[10] In Arab sources the finest-quality camphor is known as *Fansuri,* and Arab geographical texts from the ninth century onwards refer to Fansur as the source of this and other high quality grades of camphor and benzoin.[11] There is evidence to suggest that, in the tenth century, Arab merchants visited Fansur via Ceylon, in trading expeditions which were specifically aimed at purchasing the region's famous camphor.[12]

Archaeological findings may prove to be the most fruitful sources for the early trading history of Barus. An inscribed hexagonal pillar found at Lobo Tua near Pansur has been dated to AD 1088, and identified as carrying an inscription which indicates that it was erected by a Tamil trading guild thought to have been based in the region.[13] Preliminary archaeological investigations suggest that ceramic finds in the vicinity of Lobo Tua may provide evidence of an early trading settlement there.[14]

---

[9]Fansur/Barus is by no means the only Sumatran center to have borne more than one name; the names Deli and Aru may both have referred to the same place. See A. C. Milner, E. Edwards McKinnon, and Tengku Luckman Sinar S.H., "A Note on Aru and Kota Cina," *Indonesia* 26 (October 1978): 4–7; and D. Lombard, *Le Sultanat d'Atjéh au Temps d'Iskandar Muda, 1607–1636* (Paris: École Français d'Extrême-Orient, 1967), pp. 92–93 and 98. Semudra-Pasai is another Sumatran example of a name change, over time, for the same region. On the change in capital from Semudra, on the coast, to Pasai, further inland, see K. R. Hall, *Maritime Trade and State Development in Early Southeast Asia* (Honolulu: University of Hawaii Press, 1985), pp. 214–15.

[10]The name probably originated from *pancur/pancuran,* a Malay word for spring, or a place where water flows. For reference to Pansur as a Batak version of the word see van Vuuren, "De Handel van Baroes," pp. 1391–93. On his map, van Vuuren places "Pansoer" close to "Loeboek Toea," inland and slightly to the west of *kampung* Hilir and *kampung* Mudik. More modern references to Pancur, however, locate the place-name in the vicinity of a hill called Papan Tinggi, which lies further inland and to the east of the main Barus settlements. See Lukman Nurhakim, "Makam Kuno di Daerah Barus. Sumbangan Data Arkeologi Islam" (MA thesis, Facultas Sastra, Universitas Indonesia, 1977), p. 26; and an annotated map from the collection of Rusdin Tanjung, Jakarta. One of the Malay chronicles examined below treats Fansur as a name which was associated with the settlement of Lobo Tua and with the pre-sixteenth century period of Barus history. The name Fansur may have derived from a *pancur* close to Lobo Tua, have fallen into misuse, and later have been applied to a settlement in the vicinity of Papan Tinggi, see p. 68 below.

[11]See Jane Drakard, "An Indian Ocean Port. Sources for the Earlier History of Barus," *Archipel* 37 (1989): 58–65, for a summary of Arab references to Fansur and the high-quality resins found there. Translations of the relevant Arab texts are contained in G. R. Tibbetts, *A Study of the Arabic Texts Containing Material on South-East Asia* (Leiden and London: Brill for the Royal Asiatic Society, 1979); and G. Ferrand, *Relations de voyages et textes géographiques arabes, persans et turks relatifs à l'Extrême-Orient du VIIIe au XVIII siècles,* 2 vols. (Paris: Leroux, 1913–14). See also J. Sauvaget (trans.), '*Ahbār aṣ-Ṣīn wa'l-Hind. Relation de la Chine et de l'Inde, rédigée en 851* (Paris: Belles Lettres, 1948).

[12]Drakard, "Indian Ocean Port," pp. 62–65.

[13]K. A. Nilakanta Sastri, "A Tamil Merchant Guild in Sumatra," *TBG* 72 (1932): 314–27 and G. J. J. Deutz, "Baros," *TBG* 22 (1874): 156–163.

[14]Details of the archaeological investigations which have taken place in Barus can be found in Lukman Nurhakim, "Makam Kuno di Daerah Barus," and in a draft report prepared by the Pusat Penelitan Arkeologi Nasional, Jakarta. For a discussion of the possible age of ceramics

Scattered early references to the place name Fansur, and to this region as a source of camphor and benzoin resins, allow us to infer that Batak collectors were gathering the resins and bringing them to the coast, where a trading community must have existed, but they tell us little more. The early trading history of Sumatra, and the manner in which Indian and other influences reached the isolated Batak lands, are not of central concern here, although some reference to the early period, and to the presence of a trading center and of Tamil merchants there, is made in the Malay chronicles from Barus, and this will be considered below.

By the sixteenth century it is clear that Barus was a busy and prosperous port. In his *Suma Oriental* Tomé Pires mentions the "... very rich kingdom of Baros, which is also called *Panchur* or *Pansur*."[15] On the question of Barus's dual nomenclature, Pires further remarks that "The Gujerat people call it *Panchur*, and so do the Persians, Arabians, Kling, Bengalees, etc. Sumatra calls it Baros (Baruũs). It is all one kingdom, not two."[16] This statement provides a glimpse of the wide range of merchants who visited the port in this period and who contributed to the prosperity described by Pires.

The sixteenth century may indeed have seen Barus in its heyday. Brakel pictured Fansur/Barus as the cosmopolitan and polyglot center which gave birth to the Malay mystic poet, Hamzah Fansuri.[17] Hamzah often mentioned Fansur in his poetry and used camphor and the camphor tree in his imagery.[18] The large number of Muslim grave sites at Barus also suggest that it was a prominent center during this period, prior to the establishment of a European presence. Although, as yet, we know little about the many old gravestones in the Barus area, there are indications of a sixteenth century date for some of them at least.[19]

Concerning Minangkabau, Pires writes that Fansur/Barus, Tiku, and Pariaman were the "... key to the land of Menangkabau, both because they are all related, and because they possess the sea coast."[20] Traditionally, the rulers of Minangkabau had strong links with key ports on the east and west coasts of Sumatra.[21] Although little is known about the character of these relations before the sixteenth century, there are indications that Minangkabau was important for the inhabitants of the Barus region, both Batak and Malay. When the Dutch East India Company (VOC) first arrived in

---

found at the Lobo Tua site, see also E. Edwards McKinnon, "A Note on the Discovery of Spur-Marked Yuen-type Sherds at Bukit Seguntang, Palembang," *JMBRAS* 52, 2 (1979): 43.

[15] A. Cortesão (ed), *The Suma Oriental of Tomé Pires* (London: Hakluyt Society, 1944) vol.I, pp.161–62.

[16] Ibid. Arab sailing accounts, dating from early in the sixteenth century, also refer to the number of foreign merchants visiting this area and hint that west coast trade may have been on the upturn for some years. In 1511 Sulaimān-bin Aḥmad al-Mahrī described Fansur as one of the best known ports on the west coast where camphor, gold and other products could be obtained. His sailing directions indicate that traders from South India, Gujerat and Hormuz were also visiting the coast. Tibbetts, *A Study of Arabic Texts*, pp. 189–193, 216, and 223–29. See also the account of Shihāb al-Dīn Aḥmad ibn Mājid on pages 198, 206 and 208.

[17] Brakel, "Hamza Pansuri," p. 92.

[18] Syed Naguib al-Attas, "New Light on the Life of Hamza Fansuri," *JMBRAS* 40, 1 (1967): 42–51 and L. F. Brakel, "The Birth Place of Hamza Fansuri," *JMBRAS* 42, 2 (1969): 206–12.

[19] For a discussion on the literature concerning these stones see Drakard, "Indian Ocean Port," pp. 73–74.

[20] Pires, *Suma Oriental*, p. 161.

[21] P. E. de Josselin de Jong, *Minangkabau and Negeri Sembilan* (The Hague: Nijhoff, 1952), pp. 7-9.

Barus it sought, as with other west coast ports, to use the prestige of the ruler of Minangkabau among the coastal people to draw them into alliances with the Company.[22] Marsden has remarked on the reverence in which the Minangkabau royal family was held among coastal Malays[23] and also among the Batak population of the interior:

> Notwithstanding the independent spirit of the Battas, and their contempt for all power that would affect a superiority over their little societies, they have a superstitious veneration for the Sultan of Menangkabau, and show a blind submission to his relations and emissaries, real or pretended, when such appear among them for the purpose of levying contributions.[24]

In the early nineteenth century Burton and Ward found, during their expedition to Silindung, that the Bataks of Tapanuli would still submit to the ruler of Minangkabau.[25] Robert Heine-Geldern has also commented upon Batak reverence for the Minangkabau rulers, referring in detail to Batak legends which cite the Raja of Barus as intermediary between the Toba Bataks, the Si Singa Mangaraja kings, and the ruler of Minangkabau to whom they paid tribute.[26]

In the seventeenth century when the VOC invoked Minangkabau royal prestige in Barus, therefore, the idea of Minangkabau sovereignty was probably meaningful and important to the rulers and people. The seventeenth century letters which Barus rulers sent to the Dutch Governor of the West Coast at Padang addressed him as a representative of the Minangkabau ruler whose many resonant titles were recorded in full.[27] When the Governor replied, he, too, wrote in the name of the Yang Dipertuan and he had the use of the royal seal or *cap* of Minangkabau.[28] Such details held significance for the Barus rulers. In 1669, when a Company official arrived in Barus with a letter from the Governor, the rulers of the port were concerned and suspicious because the letter did not bear the usual seal.[29] Minangkabau royal seals and titles were also included, as we shall see, in a local Barus manuscript belonging to the Raja di Hilir family.

---

[22]H. Kroeskamp, *De Westkust en Minangkabau 1665–1668* (Utrecht: Academisch Proefschrift, University of Leiden, 1919), Ch. VI, especially pp. 100–110. According to Kroeskamp, despite Acehnese mastery over the west coast for the past hundred years, the idea of Minangkabau royal authority had never worn off and rested on "time honoured traditions out of a misty past."

[23]William Marsden, *The History of Sumatra* (Kuala Lumpur: Oxford University Press, Reprint of the third edition, 1975), p. 337.

[24]Ibid., p.376.

[25]Burton and Ward, "Report of a Journey into the Batak Country in the Interior of Sumatra, in the year 1824," *Transactions of the Royal Asiatic Society* 1 (1827): 495.

[26] R. Heine-Geldern, "Le Pays de P'i-k'ien, Le Roi au Grand Cou et Le Singa Mangaradja," *BEFEO* 49 (1959): 25 ff.

[27]See, for instance, VOC 1268, f. 850r.

[28]VOC 1264 (1668), f. 294v. Cited in Kroeskamp, *De Westkust*, p. 110.

[29]VOC 1272, f. 1066v. As Barbara Watson Andaya has pointed out, in relation to another part of the Malay world, the incorrect placing of a seal was regarded as "a studied insult." It offended a Malay sense of propriety in the observance of custom and prescribed forms. See B. W. Andaya, *Perak: The Abode of Grace* (Kuala Lumpur: Oxford University Press, 1979), pp. 90 and 81.

The role of Minangkabau in Barus, at least from the sixteenth century onwards, appears to have been a question of special loyalties rather than of physical control and domination. This did not apply, however, to Barus's relations with its other powerful neighbor, Aceh. In the first part of the sixteenth century Barus seems to have flourished; however the rise of Acehnese territorial ambitions in the same period led to a challenge which was to curtail the kingdom's apparent independence and cut across its links with Minangkabau. From the end of the sixteenth century, Acehnese ambitions on the west coast were an important and seemingly oppressive factor in Barus history. As J. Kathirithamby-Wells has demonstrated, other west coast kingdoms were also linked with Aceh in the same period and by 1568 Acehnese influence had spread as far down the west coast as Pariaman.[30] Acehnese practice was to station a Panglima (or governor) in these frontier ports in order to oversee trade and protect Acehnese interests. Barus was no exception in this. As early as 1539, during a campaign against east Sumatran Bataks, one of the Acehnese army's generals was said to have been governor "and *Mandara*" of the "Kingdom of *Baarros*" and brother-in-law to the Sultan of Aceh. According to the Portuguese adventurer, Pinto, this general's name was Herodin Mahomet, and the Sultan of Aceh later rewarded him with the title, "Sultan of *Baarros*."[31] Aceh dominated west Sumatran trade during this period and foreign merchants were only allowed to call at Barus and other ports with Acehnese permission. This practice favoured Gujerati, rather than European, shipping which accounts for the superficial knowledge European traders possessed of Barus in the late sixteenth and early seventeenth centuries. When the Dutch East India Company (VOC) finally entered Barus and became involved in politics there in 1668, it was only after they had ousted the resident Acehnese Panglima.

* * *

The present study will concentrate on the previously unexplored period from the seventeenth to nineteenth centuries, and, among other things, it will be concerned with the significance of the hill-coastal relationship for the *pesisir* port of Barus, which will be seen as lying on the fringes of the Malay cultural world and as a frontier on which important contact was made with the people beyond it.

It is not unusual to stress the importance of hill and coastal distinctions in northwestern Sumatra. Travelers in past centuries have pointed out the differences in culture and religion which existed between the Batak people of the interior and the trading population of the coast. In 1761, for instance, J. L van Bazel divided the inhabitants of the west coast into two types, hill and coastal dwellers. The hill people, he wrote, were the old inhabitants of Sumatra. They were "uncivilized pagans" who brought their goods to the shore to barter, but who sometimes became more tractable and civilized as a result of their intercourse with coastal dwellers and foreign

---

[30]On rise and expansion of Aceh, see R. H. Djajadiningrat, "Critische overzicht van de in Maleische werken vervatte gegevens over de geschiedenis van het Soeltanaat van Atjeh," *BKI* 65 (1911): 135–265. For a description of the kingdom's expansion into west Sumatra, see J. Kathirithamby-Wells, "Achenese control over West Sumatra up to the Treaty of Painan, 1663," *JSEAH* 10, 3 (1969): 453–70.

[31]H. C. Gent (trans.), *The Voyages and Adventures of Fernan Mendez Pinto* (London: Printed by J. Macock for Henry Cripps and Lodowick Lloyd, 1653), pp. 32 and 34. The title *"Mandara"* is discussed on pages 31 and 43–44 below.

traders.[32] In contrast to the highly structured and isolated society of the Batak clans, the coastal community was heterogeneous. Malays originating from Minangkabau appear to have formed the largest population group, but, as we shall see, observers from the seventeenth century onwards have also taken account of the presence of Acehnese, Kerinci, Chinese, Javanese, and others, as well as Bataks who had made the cultural transition to the coast. The culture of this coastal world was very different from that of the interior. Religion is one difference noticed by those who have commented on the region, but the language, dress, and manners of the coastal Malays are also contrasted with those of the Bataks.

Drawing a distinction between the inhabitants of the coast and of the interior in the eighteenth century, Marsden noted that Barus was "...properly a Malayan establishment."[33] Marsden went no further in his description, but in 1855 H. Van Rosenberg commented that the inhabitants of Singkel and Barus were a mixture of Acehnese, Malays, Bataks, and people of Nias. They were usually Muslims, he said, and their customs and manners were for the most part Malay.[34] On the same topic, M. Joustra also noticed the mixed foreign population of Barus and commented on the elasticity of the term "Malay." The population of Barus, he said, could be described as a mixture of Malays, Buginese, Acehnese, Chinese, and others. But, in referring to Barus Malays, he warned that what was meant in many cases was a "Malayized" Batak population. Many of the people, including their rulers, had Batak origins but had accepted Islam and lived like the Minangkabau Malays of Sumatra's west coast.[35] Van Bazel wrote an account of the character and customs of these coastal dwellers in the eighteenth century; despite its prejudice his report suggests that their preoccupations were consistent with a concern for ritual and ceremonial, which has recently been shown to be such an important dynamic in traditional Malay society.[36] Their learning, he claimed, consisted of reading or chanting from Malay books "filled with fables and trifles," as well as "superstitious traditions and ridiculous ceremonies." Their religion was the "doctrine of Mohammed," but in this they were but poorly educated, and they adulterated it with many "foolish superstitions, ceremonies and talismans against bad luck and sickness." Their greatest prize, he wrote, consisted of a kris with a golden handle, and the most important of their ceremonies lay in the carrying of a large sunshade which was used to accompany only "chiefs and statesmen."[37]

The tendency, which was noticed by observers from the seventeenth century onwards, for Bataks to move to the coast and undergo Malayization is not unique to Barus. Malay kingdoms frequently absorbed non-Malay peoples living on their fringes, and in east Sumatra during the nineteenth century the Malay sphere was

---

[32]See E. B. Kielstra's summary of Van Bazel's manuscript in E. B. Kielstra, "Onze Kennis van Sumatras Westkust, omstreeks de helft der Achttiende Eeuw," *BKI* 36 (1887): 508–9. Van Bazel wrote a two-part survey of West Sumatra in 1761. The first part, his "Radicaale Beschrijving," concerns culture and history and exists only in manuscript form. A copy is held in the Arsip Nasional, Jakarta. The second part, on Dutch trade with the west coast, was published in *TNI* 9, 2 (1847): 1–95.

[33]W. Marsden, *History of Sumatra*, p. 367.

[34]H. van Rosenberg, "Beschrijving van het Distrikt Singkel," *TBG* 3 (1855): 410–11.

[35]M. Joustra, *Van Medan naar Padang en Terug* (Leiden: van Doesburg, 1915), p. 85.

[36]A. C. Milner, *Kerajaan: Malay Political Culture on the Eve of Colonial Rule* (Tucson: University of Arizona Press, 1982), passim.

[37]Kielstra, "Onze Kennis van Sumatras Westkust," pp. 510–11.

noticed to be expanding into what was previously Batak territory.[38] In modern Malay society the acceptance of Islam is considered to be equivalent to becoming Malay, to "*masuk Melayu.*" But, in the past, and in Sumatra apparently, religion was by no means the only indicator of Malay identity. Anthony Milner has argued that, in east Sumatra, to be a Malay was a cultural identification based on language, dress, attitudes, and etiquette. According to Milner, to be Malay ". . . was to behave and think in a particular way, that is, to participate in Malay culture. By adopting Malay culture it was possible to become Malay."[39] The transition between Batak and Malay cultural identity may sometimes have been flexible. In nineteenth century east Sumatra, it appears, a Malay ruler might even claim Batak ancestry.[40] It may have been that on the edges of cultural identity, new Malays or old Bataks slipped easily between the two; in the early twentieth century, Pleyte reported that Bataks living on the fringes of the largely Malay "government territory" in Barus dressed scantily, according to their own custom, in their own small settlements (*huta*), but adopted Malay dress when they went into the *kota*.[41]

In Barus, the questions of Batak and Malay identity and of the borderline between them were important and relevant. In the local sources for Barus history, these ethnic distinctions and cultural boundaries are frequently alluded to, and it will be necessary to explore such references with care in order to appreciate them in context. In Barus, moreover, we shall see that interaction between Bataks and Malays involved not only a change in cultural identification on the part of the Bataks who had moved to the coast, but also encompassed a degree of adaptation and local redefinition of Malay cultural categories themselves. Scholarly works which have been concerned to define a traditional Malay cultural ethos and political ideology allow us to talk with some confidence about Malay political culture,[42] and it will be necessary, in the course of this study, to consult these analytical works as well as Malay sources in order to place Barus concerns in the context of a Malay-Sumatran tradition. Barus concerns, in turn, may then offer new perspective to our existing cultural and political models. A central concern of this study is the way in which Malay ideas of authority, in particular, may have been subject to restatement in the Barus context.

---

[38] Milner, *Kerajaan*, pp. 87–88. For an example of entry into Malay culture in another "frontier" situation, see Douglas Miles' study of Banjarese Malays and Ngaju Dayaks in *Cutlass and Crescent Moon: A Case Study in Social and Political Change in Outer Indonesia* (Sydney: Centre for Asian Studies, University of Sydney, 1976), especially Ch. 8, pp. 100–101 and 147. Miles found that "Bandjarese-Malay society will accept new recruits only on the condition that they relinquish their right and obligations as Ngadju Dayaks." Ibid., p. 100.

[39] Milner, *Kerajaan*, p. 89.

[40] Ibid., p. 88.

[41] C. M. Pleyte, "Herinneringen uit Oost-Indie," *TAG* 17 (1900): 38–39. Batak men appear to have dressed in one sarong covering the lower part of the body and another thrown over the shoulders like a shawl. Their headdresses were also different from those of Malays, who commonly wore sarong or trousers with a type of jacket. See Milner, *Kerajaan*, p. 89; and the *Encyclopaedie van Nederlandsch Oost-Indië*, sv. Kleeding.

[42] See, for instance, J. M. Gullick, *Indigenous Political Systems of Western Malaya* (London: University of London The Athlone Press, 1958); A. C. Milner, *Kerajaan*; V. Matheson, "Concepts of Malay Ethos in Indigenous Malay Writings," *JSEAS* 10, 2 (1979): 351–71; B. W. Andaya, "The Nature of the State in Eighteenth Century Perak," in *Pre-Colonial State Systems in Southeast Asia*, ed. Reid and Castles, pp. 22–36; and *Perak: The Abode of Grace*; also Leonard Andaya, *The Kingdom of Johor, 1641–1728* (Kuala Lumpur: Oxford University Press, 1975).

Reference to Malay cultural categories and political models in Barus, however, must also take account of a further subtlety. Mention has already been made of the "elastic" nature of the term Malay in the Barus context, and several quotations have been made from works which speak variously of the Malay population of the port, of Minangkabau Malays, and of Minangkabaus. An examination of Malay culture in Barus must consider what is meant by the terms "Malay," "Minangkabau" or "Minangkabau/Malay" in Barus. We shall see that this is an issue which presents itself in the study of Malay texts from the region.

To explore the meaning of the terms Malay and Minangkabau in Barus involves a consideration of the population of the west Sumatran coastal regions, known as the *pesisir* and also as the western *rantau* of Minangkabau. The distinction, in Minangkabau society, between the *darat*, or the inland, mountainous, heartland of Minangkabau, and the *rantau*, coastal regions in Sumatra and further afield, is recognized in the scholarly literature on Minangkabau. Also well recorded is a pattern of temporary and permanent migration, among Minangkabau men in particular, from the *darat* to the *rantau*, a process known as *merantau*.[43] The question of whether those who have, over time, established themselves in the coastal regions, are still to be described as "Minangkabau" is a complicated and delicate one, answers to which may vary from time to time and place to place.

We have seen that, in 1811, Marsden described Barus as "properly a Malayan establishment,"[44] whereas a twentieth century author, Christine Dobbin, describes Barus and the other northern ports of the west coast of Sumatra in the seventeenth and eighteenth century as inhabited by "Minangkabau traders" as well as Bataks.[45] Dobbin distinguishes between "Malays" and "Minangkabaus" whereas Marsden appears to consider that these terms represent the same thing in a Sumatran context. According to him, the Minangkabau "are distinguished from the other inhabitants of this island [Sumatra] by the appellation of *Orang Melayo*, or Malays, which, however, they have in common with those of the coast of the Peninsula, and of many other islands."[46] Van der Toorn, who compiled a Dictionary of the Minangkabau language in the nineteenth century, describes Minangkabau as a "patois" of Riau Malay,[47] and R. J. Wilkinson defined Minangkabau itself as "an important Malay territory."[48]

A tendency by modern authors to refer, with more precision than those of earlier centuries, to coastal inhabitants whose families originally came from the *darat* as "Minangkabau," may be due to a heightened, modern, awareness of some of the main features of Minangkabau society. Until the Padri War in the early nineteenth century, Europeans knew little about society in the interior of Minangkabau. Since that time scholarly work has multiplied so that we now have a detailed understand-

---

[43]See in particular Mochtar Naim, "Merantau: Minangkabau Voluntary Migration" (PhD thesis, University of Singapore, 1973). Published in Indonesian as *Merantau: Pola Migrasi Suku Minangkabau* (Yogyakarta: Gadjah Mada University Press, 1979).

[44]Marsden, *History of Sumatra*, p. 367. "It is properly a Malayan establishment, governed by a *raja*, a *bandhara*, and eight *pangulus*, and with this peculiarity, that the *rajas* and *bandharas* must be alternately and reciprocally of two great families, named *Dulu* and *D'ilhir*."

[45]Christine Dobbin, *Islamic Revivalism in a Changing Peasant Economy. Central Sumatra, 1784–1847* (Copenhagen: Scandinavian Institute of Asian Studies, 1983), p. 170.

[46]Marsden, *History of Sumatra*, p. 41 also p. 325.

[47]J. L. van der Toorn, *Minangkabausch-Maleisch-Nederlandsch Woordenboek* (The Hague: Martinus Nijhoff, 1891), p. v.

[48]R. J. Wilkinson, *Malay-English Dictionary (Romanised)* (London: Macmillan, 1959), 2 vols.

ing of specialized features of Minangkabau society, such as its matrilineal descent pattern, *nagari* organization, and its division into two moieties, or *laras*. These have become major indices for defining Minangkabau society. Our increased, twentieth century, precision in the appreciation of such indices may lead us, with hindsight, to emphasize Minangkabau ethnic identity in contexts outside the *darat* where early travellers saw a more loosely defined society which they described as Minangkabau/Malay.[49]

Scholars of Minangkabau tend to define the western *rantau* or coastal region of Sumatra as more thoroughly Minangkabau than society on the east coast. Tsuyoshi Kato's description of the eastern *rantau* distinguishes between Minangkabau and Malay as ethnic groups, while simultaneously hinting at the difficulties entailed in such a distinction:

> The rantau hilir, with its commercial centers, was neither entirely Minangkabau nor exactly non-Minangkabau—a quality which was partly responsible for the sense it gave of expansiveness. It was not an empty space to be Minang-kabauized, for the existence of other ethnic groups, such as Malays and Batak, in the area was long recognized.[50]

On the west coast, ports such as Pariaman, Tiku, and Inderapura had close historical and kinship links with the interior, but even here Minangkabau from the *darat* who had moved to the coast are observed to have lived "as Malays rather than Minangkabau."[51]

Barus is located in the far north of the west coast *rantau*, and one might expect that the "Minangkabau" component of Malay society there may have been less marked. Modern Minangkabau scholars, however, classify the Barus region as part of the Minangkabau *rantau* and term its inhabitants "Minangkabau," on the basis of migrations which are thought to have taken place in the sixteenth and seventeenth centuries.[52] While the present study will offer evidence of the importance of such migration for the history of Barus, the question of whether the Malay population of Barus should be termed "Minangkabau" in subsequent centuries seems less certain. Mochtar Naim refers to the use of Minangkabau *adat* in the northern *rantau* regions, including Barus, and to Minangkabau *suku* affiliation, but no detailed study has been

---

[49]James Boon has observed that, "Experience across cultures, like communication across languages, is neither unique nor universal. Its advantage lies rather in the sense of exaggeration it ensures. Every culture appears, vis-à-vis every other, exaggerated." This may apply to the distinctions which are both made and ignored between Minangkabau and Malay culture. James A. Boon, *Other Tribes, Other Scribes. Symbolic Anthropology in the Comparative Study of Cultures, Histories, Religions, and Texts* (Cambridge: Cambridge University Press, 1982), p. 26.

[50]Tsuyoshi Kato, *Matriliny and Migration. Evolving Minangkabau Traditions in Indonesia* (Ithaca: Cornell University Press, 1982), pp. 91–92.

[51]This observation is made by Kato on the basis of a narrative describing the life a Minangkabau merchant on the west coast in the late seventeenth and early eighteenth centuries. See ibid., p.92, note 20; and W. Marsden, *Memoirs of a Malayan Family* (London: Oriental Translation Fund, 1830).

[52]Naim, *Merantau*, pp. 107 and 109–13. Naim cites Hamka, "Adat Minangkabau dan Harta Pusakanja," in *Menggali Hukum Tanah dan Hukum Waris*, ed. Mochtar Naim (Padang: Centre for Minangkabau Studies, 1968), p. 28, where Hamka refers to the Minangkabau origins of inhabitants of northwest Sumatra.

undertaken which would indicate how widespread this is.[53] Van Vollenhoven described Batang Natal and Barus as "principally Minangkabau" in his *Het Adatrecht van Nederlandsch Indië*, but the evidence upon which he bases this assertion is uncertain.[54] Naim cites *suku* affiliation as the principal qualification for a member of Minangkabau society[55] and he also quotes the following passage from P.E. de Josselin de Jong's study of Minangkabau and Negeri Sembilan:

> Whether the inhabitants of these regions [the rantau] should also be called Minangkabaus is hard to say; the only satisfactory way of deciding this question would be to find out whether they consider themselves to be so, or whether they call themselves "Malays."[56]

Insufficient anthropological work has been done in Barus to answer this question for the modern period. Both of these definitions, however, may be borne in mind in considering the nineteenth century Malay chronicles of Barus.

The question of Minangkabau and Malay identity is, then, a subtle and difficult one.[57] As P. Voorhoeve has put it with regard to the study of literature, "the dividing-line between real Minangkabau texts and Minangkabauising Malay texts cannot be sharply drawn."[58] The conceptual and practical boundary between Minangkabaus and Malays on the northwest coast of Sumatra was probably an amorphous and mobile frontier, in which the two categories were not mutually exclusive. It is not an unimportant frontier, however, for our understanding of Sumatran history and one of the aims of the present study will be to consider the process of interaction between different ethnic identifications in the Malay texts from Barus. By avoiding simple classifications and attempting to tease out features which relate to the various ethnic groups present in Barus, we may better understand how cultural interaction operated in these frontier regions.

A further point to be made on the subject of Barus's geographical position is that relations between Bataks and Malays in Barus involved not only those Bataks who moved to the coast and became, to a greater or lesser extent, Malay. There is also the question of coastal interaction with the Bataks of the interior who were involved in the collection and transportation of resins which they brought to Barus to sell. At this level of interaction, between groups who remained culturally distinct and geographically separate, hill and coastal contacts in Sumatra have been little studied.[59] It is in

---

[53]Naim, *Merantau*, p. 107.

[54]C. van Vollenhoven, *Het Adatrecht van Nederlandsch Indië* (Leiden: Brill, 1918), vol. 1, p. 227.

[55]Naim, *Merantau*, p. 39.

[56]De Josselin de Jong, *Minangkabau and Negeri Sembilan*, p. 7, cited in Naim, *Merantau*, p. 112.

[57]Mochtar Naim's sensitive description of the "shared *rantau*" between Minangkabau and the Bataks of Mandailing is illustrative of the complexity such cultural meetings involve. According to Naim the inhabitants of this *rantau*, "borrowed each others culture and spoke both dialects, frequently intermarrying, and yet preserving their own traditions." Naim, *Merantau*, p. 92, see also p. 76.

[58]P. Voorhoeve, *Critical Survey of Studies on the Languages of Sumatra* (The Hague: Nijhoff, 1955), p. 16.

[59]A contribution to the general topic which should be mentioned here is Bennet Bronson, "Exchange at the Upstream and Downstream Ends: Notes Toward a Functional Model of the Coastal State in Southeast Asia," in *Economic Exchange and Social Interaction in Southeast Asia*, ed. K. L. Hutterer (Michigan: 1977), pp. 39–52. Two historians who have concerned themselves

the fields of archaeology and early history that most attention has been paid to the geographical, economic, and political relationship between coast and interior in Sumatra. In a recent essay reviewing the progress of Srivijayan studies, for example, Wolters has suggested that a useful category for expanding our understanding of coastal kingdoms like Srivijaya might be to think in terms of riverine neighborhood networks which stretched inland, rather than large immobile coastal capitals.[60] He pictured a situation in which shared spiritual values would link a ruler with the riverine landscape surrounding him and enable him to secure loyalty and mobilize manpower.[61] Riverine traffic, Wolters suggested, would unite the scattered inhabitants of a region and encourage neighborly obedience.[62] In an article published in 1980, J. Miksic took up Wolters' point and further suggested that a search for "clues to the social bonds that rulers were able to manipulate" in order to mobilize a region should begin in the hinterland and along traditional communication routes.[63] Miksic's own research, based upon archaeological evidence, suggests that Sumatran ceremonial centers tend to be situated apart from coastal areas of habitation and commerce; rather, they often occur inland in positions which may mark traditional transport routes and where they may have served to "regulate and safeguard" intercourse between highland and lowland peoples. Inscribed oath stones, such as those found at Palembang and elsewhere in south Sumatra, may be evidence of this.[64] Another scholar who has used written sources to make a similar point is K.R. Hall. In a recent article he has pointed to the role of the hinterland population in giving substance to the claims of coastal rulers.[65] Hall illustrates the point with an episode from the north Sumatran chronicle, the *Hikayat Raja-Raja Pasai*, where a prince called Merah Silu was acknowledged in the interior and then used that authority to gain control over the coast and the kingdom of Samudra. Such group acclamation, Hall suggests, was an important feature of Sumatran political tradition.[66]

These searches for a better understanding of so called coastal Sumatran states and their relationship with the interior have relevance for our Barus inquiry. We shall see that the interior was of more than purely economic significance for the coastal population of Barus, and that relations between rulers on the coast and the hill people were important in the political life of the kingdom. It is important to note that in northwest Sumatra pathways rather than waterways provided the most important means of communication with the interior, but the concept of neighborhood networks which linked these distinct geographical spheres is appropriate to the Barus setting. Not only do categories used in archaeology and early history add to our understanding of Barus history, but Barus history may itself help to develop our understanding of the process of hill-coastal interaction in Sumatra.

with the relationship between coastal Malays and Bataks of the interior in east Sumatra are A. Reid, in *The Blood of the People* (Kuala Lumpur: Oxford University Press, 1979), see in particular Chapters I and III; and Milner, *Kerajaan*, especially Chapter V.

[60] O. W. Wolters, "Studying Srivijaya," *JMBRAS* 52, 2 (1979): 1–33.

[61] Ibid., p. 30.

[62] Ibid., p. 21.

[63] J. Miksic, "Classical Archaeology in Sumatra," *Indonesia* 30 (1980): 43–44.

[64] Ibid., pp. 50–54.

[65] K. R. Hall, "The Coming of Islam to the Archipelago: A Reassessment," in *Economic Exchange and Social Interaction*, ed. Hutterer, pp. 213–32.

[66] Ibid., pp. 223–26.

* * *

Coast-hinterland relations in Barus were in part shaped by economic considerations, by the role of the region, that is to say, in supplying forest resins. We have seen that the presence of camphor and benzoin in the hinterland of Barus, and the high quality of the resins found there, has led to a permanent association between the name Barus and camphor in the archipelago where camphor is known as *Kapur Barus*. Tapanuli has been described as the camphor and benzoin growing area of Indonesia *par excellence*,[67] and, from the seventeenth century onwards, information is available concerning the areas in which these resins were produced and the means by which they reached the coast. Camphor and benzoin collection in the Barus region was the preserve of Batak hill dwellers, who brought their produce to the coast.[68] Traditionally these people undertook the difficult and specialized job of deciding which trees to use and when they were ready. Much mystery, as well as a special language, surrounded the art of camphor gathering, which may have helped to keep its collection as an exclusively Batak preserve.[69] In addition, the areas in which camphor trees appear to have developed best lie in difficult terrain on hills and above deep gullies. Benzoin gardens were kept in some areas, but camphor trees do not take well to cultivation, and resin-bearing trees had to be sought out on the hillsides.[70] Coastal dwellers seem rarely to have ventured into the difficult and forbidding interior, and Bataks from different parts of the hinterland brought these resins to the coast.

Descriptions by foreign observers of the Barus region between the seventeenth and early twentieth centuries show that the hills to the northwest and northeast of Barus were particularly important in the supply of resins to the coast. By the seventeenth century the most fruitful camphor trees appear to have grown in the eastern part of upper Singkel, in the lands of the Dairi Bataks, along the banks of the Sungai Cenendang in the region known as Kelasan.[71] According to van Vuuren, a Dutch administrator who worked in the area during the early twentieth century, this stretch was particularly suitable because of its warm climate. The camphor tree, he wrote,

---

[67]Wolters, *Early Indonesian Commerce*, p. 114.

[68]VOC records from the seventeenth century confirm that it was the Batak hill population who collected resins, but these records provide little detailed information. See, for instance, Melman to Pits (1670) VOC 1272, f. 1082r. Specific information on camphor collection, and the whereabouts of growing areas comes mostly from nineteenth and early twentieth century accounts.

[69]See Kreemer, "De Winning van Kamferhout," pp. 886–87; van Vuuren, "De Handel van Baroes," p. 1397; and J. de Ligny, "Legendarische herkomst der Kamfer Baroes," *TBG* 63 (1923): 549–55. Honey collection ceremonies of northeastern Sumatra are an example of similar ritual collection procedures. See David Goldsworthy, "Honey Collecting Ceremonies of the East Coast of North Sumatra" in *Studies in Indonesian Music*, ed. M. J. Kartomi (Clayton: Centre of Southeast Asian Studies, Monash University, 1978), pp. 1–45. A *tabu* camphor language is also used by camphor gatherers in the Malay Peninsula. See W. W. Skeat and C. A. Blagden, *Pagan Races of the Malay Peninsula* (London: Cass, First Edition 1906, Reprinted 1966), vol. 2, Ch. 2.

[70]See van Vuuren, "De Handel van Baroes," pp. 1397–99. On planting benzoin, see especially p. 1399. For problems relating to the cultivation of camphor, see Kreemer, "De Winning van Kamferhout," pp. 880–81.

[71]Van Vuuren, "De Handel van Baroes," p. 1395 and Kreemer, "De Winning van Kamferhout," p. 880.

was more likely to produce resin when growing on warm, low-lying hills.[72] From the growing area, the camphor was brought overland to Barus, through Kelasan and Rambe. Some was also taken to Singkel, but even as late as the twentieth century the Batak collectors were keen to take their produce to Barus, "lest it be thought anything less than the famous Camphor Barus."[73] Seventeenth century Dutch sources suggest that a certain amount of benzoin was also collected in the Dairi region.[74] The most important benzoin territory, however, appears to have lain to the northeast of Barus, in the general area covered by Si Manulang Taruan, Parbutihan, Si Bulan, Bonan Dolok, Si Tapongan, Sanggaran, Huta Tua, and in the more westerly areas of Rambe and Pusuk.[75] Also, in the seventeenth century VOC sources report that large quantities of benzoin were brought down to Barus and Sorkam from the upland valley of Silindung, which is bordered by these eastern hills.[76] Links between these easterly hill areas and Barus were strong. In the late nineteenth century, for instance, when Dutch administrators began to move into the interior, there was said to be considerable local disquiet among the Bataks when it was proposed that areas such as Si Manulang Taruan should be linked administratively with the Toba lands instead of the coast.[77]

In the immediate hinterland of Barus, the flow of resins could be controlled by regulation of pathways and coastal routes. Camphor and benzoin on its way to Barus was often brought through Rambe and down to Tukka, which acted as a collecting center. This seems to have been the route which the Dairi Bataks were obliged to follow. Nineteenth and early twentieth century evidence suggests that resins of the hinterland were subjected to taxation by the inhabitants of these places.[78] The collectors were also frequently denied passage and were forced to sell their produce in the upland markets (*onan*), from whence it was brought downhill by others. The inaccessibility of the mountainous interior meant that the groups able to control the valleys and key access routes, such as Rambe, Tukka, and Pasaribu, might profit from the intercourse between hill and coast.[79] Influence over these regions and their populations was therefore important for the coastal inhabitants of Barus, and we shall see that such connections between the peoples of the coast and the hinterland took more than one form.

* * *

---

[72]Van Vuuren, "De Handel van Baroes," p. 1395.

[73]Ibid., p. 1395 and, for a similar point about the prime benzoin growing areas, see p. 1396.

[74]See Chapter 2 below.

[75]Van Vuuren, "De Handel van Baroes," p. 1395. See Map 2.

[76]Melman to Pits (1670) VOC 1272, f. 1077r.

[77]Van Vuuren, "De Handel van Baroes," p. 1396; and Anon., "Verslag van een reis van den Controleur van Baros naar de Beoosten Baros Gelegen Onafhankelijke Landschappen in het Jaar 1883," *TBB* 52 (1917): 195–205 and 252–65.

[78]See van Vuuren, "De Handel van Baroes," p. 1396.

[79]On the presence of *onan* in Rambe and Tukka, see W. H. K. Ypes, *Bijdrage tot de Kennis van de Stamverwantschap, de inheemsche rechtsgemeenschappen en het grondenrecht der Toba-en Dairibataks* (Leiden: Uitgegeven door de Adatrechtstichting te Leiden, 1932), p. 503. An *onan* in Pasaribu which was intended to intercept the passage of resins to Barus is mentioned in a local manuscript translated into Dutch by K. A. James, "De Geboorte van Singa Maharadja en het ontstaan van de Koeria (District) Ilir in de Onderafdeeling Baros," *TBG* 45 (1902): 138.

Barus, then, was set on a frontier of the Malay world. Hinterland relations and intercourse between different localities and social groups were necessarily important preoccupations, and an appreciation of cultural and political life in the region must take account of these relationships. It is within this context that the existence of two royal houses in Barus must be considered. Not only did the two royal families originate from different ethnic groups and different parts of Sumatra, but we shall see that they each had special ties with different parts of the Barus hinterland which were based, it seems, upon different political principles. The issue of duality in Barus is often discussed in the local sources in terms of these relationships, and, in turn, the terms of the discussion were probably influenced, as we shall see, by the political traditions of different parts of Sumatra. This study will argue that the existence of two kings and two royal dynasties was an important political issue within the Barus polity, and, before looking more closely at the Barus situation, it will be helpful to consider dual government and coastal/hinterland relations in a wider context.

The use of the terms Hulu and Hilir to refer to different parts of a state is not uncommon in the Malay world, where the importance of riverine communications leads naturally to the use of geographic expressions such as "upstream" and "downstream."[80] Similar terms occur in Batak languages, for instance *dolok* (hilly area), *holbung* (low-lying), while *tobing* suggests "towards the river" and *dolok* indicates the opposite direction. *Julo* (which is similar to the Malay word *hulu*) suggests inland, while *jae* indicates a coastal direction.[81] These words are often used in conjunction with ordinary place names where an area contains different types of landscape; for instance in the Barus hinterland are Tukka Holbung and Tukka Dolok, and Pasaribu Dolok and Pasaribu Tobing.

An active awareness and use of such distinctions is by no means surprising in north and west Sumatra, where the hilly interior reaches almost to the seashore and produces numerous fast and often unnavigable rivers, which ribbon the flat coastal stretch known as the *pesisir*. Economic life, communications, and political boundaries are all vitally linked to the lie of the land. What is more unusual is to find such geographical distinctions linked to a dual government.

In the typical Malay state it is customary for one Raja to head government, and Malay political theorizing is usually emphatic in insisting upon the indivisibility of Rajaship. As the polity is usually portrayed in Malay descriptions there could, in the nature of things, be only one ruler at the apex of political life. As Gullick has

---

[80]Wilkinson states that the word hulu is "common in the sense of 'upper part' e.g., *ka-hulu* (upstream) ... *orang hulu* (man from the hinterland, rustic).... The higher portion of the watershed of any river State is known always as its *hulu* or *ulu*." Hilir represents a "Flowing down; movement or situation downstream...." And also, "Radja di Hilir: 'Ruler in the Lower Reaches,' i.e., Prince of Lower Perak." The precisely opposite motion to ke Hilir is known as "*Mudek*—Progress upstream; going back against the current ... in contrast to drifting down with the current (*hilir*)." R. J. Wilkinson, *Malay-English Dictionary* (London: Macmillan, 1959), pp. 408 and 783. [In Barus the Raja di Hulu's village (*kampung*) is, and was in the past, known as Mudik.]

[81]A list of these geographical terms and their definitions may be found on a map published by C. M. Pleyte, "Schetskaart der reisrouten ter ontdekking van het Toba-Meer," in conjunction with his article "De Verkenning der Bataklanden," *TAG* 12 (1895): 71–96 and 727–40. See also J. H. Meerwaldt, *Handleiding tot de Beoefening der Bataksche Taal* (Leiden: Brill, 1904). A difference between Batak and Malay geographical orientations has been noticed in the placing of the right- or left-hand side of a river according to whether one faces upstream, in the Malay case, or downstream, in the Batak case. Milner, *Kerajaan*, p. 89.

observed, "Government was *kerajaan,* the state of having a ruler, and they [the Malays] visualized no other system."[82] In order to set Barus and its preoccupations in context, it is necessary, therefore, to give some attention to Malay ideas of sovereignty and *kerajaan* and to consider how appropriate these may be in localities such as Barus which lay on the fringes of the Malay cultural world.

Indivisibility of the ruler's position appears to have mirrored the unity and the very existence of the corporate Malay body. According to Gullick's analysis, the ruler's role was to "symbolise and to some extent to preserve the unity of the State."[83] His presence counteracted the centrifugal and disintegrative forces at work in the unruly life of Malay kingdoms. Gullick does not believe that the ruler (known usually as Sultan, Raja or Yang Dipertuan) exercised substantial administrative authority; his role, rather, was to invest the unity of the group with an "aura of sanctity and supernatural power."[84] This aura was known as *daulat,* a quality which was exclusive to enthroned rulers. *Daulat* distinguished the ruler from ordinary men, and this position of apartness was marked by a variety of prohibitions, ceremonies, and insignia which were exclusive to the ruler.[85] The ruler's relations with his subordinate chiefs were marked by an elaborate obeisance ceremony *(menghadap)* which symbolized absolute submission to the ruler's *daulat.* The *kebesaran,* or regalia, of a sultan were invested with spiritual powers: elephants, the color yellow, and the use of state umbrellas were the absolute preserve of the ruler, and the different grades of honor and distinction which he awarded to his subjects were all carefully defined.[86] As Winstedt has pointed out, many Malay practices concerned with the observance of royal *daulat* have been influenced by Hindu, Buddhist, and Islamic ideas. After the acceptance of Islam in the archipelago, Malay rulers were considered to be the "Shadow of God on Earth."[87] The Sultan's person was sacrosanct, and Malays had a special word, *derhaka,* to convey disloyalty and disrespect towards a ruler.[88]

Milner, whose study of *kerajaan* explores Malay attitudes towards sovereignty, portrays the Malay Raja as the idiom through which men experienced the world.[89] He suggests that the indispensability of a Raja in Malay life is expressed in Malay responses to a situation of Rajalessness.[90] In Malay writings the possibility of a kingdom without a Raja is equated with "utter confusion [*sangatlah huru-haranya*]."[91] "Anarchy," Milner observes, "was the natural outcome of the disappearance of soci-

---

[82]Gullick, *Indigenous Political Systems,* p. 44.

[83]Ibid., p. 44.

[84]Ibid., pp. 44–45.

[85]Ibid., pp. 45–46. See also Andaya, *Perak,* p. 27.

[86]Gullick provides a brief description of the regalia and ceremonies with which Malay rulers were honored; ibid. A more detailed treatment of Malay ceremonial is to be found in R. O. Winstedt, "Kingship and Enthronement in Malaya," *JMBRAS* 20, 1 (1947): 129–40.

[87]Winstedt, "Kingship and Enthronement," p.130.

[88]Andaya, *Perak,* p.27.

[89]Milner, *Kerajaan,* p. 113.

[90]Ibid., p. 94.

[91]Ibid., p. 109.

ety's focal point."[92] Similarly, the possession of a Raja is portrayed as "the essential concomitant of a [Malay] polity."[93]

The importance of the ruler to Malays lay, Milner suggests, in those aspects of government which colonial observers often took to be the mere trappings of authority—that is to say in his ceremonial role. On the basis of traditional Malay literature, Milner argues that, politically, Malays were preoccupied not with coercion and social control, but with the ordering of public and ceremonial life where reputation and rank were what mattered. In a world where proper (*patut*) behavior and custom (*adat*) were crucial, the ruler's role was to confirm identity by means of the distribution of titles (*nama* or *gelar*) and the observance of proper ceremonial form. Milner argues that Malays believed service to a Raja was a means of acquiring and enhancing *nama* or reputation in this and the next life. Raja and subject were bound together in a system where the ruler's *nama* was enhanced by the possession of numerous subjects, and subjects achieved *nama* by means of loyal service to their Raja. For Malays, Milner suggests, this relationship was central to the very notion of a political system, of being in a *Kerajaan* or "to be in the condition of having a Raja."[94]

The possession of an illustrious genealogy was an essential aspect of a Malay ruler's *daulat*. Barbara Watson Andaya notes that, according to Malay ideas of government, "The pre-eminent figure in the theoretical political system was the Sultan, whose right to the throne was primarily based on his unbroken descent from a glorious ancestor."[95] A genealogy which established the ruler's sovereignty was a reflection of "moral order" in the kingdom, or, as Milner puts it, "an organization of the past."[96] This ordering and elevation of the ruler's position adds to the monolithic quality of his role. No two could be so fitted to rule. According to Andaya, "The doctrine of the pre-eminent genealogy precluded any possibility of equal claims [to sovereignty]; each *negeri* had a raja, and a divided state was anathema."[97] The extent to which duality is abhorred in Malay texts may, however, be an indication of how immediate the practical threat of divisiveness was in traditional Malay states.

Malay writings reveal just how unthinkable dual Rajaship was considered to be. Like a state of Rajalessness, such division is depicted as *huru-hara*, the most extreme confusion and disarray; an abandonment of custom and moral order. When, for a short time in 1746, Perak was divided under two rulers, the *Misa Melayu* states that there was complete confusion, *huru-hara*.[98] According to Andaya, the rulers were reconciled because it was "impossible that there should be *negeri sebuah, Raja dua*,"[99] one state with two Rajas. Similarly, in the *Tuhfat al-Nafis*, a text which pays close attention to the integrative and disintegrative forces within a kingdom, the possibility of two rulers is equated with calamity.[100] When Raja Kecil attacked Johor in 1718 and

---

[92]Ibid., p. 104.

[93]Ibid., p. 95.

[94]Ibid., passim.

[95]Andaya, "The Nature of the State in Eighteenth Century Perak," in *Pre-Colonial State Systems,* ed. Reid and Castles, p. 24.

[96]Ibid., p. 24 and Milner, *Kerajaan,* p. 103.

[97]Andaya, "Nature of the State," p. 24.

[98]Raja Chulan, *Misa Melayu* (Kuala Lumpur: Pustaka Antara, 1966), p. 22.

[99]Andaya, "Nature of the State," pp. 24–25.

[100]Virginia Matheson, "Concepts of State in the *Tuhfat al-Nafis*," in *Pre-Colonial State Systems,* ed. Reid and Castles, pp. 18–19. I am grateful to Dr. Matheson for discussing the concept of

made himself ruler there, the text describes a situation where both Raja Kecil and the newly deposed Sultan were still at court.[101]

> ... there were many slanderous rumours circulating because in effect the state had two kings. The people were divided, some siding with Raja Kecil, others siding with Sultan Abd al-Jahil. Every day the rumours grew worse, eventually raging like a fire that blazes out of control.[102]

Fitnah, which can be translated as calumny or malicious report, has particularly disruptive associations in the *Tuhfat al-Nafis.* According to Virginia Matheson, "It was used to spread dissension and worsen a turbulent situation. . . . Its potency as a weapon and an inflammatory source in a close community is difficult to overrate."[103] Elsewhere in the *Tuhfat, fitnah,* like *huru-hara,* is associated with the dislocation caused by the existence of more than one ruler. When conflict broke out between Malays and Bugis in Riau, the text describes the possibility of divided rule in graphic terms:

> In these circumstances, there were misunderstandings between the two sides. You know how it is in a *perahu* with two captains, and in a country with two kings. This provided grounds for malicious rumours between the two sides, and the longer it went on the greater they became. It was like a fire which blazes unchecked until it rages out of control and only dies down after consuming everything.[104]

The implication here is that the state would be destroyed if such a situation were allowed to persist. It was not. The dangers inherent in duality were recognized and harmony was restored through a renewed oath of loyalty.

Another Malay text, this time from Kedah, the *Hikayat Marong Mahawangsa,* makes a similar point concerning the impropriety of two Rajas and the indivisibility of Rajaship. A Syeikh advises the aged Sultan of Kedah that it would be appropriate for him to retire in favor of his son.

> Now, said Sheikh Abdullah, since there is a Sultan for that country, and your Majesty is old, it would be proper that your Majesty should abdicate in his favour [his son's], and assume the dignity of Marhum. Very true, said the Sultan, aged rulers should retire into the dignified state you have mentioned. There cannot safely be two princes in authority at the same time. True, replied the other, for such is written in a book.[105]

Rajaship and dual government in Malay thought with me and for directing me to this and other examples of Malay thinking on the subject.

[101]Cited in Matheson, "Concepts of State," p. 19, see also L. Andaya, *Kingdom of Johor,* passim.

[102]Virginia Matheson and Barbara Watson Andaya (eds.), *The Precious Gift—(Tuhfat al-Nafis) by Raja Ali Haji ibn Ahmad* (Kuala Lumpur: Oxford University Press, 1982), p. 52 fol. 61:1.

[103]Matheson, "Concepts of State," p. 19.

[104]Matheson and Andaya, *Precious Gift,* pp. 203–4.

[105]J. Low, trans., *Marong Mahawangsa: The Kedah Annals* (Bangkok: American Presbyterian Mission Press, 1908), pp. 186–87.

This was more than a matter of indicating the disaster which would, in fact, accompany any division of royal authority. It was a matter of essence, of the nature of a polity. In a Sumatran text, the *Hikajat Potjut Muhamat*, the hero leaves Aceh because of the brief existence of two rulers in the country. This was

> Because he is ashamed at what he witnesses here. He cannot abide the sight of two princes. What never happened to others has now happened to us: one country, two kings.[106]

According to the Malay ideal of government, the very nature of a state involved the indivisibility of Rajaship.[107]

In these quotations the alternative to unified rule is presented graphically and equated with disaster and disintegration. The very urgency of these statements, however, may suggest an underlying tension in these Malay works concerning the centrifugal and centripetal forces within the traditional Malay polity. The view that anything other than a single ruler is unthinkable may, indeed, stem precisely from the fact that often division was only too possible. This is partly a philosophical and partly a practical issue. The texts we have cited have, simultaneously, described monarchy in terms of necessary indivisibility and pointed to the practical consequences of division. Safety is equated with one ruler and danger with more than one, shame is equated with two rulers as is confusion, both of which are presented as anathema and are juxtaposed with the proper order of things. The repetition of these equations suggests a preoccupation in the texts with disruption and diversity. There are many indications of forces within Malay kingdoms which pulled away from the center, and these may be reflected in the insistence on unified rule in traditional Malay literature.

Among these suggestions of division is the presence of dualistic tendencies which may be reflected in complementary lineages such as the Malay/Bugis

---

[106]G. W. J. Drewes, ed. and trans., *Hikajat Potjut Muhamat* (The Hague: Nijhoff, 1979), p. 49. Also in the text Potjut Muhamat declares, "I cannot bear the sight of two kings. That is what I cannot stand. The country goes to ruin and is thrown into disorder. We shall see that the royal compound has become a wood, and the square a jungle. The main mosque is in complete disrepair and the country is doomed because of the two kings. People do not give notice of marriage and divorces any more, because they see that there are two kings. . . . Thieves are not kept in check because there are two kings. When people see that disorder prevails, they say that Acheh is a most unholy country." And so on. Ibid., p. 41. See also James Siegel, "Awareness of the Past in the Poetjoet Moehamat," in *Southeast Asian History and Historiography*, ed. C. D. Cowan and O. W. Wolters (Ithaca: Cornell University Press, 1976), p. 322.

[107]In Java, too, division of the state did sometimes occur, but this appears to have been contrary to accepted notions of sovereignty. Comparing Malay and Javanese attitudes to division, Barbara Watson Andaya has indicated the example of eleventh century Java, when Airlangga divided the kingdom in two, although "the existence of two kings was unusual and against adat." Andaya, "The Nature of the State," p. 25 note 18. Buchari argues that this was against the norms of the time and "a disruption of the cosmic order." Buchari, "Sri Maharaja Mapanji Garasakan," *Madjalah Ilmu-Ilmu Sastra Indonesia* 4, 1 and 2 (1968): 8–9 (also cited by Andaya). For a survey of studies on this subject and a consideration of its spatial implications, see also Max Nihom "Ruler and Realm: The Division of Airlangga's Kingdom in the Fourteenth Century," *Indonesia* 42 (1986): 78–101. Later, during the eighteenth century when division of the kingdom of Mataram took place, "the crisis was immense" because there could only be one "true king"—one legitimate ruler. M. C. Ricklefs, *Jogjakarta under Sultan Mangkubumi 1749–1792* (London: Oxford University Press, 1974), p. 34.

Sultan/Yang Dipertuan Muda families of Johor-Riau.[108] Scholars have also commented upon the special and ambiguous position of the Bendahara family at the Melaka court. The Bendahara was drawn from a lineage which seems to have been in some senses complementary to that of the Sultan and which provided the royal lineage with brides.[109] According to John R. Bowen, "From the Generation of Iskandar Syah to the time of the Kingdom of Johor, the relation between the royal descent line and the line of the Bendahara is portrayed as an asymmetrical marriage alliance."[110] The *Silsilah Raja Brunei* also records not only tension between Raja and Bendahara lineages in Brunei, but also a period when a Bendahara usurped the throne.[111] At this stage Brunei is described in the *Silsilah* as having two Rajas, although one was not "of the line of the Yang Dipertuan" and was neither "*nobat* nor crowned."[112]

Division did take place in Malay kingdoms. Perak, for instance, was divided at times between Hulu and Hilir. In 1746 and between 1773 and 1788, the kingdom was divided between a ruler living upstream and a ruler living further downstream, although in both these cases the two princes were members of the same royal family.[113] Jambi, too, is said to have been divided for a time between two rulers who were brothers and who disputed the succession. One of these established himself as

---

[108]Virginia Matheson has described the role of Bugis and Malay lineages in the government of Johor-Riau as a "dual court system," "Tuhfat Al-Nafis (The Precious Gift). A Nineteenth Century Malay History Critically Examined" (PhD thesis, Department of Indonesian and Malay, Monash University, 1973), p. xvii. In her thesis Vivienne Wee elaborates the "complementary distribution" of lineages descended from Malay and Bugis factions in Riau, the *keturunan tengku* and *keturunan raja*. After 1722 Wee writes, "The sultan's office of *yang dipertuan* 'he who is made lord' was effectively divided into two: the post of *yang dipertuan besar* 'senior lord' was to be the monopoly of the post-1722 faction, and the post of *yang dipertuan muda* 'junior lord' was to be the political monopoly of the post-1722 faction." Vivienne Wee, "Melayu: Hierarchies of Being in Riau" (PhD thesis, Australian National University, 1985), pp. 201 and 199–202.

[109]C. H. Wake, "Melaka in the Fifteenth Century: Malay Historical Traditions and the Politics of Islamization," *Melaka. The Transformation of a Malay Capital c.1400–1980*, ed. Kernial Singh Sandhu and Paul Wheatley (Kuala Lumpur: Oxford University Press, 1983), p. 144 and passim.

[110]John R. Bowen, "Cultural Models for Historical Genealogies: The Case of the Melaka Sultanate," in *Melaka*, ed. Singh Sandhu and Wheatley, p. 166. Bowen traces what he describes as a "classificatory shift" between the Raffles 18 and Shellabear editions of *Sejarah Melayu*, in which the principles of descent upon which this alliance was based alter to reflect the changed circumstances of the Sultanate. In the later, Shellabear, edition, "The Bendahara now figured as junior royalty by descent rather than as a pre-eminent subject by alliance," p. 171.

[111]See Hugh Low, "Selesilah (Book of Descent) of the Rajas of Bruni," *JSBRAS* 5 (1880): 11, 13.

[112]Ibid, pp. 13–15. See also P. L. Amin Sweeney, "Silsilah Raja-Raja Berunai," *JMBRAS* 41, 2 (1968): 62.

[113]Dissension within the Perak royal family was a particular problem for the ruler, which was accentuated by the *waris negeri* system. The *waris negeri* were the royal princes who were closest in line of descent to the ruler and they were often difficult to control. Foremost among them was the Raja Muda, the next in line to the throne, who was responsible for the administration of government. The Raja Muda was, in the usual course of events, the ruler's successor, and this could easily lead to his becoming a focus for discontent. Barbara Andaya describes instances in the eighteenth century when the country was divided between the Hulu and Hilir as a result of this dissension, see Andaya, *Perak*, pp. 32–34.

ruler in the interior, after obtaining support in the form of a title from the ruler of Pagaruyung.[114]

Duality does not always appear as a source of tension in societies of the Archipelago however. In Eastern Indonesia many examples of diarchic forms of government such as that of the Atoni have been shown to be based upon an established structure of complementary oppositions—of sacral and secular lords.[115] And dyadic forms have been shown to be widespread in these societies.[116] The partnership between the rulers of Goa and Tallo' in the sixteenth and seventeenth centuries is said to have been one of cooperation, marriage alliances, and something like a rotation of sovereignty between the ruling dynasties of two separate kingdoms.[117]

Much closer to Barus were the three kings of Minangkabau, the Rajo nan Tigo Selo, who were entitled Raja Ibadat, Raja Adat, and Raja Alam. This division of roles, about which we know very little, is also said to have existed along the reaches of the Batang Hari river.[118] There are also numerous other references in Dutch records to the existence of more than one ruler in smaller Sumatran centers and to the use of the title Raja di Hilir in particular. Little published work is available on the subject, but examples abound. In the eighteenth century, for instance, there were two Tuanku at Natal,[119] two Tuanku were also required to sign treaties in Sorkam in the eighteenth century, and, in the nineteenth century, de Klerck referred to the existence of a "Raja Oedah" and a "Raja Toeha" in Singkel.[120] According to Marsden, the sovereignty of Pasaman in the eighteenth century was "divided between the two *rajas* of *Sabluan* and *Kanali*, who, in imitation of their former masters [the rulers of Minangkabau], boast an origin of high antiquity."[121]

---

[114]See J. Tideman and Ph. F. L. Sigar, *Jambi* (Amsterdam: de Bussy, 1938), p. 67 and H. M. M. Mennes, "Eenige Aanteekeningen Omtrent Djambi," *Kolonial Tijdschrift* (1932), p. 30.

[115]Clark E. Cunningham, "Order and Change in an Atoni Diarchy," *Southwestern Journal of Anthropology* 21 (1965): 359–81. See also James J. Fox, "Obligation and Alliance: State Structure and Moiety Organization in Thie, Roti," in *The Flow of Life*, ed. James J. Fox (Cambridge, Mass.: Harvard University Press, 1980), pp. 98–133.

[116]James J. Fox, "Models and Metaphors: Comparative Research in Eastern Indonesia," in *Flow of Life*, ed. Fox, pp. 327–33; and James J. Fox, ed., *To Speak in Pairs: Essays on the Ritual Languages of Eastern Indonesia* (Cambridge, Mass.: Cambridge University Press, 1988).

[117]See A. Reid, "A Great Seventeenth Century Indonesian Family: Matoaya and Pattingalloang of Makassar," *Masyarakat Indonesia* 8, 1 (1981): 1–28; and "The Rise of Makassar," *RIMA* 17 (1983): 135–36.

[118]De Josselin de Jong, *Minangkabau and Negeri Sembilan*, pp. 101–2.

[119]*Memorie door den Commandeur van der Wall*, 1760 Arsip Nasional, Jakarta, SWK 8, p. 9.

[120]E. S. de Klerck, *De Atjeh Oorlog*, 2 vols. (The Hague: 1912), vol. 1, p. 229. A further type of dualistic division which was common in Sumatra is that between right and left which usually relates to settlements on either side of a river or of one river which has branched in two. Sorkam Kiri and Sorkam Kanan and Batu Bara Kiri and Batu Bara Kanan are examples of the former. Examples of the latter type of division are the Kampar river in east Sumatra and the Simpang inland of Singkel.

[121]Marsden, *History of Sumatra*, pp. 335–36 cited by Dobbin, "The Exercise of Authority in Minangkabau in the Late Eighteenth Century," in *Pre-Colonial State Systems*, ed. Reid and Castles, p. 87. Externally imposed power sharing and division does not appear to have been successful, for instance in Anak Sungai where the British attempted, in the seventeenth century, to divide contested authority between a ruler in Menjuto and in Anak Sungai, see J. Kathirithamby-Wells, *The British West Sumatran Presidency [1760–85]* (Kuala Lumpur: University Malaya, 1977), p. 26.

To some extent, these examples may be found to reflect social divisions based upon an accommodation between groups from different regions or who derived from different ethnic and religious backgrounds. In Negeri Sembilan, dual Hulu and Hilir lineages were formed as a result of interaction between Sumatran migrants and the original inhabitants.[122] Even more relevant for this study may be the dualistic rivalry in Minangkabau society described by Josselin de Jong and expressed in a "hostile friendship" between the two principal Minangkabau descent groups or *laras* (also *lareh*), Bodi Caniago and Koto Piliang.[123] These *laras* embody two pairs of four *suku* which are usually described as representing respectively the "egalitarian" and "aristocratic" or hierarchical elements in Minangkabau society.[124] This pattern of two sets of four *suku* is also represented in other parts of Sumatra, where it reflects local social divisions. The administrative system of Padang accommodated representatives of each of the two Minangkabau *adat* traditions in eight panghulu positions, representing four of the principal lineages from each of the two groups.[125] The Batak population of the east Sumatran kingdom of Deli was also divided by two sets of four *suku* who acknowledged the Sultan of Deli; four were lowland and four interior *suku*.[126]

The presence of two royal families within one kingdom can, therefore, be viewed from more than one perspective. According to the principles enunciated in several well-known Malay *hikayat* it was an impossibly shameful occurrence, and dual kingship does, indeed, appear to have flown in the face of traditional Malay ideas on government. Elsewhere, in regions less immediately linked with the Melaka tradition, prevailing ideologies may have offered more flexible approaches to dealing with ethnic and geographic diversity and to the systems of government which reflected these. Barus was set on a frontier in the Malay world in several senses, not least of these being the cultural frontier between Bataks and Malays. In considering the issues posed by dual royal lineages in Barus it will be necessary to read the Barus, material in the context of these various approaches to duality and to the resolution of conflict in Malay societies.

* * *

In order to examine these questions in more detail, attention will be given in the next chapter to the situation encountered by the VOC in 1668, and to the attempts of Company officials to change it.

From this examination three conclusions will emerge. It will appear, first of all, that the existence of two rulers was a source of considerable tension in Barus. VOC sources frequently refer to "groote jealousie" between the Rajas, and the constant friction this produced eventually led to the Company attempting a resolution of the situation. Secondly, and in spite of that friction, the presence of duality within Barus

---

[122]M. B. Hooker, *Adat Laws in Modern Malaya* (Kuala Lumpur: Oxford University Press, 1972), pp. 185–89 and passim.

[123]De Josselin de Jong, *Minangkabau and Negeri Sembilan*, p. 71. On rituals involving dualistic rivalry in Minangkabau see pages 76–80.

[124]Ibid., p. 74.

[125]F. W. Stapel, "Een verhandeling over het ontstaan van het Minangkabausche rijk en zijn Adat," *BKI* 92 (1935): 461–66. Cited in Dobbin, *Islamic Revivalism*, p. 80.

[126]E. Netscher, "Togtjes in het gebied van Riouw en Onderhoorigheden," *TBG* 14 (1864): 349.

had great survival value. The VOC attempted to create a monarchical state and eliminate one of the families, but achieved only partial success. Both families survived and played a part in the government of the kingdom until the early nineteenth century when, for a short time, a situation of actual dual government was revived. Despite the tensions it provoked, then, the existence of two rulers deriving from distinct royal families seems to have been appropriate in some way to the kingdom of Barus. Finally, the Hulu-Hilir distinction is not a simple hinterland/coast distinction. It will be seen that both families, in fact, had hinterland links. Each of them derived significant support and recognition from different sections of the upland population, and lines of loyalty existed between hinterland and coast which, in some degree, explain the survival of both families.

A survey of these relationships as they are presented in the external sources for Barus history will serve as a prologue to a consideration of the Malay sources from Barus.

2

EUROPEAN PERCEPTIONS OF BARUS
1668–1840

A detailed examination of European sources for Barus history is not the purpose of this chapter. Neither is it intended to write the political, social, and economic history of Barus on the basis of VOC and later Dutch and British sources. The European records which are analyzed here do, however, provide one description of that period of Barus's past which forms the subject of a large part of the Malay chronicles considered below. Not only is it possible to locate, in the European historical record, events which are described in the Malay sources, but many of the same issues, such as dual government, relations between the two royal families, between Bataks and Malays, and between coast and hinterland are given close attention in both the insider and the outsider accounts. The intention here, however, is not to use European sources to verify the Malay texts, but rather to enable us, by reading the chronicles in the context of contemporary accounts, to understand further the past to which they refer and the perspectives within which they view it.

The European records are, of course, often contemporary with the events they describe, whereas the Malay sources are from a later period and are written for a different purpose. In addition to embodying their own perspective on events, the European records therefore possess chronological advantages which have been exploited in this chapter. European records, however, do not hold the only chronological and interpretative key to Barus's past and subsequently we shall see that the Malay sources can be used in turn to assist a reading of the Dutch record. The Malay chronicles show us how local historians wished to present Barus' past. The European sources, though they disguise and ignore issues for their own purposes, show how those observers saw their own present. As such they may themselves be considered as a text on Barus and as another voice from that past with which the Malay chronicles are concerned.

VOC records offer the historian a first detailed insight into the political life of Barus. What is particularly important and relevant here is that they describe the position of the two rulers as seen through the eyes of VOC servants, and offer a glimpse of local government in Barus during a critical period when Europeans sought to alter the political structure of the state.

As with any text, caution must be exercised in the use of these seventeenth century documents. Although the reports of the first VOC officials to visit Barus describe conditions there before Company trade became established, they also present problems. The Company's servants who were sent to northwest Sumatra were by no means the best available, even by the standards of the VOC. In addition to their

sometimes doubtful honesty and lack of sympathy with local affairs, their understanding of events was hindered by their linguistic and cultural limitations. J. J. Pits,
during his period of office as Stadhouder of the Westkust, was far from satisfied with
his subordinates, among whom fraud and maltreatment of the local population was
common.[1] They were often obliged to rely on local intermediaries from Padang and
elsewhere who, no doubt, looked after their own interests and represented the local
situation from their own point of view. Company visits to Barus were sporadic at
first and, in these early days of Dutch contact with west Sumatra, it is unlikely that all
the nuances and subtleties of local affairs revealed themselves to the mixed bag of
people who worked for the VOC.[2] It was not, for instance, until the mid-nineteenth
century that European travelers entered the inland Batak regions behind Barus, and
in the seventeenth century the Company's knowledge of these people, who had a
large effect on Barus affairs, was only superficial.[3]

The Company's interest in Barus and the west coast ports was principally commercial and the reports of its servants reflect this.[4] Seventeenth century Dutchmen
cannot be expected to have viewed events from the same perspective as the local
population, and much of the internal, political and cultural life of the kingdom is
ignored or only hinted at in official reports, the bulk of which are concerned with
trade.[5] There were, however, aspects of the government of this kingdom which
proved to be very troublesome from the Company's point of view. VOC correspondents were forced to concentrate on these issues, and the information which emerges
from their letters allows the identification and description of an unusual local situation: a Sumatran polity which operated in its own way, which was governed by two
rulers, and which failed to conform, in this respect, to the familiar pattern of Malay
government.

POPULATION AND GOVERNMENT IN BARUS IN THE SEVENTEENTH CENTURY

VOC reports present Barus as a *pesisir* port which was, in many respects, Malay
in character, despite the presence of a large Batak population. The population,
according to Arendt Silvius, consisted of "Malays from this coast and from other
regions who, over time, had also blended in some degree with the Bataks."[6] "Like

---

[1] See H. Kroeskamp, *De Westkust en Minangkabau 1665–1668,* Academisch Proefschrift,
University of Leiden (Utrecht: Schotanus and Jens, 1931), p. 147. For a more detailed discussion
of the limitations of VOC reports on Barus in the early years of contact see J. E. Drakard, "A
Malay Frontier: The Adaptation of Political Culture in Barus" (MA thesis, Monash University,
1984), pp. 35–38.

[2] It is now well understood that the VOC's representatives in the region were not all
Dutchmen. Europeans from elsewhere, Asians and Eurasians, were also among the Company's
ranks. See, for instance, M. C. Ricklefs, *A History of Modern Indonesia* (London: Macmillan,
1981), p. 25. The terms "Dutch" and "Dutchmen" have, nevertheless, been used in the following pages for convenience.

[3] Kroeskamp comments that the interior remained "terra incognita" for the Company and that
its servants were only familiar with a small stretch of the coast. Kroeskamp, *De Westkust*, pp.
156–57.

[4] Political and not just commercial aims motivated the VOC's alliance with Barus, but once the
Contract had been signed trade dominates the reports of Company servants there.

[5] See Barbara Watson Andaya's comments on the "inherent biases" of the VOC material she
used for her study of eighteenth century Perak. Andaya, *Perak,* p. 5.

[6] ". . . van Meleijers die van deze cust ende andere gewesten sig door de tijt ook eenigsins met
de Battas vermengt hebben." Silvius to Pits (1677), VOC 1322, f. 1328r. References in this

most Malays their religion was Mohommedanism."[7] François Backer, one of the first VOC servants to visit the port, thought that in "reasonableness, judgement and understanding" the inhabitants of Barus were superior to many other west coast groups: "They are more like chief Rabbis than brutal folk," he declared.[8] Another official described the people of Barus as "puffed up with pride."[9] Malay was the language of the port, although seventeenth century sources make no mention of whether the Minangkabau dialect was used. Company reports mention no special language difficulties in Barus and the letters sent from the Barus rulers to Pits were translated by Company scribes from Malay.[10]

The 1668 Contract negotiations reveal there were Acehnese resident in Barus, some of whom had married members of the local nobility.[11] A group of Chinese were established in the trading area, referred to in VOC reports as the *barung-barung* (*warung*, shop or stall), near the shore.[12] Another group whom the Dutch describe as *strandbewoonders* (beach or coastal dwellers) are reminiscent of the *orang laut* of peninsular Malaya.[13] According to VOC reports, these people formed a distinct community under their own leader, the Malim Muara (Captain or chief of the river mouth). Their *adat* or custom was said to be different from that of the Malays.[14] The *strandbewoonders* may have been composed, at least in part, of islanders who earned

---

chapter to documents from the Overgekomen Brieven en Papieren, Batavia's Inkomend Brievenboek (Sumatra's Westkust) which is held in the Algemeen Rijksarchief, The Hague, are given according to the new VOC classification which has been attributed by the Rijksarchief. A list which reconciles VOC numbering with the old KA system is available from the Eerste Afdeeling of the Rijksarchief.

[7] Ibid., "Hunne religie is als te gros der Maleijers Muhummetisch."

[8] Backer to Pits (1669), VOC 1272, f. 1066v. This remark is also quoted by Kroeskamp who puts a similar interpretation on it. (*De Westkust* , p. 149). Kroeskamp also cites an earlier VOC expectation that the Barus people would be "brutale volck," Ibid., p. 135. Silvius described the people of Barus as "deceitful, self-interested, subtle and diplomatic . . . ," Silvius to Pits (1677), VOC 1322, f. 1328r.

[9] "Opgeblazen hoogh moedig," Silvius to Pits, Ibid.

[10] See, for instance, VOC 1268, f. 849: a translated letter from the rulers of Barus to Pits, in which the scribe explains that he has skipped the elaborate Malay courtesies with which the letter opened.

[11] Kroeskamp, *De Westkust*, p. 138. One of the stumbling blocks encountered during the first treaty negotiations was local opposition to the VOC demand that all of these Acehnese be expelled from Barus. The Company was forced to back down because of the strength of local feeling on this matter. Ibid., pp. 141–42.

[12] Melman to Pits (1668), VOC 1268, f. 857v. Also Kroeskamp, *De Westkust*, pp. 138–39.

[13] For a description of the *orang laut* see Andaya, *Kingdom of Johor*, pp. 80–83. A modern researcher noted the possible presence of *orang laut* in the Barus coastal area during 1981. Margaret J. Kartomi, "Kapri: A Synthesis of Malay and Portuguese Music on the West Coast of Sumatra," in *Cultures and Societies of North Sumatra*, ed. Rainer Carle (Berlin and Hamburg: Dietrich Reimer Verlag, 1987), p. 385, n. 51.

[14] F. W. Stapel and J. E. Heeres, eds., *Corpus Diplomaticum Neerlando-Indicum*, vol. 4 (1691–1725) in *BKI* 93 (1935): 82–83. By the 1690s the Company had enlisted these people for its own service, and the Contract of 1694 stipulated that the *strandbewoonders* should be available to perform services for the VOC resident.

their livelihood in the trade between Barus, Nias, and the smaller offshore islands.[15] Another population group not mentioned in the earliest Dutch reports but which made itself felt at a later stage were the *strandbataks*, Bataks of the beach or coastal areas.[16] They are mentioned most frequently in connection with Sorkam and Korlang which may have had much larger Batak populations than Barus.[17] VOC officials were critical of the *strandbataks*, who are described as engaging in robbery and marauding in the Barus region and as far north as Singkel.[18] The group is not described in detail in the Company's records, but it may have consisted of hill people who had made the transition to the coast, while retaining their Batak identity.

In its political life, Barus is depicted exhibiting many of the familiar features of a Malay polity,[19] but there are also indications of a less than autocratic style of government there which is reminiscent of the so called "republican" or "democratic" style of Minangkabau political life. The center of political life was the *balai* (audience hall or public meeting house, as distinct from the ruler's palace, or *istana*).[20] VOC reports mention decisions which were made and announced in the *balai*, and this was also the place to which the population took their complaints and where they made their wishes known.[21] The citizens, or *gemeente* as the Dutch called them, appear to

[15]According to Kroeskamp's interpretation, Barus, Singkel, and Nias formed a symbiotic community (*levensgemeenschap*), and the Company found that it was not possible to be involved with one without developing similar contacts with the other two. Kroeskamp, *De Westkust*, p. 150. In 1672 a contract was signed with Singkel and during 1693 and 1694 a series of contracts with different parts of the island of Nias were entered into. Stapel and Heeres, eds., *Corpus Diplomaticum*, vol. 4, pp. 25–54.

[16]N. Macleod, "De Oost-Indische Compagnie op Sumatra in de 17e eeuw," *Indische Gids* (1905), No. 1, p. 127.

[17]VOC 1294, f. 418v.–421r.

[18]Macleod, "Oost-Indische Compagnie op Sumatra," p.127.

[19]Important officers of state were the four *Hakim* (judges), three *Imam* (elders or leaders in religious matters, who commonly led Friday prayers), and three *Khatib* (preachers who performed recitations in the mosque). Pits to Barus (1668), VOC 1268, f. 851r. For mention of these religious officials in nineteenth century Malay political life, Gullick, *Indigenous Political Systems*, pp. 36–37. In Barus the *Hakim* were active in public life and, along with other members of the *gemeente*, they took part in the decision to become allies of the Company. In government the two Rajas were assisted by several high-ranking ministers. Three added their names to the 1668 Contract, the Orangkaya Balai, Maharaja Muda, and Raja Sittia Lilla [Setia Lela?], but in later contracts and VOC records four senior ministers are usually named, and one may therefore have been absent or unwilling to sign in 1668. See Stapel and Heeres, eds., *Corpus Diplomaticum*, vol. 2 (1650–1675), in *BKI* 87 (1931): 383–89. See pp. 482–86 for a Barus contract which was signed by four senior ministers. Four was the usual number in Malay kingdoms. See Gullick, *Indigenous Political Systems*, p. 10.

[20]For mention of the *balai* see VOC 1272, f. 1066v. The term *balai* is often qualified by other terms which define its use. In particular, there is a distinction between its use in Minangkabau and on the Malay peninsula. In the latter case the *balai* was usually attached to the ruler's palace or *istana* and served as his hall of audience. In Minangkabau, the *balai* is more generally understood as a council hall or public meeting place. See Wilkinson, *Malay-English Dictionary*, vol. 1, pp. 71–72 and van der Toorn, *Minangkabausche-Maleisch-Nederlandsch Woordenboek*, p.48. The presence of a *balai* is considered to be one of the defining characteristics of a Minangkabau *nagari*. See L. C. Westenenk, *De Minangkabausche Nagari* (Weltevreden: Visser, 1918), p. 11.

[21]VOC 1272, f. 1066r.

have played an active role in the affairs of the kingdom.[22] The Dutch word *gemeente* appears to indicate citizenry, and the same group in Barus was also referred to as *burgers* (citizens or middle class men).[23] According to Melman's report of the initial Contract negotiations, it was the *gemeente* which bullied the rulers of Barus into making an agreement with the Company, despite their fear of Acehnese reprisals.[24] In fact, according to Melman's report, there was "uproar" during the *"pitscharingh"* (or *bicara*) held in the *balai* when the two Rajas declared their continued loyalty to Aceh.[25] The *gemeente* are presented as being attracted by the relative freedom in trading arrangements initially offered by the Company and by the promise of an escape from the harsh rule of the most recent Acehnese Panglima.[26]

Although VOC correspondents do not make this connection, it is possible that an apparent lack of central and autocratic authority in Barus was linked to the presence in the kingdom of two rulers, rather than the usual single and pre-eminent ruler. When Melman and his colleagues first arrived and began negotiations to bring the kingdom into their system of west coast alliances, they encountered both the Raja di Hulu and the Raja di Hilir of Barus. Despite the geographical distinction implicit in these titles, both of the rulers lived on the coastal flat, though in separate *kampung*, Kampung Hulu (or Mudik, upstream) and Kampung Hilir.[27] Despite being ruled by two kings, Barus was, nevertheless, considered to be one kingdom. The two princes were joint signatories to the first Contract with the VOC in 1668.[28] The rulers apparently recognized each other's right to rule and they both signed other documents, such as letters to the Company, jointly.[29] The earliest VOC reports make some attempt to distinguish them on grounds of status and one correspondent writing in

---

[22]By *Gemeente* in the Barus context VOC officials may have been referring to the *Orang Kaya*, powerful and wealthy men who played an important role in the political life of Malay kingdoms. On the role of the *Orang Kaya* in Malay kingdoms see Milner, *Kerajaan*, p. 25.

[23]*Gemeente*—"de gemene burgerij, al de burgers van stad, in tegenstelling van de regeering," C. Kruyskamp, *Van Dale Groote Woordenboek der Nederlandse Taal* (The Hague: Nijhoff, 1961).

[24]In answer to an inquiry by Melman and Backer when the *gemeente* visited their ship, the *Hakim* and the whole *gemeente* are said to have declared, "Yes, we will trade with the Dutch and with them we will live and die." (Ya, wij willen met de Hollanders handelen, en met haer leven en sturven.) Backer to Pits (1669), VOC 1272, f. 1066r.

[25]Ibid. A member of the *gemeente*, whose relatives were held as hostages of the Company attacked the Raja di Hilir with his *kris* and, according to the account which was given to Melman, the rulers would have been killed if some of the women had not intervened and they had not managed to escape. This incident is cited in Kroeskamp, *De Westkust*, p. 140. In Malay works from the Peninsula the slaying of a ruler is presented as an unthinkable crime. If it is true, this incident may be an indication of the authority of the *gemeente* in Barus, and the unusually tenuous position of the rulers.

[26]Pits described this Panglima as a brother-in-law of the "aarts-bisschop" of Aceh. Ibid., p. 137. Several European travelers who visited Aceh in the seventeenth century mention a "Bishop" or "Arch-bishop" there. Probably referring to the office of *kadi* or judge, the earliest of these references have been supposed to refer to Shamsu'l-Din al-Sumatrani and later mentions of the same office to Nuru'l-Din Al-Raniri. See B. Schrieke, *Indonesian Sociological Studies* (The Hague and Bandung: van Hoeve, 1957), vol. 2, p. 393 note 149 and Syed Muhammad Naguib Al-Attas, *Raniri and the Wujudiyyah of 17th Century Aceh* (Kuala Lumpur: Malaysian Branch of the Royal Asiatic Society, 1966), p. 9.

[27]Melman to Pits (1669), VOC 1272, f. 1082v.–1082r..

[28]Stapel and Heeres, eds., *Corpus Diplomaticum*, vol. 2, pp. 383–89.

[29]See, for instance, VOC 1369, ff. 1074–79, which is a letter to Pits from the Raja di Hulu, the Raja di Hilir, and their chief ministers.

1669 described the Raja di Hilir as the second (*tweeden*) ruler.[30] Another Dutchman writing in the same year, however, made no such distinction. To him the Raja di Hulu was *opper-Regent* and the Raja di Hilir was *mede opper-Regent*.[31] According to Melman who made the distinction between *opper* and *tweeden* kings, the former had most influence in "government" (*regeering*), whereas the latter had many supporters among the *gemeente*.[32] We shall see that VOC servants soon dispensed with attempts to categorize the two rulers in this way and that in later accounts both rulers and their families were, if not always evenly matched, consistently supported by certain sections of the Barus population.

The rulers do not appear to have divided their duties and responsibilities. Rather, as their titles indicate, they had different areas of geographical influence. One of the earliest Dutch reports, written by Melman in 1669, identifies the distinct spheres of authority suggested by the rulers' titles. The Raja di Hulu, he said, ruled over the highland and most distant areas of the kingdom and in those which were separated from Barus by "impassable" hills. The Raja di Hilir, on the other hand, governed the closest lying settlements and also those stretching down the west coast as far south as Batahan.[33] All of these small ports were centers for the delivery of resins which were transported to the coast from the hills lying behind them. In theory, then, the Raja di Hulu was responsible for the inland groups, the Bataks, and the Raja di Hilir ruled over the mixed Malay population of the coastal area. We shall see, however, that this initial picture is somewhat misleading. Subsequent reports from the second half of the seventeenth century depict both rulers enjoying contact with, and influence upon, different parts of the Batak interior and, to some extent, they competed for control over trade with these people.

Company servants appear to have recognized the unusual nature of this situation, and they attempted some explanation of the presence of two rulers. According to Silvius, the first Malay inhabitants of Barus came as "refugees from Tarusan, south of Sallido."[34] The Raja di Hilir and the Orang Kaya Balai considered themselves to be "loosely descended from this source."[35] Backer also mentioned, in 1669, that the Raja di Hilir was a "Tarousangger."[36] The Raja di Hulu, whom Silvius described as the "less pretentious" of the two, was said to be descended from a mixture of local Malays and Bataks.[37]

VOC accounts of the origin of power sharing in Barus are confusing. The Sultan of Aceh is regarded as having had a role in instituting dual government, but the full extent of Acehnese involvement is not clear. Silvius noted that the Raja di Hulu had been given that title by the ruler of Aceh,[38] whereas according to Melman the Sultan of Aceh was responsible for appointing both rulers.[39] Melman attempted an

---

[30]Melman to Pits (1669), VOC 1290, f. 1180v.

[31]Or co-*opper-Regent*. Backer to Pits (1669), VOC 1290, f. 600r. and 599v.

[32]Melman to Pits (1669), VOC 1272, f. 1065. Also cited in Kroeskamp, *De Westkust*, p. 152.

[33]Melman to Pits (1669), VOC 1272, f. 1082.

[34]Silvius to Pits (1667), VOC 1322, f. 1328r.

[35]Ibid.

[36]Backer to Pits (1669), VOC 1272, f. 1066 v.

[37]Silvius to Pits (1677), VOC 1322, f. 1328r.

[38]Ibid.

[39]Melman to Pits (1669), VOC 1272, f.1082v.

historical sketch of Barus in 1669 and, according to his account, Barus had, latterly, come under Acehnese domination. The kingdom had been reduced to a position of "homage and tribute" by means of violent attacks from Aceh. In the process, he wrote, some of the population had been converted from "heathens to Moors." Great unrest resulted from this Acehnese tyranny including "massacres, robbery and violence." It was in an attempt to improve this situation and to ensure resin supplies, that the ruler of Aceh, according to Melman, appointed two rulers over the kingdom. He chose those who appeared to be the "oldest established" and gave them the titles Raja di Hulu and Raja di Hilir.[40] In this connection, it is worth recalling Pinto's reference to a former *"Mandara"* of Barus, to whom the ruler of Aceh gave the title Sultan of Barus in 1539.[41] Pinto is not always given a great deal of credence for his accuracy; however the term *"Mandara"* appears to be an equivalent of Bandara or Bendahara.[42] In later years the Barus royal families shared the titles Sultan and Bendahara/Bandara and it is not impossible, therefore, that Pinto was referring to an earlier version of that arrangement which was altered by the Sultan of Aceh when he awarded the title Sultan or Raja to one family. Another early reference which may hint at the existence of dual kingship in Barus prior to the seventeenth century is Pires' statement (1512–1515) that Fansur/Barus was "all one kingdom not two."[43] Pires is usually taken here to be referring to the dual nomenclature of Barus, but we shall see that there are arguments for believing that the name Barus may have been brought from Tarusan, in southwest Sumatra, by the Malays who migrated from that region. This is the interpretation offered in the local, Malay, sources.[44] If this is, indeed, the case and the name Barus was first used by Malays from Tarusan, then the Tarusan migration would have had to have taken place before Pires wrote.[45] Pires' "One kingdom not two" might then apply not only to two names, but also to two kings.

Friction between the two rulers was noticed by Company officials very soon after the initial Dutch contact with Barus. It manifested itself, in the first instance, in the rulers' different attitudes toward Aceh and towards the Company itself. The Raja di Hulu was initially hostile towards the Company and was reported to be unwilling to cast off his Acehnese loyalties. For some time he refused to co-operate with the VOC and reportedly waited for help from Aceh.[46] The Raja di Hilir, on the other hand, encouraged the Company's presence in Barus and appeared to be anxious to be free of Aceh. He is described in reports as "our patron,"[47] and once the Dutch were

---

[40]Ibid.

[41]See footnote 31, ch. 1, above.

[42]See pp. 43–44 below.

[43]See p. 5 above.

[44]See p. 5 above and also Drakard, "An Indian Ocean Port," pp. 56–60 and 71–74, for a discussion of this point and a consideration of the use of the place name "Barus" in north Sumatra.

[45]We have seen that Wolters considers that there is no evidence for the use of the name Barus in north Sumatra prior to the account of Pires. Van der Tuuk also believed that the name Barus came to this region from Tarusan where there is a small river called Sungei Barus. H. N. van der Tuuk, *Bataksch-Nederduitsch Woordenboek* (Amsterdam: Muller, 1861), p. 375. See also pp. 3–5 above.

[46]Kroeskamp, *De Westkust*, p. 153 and Backer to Pits (1669), VOC 1272, f. 1065.

[47]Ibid., f. 1067v.

established in their fortified position he visited them frequently, with assurances of his loyalty and promises of prosperity and flourishing trade.[48] He also complained to them about the "bad faith" of the Raja di Hulu, who had publicly denounced him in the *balai* for mixing with the Company.[49]

These indications of Hilir hostility and Hulu loyalty to Aceh suggest that Silvius may have been more accurate than Melman in suggesting that it was the Raja di Hulu who owed his position to Aceh and not both rulers. The precise role of the Sultan of Aceh is not described in the reports, but, as we have seen, it seems likely that Aceh's part in creating this unusual situation may have been to formalize an existing arrangement rather than create it. As Melman points out, there already seem to have been two "oldest established" families, and, unless there already were two existing influential royal lines in Barus, it is hardly to be supposed that the Sultan of Aceh should create two rulers in the interest of peace and harmony. A likely, though necessarily tentative, explanation of the discrepancy between the reports of Melman and Silvius is that, in order to counter the influence of the anti-Acehnese Malays who had settled in Barus from Tarusan, the ruler of Aceh may have offered his support to the existing Batak Raja there and have formalized his position.

These Dutch reports, in spite of the differences between them, seem to have recognized the special nature of a situation in which two kings ruled jointly, and recognized a need to explain the circumstances by which it came into being. The VOC's main interest in Barus was, however, to make a profit from the purchase of resins and the sale of cloth and other items which were in demand in the interior. The letters of Company officials to their superiors are not, therefore, ideal sources for a study of the political life of the kingdom, and they do not contain satisfactory answers to many of the questions which arise as to how duality worked in Barus, and whether it should properly be called a dual system. Because of their preoccupation with trade, however, the VOC letters do contain information about the relationship between the rulers and the Batak population of the interior which helps to explain why both royal families survived in positions of authority despite their mutual antagonism.

On the basis of VOC accounts, the Hulu-Hilir distinction in Barus does not appear to have been a simple hinterland/coast distinction. On the contrary, both families are presented as possessing hinterland links. Each of them derived significant support and recognition from different sections of the hinterland population, and lines of loyalty existed between hinterland and coast which, in some degree, may explain the survival of both families.

The friction apparent in the conflicting attitudes of the rulers toward the Company and toward Aceh was also manifested in competition between them for control over upland paths and inland produce. It is unlikely that this rivalry sprang

---

[48]See, for instance, Backer to Pits (1671), VOC 1290, passim.

[49]Backer to Pits (1669), VOC 1272, f. 1065. "radja d'oulou die publijckelijk op d'algemene balai radja d'ilheer van alte groote patrocinatie beschuldijde." "Patrocinatie" does not occur in this form in any of the Dutch dictionaries consulted here. It appears to imply the possession of a patron or protector. The *Woordenboek der Nederlandsche Taal* of G. J. Boeklenoogen and J. H. van Lessen (The Hague: Nijhoff, 1931), gives *patrocinator* among the derivatives of the word *patroon*. "Patrocinatie" may be a version of the Latin word *patrocinium*, see C. Kruyskamp, *Groot Woordenboek der Nederlandse Taal* (The Hague: Nijhoff, 1961) and P. G. W. Glare, ed., *Oxford Latin Dictionary* (Oxford: Clarendon Press, 1977), vol. 6, where "patrocinium" and "patrocinor" are listed.

from a situation which was the simple product of Acehnese interference in Barus affairs, imposed from the outside upon the inhabitants of Barus. On the contrary, the hostility was able to endure because each Raja and his family received support from different sections of the hinterland population.

COASTAL-HINTERLAND RELATIONS

In the 1660s, Melman and Silvius commented on the links they observed between coast and interior and on the way in which these relationships involved the rulers of the port. Melman drew attention to the rivalry existing amongst the Batak peoples themselves, but he noticed also the fact that, in spite of their rivalries, all groups were concerned to have access to the port. The Bataks brought resins to the coast not only from the hills immediately inland from Barus, but also from those bordering the small coastal settlements between Barus and Air Bangis. In this area, benzoin was plentiful in Sibuluan, Batang Toru, Batu Mundam, Tabujang, Natal, and Batahan.[50] Melman observed that Barus would be unable to withstand an attack if the Bataks ever wanted to destroy it, but added that there were several reasons why this could never happen. The Bataks, he wrote, frequently engaged in local wars, and it was impossible that they would join together to attack Barus. One group would prevent another from launching an assault, he suggested, by refusing to allow passage through their territory, thereby blocking the route to the coast.[51] A second overwhelming reason why the Bataks would never wish to attack Barus was, in Melman's view, their dependence on the port as an outlet for their goods and a source of foreign materials.[52] And here the role of the rulers was important.

Company servants soon realized that contact and influence with the inland people was necessary for the success of their trade in Barus; but since the Bataks were sometimes unwilling to travel past the foothills and across the coastal flat, direct contact was difficult. They were forced, initially, to rely on the local population and the rulers of the port, who acted as intermediaries with the hill people. Early Dutch descriptions of Barus illustrate the manner in which such trade and intercourse between hill and coastal dwellers took place. According to Melman in 1670, the Barus rulers purchased the resins which had been brought down by the Bataks and, because the hill people feared to take their goods to the seashore themselves, the rulers and their followers arranged the transport of resins to the beach, where they were sold for a modest profit to foreign merchants.[53] Melman advised his superiors in Padang that the Bataks trusted the "Barusers," or the Barus *grooten*, as he described them, and by this, it seems, he meant the rulers, or *grandees* of Barus.[54] He described these *grooten* as more like brokers (*makelaars*) than merchants.[55] Similarly Silvius, eight years later, described the rulers of Barus as "mediators" with the Bataks.[56] The resins were exchanged for salt—which was in great demand inland, cloth—especially

---

[50]Melman to Pits (1669), VOC 1272, f. 1083r.

[51]Ibid., ff. 1083r.–1084v.

[52]Ibid., f. 1084v. "Overmits door deze attacque de bander der uitheemse volkeren tenemaal verdestrueert end uit geroijt soude worden waer door hun de gelegentheijt om hare wieroocken ter merckt te brengen."

[53]Melman to Pits (1669), VOC 1272, f. 1087r.

[54]Ibid.

[55]Ibid., f. 1088v.

[56]Silvius to Pits (1677), VOC 1322, f. 1328v.

the prized Indian varieties, and iron.[57] The rulers of Barus had the first opportunity to buy cloth and other merchandise from foreign traders and appear to have taken a direct part in trading with the Bataks.[58]

Dutch reports on the Barus situation, and letters from the rulers which were sent to Padang, suggest that the pathways immediately surrounding Barus were often made unsafe for the Bataks by the threat of plunder, and, at such times, trade stopped for long periods.[59] To some extent, the coastal rulers seem to have been responsible for ensuring the safety of the Bataks, for securing the pathways and protecting them from rapacious merchants. They also sent messages inland to inform the Bataks when ships had put into port and resin supplies were required. The hill people had to be tempted to come to port, and it seems that they did have cause to fear mistreatment on the coast, from the *strandbataks* in particular. Nevertheless, the Dutch sources present this as a reciprocal arrangement. The Bataks needed an outlet for their goods, and it was their link with Barus and her rulers which ensured their safety on the roads and the sale of their goods. Such was Melman's assessment.

Local attitudes toward the interior may be detected in the many assurances which the rulers gave to the Company concerning their ability to command resin supplies. And this meant both rulers, not merely the Raja di Hulu. Melman and Backer report that, while the Raja di Hulu remained aloof from the Company during the early months of their contact with Barus, the Raja di Hilir promised supplies of benzoin.[60] He and his brother visited Company officials and made frequent assurances of their "good faith" and their eagerness to trade with the Company. The Raja di Hilir acted as a go-between in 1670 when a Batak Raja came down from the hills with a large following which included the chiefs of Silindung and Korlang. According to Melman, these Batak chiefs brought large quantities of resin to the Company store and, through the Raja di Hilir, they promised not only that they would be loyal to the Company but that, along with their fellow chiefs, they would attempt to see that all the hill people who were subject to the Government of Barus, and to the Raja di Hilir, ceased their conflict with each other and returned again to their occupations of planting benzoin bushes and collecting resins.[61] By 1671 the Raja di Hulu is said to have acknowledged that help from Aceh was unlikely, and he, too, agreed to cooperate with the Company. He also gave assurances that he could guarantee resin supplies and boasted of his influence with the Bataks. He told Backer that he could provide the best quality white benzoin, because the Bataks obeyed him.[62] Backer reported that, on the last day of the month, a hundred or so Bataks

---

[57]Melman to Pits (1669), VOC 1272, f. 1082v.

[58]Ibid., f. 1087–88 v.

[59]See, for instance, Melman to Pits (1673), VOC 1294, f. 418v.

[60]According to Backer, the Raja di Hulu publicly forbade his people to have anything to do with the Company. Backer to Pits (1671), VOC 1272, f. 1066 and Backer to Pits (1673), VOC 1290, f. 599v.

[61]Melman to Pits (1669), VOC 1272, f. 1077r. ". . . alle bergleiders die nu onder de Barosse heerschappij ende Raja di Hilir sorteren." Backer also mentions this visit by the "Raja Batta" in Backer to Pits (1671), VOC 1272, f. 1067r. In another report Backer again mentions the assurances given to the Company by the Raja di Hilir that he was in touch with the Bataks. The Bataks were at peace, the Raja di Hilir said, and he had hopes of receiving plentiful supplies, Backer to Pits (1671), VOC 1290, f. 600.

[62]Ibid., f. 600r. "Dat ze hem gehoorzaemde."

arrived with a considerable quantity of benzoin "as promised by the Raja di Hulu."[63] Influence with the inland population appears, then, to have been crucial to trade in Barus and both rulers, not merely the Raja di Hulu, claimed to have authority in the interior. The Dutch acknowledged this relationship and, indeed, one Company servant even commented that the rulers of Barus appeared to have more authority inland than among their own people on the coast.[64]

THE VOC RESPONSE TO DUAL GOVERNMENT

The dependence of Company officials upon the Barus rulers for contact with the Batak population and access to the resin trade resulted in increasing VOC irritation. Company trade was also frequently disrupted by political disturbances within Barus. Immediately after the 1668 Contract had been signed, Pits had interfered with the local government by appointing and promoting ministers of state.[65] But, in spite of its having its "own men" in positions of power, things still did not go smoothly for the Company. From the VOC perspective, it was essential to maintain peace within the kingdom in order to ensure the free flow of goods and obtain the largest possible profit. In the Company's eyes there were two reasons why things did not always go as they wished and why the kingdom was troubled by unrest, petty disputes, and the consequent standstill of goods. First was the disturbing influence of Aceh and second the mutual hostility of the two rulers. The Company's identification of these problems, its analysis of the situation, and its methods of dealing with it, were to lead to much deeper interference in the affairs in the kingdom than was represented by the mere appointment of ministers.

The two problems appear to have been intertwined. As we have seen disagreement over whether to support the VOC or to remain loyal to Aceh was reportedly a cause of friction between the rulers when the Company first entered Barus; and in later years, if either Raja was disillusioned with his co-ruler and with the Company, his hostility often expressed itself in terms of his renewed support for Aceh. At least this was the Company's perception of his actions. There were many other reasons why the rulers and peoples of Barus and her hinterland might have come to resent Company control and be reluctant to cooperate with their new overlords: Company interference in political affairs, the banishment of members of the ruling families, monopoly trading tactics and prices, refusal to accept lower grades of benzoin and camphor, the low quality of fabrics offered in exchange, restrictions on travel, and the use of armed force to quell disturbances must all have contributed to creating bad blood between Barus and the Company.

Against the background of the Company's dissatisfaction with the situation in Barus, the VOC soon decided that dealing with two rulers was troublesome and inconvenient. A regular feature of Company policy throughout the archipelago was its tendency to identify and isolate a single indigenous authority through whom it might influence and direct affairs. Barus was no exception, and the Company was

---

[63]Ibid., f. 601 "...de gedane beloften bij Raja d'oeloe op dato 23 gedoen, gevolg genoomen hadde."

[64]Silvius to Pits (1677), VOC 1322, f. 1328v.

[65]He appointed Abu Bakar, who had played an important part in persuading the rulers to sign the 1668 Contract, to the position of Bendahara Muda, replaced the banished Acehnese Panglima by a Malay servant of the Company, and appointed Maharaja Lilla to the position of Temenggong. Pits to Barus (1669), VOC 1268, ff. 850v–851r.

soon involved in playing off one ruler against the other. It was not long before the removal of one of the Rajas became a major aim of VOC policy toward Barus. Interference of this sort would be expected to increase whatever suspicion and tension already existed between the rulers, superseding and disguising the original cause of friction. Once the Company began to meddle with the structure of government and to upset whatever natural equilibrium had existed, it becomes impossible to distinguish original sources of tension from those inspired by the Company. The Company threatened to leave Barus because of the troubles caused by jealousy between the rulers and, according to the reports of Backer and Melman, Company officials frequently sought assurances from the Rajas that they would cooperate with each other. Almost without exception, the frequently renewed contracts made between the Company and Barus stressed that the rulers should cooperate and live in peace, so that goods might flow and the trade of Barus might flourish.

In February 1680 Silvius submitted a report to Commander Hurdt and the Council at Padang which suggested that the Company allow the dual Rajaship to disappear.[66] Silvius pointed out that continued warfare was damaging to trade, and it was in the Company's interest that the fighting should stop. Silvius suggested that the VOC should covertly allow the Raja di Hulu, who was, he said, rich enough to command considerable authority, to oust the Raja di Hilir altogether. Silvius concluded that ultimately it would be most advantageous for the Company to "pull out" the whole Hilir family. All this, he proposed, should be accomplished under the assumed authority of the Raja di Hulu. In view of the Raja di Hilir's large following and considerable authority among the Bataks, the Company would not be strong enough to act alone.[67]

The opportunity to bring about this change came in the course of a drawn out wrangle between the two ruling families concerning control over access to the interior. There was a crisis in 1693 which led to decisive Dutch action. Following an attack by the Hulu family on the VOC post, in which a number of Company servants were killed and as a result of which a military force was sent to Barus, the Company forced the rulers into an agreement to abolish the dual Rajaship. Henceforth, the Company decreed, there should be but one Raja, called Raja Barus, who was, on this first occasion, to be drawn from the Hilir family.[68]

This agreement brought about the fulfillment of Silvius' plans. The Hilir family had not been eliminated, but the dual Rajaship had. From that time onwards, the Company insisted, Barus would be ruled by one Raja with four *penghulu*. The Raja di Hilir was named Raja Barus, and Raja Minuassa [Menawar Syah?], the grandson of the old Raja di Hulu, became the first *penghulu*. Among the various articles of the contract which formalized the new arrangement, it was specified that the individual territory of the Raja di Hilir and the Raja di Hulu, and the people who grouped themselves on either side, should, henceforth, be known as Negeri Barus and be subject to the Raja Barus. No further reference was to be made to a dual government.[69]

The 1694 agreement formally put an end to dual government for the remainder of the VOC period, but it did not succeed in "pulling out" either of the two royal families. Indeed, contrary to Silvius' original plan it was the Raja di Hilir and not the

---

[66] Macleod, "De Oost-Indische Compagnie op Sumatra," *IG* 2 (1905): 136.

[67] Ibid., pp. 136–37.

[68] Ibid., p. 1435, and *Corpus Diplomaticum*, vol. 4, pp.71–83.

[69] Ibid.

Raja di Hulu who became Raja Barus in 1694. This interchangeability between the two families was to continue, and it suggests that a "dual system" as such was not in place in Barus. Rather than a case of institutionalized power sharing, what the VOC seems to have encountered in Barus was a situation in which two prestigious families competed for influence, subjects, and wealth in the hinterland. "Control" over the coastal regions, was not, according to the VOC picture, an element in the authority of the two rulers. Given that the Company's presence must itself have been an influential factor in Barus affairs from 1668 onwards, it is difficult to use VOC sources to make judgments concerning the political situation there which do not take this relationship into account. This applies particularly to the question of hostility between the two ruling families. What the VOC sources do reveal clearly, however, is the role that hinterland links played in the position and influence of the two royal families.

The importance of their inland, Batak, constituencies for both the rulers is also evident in the years after 1694. The Company was soon forced to face the fact that it could not manage without the authority of the Hulu family, and, before long, a revision had to be made of the drastic measures taken in 1694. During the 1693 military expedition, the Hulu family had been given help by the Batak chiefs in the Dairi hills.[70] After the contract had been signed, Raja Minuassa returned to the Dairi lands and went into temporary exile in the hills behind Singkel.[71] In 1698, a new agreement recalled him to Barus, and he was appointed by the Company as their intermediary with the Dairi Bataks, who had not been satisfying the Dutch demand for resins. This was despite a Contract signed in 1694 with the Dairi chiefs, in which the Company attempted to persuade them to transfer their loyalty from the Hulu family to the new Raja Barus.[72] It appeared that, while it was possible to eliminate the dual Rajaship in formal terms, the absence of a Hulu Raja within the kingdom was not in the Company's interest. His important role in the movement of goods was simply not to be ignored. The Company did not restore the royal title of the Hulu family, but Minuassa was made *bara-antara* (mediator) with the Dairi Bataks.[73] The incident clearly implies the importance of the links between the coastal rulers and the inland producers of resins. Little, it seems, had really changed. A Raja di Hulu was still needed, even if under another title.

Reports from the early eighteenth century suggest the continued strength of these loyalties and the apparent durability of the two ruling families. In particular, each of the royal families appears to have enjoyed special influence in distinct areas of the hinterland and among distinct groups of Bataks. By 1706 the Raja Minuassa was using his influence with the Dairi and in Singkel to regain his family's royal status. Trade was disrupted and the kingdom was once again thrown into confusion.[74] In 1709 Minuassa's uncle, Megat Suka, or Raja Bongsu as he was also called (he was the youngest son of the old Raja), took up the cudgels on behalf of his family's rights, and with an Acehnese ally he succeeded in unnerving the Raja Barus.[75] The Raja wrote to Padang claiming that the kingdom was in confusion and was no longer like

---

[70]Macleod, "De Oost-Indische Compagnie op Sumatra," *IG* 2 (1906): 1435.

[71]Ibid., pp.1437–38.

[72]*Corpus Diplomaticum*, vol. 4, pp. 83–86.

[73]Ibid., pp. 142–44.

[74]Instruction to Onderkoopman Hendrik Disselbrink (1707), VOC 1760, f. 125–29.

[75]Resident Ijsbrand Induis to Padang (1710), VOC 1777, f. 39, and Gezaghebber Hofman at Barus (1711), VOC 1827, f. 17–30.

a monarchical state; owing to Megat Suka's wickedness, he said, it was as if there were once again two rulers of Barus.[76] Company officials assessing the situation advised Dutch help for the Raja Barus because as long as the Dairi supported the Hulu family, members of the family would be able to make trouble, and because of the loyalty these Dairi Bataks traditionally owed to the Hulu family VOC servants foresaw no possibility of this support dwindling.[77]

Officials also remarked on the relationship between the Hilir family and the Pasaribu Bataks (resident in Silindung, Sorkam, and Korlang). If the Hulu family were allowed to overcome the Raja Barus, one wrote, the Pasaribu would consider themselves to be unprotected and would "fall away" from Barus.[78] In 1683 the then Raja di Hilir is said to have left Barus for Sorkam, where he was "much loved" by the population who held him to be "nearly holy."[79] When he died in Sorkam in 1689 the Bataks refused to give up his corpse to the Raja di Hulu who wanted to bury him in Barus.[80] Again, during 1709, as the Hilir Raja Barus sought to strengthen his position, it was to the Pasaribu hills that he traveled with a large retinue. He remained away for some months and sent several letters to the residents and local government in Barus.[81] In 1714, the Raja Barus died and, since there was no suitable successor in the Hilir family, Raja Minuassa was appointed Raja Barus. He is said to have been unanimously chosen by the older people in Barus. In order to appease the Hilir family supporters and maintain some balance between the two rival parties, a nephew of the old Raja Barus was made Bendahara.[82] Despite the accession of the Hulu family, the resident of Barus in 1720 commented on the enduring distinction between the two families and that the "southern Bataks," though nominally subject to the Raja Barus, were, in fact, more inclined toward the Hilir family and its current representative, Raja Ibrahim.[83]

---

[76]Translated letter from the Raja of Barus (1709), VOC 1777, f. 43. "in de negorij Baros door dien UES dienaar in een gants swaeke gesteltheijt is, nadermaal hem ontbreekt de hulp van de Comp en het niet is als ten tijde van de Commander Boudens wassen maar een hooft en nu is t gelijk . . . twee hoofden zijn."

[77]Ijsbrand Induis to Padang (1710), VOC 1777, f. 39.

[78]Ibid.

[79]Macleod, "De Oost-Indische Compagnie op Sumatra," p. 486.

[80]Ibid., p. 1423.

[81]Resident Ijsbrand Induis to Padang (1710), VOC 1777, f. 29.

[82]P. Th. Coolhaas, ed., *Generale Missiven van Gouverneurs-Generaal en Raden aan Heren XVII Der Verenigde Oostindische Compagnie*, Deel VII, 1713–1725 (The Hague: Nijhoff, 1979), p. 101. ". . . om door de jalousie van die vermogende familien de saeken aldaar des te beterin balans te konnen houden."

[83]Memorie of Resident Pouw at Barus (1719), VOC 1926, f. 88. A contract from the year 1731 appears to contradict the general impression in VOC sources of an exclusive bond between the Hilir family and the Pasaribu Bataks. During the reign of Raja Minuassa the Pasaribu Bataks are said to have been at odds with the administration in Barus. In a Dutch contract they were required to agree that henceforth they would be loyal to the Raja Baros instead of the Raja di Hulu, "Sullen radja-Baros in plaats van radja de Houlou onder het hooger gesagh van de E. Comp. voor onsen konink erkennen, eeren en respecteeren, en alles toebrengen wat wy voorheen aan radja de Houlou gedaan hebben." The text of this article (no. 4) in the published version of the VOC contracts is consistent with the MS copy of the document held in The Hague. I believe, however, that this is either a mistake in the original contract or a scribal error in the copy send to Holland, since there is no evidence in earlier Company reports for such a relationship between the Pasaribu Bataks and the Hulu family. Neither does it make sense since the Raja Barus in question was already a member of the Hulu family. Raja di Hilir is

Each of the two royal families appears, then, to have had a special and enduring relationship with particular sections of the Batak population. As we have seen, the Hilir family had a long lasting relationship with the Bataks of Sorkam and Korlang. The groups in the Pasaribu and Silindung hills behind Sorkam were also a special constituency of the Hilir family, and it was among these people that the Hilir rulers were able to command resin supplies. The Hulu family, on the other hand, appear to have enjoyed a close relationship with the Batak areas to the northwest of Barus in upper Singkel and in the Dairi hills. It was to these areas that members of the Hulu family resorted in times of trouble and among the Dairi that Hulu Rajas secured resin supplies. Apart from their commercial nature, Dutch sources tell us little about the basis and character of these relationships; they do indicate, however, that lines of loyalty seem to have existed between each of the Barus royal families and particular Batak groups in the interior. We shall see that these bonds are prominent not only in VOC sources, but also in local sources which chronicle the history of Barus and its two ruling families.

At a formal level, the elimination of two kings was successfully accomplished by the treaty of 1694. VOC sources do not, however, reveal how this change was perceived within Barus. As we have seen, the first Raja Barus wrote to Padang in 1709 with the complaint that the Hulu family were behaving as though there were still two rulers in Barus, and that Barus was no longer a monarchical state. Perhaps both families were in favor of monarchy as long as they held the throne. During the remainder of the VOC period Raja Barus was the formal ruler of the kingdom and foremost client of the Company. The ruler's authority, however, appears to have become increasingly dependent upon VOC support. Company records show that during the eighteenth century the Raja Barus, his "Bendahara" and the other important *penghulu* all received regular payments from the Company according to their rank.

Despite the decisive nature of the 1694 agreement, each of the ruling families seems nevertheless to have retained its claims to royal status. Each family, that is to say, appears to have retained its qualification to fill the Raja Barus position, and dual royal claims were not eliminated. The exact details of succession to the Raja Barus position in eighteenth century Company records are difficult to determine. There are several reasons for this; one is the lengthy reign of the second Raja Barus, which may have obscured Hulu and Hilir relations as an urgent issue in Barus politics. Another is the use, in later Company records, of the title "Raja Barus" in preference to any other royal title or *gelar*. Perhaps as a result of the VOC insistence in the 1694 contract that dual government was no longer to be an issue in the kingdom, the Hulu and Hilir families are rarely mentioned in later VOC reports, and this makes it difficult to identify individual incumbents.

Insofar as it has been possible to determine the succession according to Dutch records, however, the two families did not disappear and a degree of rotation between them seems to have taken place, with the actual position of Raja alternating between them. We have seen that a Raja di Hilir became the first Raja Barus and he was succeeded by the Hulu prince Minuassa or Menawar Syah. At that time a Hilir representative, Raja Ibrahim, was made Bendahara in order to satisfy Hilir claims and to retain a balance between the two families. Raja Minuassa lived until about

---

surely what is intended here. See *Corpus Diplomaticum*, vol. 5, pp. 98–101, and VOC 2194 (1731), ff. 649 and 568.

1739 and was succeeded by Raja Ibrahim.[84] Raja Bongsu became Bendahara or next in command and next in order in the Company's list of gift payments.[85] Whether or not Raja Bongsu later became ruler is not clear. By 1759 the succession had changed again and a letter refers to Raja Barus and the second regent, Raja Ibrahim. In the local, Malay, sources from Barus "Raja Ibrahim" is a name which is used exclusively by the Hilir family, and it is likely, therefore, that this second regent was a Hilir representative. Local sources also record that Sutan Marah Pangkat became Raja Barus in 1756. Marah Pangkat is mentioned as 3rd Penghulu in a Company letter of 1747 which indicates that he was in line for the succession and probably did succeed to the Raja Barus position.[86] Malay sources also state that Marah Pangkat was the son of the previous Raja Barus, Raja Bongsu, but it has not been possible to confirm this in VOC records. Malay sources, as we shall see, give a more thorough account of royal succession in these years, including detailed reign dates. Like Company records, however, these narratives have their own perspectives and their own structures for ordering the past. Later in this study it will be possible to consider more carefully the relationship between the historical perspective of the Dutch and Malay sources.

Although the precise details of royal succession in this confusing period are difficult to determine, the position of Raja Barus does seem to have alternated between the families for some time. A Dutch account from 1760 states that the Raja of Barus was chosen in turns from the families of "D'Oulue en D'Ilir," and that whichever family was excluded from the Raja Barus position provided the "Bandahara."[87]

As the eighteenth century progressed, Company trade on the northwest coast became increasingly hampered by Acehnese "smuggling" and the presence of English traders in the area. There are also indications in Dutch and British records that the increasing dependence of the Barus *regeering* upon the VOC for their positions and status had a harmful effect on the ability of the royal families to appeal to the Bataks of the interior. Company reports in the first half of the eighteenth century reflect frequent unrest among the hinterland population and competition from other trading centers. Between 1736 and 1740 there are reports of an influential Minangkabau prince or Yang Dipertuan who called upon the loyalty of the Barus rulers and of the populations of Sorkam and Korlang in an uprising against the Company. For a period, this prince and a holy man who accompanied him are said to have won the support of the Barus rulers and caused trouble between the VOC establishment at Barus and the population of Sorkam.[88] In addition the presence of two strong-minded chiefs in neighboring regions seems to have further eroded the

---

[84]Unfortunately the set of Overgekomen Brieven used for this study does not hold Sumatra's Westkust records for the years 1740–1741. In a letter of 1739 the Raja Barus was said to be "deathly ill," and by 1744 the succession had changed, VOC 2468, f. 711.

[85]VOC 2701, f. 289.

[86]See VOC 2571, f.432.

[87]This information comes from a report written by van Basel in 1761. The manuscript which has been consulted here is held in the Arsip Negara of the Republic of Indonesia, SWK 10 , p. 37. The information in van Basel's report is also summarised in Kielstra's "Onze Kennis van Sumatra's Westkust," p. 514. The same information is also mentioned in Marsden, *History of Sumatra*, p. 367.

[88]VOC 2347, ff. 614–37 and f. 425

authority of the Barus *regeering*. These were Raja Simorang a chief of Tapanuli[89] and Raja Bukit, an Acehnese who had settled in Sorkam and who was officially the subordinate of the Ruler of Barus. Raja Bukit's following, however, by the middle of the eighteenth century is said to have been considerable and larger than that of the Raja Barus.[90] Competition from the English settlements at Natal and Tapanuli, and from Singkel, where many of the Bataks began to take their resins in preference to Barus, further exacerbated the decline in Barus' trade and the authority of her rulers. Rather than promoting Barus and its position in the resin trade, the attempts of the VOC to control the political situation and the way in which trade was conducted undoubtedly damaged the existing political and commercial balance, and contributed to the demise of Barus as an important and authoritative local center. In 1778 the Company withdrew from Barus.

THE HULU AND HILIR FAMILIES IN THE NINETEENTH CENTURY

After the Company's departure, Barus is only a shadowy presence in European records of Sumatra until 1814, when John Canning, a representative of the English Company, visited the port. The ruler of Barus was also in communication with John Prince of the British post at Natal, and on the basis of reports from these English observers it is once again possible to identify individual rulers of Barus and to form a picture of conditions within the kingdom.

Canning's mission to the northwest coast was specifically aimed at discovering the extent of Acehnese sovereignty and authority over the ports north of Tapanuli bay.[91] According to European accounts, the rulers of Barus and other ports such as Singkel were afraid of Acehnese aggression, and sought the protection of a European presence. Viewed in this light, the conversations between Canning and the Raja Barus, which are described by Canning and included in his report, must be treated cautiously. Whatever the Raja told his English visitors was likely to have been colored by his desire for their support.[92] By 1814 the Raja Barus appears to have been a member of the Hulu family called Sutan Baginda Raja. According to Canning, he was an old man who claimed to have ruled for many years. Canning reported that this ruler had for some time been under intense pressure from Acehnese traders who had settled in nearby Tapus and who were threatening to overwhelm the trade and

---

[89]Raja Simorang was an influential chief who is often mentioned in Dutch and English Company records during the middle of the eighteenth century. For frequent references to Raja Simorang see Anne Lindsey Reber, "The Private Trade of the British in West Sumatra 1735–1770" (PhD dissertation, University of Hull, 1977), p. 122 and passim.

[90]Raja Bukit and his relations with the ruler of Barus are a subject of concern in the Malay chronicles from Barus which are considered below. See Chapter Four. Raja Bukit's relations with Aceh and the VOC are discussed in Reber, "Private Trade," Appendix XII. The size of his following, including a dispute with the Raja Barus, is mentioned on pp. 300–2.

[91]Captain J. Canning, 24 November 1814, Sumatra Factory Records, vol. 27.

[92]Some of the ruler's assurances to Canning are open to doubt in light of the earlier history of Barus. The ruler may have thought himself to be at an advantage since the British had never occupied Barus and probably knew little about its past. The ruler, for example, assured Canning that he was harassed by his fear of Aceh and of Acehnese merchants in the region. Having obtained Canning's assurance of protection, however, he attempted to persuade Canning that the British should "win back" Taruman for him. Canning 1814, Paragraph 24. It is unlikely, however, that the authority of the Barus rulers had ever stretched as far north as Taruman.

political independence of Barus.[93] Singkel, which was under the independent rule of "Lebbee Dappah," was by this time a flourishing northern center, as was Taruman. Barus, on the other hand, appears to have declined in importance. According to Canning, the principal political importance of Barus in 1814 was as a barrier against the influence of Aceh on the west coast.[94]

The ruler of Barus told Canning that he was descended from a family of Bataks from Toba and that he was presently considered to be the chief of Toba. According to an appendix to Canning's report written by John Prince, the ruler belonged to the Pohan *marga*.[95] There is no mention in Canning's account of the Hilir family, and, in seeking to assert his independence from Aceh, the Tuanku of Barus assured Canning that his family had ruled Barus as "undisputed sovereigns" for many years. The Tuanku appeared to be extremely anxious for protection against Aceh, and, according to Canning, he was overjoyed when Canning gave him a certificate which attested that he was an ally of the English. In a letter to John Prince, the Tuanku described Barus as "but a village compared to its former state."[96]

The impression created by Canning's report, that the Hilir family was no longer influential in Barus affairs, is contradicted by a Dutch report written just a decade later. Dutch contact with Barus was resumed in the 1820s and 1830s as the war against the Padri moved up the west coast and into the interior. Direct control over Barus was not established until 1839 following the fall of Bonjol in 1837, but visits to the north had been made over the preceding years, and information about the state of affairs in Barus is available from that period. These scattered reports offer new insight into the political situation within Barus and the exercise of royal authority there.

In a report written in 1825, Ridder de Steurs states that at the beginning of that year the Dutch Resident at Padang had received a letter from the Raja Barus, in which he asked for assistance in settling a dispute between the Rajas of "Moedik en Ilier." A Dutch official visited the port and brought about an agreement between the Rajas, resolving what de Steurs describes as a succession dispute. In his report he gives an account of the history of this quarrel.

According to de Steurs, Barus in 1825 consisted of two settlements, Kampung Mudik and Kampung Ilir. The Raja Barus was Sutan Sailan[97] who lived in Kampung Mudik. Kampung Ilir lay at the river mouth and was governed by "Radja Bandhara" whose name was "Soetan main allam." This settlement had previously been insignificant, but its population had grown since the dispute between the two princes.[98] In about 1819 the old Raja Barus had died. According to de Steurs, this ruler had belonged to the family of the ruler of Tarusan, from which we can deduce

---

[93]Canning writes of the threat to Barus from Tapus in the following terms: "These threats, however, and the perpetual fear of being attacked by the Acehnese from Tapoos operated so powerfully on the Tuanku's mind that in the year 1809 he made an offer of the sovereignty of his country to the Company on the sole condition of protection from his enemies, which was, however, declined." Canning, 1814 paragraph 19.

[94]Ibid.

[95]Canning, 1814 Enclosure No. 9.

[96]Canning, 1814, Enclosure no. 10.

[97]Spelt Seilan by de Steurs.

[98]In P.H.van der Kemp, "Eenige Bijdrage tot E. B. Kielstra's Opstellen over Sumatra's Westkust," *BKI* 44 (1894): 551.

that he was a member of the Hilir family. There is reason to doubt this information, however, since the Raja Barus in 1815 was definitely a member of the Hulu family and had a Batak *marga* name. He was also an old man, and none of the available sources mention two rulers dying in this period. Whether or not the old Raja came from the Hilir or Hulu lines, two nephews, according to de Steurs, had claims on the succession. And this implies a marriage relationship between the families at the time, since the two are said by de Steurs to have been the uncle of Sutan Main Alam and the current Raja Barus, Sutan Sailan. According to de Steurs' account, Main Alam's uncle renounced his claim on the succession and Sutan Sailan succeeded as Raja Barus. He is said to have reigned peacefully for five years.

In about 1824, according to de Steurs, Sutan Main Alam left Kampung Mudik where he had been living and challenged the ruler's authority by establishing himself as an independent royal authority in the coastal kampung. He was supported, and according to de Steurs also incited, in this by Acehnese merchants living in Barus. A long drawn out series of hostilities between the two rulers followed. Foreign merchants and the Acehnese resident in Barus participated on the Hilir side, while the Hulu Raja Barus, Sultan Sailan, appealed for Dutch help.[99] In the peace brought about when a junior Dutch official visited Barus it was agreed that two settlements should exist.[100] De Steurs indicates that one reason for the outbreak of hostilities between the two families was the "despotic" nature of the Hulu Raja who had antagonized the trading community. The rulers of Barus, he reports, still took part in trade and had the right to first purchase of any goods which arrived in Barus by ship. Although the Rajas were, potentially, able to monopolize trade, they are said to have had limited means and the Acehnese and Meulaboh merchants living in Barus were in a powerful position.[101]

The outcome of this dispute was described by two separate observers who visited the west coast in 1837 and who record that the kingdom was still split in two, but that some regularization of the arrangement had taken place. W.L. Ritter reported that Barus was still divided into two principal settlements, Kampung Hilir and Kampung Mudik, which were governed by their own chiefs.[102] Only on exceptional occasions and in times of mutual need, such as a war against Aceh or against the inland Bataks, he said, did these chiefs cooperate with each other. According to Ritter, "In earlier times they had often disagreed which led to some bloody fighting, but now they lived together in friendship which had increased their prosperity."[103] Ritter added that the Raja Mudik "was, as it were, the king," while the Raja of the Hilir kampung bore the title Mandara.[104] As we have seen, Pinto referred to a

---

[99] Ibid., pp. 551–52.

[100] Ibid., p.155.

[101] Ibid. In 1814 the Raja Barus had told Canning that there were no Acehnese living in Barus and never had been.

[102] W.L.Ritter. "Korte Aanteekeningen over het Rijk van Atjin," *TNI* 2,1 (1839): 20–21.

[103] Ibid., pp. 21–22. Fortifications around the two principal kampung were still evident when Ritter visited. According to him, the Hilir settlement was situated on the path to Kampung Mudik, which could thus be obstructed by those living downstream.

[104] Ibid.

Mandara or governor of Barus in the sixteenth century and in 1669, Pits appointed a Raja Bandara of Barus.[105]

In the same year another observer, Francis, reported that the Raja was chosen in turn from the Hulu and Hilir families and the leading member of the other family bore the title Bendahara.[106] At that time there were still many foreign merchants in Barus, and Francis mentions a community of 100 wealthy Meulaboh traders who wielded considerable influence in the kingdom.[107] A community of Acehnese merchants who had settled in Tapus, north of Barus, were also very powerful, and the Rajas of Barus had appealed to the Dutch for assistance in preserving what was left of their independence from Aceh.[108] The leader of the Acehnese community in Tapus, Tok Ku Raja Uda, was said by G. Strup to be involved in a dispute with the Hulu ruler concerning certain valuables.[109] We shall see that Tok Ku Raja Uda is also mentioned in the Malay chronicles from Barus.

Although the description of these events which can be gleaned from nineteenth century Dutch sources is fragmentary, it does offer evidence that both the Hilir and Hulu families maintained their claims to rule into the nineteenth century. It also suggests continued recognition within Barus of alternate succession as a possible option when a ruler died. Incomplete and scattered as they are, the available sources do suggest that even after the formal elimination of dual government in 1694, the royal families of Hilir and Hulu Barus both maintained the sovereign claims of their ancestors and neither was eliminated as an alternative source of authority in Barus. The Malay sources chronicle the events of the early nineteenth century and present their outline much as they appear in Dutch accounts. The Malay chronicles, however, offer individual perspectives which help us to discern how these issues were approached within Barus and how local historians from the two families wished them to appear.

THE REESTABLISHMENT OF DUTCH AUTHORITY IN BARUS

According to an unpublished Dutch manuscript which draws on official reports from Barus, the final outbreak of hostilities between the Hulu and Hilir families took place in 1830. In this account, Sultan Main Alam is also called "Soeltan Troesan." In about 1834 he was succeeded by Sutan Ibrahim, who also carried the title Tuanku Bendara. When the Hulu Raja died soon after, there was a dispute between his family members, "Soeltan Limba Tua" and Marah Sultan. The former became Tuanku, while the latter was recognized by the Acehnese at Tapus and led them in attacking Barus and the coastal regions. Because of these disturbances, the document asserts, both Tuanku Mudik and Tuanku Ilir appealed to Kolonel Michiels, the Dutch Commander of the west coast, for help.[110]

---

[105]VOC 1268, f. 850v.; Gent, trans.,*Voyages and Adventures of Fernand Mendez Pinto*, p.34; and p. 7 above.

[106]Francis, "Korte Beschrijving van het Nederlansche Grondgebeid ter Westkust van Sumatra in 1837," *TNI* 2 (1839): 35.

[107]Ibid., p. 88. Francis calls them "Analaboes."

[108]P. J. Veth, *De Vestiging en Uitbreiding der Nederlanders ter Westkust van Sumatra door Generaal-Majoor H.J.J.L. Ridder de Steurs*, 2 vols. (Amsterdam: van Kampen, 1849–50), 2: 132–33.

[109]H. M. Lange, *Het Nederlandsch Oost-Indisch Leger ter Westkust van Sumatra, 1819–1845*, Vol. 2 (s'Hertogenbosch: Muller, 1854), p. 328.

[110]"Onze Verstiging te Barus," Instituut voor de Tropen, Amsterdam, Broch Onz 93=542, p. 7.

The Netherlands Indies government was initially reluctant to become too closely involved with Barus, and it was not until after the fall of Bonjol that the administration was willing to reoccupy Barus as part of its policy of driving the Padri inland and pushing back Acehnese influence on the west coast.[111] A military force arrived in Barus in 1839–1840 and, with the help of the local population, succeeded in driving back Acehnese attacks from Tapus and Singkel. A government official was posted at the port which was incorporated by the Netherlands Indies government.

With the promotion of Sibolga as regional administrative center and the advent of modern shipping, Barus declined in importance, as did the authority of its rulers.[112] They became salaried officials of the Netherlands Indies government and, in the manner of other local rulers, they came to be described as merely the *kuria*, or district, chiefs of Barus Mudik and Barus Hilir.[113] By 1852 the rulers of Barus appear to have undertaken no longer to use their royal seals. These seals are reproduced here on page 48. They are contained in a bundle of material in the Tropen Instituut in Amsterdam and were sent in a letter of 1909 from Ismail, the Kadi at Barus, to P. C. Arends, the recently departed Controleur there. A note in *jawi* accompanying each of the seals records that the seal of Tuanku Mudik was prohibited from use in 1851, and that of Raja Barus Tuanku Ibrahim in 1852.[114] No explanation of this prohibition is included with the seals or with the letter they accompanied. The existence of two royal *cap*, however, and the order that they were no longer to be used, may stand as a metaphor for the history of dual royal claims in Barus and for the impact of European colonial authority upon those aspirations.

*   *   *

This chapter set out to consider how European sources present the political history of Barus between 1668 and 1840. What these records reveal is that the presence

---

[111] E. B. Kielstra, "Sumatra's Westkust van 1826–32," *BKI* 37 (1888): 221 and 327.

[112] See, for instance, Tengku Luckman Sinar, "Sibolga dan Pantai Barat Sumatera Utara dalam Lintasan Sejarah," Unpublished paper, Medan 1980; and van der Kemp, "Een Bijdrage tot E. B. Kielstra's Opstellen," p. 612.

[113] According to the "Onze Vestiging" MS the salary of the chiefs was very small, as was their authority, p.12.

[114] Ijzeren Kastlijst 112.4, 134. The seals can be found on page 48.
There is insufficient evidence concerning the use of these royal *cap* to be precise about their age and use. One, more decorative, *cap* contains the following inscription: "Tuanku Raja Barus Dalam Pansur." A note in *rumi*, possibly by Ismail, on the same scrap of aged paper, reads, "Inilah cap Toeankoe Radja Moedik di Baroes"—"this is the seal of Tuanku Mudik in Barus." On the back of the same paper is written in *jawi* script: "Ini cap diambil dari surat yang sudah apkir tidak dipakai lagi dari tahun 1851."
The other, rougher and more damaged *cap* is less easily legible and more ambiguous. It reads: "Inilah cap[2] Raja Barus Tuanku Ibrahim wakil[nya?] Tuanku Bendahara Raja Barus." The *angka dua* after c-p and the ending of the word *wakil* are not clear and it is, therefore, hard to be sure whether this is the seal of one or two people. It may, however, simply be the seal of the Hilir ruler, Tuanku Ibrahim, who, we saw, was also called Bendara or Bendahara and who may also have used the title *wakil* (see p. 179, n. 21 below for a reference to the use of *wakil* as a title). The *jawi* message on the back of this seal reads, "Inilah cap diambil dari surat perjanjian yang sudah apkir tidak dipakai lagi dari tahun 1852." And, on the top side of the paper is written in *rumi*, "Cap Toenkoe Koeriah Ilir di Baroes." Below the word Ilir the word "Moedik" has been crossed out. The use of the name Ibrahim does indicate that this *cap* applied to the Hilir family.

of dual sources of authority in Barus was an issue for Europeans who wrote about the kingdom, just as it is in the Malay chronicles.

We may draw some conclusions on the basis of this survey of the European text. The two royal families of Barus clearly maintained their separate identities for a considerable period. The Dutch noted friction and competition between the two royal houses, but despite this apparent hostility, neither family succeeded in eliminating the other. VOC interference in the affairs of the kingdom may have influenced not only the relationship between the families, but also their ability to survive politically. Each of the royal families, however, also appears to have possessed its own base of support among the population of Barus, and particularly among the Bataks of the interior. Rather than a distinction between an inland and a coastal ruler, what we have found in Barus is a situation where two coastal rulers each commanded distinct lines of loyalty with different sections of the Batak population. These special bonds endured for a considerable time, and they may have contributed to the ability of both families to maintain their royal claims into the nineteenth century.

Reference to "special bonds" and to "lines of loyalty" may help to make the point that coastal-hinterland relations in Barus had a more than merely commercial dimension, but Dutch sources provide little scope for an inquiry into how such bonds were perceived locally and how duality was regarded in Barus. These questions can be most fruitfully pursued in the Malay texts. It is time now to turn from the chronologically ordered and familiarly phrased perceptions of Europeans and to seek entry into a local discourse on interaction between coast and hinterland, Bataks and Malays, and "Hulu" and "Hilir" rulers in Barus.

The Royal Seals of Barus

3

TWO MALAY TEXTS

The references made in the last chapter to Malay sources concerned with Barus's past may give the impression of a homogeneous body of Malay textual tradition. Such an impression would be misleading. The material from Barus represents nothing so unitary or simple as *a* Malay view. This chapter will introduce two Malay texts from Barus and will argue that these texts represent two traditions and two different approaches to Barus's past.

The chronicles considered here are the royal chronicles of Hulu and Hilir Barus and we find in them local perceptions of the relationship between the two royal families and of the issue of royal authority in Barus. The texts are similar in length, subject matter, and narrative structure, which makes them eminently comparable. And comparison reveals important differences between them which have been categorized here as Hulu and Hilir approaches to Barus's past. The terms "Hulu" and "Hilir" are intended as archetypes which describe the orientation of these two traditions. Of course the texts analyzed here may not be the only examples of an "Hulu" or "Hilir" perspective; neither can all texts from Barus necessarily be categorized in this way. Indeed the very texts with which we are concerned may also be read in other ways. However in the following chapters a systematic comparison of these two chronicles will reveal important differences in the way they chronicle a common past, and present the issues of authority and sovereignty.

The history of Barus is not momentous in the sense of having an impact upon Sumatran history or upon that of the archipelago as a whole. It does, however, raise important issues which are reflected in the political thought, social structure, and literature of much of island Southeast Asia. In their treatment of duality and of relations between different ethnic groups and different geographical spheres, the Malay texts from Barus offer two different approaches to questions of universal significance. An appreciation of these differences may prompt us to consider the chronicles not only side by side, but in the context of other Barus texts, of the literature of Sumatra and the Malay archipelago, and of the chronicles' Batak and Malay ancestries.

The following chapters attempt such a reading. The aim will be to elucidate the categories of explanation employed in the texts, to compare the two and consider them in the context of "Malay perceptions" revealed in other works of Malay literature. To this end close attention will be paid to the form and structure of the two chronicles. It will be necessary to consider the genre expectations aroused in a reader of, or listener to, the chronicles. The function of rhetoric and dialogue and of local use of the Malay, Minangkabau, and Batak languages must all be of concern in the attempt to understand the messages embodied in these works. This approach may offer a means of identifying local priorities and concerns which might not, otherwise, be discoverable.

First, however, it is necessary to examine what is known about these texts, their composition, their relationship to each other and to the two royal families of Barus.

THE HULU AND HILIR CHRONICLES

The manuscripts in question are the *Asal Keturunan Raja Barus*, and the *Sejarah Tuanku Batu Badan*. Both works were compiled in their present form in the nineteenth century. The *Asal* is held in the manuscript collection of the Museum Nasional in Jakarta, and the *Sejarah* is kept in Barus where it is in the possession of the descendants of the Hilir royal house. The two manuscripts have recently been transliterated into romanized Malay and published, together with an introduction which summarizes their contents and describes the various versions of the MSS, their physical state, and language.[1] Not all of this information has been repeated here and the present introduction to the chronicles will concentrate on identifying the texts and their relationship to the two royal families, as well as pointing to important features of their spelling and language use.

The two manuscripts have a similar structure and tell a recognizably similar story. Each describes the origins of the ruling family with which it is concerned, and then proceeds to relate the foundation of the kingdom of Barus, an agreement to share the kingdom between the two families and other incidents in Barus's past. Both conclude with an account of the nineteenth century conflict between the Hulu and Hilir families, which was reported by Dutch observers and was mentioned in the previous chapter. Each takes the form of a genealogical chronicle of one of the ruling families, and both appear to have belonged to the descendants of the appropriate ruling line.

HULU CHRONICLE

The *jawi* MS of *Asal Keturunan Raja Barus* belongs to a larger group of Malay MSS from Barus held in the Museum Nasional in Jakarta. These are catalogued as ML. 162 under the general title *Asal Turunan Raja Barus*.[2] Elsewhere I have argued that this item should not be regarded as a single text, but as a collection of texts and romanizations of texts from Barus, possibly gathered by an interested European and bound into one exercise book. In his catalogue of the Bataviaasch Genootschap collection, van Ronkel divided what was then Bat. Gen. 162 into nine separate sections.[3]

There is no specific title for the whole, and the exercise book has been numbered from 1–322 in pencil. It seems likely that these pencilled numbers were added at a date after the collection first came into being. The text is written in ink not pencil and the pencil numbers run straight through the book, regardless of blank pages between sections and in a fashion which results in *jawi* sections being numbered back-to-front.

The argument that ML. 162 should be considered as a collection of texts from Barus rests upon several points. These are: the presence of *jawi* sections which are later repeated in romanized form, summarised and, in one case, translated into Dutch; the repetition of sections of narrative in a different and abbreviated form; the

---

[1]Jane Drakard, ed., *Sejarah Raja-Raja Barus. Dua Naskah dari Barus* (Jakarta: Ecole Française d'Extrême Orient, 1988).

[2]*Katalogus Koleksi Naskah Melayu Museum Pusat* (Jakarta: Dept. Pendidikan dan Kebudayaan, 1972).

[3]Ph. S. van Ronkel, "Catalogus der Maleische Handschriften in het Museum van het Bataviaasch Genootschap van Kunsten en Wetenschappen," *VBG* 57 (1909): 281. For a slightly revised version of this division, see Drakard, ed., *Sejarah Raja-Raja Barus*.

use of different dates attributed to separate sections of the collection; and the fact that sections are written on paper which appears to vary in age if not type.[4] The different parts of the manuscript are distinguished in some cases by their individual openings and in others by the blank pages which separate them.

It is unfortunate that no information is available as to how the collection came into being. The presence of Dutch translations within the manuscript, and the transliteration of parts of the *jawi* text, may suggest that the copying and transcription of the sections in the collection were organized for the benefit of a European collector. Several of the Dutch administrators who served in Barus during the later nineteenth and early twentieth centuries showed an interest in local traditions and even published articles about them, and it is, therefore, possible that the collection found its way to Jakarta in its present form as a result of the efforts of one of these men.[5] Detailed philological and literary analysis of the collection's different parts may help, in the future, to clear up these problems.

For the purpose of this study three sections of the collection have been identified as representing individual works, as opposed to copies or summaries of works. These are sections 1, 2 and 6. These sections can be described as follows:

1) :58–1. A history of the Hulu royal family of Barus, written in *jawi* script, entitled *Sarakatah Surat Catera Asal Keturunan Raja Dalam Negeri Barus.*

2) :92–71. A version of the Hilir royal chronicle of Barus and its establishment in Barus, written in *jawi* script. Untitled.

6) :137–252. A section in *rumi* Malay, beginning "Inilah Hikayat Tjarita Baros parmoelaanya batak datang darie Tobah darie Soekoe Pohon sapartie tersaboet di bawa ini." This is an account of the history of the Hulu royal family, broadly similar in emphasis to that found in *jawi* pages 58–1, but it is not the same narrative. The writing here only covers one half of one side of each page.[6]

In the case of the two *jawi* sections of the *Asal* there is independent evidence for the existence of these chronicles in written and oral form within Barus. These two sections will be referred to as *Asal 1* and *Asal 2*. They are self-contained and possess independent openings. *Asal 2* contains an abbreviated version of the narrative contained in the Hilir chronicle and it is discussed below with reference to that text. Section 6 describes itself as *Hikayat Tjarita Baros parmoelaanya batak datang darie Tobah darie Soekoe Pohon*. Like the *Asal 1* text this *Hikayat Carita*, as it will be referred to here, commences with the origins of the Hulu royal family of Barus, but it diverges from the *Asal 1* narrative and includes different incidents. The *Hikayat Carita* carries the date AD 1873 for the "present" (*sekarang*) and it may have been based, at least in part, upon the earlier text of the *Asal 1*. The *Hikayat Carita* section of ML. 162 deserves more detailed consideration on another occasion, although it will be referred to here in the context of our reading of *Asal 1*.

It is the text contained in section *Asal 1* which has been identified as the most complete available version of Hulu family history. The original *jawi* form of the MS,

---

[4]These arguments are developed more fully in Drakard, ed., *Sejarah Raja-Raja Barus.*

[5]See, for instance, James, "De Geboorte van Singa Maharaja," pp. 134–45, and Deutz, "Baros," pp.156–63. Neubronner van der Tuuk, the great scholar and collector of manuscripts, lived in the Barus area between 1851 and 1857, and he, too, collected Malay as well as Batak manuscripts from the region.

[6]For a description of the remainder of the ML. 162 collection see Drakard, ed., *Sejarah Raja-Raja Barus.*

its title, early date and the fact that it appears to form the basis for other parts of the *Asal* collection are all factors which appear to justify extracting it from the ML. 162 collection for the present exercise and considering it separately as *a* Hulu family history. Like the Hilir text this MS records the genealogical history of its ruling family from its arrival in Barus until the nineteenth century. The *jawi* text has an underlined title, *Sarakatah Surat Catera Asal Keturunan Raja Dalam Negeri Barus* (which has been abbreviated here to *Asal Keturunan Raja Barus*). It possesses a distinct beginning and end and is separated from the next section of the collection by six blank pages. The chronicle contains a statement which suggests something of its origins. No specific copyist is mentioned, but the text relates that the story it offers is "told by all of the older people in *negeri* Barus."[7] There is a detached tone about the way this statement is made which differs from the main body of the story and suggests that it may be a copyist's or compiler's note. The chronicle makes frequent use of dates, and Sutan Marah Tulang, the last Hulu Raja mentioned in the narrative, is said to have been installed in AD 1853 (1270 H.).[8] The text includes a list of all the Raja di Hulu who assumed authority in Barus from the acceptance of Islam "until the present" (*sampai sekarang*) which reads as 1283 H.[9] The Christian era equivalent of this date is AD 1866.

External evidence for the existence of this narrative within Barus can be found in European sources. In 1874 a Dutch official in Barus, G. J. J. Deutz, published an article in which he discussed not only the archaeology of Barus, but also local traditions concerning the rulers of the kingdom. The account he gives is much the same that offered in *Asal 1*.[10]

Another piece of external evidence helps to locate the chronicle. In 1932, in his important ethnographical study of the Dairi and Toba regions, W. K. H. Ypes mentions a composition which he found in the possession of the district head of Barus Mudik. Ypes cites only the part of this manuscript which is relevant to a point of his own concerning the establishment of the Pardosi *marga* in upper Barus. But, on the basis of his summary, the composition closely resembles *Asal 1*. It includes a version of the Hulu origin story very similar to that contained in *Asal 1*.[11] Enquiries in Barus suggest that this manuscript is likely to have been an original of the Jakarta text. According to local informants a Hulu royal chronicle certainly existed and it is only in recent years that the descendants of the family have lost track of it.

HILIR CHRONICLE

The *jawi* text of the *Sejarah* is in the possession of the Pasaribu family in Barus.[12] The Pasaribu family claim to be descended from the Hilir rulers of Barus, and Tuanku Batu Badan is the local name for their founding ancestor, the first Hilir Raja,

---

[7] *Asal*, p. 45(15). Bagitu carita yang kami dapat dari segala orang tuha-tuha di dalam negeri Barus. All future references made to the 58-page *Asal* text reflect the pencilled-in reverse order numbering on the MS in brackets. See also Drakard, *Sejarah Raja-Raja Barus*, p. 93.

[8] *Asal*, p. 42(16).

[9] Ibid.

[10] Deutz, "Baros," pp. 156–63. It may be more than a coincidence that Deutz published this article only one year after the date on the *Hikayat Carita* in the *Asal* collection.

[11] W. K. H. Ypes, *Bijdrage*, p.508.

[12] I consulted this MS in Barus on two occasions, in 1981 and 1982, and I should like to thank Zainal Arafin Pasariburaja and his family for their permission to photograph it.

Sultan Ibrahim, who came from Tarusan and established himself in Barus.[13] The manuscript is regarded as a family heirloom (*pusaka*). It is treated with great care and has been handed down by successive generations.

Sejarah Tuanku Batu Badan, the title used for the MS here, comes from the modern local name for the chronicle. No title or title page appears on the manuscript, but a copyist's note at the end records that the present copy was made in AD 1872 (1289 H.) by Sutan Marah Laut bin Sultan Main Alam.[14] He describes the work as a *kitab tambo*, which is a Minangkabau term for a written account of ancestry and origins, and he states that he copied it from a version which was old and used. A new copy was made in order that the story should be preserved for future generations.[15] If Marah Laut made the extant copy in 1872 from an earlier version, the original must have been composed at some point between the close of the narrative and 1872. The narrative concludes with the nineteenth century conflict between the Hulu and Hilir families and with the death of Sultan Main Alam, the ruler who had challenged the authority of Raja Barus and established himself in the Hilir *kampung*. This was Sutan Marah Laut's father, as we can see from his full title quoted above. Sultan Main Alam (who was also known as Sultan Tarusan[16]) died in 1834[17] and the original from which Sutan Marah Laut made his copy must therefore have been composed or compiled between 1834 and 1872. In the absence of additional evidence it is not pos-

---

[13]The Pasaribu family possess extended genealogies which trace their relationship with Sultan Ibrahim. Pasaribu is a Batak family name, although the Pasaribu family in Barus are Muslims and have probably been so for a long time. The nature of the relationship between the Malay, Sultan Ibrahim, and earlier generations of the Pasaribu family will be examined below. Today the Pasaribu family in Barus hold great pride in their family's past and have a considerable interest in local history.

The Tarusan origins of the Hilir family are mentioned in VOC sources from 1668, although there was no specific reference to Sultan Ibrahim. Ibrahim is, however, a name which the Hilir family used frequently in the seventeenth and eighteenth centuries. A pair of decorated gravestones in Si Gambo-Gambo near modern Barus are believed, locally, to mark the graves of Sultan Ibrahim and his wife. The larger stone is uninscribed, but the other bears an inscription which indicates that it is the grave of a woman called Tuhan Amrsura who died in Safar 972 or AD 1565; see P. Voorhoeve, "Gescheidenis van Baroes," *TBG* 70 (1930): 92; and Hasan Muarif Ambary, "Catatan tentang penelitian beberapa situs 'masa' Sriwijaya," in *Pra Seminar Penelitian Sriwijaya* (Jakarta: Pusat Penelitian Purbakala dan Peninggalan Nasional, 1979), p. 13.

[14]*Sejarah*, p. 60.

[15]*Sejarah*, p. 60 "Tamat ini kitab tambo pada hari bulan Rabi'ul 'akhir tahun Al-Hijrah Nabi Muhammad Rasullullahi Salallahu 'alaihi wassalam pada sannat 1289 adanya." This statement is followed by a two and a half page genealogical list and a further *jawi* colophon which, although now torn and difficult to read, makes it clear that AD 1872 (1289 H.) is not the manuscript's original date, but rather the date when Sutan Marah Laut copied an already aged original. The colophon reads: Saya yang bergelar Sutan Marah Laut bin Sultan Main 'Alam yang menyalin ini kitab tambo. Karena disalin sebab sudah tuha (sudah) sebab lama terpakai. Dari itu aku salinkan kepada kitab ini supaya jangan hilang sampai sekarang. Adapun terbuat ini surat tatkala saya duduk berdagang dalam negeri Sorkam. Demikianlah sebabnya maka aku Sutan Marah Laut anak Barus kampung selama-lama berdagang di negeri Sorkam [Torn]. Tamat pada tahun . . . [Torn] . . . pada tahun 1289 pada bulan sepuluh rabi'ul'akhir tahun Belanda pada 17 juni 1872.

[16]He is referred to thus in the Dutch account contained in "Onze Vestiging te Baros," p. 6. In the abbreviated Malay text of the Hilir chronicle contained in *Asal* 2, in a genealogy contained in a *rumi* transliteration of this section, he is also referred to as Sutan Main Alam, *Asal*, pp. 287–88.

[17]See "Onze Vestiging te Baros," p. 6.

sible to date the chronicle more accurately. It is possible, however, that parts of the present text and the sections of narrative of which it is composed were extant in Barus prior to 1834, probably in oral form.[18]

The popularity of the Sultan Ibrahim narrative in Barus is indicated by the number of versions or copies of this story in circulation in the later nineteenth century. In 1902 K.A. James, a district official in the Barus area, published an article which summarized in Dutch the narrative of a Barus story dealing with the origins of the Hilir family.[19] His information was derived, James wrote, from an account written by a descendant of that house, Sultan Alam Syah, who was a district head of Barus Hilir and who had died in 1898. The story related in James's article is in fact a summary of that contained in the early part of the *Sejarah*. In a genealogy which is in the possession of the Pasaribu family, Sultan Alam Syah is said to have been the son of the last Hilir Raja mentioned in the text, Sultan Perhimpunan, and the grandson of Sultan Main Alam who was involved in the war with the Hulu family in the early nineteenth century. Alam Syah was, therefore, a nephew of Sutan Marah Laut. Alam Syah may have prepared a fresh and abbreviated version of his family's history for James's use. I have argued elsewhere that the original of Alam Syah's account is a 14 page Malay text held in the Tropical Institute of Amsterdam which bears his signature and the date 1896.[20]

In addition to the James/Alam Syah version of the "Hilir" story, there are two other texts which incorporate part of the Hilir narrative and which add to the impression not only of the amount of literary activity which took place in Barus in the nineteenth century, but also of the importance and currency of this narrative within Barus. These are *Asal 2* and a text held in the Leiden University Library called the *Hikayat Raja Tuktung*. Both texts have been described in greater detail elsewhere.[21] *Asal 2* is an abbreviated version of the Hilir narrative which is transliterated into *rumi* later in the *Asal* collection. It includes many of the names and significant events mentioned in the *Sejarah*, although it is much briefer and concludes in a list-like fashion.

The *Hikayat Raja Tuktung* was collected in Barus in the 1850s by van der Tuuk, who noted that this MS was a copy of another text which was dated 1260H or AD 1844.[22] He also refers to what may be another copy which belonged to the Tuanku of Si Gambo-Gambo. Si Gambo-Gambo was, for a period, synonymous with Barus Hilir, and it is possible that van der Tuuk was referring here to the text of the *Sejarah* MS which was kept in Si Gambo-Gambo in 1981.[23] The two texts are different however. Van der Tuuk emphasized the verse structure of *Hikayat Raja Tuktung* which is shorter than the *Sejarah*, and, although it narrates many of the same events, the

---

[18]On Malay composition see Amin Sweeney, *A Full Hearing. Orality and Literacy in the Malay World* (Berkeley: University of California Press, 1987), Chapter 3 and passim.

[19]James, "De Geboorte van Singa Maharadja," pp. 134–35. James offers little commentary on the narrative which is, with small variations, the same account of the Hilir origin story as that found in the *Sejarah*.

[20]See Drakard, ed., *Sejarah Raja-Raja Barus*, where the relationship between different versions of the Hilir chronicle are discussed in more detail. The Malay text in the Tropical Institute is catalogued Ijzeren Kastlijst G 58 –112.4 143 Sin 997=540.

[21]See Drakard, ed., *Sejarah Raja-Raja Barus*.

[22]H. H. Juynboll, *Catalogus van de Maleische en Sundaneesche handschriften der Leidsche Universiteits Bibliotheek* (Leiden: Brill, 1899), p. 315 Cod. Or. 3205.

[23]Zainal Arafin Pasariburaja had moved to Batu Garigis by 1982–1983.

language used is different. The *Hikayat* concludes at a point corresponding to two thirds of the way through the *Sejarah*. Raja Tuktung or Tutung is mentioned in both the *Sejarah* and the *Asal* as Raja of Tukka, which, as we have seen, is a region inland from Barus. Although the words used in these two works are different, some passages of the *Hikayat Raja Tuktung* and the *Sejarah* are very similar in their language and rhythm.[24] The relationship between these texts deserves closer attention.

Another text from Barus which was collected by van der Tuuk is the *Sejarah Sultan Fansuri*.[25] This MS contains a history of Barus in verse and copies of various agreements and regulations instituted in Barus. Although the MS is mentioned in Chapter 8 below, it has not been considered in detail here since it is different in narrative structure and orientation from the *Sejarah Tuanku Batu Badan* and the *Asal*. Like the *Hikayat Raja Tuktung*, the *Sejarah Sultan Fansuri* deserves more attention, especially in the light of the "Hulu" and "Hilir" traditions identified here.

For the purposes of the present study, it has been necessary to identify one version of Hilir history which can be compared with the Hulu chronicle. For this the *Sejarah Tuanku Batu Badan* is highly appropriate. It is the only extant *jawi* manuscript of the Hilir story which records the earliest history of the Hilir family and which also takes its narrative and genealogy into the nineteenth century. The *Sejarah Tuanku Batu Badan* also belongs to the Hilir family, who regard it as their own royal history.

ROMANIZATIONS OF THE SEJARAH TUANKU BADAN

Several romanized versions of the *Sejarah* MS exist. The Pasaribu family considered the chronicle to be sufficiently important to justify preparing, in 1973, a romanized copy which they had printed under the title *Sejarah Kedatangan Tuanku Batu Badan Ke Daerah Barus*. This is the basis for the title *Sejarah Tuanku Batu Badan* used here. It is not an authentic title, and the chronicle might also be called *Tambo Raja Barus*. However, in the absence of a formal title on the MS itself, I have chosen to respect the choice made by the descendants of the Raja di Hilir family and have used their title. The romanization was made by a member of the Hilir family, Azhar bin Mara Hasyim Gelar Namora Ladang, in whose possession the manuscript remained until his death. The printed text was circulated within the family and among friends and interested people in Barus and elsewhere, but, because of a number of printing errors, it was not offered for sale as had originally been intended.

In addition to this modern romanization and partial Indonesianization of the MS, there are also three romanizations of the MS held in the V.E. Korn collection.[26] These all differ, and they have been discussed in detail in my own edition of the two Barus chronicles. One of these romanizations carries a note which indicates that it was prepared in 1900 at the request of J. J. Plas, a Dutch official in Barus. Unfortunately, little is known about why or how the other versions came to be in the collection. There is, however, a Dutch letter kept with the *jawi* manuscript of the *Sejarah* which indicates that it was taken out of Barus at some stage and was returned to the Pasaribu family via the Resident of Tapanuli in 1939. The text is referred to in this letter as the *Tambo Barus Hilir* (Chronicle of Barus Hilir). It seems likely that the manuscript was taken out of Barus either for a copy to be made or to enable a Dutch

---

[24]See Drakard, ed., *Sejarah Raja-Raja Barus*, pp. 101–3.

[25]Leiden University Library, Cod. Or. 3303.

[26]V. E. Korn Collection, catalogue number 436; see also Drakard, ed, *Sejarah Raja-Raja Barus*, pp. 105–7.

enthusiast to examine the chronicle. In the catalogue of manuscripts held in the Lembaga Kebudayaan Indonesia is a list of manuscripts which were found to be missing in 1948, after the Japanese occupation. Among these is mentioned a copy of a chronicle from Barus. The original of this lost copy may have been the *Sejarah Tuanku Batu Badan* manuscript.[27] Of the two other Korn romanizations, one was prepared in Barus in 1926 and the other is unfinished and undated. In the present study the Malay used in all quotations comes from my own romanization of the chronicle, aspects of which are discussed below.

* * *

These two Malay texts, then, represent two distinct royal histories and two versions of Barus's past, each of which existed in the nineteenth century and each of which had the status of royal traditions which were reproduced in various forms. It is by no means unusual for Malay royal genealogies to be treated as precious objects and heirlooms. Observers have noticed that such genealogies might be wrapped in cloth and treasured as part of the state regalia.[28] The composition of a *hikayat*, or royal genealogy, might also be a part of the process of establishing and eulogizing a Malay kingdom.[29] That these chronicles should be preserved by the descendants of the royal families of Barus is not surprising in view of their contents, since both deal directly with the past relationship between the two families and explain their position vis-à-vis each other. Unfortunately, no specific information is available concerning the use to which these two manuscripts were put in Barus, and it is not known whether they were intended for reading aloud, as with many Malay texts, or were simply kept by the families as a testament of their royal heritage. Neither is it possible to tell to what extent these two versions of the past were composed or compiled in their present form in relation to each other. Did they spring from an argument between the royal families? Which was composed first, and was it used in reference to the composition of the other?

Future philological research may throw light on these questions, but further historical evidence would also be necessary to reveal the whole story. We know that both chronicles were written after the conflict between the two families and that both conclude their narrative with this event. We shall see that in both, the resolution of the conflict between the families not only provides a place where the narrative stops, but also functions as a denouement through which the conclusion of the narrative is related to earlier parts of the individual histories. The way in which this dispute is treated in each chronicle encourages the view that it may have been an important impetus for the preparation of the MSS in their present form.

The prohibition of royal seals, which was mentioned in the previous chapter, may also be related to the composition of the Hulu narrative in particular. Without knowing why the prohibition took place, the earlier date for the prohibition of the

---

[27] R. M. Ng. Poerbatjaraka, P. Voorhoeve, and C.Hooykaas, *Indonesische Handschriften* (Bandung: Nix, 1950), p. 177, no. 440; see also P. Voorhoeve, "Geschiedenis van Baroes," *TBG*, pp. 92–94.

[28] See for instance W.E. Maxwell, "Notes on two Perak Manuscripts," JSBRAS, vol. II (1878), p. 184. Cited in Milner, *Kerajaan*, p.39. See also Milner s.v. Hikayat.

[29] According to Newbold, "Each state generally had its *Sila* or keturunan, containing the genealogy of the ruler." T. J. Newbold, *British Settlements in the Straits of Malacca*, 2 vols. (London, 1839; Reprint ed. Kuala Lumpur: Oxford University Press, 1971), 2: p. 333.

Hulu royal seal is puzzling,[30] but it may relate to an incident which occurs toward the close of the Hulu narrative. The last Hulu Raja Barus mentioned in the narrative is Sutan Marah Tulang, who became Raja in 1853. Before him Sutan Agama is said to have ruled for "about three years," until he was exiled to Banda Neira for murdering the child of a *panghulu*. The withdrawal of the royal seal may have been a punishment by the Dutch administration for this crime or be otherwise related to commencement of Sutan Agama's reign. Sutan Marah Tulang was presumably denied access to use of the seal, which might have provided a motivation for having his family history recorded.

Apart from these speculations as to why the Hulu MS may have been composed when it was, there is a hint within the chronicle itself that the MS was prepared with an external audience in mind. I have already mentioned the detached tone of what may be a copyist's or compiler's note in the *Asal*. In this passage not only are the *orang tuha* (elders) of Barus given as the source of the narrative, but the text also speculates upon the truth or otherwise of the account.[31] This concern with the historicity of the *carita* is unusual and may indeed be an indication that the chronicle was written down in its present form at the request of an outsider. We know that Neubronner van der Tuuk was resident in Barus until 1857 and that he was a collector of local manuscripts. It is therefore not impossible that van der Tuuk may have inspired the transcription of the MS *in its present form*, although if this were the case one would expect a copy to have reached Leiden in his collection.

Whatever the involvement of outsiders, however, the collective memories upon which the chronicle is based probably went back before the nineteenth century. In the case of the *Sejarah* narrative, the notes of van der Tuuk and the existence of the *Hikayat Raja Tuktung* seem to provide evidence that this was the case. According to van der Tuuk's handwritten notes on the *Hikayat*, it was dated 1844. We know that the *Hikayat* includes many of the same narrative episodes as the *Sejarah*, but without the nineteenth century conflict between the families. It therefore seems likely that a narrative concerning the Hilir royal family was current in Barus in some other form *before* the compilation of the *Sejarah* in its present form. It is not possible to disentangle all of these problems in this preliminary study, but when the textual traditions of Barus have been thoroughly studied and understood we may be provided with a useful insights into the way in which Malay *hikayat* are compiled.[32]

As it is, more is known about the background of these texts than about many Malay works, and for the present purpose the exact relationship between the chronicles is secondary to the character of the statements they each make about the Barus polity. We can be certain that the texts were transcribed in their present form after the war between the families and after the Netherlands Indies administration had established itself in Barus. They represent two royal views of Barus's past. They appear to have been kept in the possession of their respective royal families. It is to

---

[30]1851 as opposed to 1852 for the Hilir seal.

[31]*Asal*, p. 45(15). "Bagitu carita yang kami dapat dari segala orang tuha-tuha di dalam negeri Barus. Dan lagi tentangan dari carita itu barangkali ada batul atau tidak itu kami tidak boleh mengaku karena kami dapat pendangaran saja di dalam carita. Adapun masa dan ketika hijrah yang tertulis itu kami lihat daripada batu pekuburan orang dahulu-dahulu kiranya siapa yang mahu labih keterangan boleh tanya kepada Raja Barus."

[32]On this point see Amin Sweeney, *Full Hearing*.

be hoped, therefore, that an examination of these chronicles may reveal something of how royal authority was thought about in nineteenth century Barus.

The Scope of the Chronicles

The two manuscripts are of roughly equal length and they both deal with a period which lies approximately between the sixteenth and nineteenth centuries.[33] The subject of each is the internal history of Barus itself, and the position of, and relations between, the two royal families. Each text begins with an account of its own family's origins and first arrival in Barus. In both accounts the founders of the two lines undertake a journey which brings them to Barus. The texts thus possess structural similarities in these early sections or origin stories, even though the two origin accounts are quite different from each other. Neither chronicle acknowledges the existence of a second royal line until the families meet in Barus. From this point onwards, each chronicle acknowledges the other family's presence and deals with events and characters which are loosely identifiable in the other. Often the names used for the protagonists in the texts differ, but the individuals concerned are identifiable by means of their exploits. To this extent, after the first meeting between representatives of the two families, both chronicles recount what can be considered to be a common past, punctuated by significant events mentioned in both. The way in which the texts present this past is different, but the similarities between them are maintained throughout the narrative, as each describes an accommodation and mutual agreement between the families, a breakdown in their relations, an alliance made for their mutual protection, a further crisis, and eventual war followed by a negotiated peace.

The chronicles rarely focus on the world outside Barus. Despite the area's trading past, and, in contrast to most of the better known Malay manuscripts from the north and east coasts of Sumatra and from the Malay peninsula, the Barus texts show little interest in a wider world of archipelago affairs. It would not, of course, be surprising if west coast Sumatrans such as those of Barus should look out upon the world with different eyes from peoples of the east coast, whose geographic awareness must have been influenced by their proximity to the Melaka Straits. Looking out and around them, the inhabitants of east coast Sumatran kingdoms in the pre-modern period would have felt involved in the busy life of the Straits and would have looked also towards the old kingdoms of the Malay peninsula, the royal families of which had long intermarried with the east Sumatran rulers. Further still, these mercantile people must have been aware, on their horizon, of Thailand, Burma, Indo-China, and China itself. Civilization, no doubt, appeared for the most part to lie to the north and east. For the west Sumatran, however, looking out on the Indian Ocean would have been a very different experience. In front of the people of Barus as they looked to the west lay only Nias, a few smaller islands, and, beyond them, the ocean. Behind the coastal dwellers stretched the steep and difficult hinterland. Some three hundred miles to the north lay the commercial center of the kingdom of Aceh and, a little closer but still far distant in the South, lay the center of the old kingdom of Minangkabau.

Little comparative work has yet been done on the literatures of east and west Sumatra, yet there are suggestions that written histories and traditions may reflect this difference in geographical perspective. The *Hikayat Deli*, for example, is an east

---

[33]The *Asal* is fifty eight pages long and the *Sejarah* numbers sixty pages of manuscript and a two page genealogical chart.

Sumatran Malay text which derives from a similar period to the Barus chronicles, but which may display a "Malacca Straits" outlook. The hero of this work, Mohammad Dalek, is shown traveling round the archipelago and to the Peninsula, making conquests on behalf of the Sultan of Aceh. He visits Siak, Kedah, Perak, Selangor, Johore, Pahang, Kelantan, Trengganu, Patani, Melaka, Cambodia (Kemuya in the text), Bengkulu, and Borneo. Although the text is chronologically inaccurate in portraying all these kingdoms in existence simultaneously, it has been suggested that one of the geographical concerns of the manuscript may be to outline a map of the kingdoms in which Malay culture and proper forms were upheld.[34] Such a "map" also serves to place Deli and Aceh within the wider world of the archipelago and to suggest a relationship between its different parts.

By contrast, in the Barus chronicles little outside travel takes place. The world portrayed is a more confined one; and for the most part the protagonists are concerned with internal affairs. There are, nevertheless, some instances where travel occurs and a world outside Barus comes into focus. These episodes help us to define the geographical horizons of the texts.

The world they depict is primarily a Sumatran one. Aceh, Minangkabau, Tarusan, and the Batak interior feature in the narrative of both chronicles. Like the Dutch, Aceh plays the role of an external arbiter in the kingdom's affairs. The ruler of Aceh, as we shall see, plays the part of a potential overlord, and Aceh forms the most prominent external threat to Barus's security. Although Tarusan is mentioned in connection with the Hilir founder's origins, other centers on the west coast such as Tiku and Natal are not, despite their links with Barus at least in the sixteenth and seventeenth centuries. This, and the absence of references to the early possessions of Barus in Natal and Batahan, suggests that the geographical perspective of the chronicles was largely a nineteenth century one. This being said, however, an awareness is also evident in both chronicles of Barus's trading past. In the *Asal* the Lobo Tua settlement is mentioned, as is the presence of Tamils there, a fact which is otherwise only revealed, as we have seen, in archaeological evidence which was first published in the twentieth century. The texts also refer to Pagaruyung, the old court of the Minangkabau royal family, the influence of which is usually considered to have declined by the nineteenth century.

In particular, the manuscript of the *Sejarah* opens with references to the ruling family of Minangkabau and to other Sumatran courts which are said to have been connected with Pagaruyung.[35] These other Sumatran kingdoms are not mentioned in the narrative, but, presented in a formulaic opening, they place the text in a certain geographical and political context. The rulers of Minangkabau are said here to have been the source of all authority in Sumatra (Pulau Perca) and their glorious ancestry, often quoted in Minangkabau letters and seals, is mentioned. The text then states that the rulers of the following coastal kingdoms were descended from the Minangkabau kings whose authority and adat spread out to them: these include Jambi, Palembang, Padang, Banten, Aceh, Siak, Sungei Paguh, Indragiri, Inderapura and Pariaman.[36] These, or a similar list of kingdoms, are sometimes referred to as the eight *bab* or gateways to the kingdom of Minangkabau and the list appears to represent a certain manner of thinking about political geography which places Pagaruyung at the center

---

[34]Milner, *Kerajaan*, Ch. 5.

[35]*Sejarah*, pp. 1–4.

[36]Ibid., pp. 4–6.

of a series of coastal dependencies.[37] Inderapura is one of these, and it is with Inderapura that the chronicle commences, since Sultan Ibrahim, the founder of the Hilir line, originally came from Kampung Barus in Tarusan, which was part of the kingdom of Inderapura. The Hilir family, therefore, originated in a coastal kingdom which possessed old and important links with the Minangkabau royal family, and these connections are emphasized at the beginning of the chronicle.

The royal *cap* of Pagaruyung and other Sumatran kingdoms occupy the first six pages of the *Sejarah Tuanku Batu Badan*. On page three above the Pagaruyung *cap* itself is a statement which helps to account for its presence in the text.

"Inilah cap Pagaruyung disalin kepada tempat ini sebab sudah tuha tempatnya jadi disalin kepada kitab ini adanya."[38]

The suggestion is, therefore, that a copy of the royal seals of Pagaruyung already existed in Barus at the time they were included in the manuscript. The form in which the *cap* appear in the *Sejarah* is similar to the opening pages of several Minangkabau MSS, but also to numerous letters of accreditation sent out by the ruler of Minangkabau in the seventeenth and eighteenth centuries, in which the ruler usually requests that the bearer be acknowledged as his representative in the coastal regions and among all those who recognized Minangkabau sovereignty.[39] We saw in Chapter 2 that a Yang Dipertuan from Pagaruyung is said to have incited anti-VOC sentiment in Barus and Sorkam in the 1740s and to have won the rulers of Barus to his cause for a time. This was a not infrequent occurrence in east and west Sumatra in the eighteenth century, and it is likely that the royal seals transcribed at the beginning of the *Sejarah* originally reached Barus in the form of a letter or edict from Pagaruyung which was carried by this or another representative of the Minangkabau royal house. They were probably transcribed at the beginning of the MS for the reason stated there, and because they were considered to be royal *pusaka* and a part of Barus's heritage. They function in the text as a potent and illustrious opening to the narrative which links the Hilir family's founding ancestor with the revered Yang Dipertuan of Pagaruyung and with other Sumatran rulers who were said to be descended from him, including the Sultan of Aceh.

The Sumatran orientation of the chronicles is also recognizable in the themes and language they employ. As royal genealogies written in Malay, these texts belong to a genre of Malay historical writing. In form, language, and style they share many of the conventions of Malay *hikayat* literature. The ceremonial language of Malay kingship is used in both, and both employ many of the formulaic phrases and expressions of the *hikayat* genre. Indeed, the term *hikayat* is used in one of the chronicles. The narra-

---

[37] According to J. Kathirithamby-Wells, the eight *bab* are Inderapura, Bengkulen, Painan, Padang, Pariaman, Siak, Inderagiri, and Jambi, "The Inderapura Sultanate: The Foundations of Its Rise and Decline, from the Sixteenth to the Eighteenth Centuries," *Indonesia* 21 (1976): 65–66. Kathirithamby-Wells cites E. M. Loeb, *Sumatra: Its History and People* (Vienna: Verslag des Institutes fur Volkerkunde der Univeritat Wien, 1935), p. 98.

[38] *Sejarah*, p.3. "This is the Pagaruyung seal which has been copied in this book because of the age of the original."

[39] See, for instance, Marsden, *History of Sumatra*, p. 337; Newbold, *British Settlements*, pp. 80–87 and J. H. Moor, *Notices of the Indian Archipelago and Adjacent Countries* (1837: Reprint ed. London: Cass, 1968), p. 261. The royal seals of Pagaruyung as they appear on letters and in manuscripts are discussed in detail in my doctoral thesis, which is in preparation.

tive of the *Asal*, as we saw, opens with the words "Bermula dihikayatkan . . ." and part 6 of the ML. 162 collection contains the statement, "Inilah Hikayat Tjarita Baros." Other terms are used, however, to describe these works, and the issues of genre and category are by no means simple in this frontier context. Words such as *carita*, *kitab*, and *tambo* are also used as self-descriptions of the chronicle. *Tambo* is a Minangkabau term for a history of origin which conventionally relates the beginnings of the Kingdom of Minangkabau and the development of Minangkabau *adat*, and which considers questions such as the ideal arrangement of society in the Minangkabau *darek* and relations with the *rantau*. Despite the presence of a Pagaruyung royal *cap* in its opening pages, the *Sejarah* text has a different subject matter, and does not appear to embody what Taufik Abdullah has called the "Tambo conception of history."[40] Nevertheless, both the *Asal* and *Sejarah* texts contain what may loosely be described as "Minangkabau influence" in their language, orthography and ideology and differ from more conventional Malay forms in ways which may frequently be characterized as "Minangkabau" in style.

Both chronicles lack the elaborate descriptive style of some "classical" Malay texts from the Melaka Straits, such as the *Sejarah Melayu* and the *Hikayat Hang Tuah*. The language used here is less elegant and might be described as countrified. Dialogue in these texts frequently lacks the elaborate niceties of expression which are common in Malay *hikayat*, and, while this is more marked in the *Asal*, both texts occasionally use language which is more appropriate to spoken than literary Malay. An example of this may be found in the use of personal pronouns. In both texts, for instance, a Raja may refer to himself as *hamba* (literally "slave") when talking to his subjects. *Hamba* is a self-depreciatory term which is usually used by subjects and inferiors who are humbly addressing their ruler or superior.[41]

A number of Minangkabau words occur in both works, and, in the case of the *Asal*, some Batak terms too. In both the *jawi* is spelt in a way which is usually associated with features of Minangkabau dialect. This applies to the spelling of common Malay words as well as to those which are only found in Minangkabau dictionaries. Such features include the frequent use of a specified *alif* or "a" in places where it is not used in "standard" Malay and the use of "a" where "e" normally occurs, for instance in the word *dangar* for *dengar*. "O" endings are represented in both works in places where the Malay reader might expect an "a," and the texts frequently omit the nasalization of prefixes which in Malay normally take a nasalized form. Other noteworthy features include the frequent use of final *hamza* and of final "h." These features have been described more fully in the romanized edition of the chronicles, where the language used in the two texts is also compared in more detail. In that romanization the non-"standard" spelling features which are specified in the *jawi* have been retained, although no attempt has been made to go beyond this and to reconstruct a fully Minangkabauized dialect. Where no specific instruction for vowels is present in the *jawi*, therefore, the romanization adopted conforms to the modern

[40]Taufik Abdullah, "Modernization in the Minangkabau World," in *Culture and Politics in Indonesia*, ed. Claire Holt, et al. (Ithaca: Cornell University Press, 1972), p.188.

[41]Matheson and Hooker have commented upon the use of *hamba* by rulers in the *Hikayat Aceh*, but in the context, they suggest, the ruler is referring to himself as God's slave. See V. Matheson and M.B. Hooker, "Slavery in the Malay Texts: Categories of Dependency and Compensation," in *Slavery, Bondage and Dependency in Southeast Asia*, ed. Anthony Reid (St. Lucia: University of Queensland Press, 1983), p. 192.

spelling rules set out in *Ejaan Baru*.[42] This method has the effect of producing a somewhat hybrid language which will appear unsatisfactory to the Minangkabau reader, but which is faithful to the form of Malay set out in the manuscripts.[43] Inconsistences and variation in spelling practice have also been retained in order to bring the reader as close as possible to the original texts. These romanizations of the two chronicles have been used consistently for quotations in this study, and the reader will be required to contend, for example, with *balun* instead of *belum; ka* for *ke;* and *baranti* for *berhenti.*

As we have seen, Voorhoeve commented that "the dividing line between real Minangkabau texts and Minangkabauising Malay texts cannot be sharply drawn."[44] Neither has this intermediate territory been much studied, and this applies as much to questions of theme and style as to language. Features of the two Barus chronicles, however, are recognizable from the vantage points of the Riau-Johor tradition of Malay *hikayat,* from the Minangkabau world and from Batak conventions. By attending to the manner in which the Barus texts employ the conventions and shared assumptions of all of these, it may be possible to identify the strands of a local tradition and to understand more fully the different and contradictory elements of political thinking in Barus. Particular attention will, therefore, be given in the following pages to the presence of conventional elements in the texts and to the presence of words and phrases which receive special, and unconventional, emphasis.

*   *   *

So far, this introduction to the chronicles has attempted to identify the broad Sumatran context in which these chronicles are set. In terms of their geographical scope, however, the most significant regional emphasis in both texts is on Barus's immediate hinterland. Batak geography plays a crucial part in this. Both texts are concerned with mapping the areas of importance in the hinterland and their relationship to the coast. The clearest geographical statements to be found appear in the passages where each family is described descending to Barus after cementing links with the hinterland. In view of the economic and political importance of Barus's interior, this emphasis on the Batak regions seems hardly surprising, but what the two chronicles emphasize is not economic exchange but the recognition of the Barus Rajas as rulers inland. These issues form the subject of the origin stories with which each text opens and which are discussed in the next chapter.

---

[42]Departemen Pendidikan dan Kebudayaan, *Pedoman Umum Ejaan Bahasa Indonesia yang Disempurnakan* (Jakarta, 1975).

[43]One of the three romanized texts in the Korn Collection uses a more fully Minangkabauized form of spelling than the others; it also employs spelling forms which depart in places from the letters signaled in the *jawi* MS used here.

[44]Voorhoeve, *Critical Survey of Studies,* p. 16.

4

TWO ORIGIN STORIES

The opening sections of each of the two chronicles are referred to here as "origin stories." They are not necessarily mythical stories of origin, and in part each has a quite pragmatic element. They have been treated separately from other sections of the narrative because of their subject matter, and the highly individual ways in which they delineate the ancestry and heritage of the two families. It is by means of these early sections of the two chronicles, where the history of each family before their meeting in Barus is presented, that they can, most readily, be identified as "Hulu" and "Hilir" chronicles. In later sections a common past may be inferred from the two accounts; in the origin stories, however, the subject matter of each is different. The two families come from different backgrounds and different geographical areas. This is drawn out in the origin accounts.

There are, nonetheless, structural similarities in the two accounts. Both are organized around a journey made necessary by a departure from the protagonist's birthplace following a family dispute. In both cases the initial subject of the story is the son of a Raja, and he is accompanied by many followers. In both stories, too, the subject, or his family, spends time traveling through the hinterland of Barus, where he becomes a Raja and where links with the coast are developed. In each text this hinterland experience is used to justify the establishment of the respective families on the coast. The claims which each text develops for the families at this point are also used to defend their positions in later episodes of the chronicles. The origin accounts, therefore, are crucial in the development of each narrative.

Despite their similarities each text develops the establishment of its own family's position in an individual way. Over and above the obvious ethnic and geographical distinctions between the families which are brought out in these sections, the manner in which each chronicle describes its family's odyssey to the coast differs. In these origin stories a difference emerges between the chronicles in the terms used to establish authority, and these differences are developed in later parts of the narrative. They are revealed in the language and style with which events are described, and this can most conveniently be demonstrated by examining the two texts separately. In quotations from the Malay an attempt has been made not to break up passages in a way which might subvert their sense. The Malay in footnotes, therefore, is often cited in greater length than the English translation quoted in the text. In the same fashion one large passage of Malay might be the source for several points or quotations, and in these instances the footnotes direct the reader back to the note containing that passage.

ASAL (THE HULU CHRONICLE)

Although the *Asal* is a Malay text employing Malay terminology, the Hulu rulers of Barus were originally descended from Toba Bataks. Not only does the origin story contained in the Hulu chronicle actually state this, but the style of the story reflects the Hulu family's Batak origins. The narrative opens by introducing Alang Pardosi/Pardoksi, the fifth son of a Raja Kesaktian from Kampung Parsoluhan in Balige area (*lua'*) of Toba.[1] The family's clan or *suku* is Pohan, which is a Batak *marga* name although the Minangkabau Malay term, *suku*, is used in the chronicle.[2] Alang Pardoksi left his family and home after a quarrel with his father, which came about because Raja Kesaktian had asked him to travel to Asahan to obtain oil for a feast (*barale'*). Raja Kesaktian, however, completed the feast before Alang Pardoksi's return. This so angered Alang Pardoksi that he left and traveled with his wife and followers towards the west. The narrative for the first ten pages of the chronicle is occupied with Alang Pardoksi's exploits, the uncultivated land (*rimbo*) he laid claim to in the frontier regions (*rantau*), the network of new settlements he founded, and his conflict with another migrant group from Toba. Alang Pardoksi journeyed until he reached Rambe. There he stopped and created rice fields (*ladang*) and a *kampung* which he called Kampung Tundang.

> After some time the *kampung* had become a *negeri* because many people came there from Toba and settled there and made a *negeri*.[3]

Alang Pardoksi became the Raja and he fixed the borders of the land which he owned (*hingga mana-mana tanah yang dia punya*).[4] The area of the territory claimed by Alang Pardoksi was large. It stretched from Kampung Tundang in Rambe, where he had settled, west to Singkel, east to the borders of Pasaribu, and downstream to the sea shore. It included, therefore, the area now known as Barus and much of its hinterland.[5] According to the text the area of Alang Pardoksi's authority (*perintahnya*) was

---

[1]The word Toba is spelled Tobah in the chronicle. After the opening page of the manuscript the spelling of Alang Pardosi's name changes to Alang Pardoksi. This spelling has been adopted here even though other versions of this narrative, such as the *Hikayat Carita* and that recorded by Ypes, use Pardosi and Pardosi itself is a Batak *marga* name used in the hinterland of Barus.

[2]*Asal*, p. 1(58). "Bermula dihikayatkan suatu raja dalam negeri Tobah sila-silahi lua' Baligi kampung Parsoluhan suku Pohan. Adapun itu raja namanya Raja Kesaktian dan beranakkan lima orang laki-laki yang tuha bernama Mage' di Pohan, yang kedua bernama Lahi Sabungan, yang ketiga bernama Raja Tumbu' Padi, yang kaempat bernama Raja Pahit Tuha, yang kelima bernama Raja Alang Sabatangan Pardosi."

[3]Ibid. "Kemudian daripada itu lamalah antaranya itu kampung pun telah suda menjadi negeri sebab suda banyak orang datang ka sana dari Tobah serta diam di sana membikin negeri itu."

[4]Ibid., p. 2(57).

[5]Ibid. "Alang Pardosi juga suda menjadi raja dan serta suda ditentukannya hingga mana-mana tanah yang dia punya pada masa itu, yaitu sehinggan Alang Pardoksi kampungnya lalu ka tepi laut. Dari sana ka sebelah barat sampai ka Sinu Todang Simpang Kiri Batang Singkel lalu ka muara ka sebelah Tunggara sehingga sampai ka perbatasan dangan tanah Pasaribu itu jauh perintahnya karena itu tanah semuhanya balun bertunggu melainkan rimbo saja semuhanya. Kemudian suda barapa lamanya di sana maka adalah masing-masing membikin kampung kecil-kecil sampai ka Dahiri dan lain-lainnya."

extensive, because none of this land was yet settled. It was all still jungle. After some time small settlements were created which stretched to Dairi and other places.[6]

The family with which Alang Pardoksi came into conflict was that of Si Namora, who also came from Toba, from the region of Simamora and the *negeri* of Dolok Sanggul. His *suku* was Simamora, which is another Batak *marga* name.[7] He too had left his home in Toba because of a family quarrel. The details of this quarrel were complex and, like Alang Pardoksi's search for *minyak*, they were odd. It involved the suggestion by one of the sisters-in-law of Si Namora's wife that her pet dog had dirtied their house. Si Namora and his wife were childless and the sister-in-law suggested that the pet dog was their child. After leaving his home Si Namora and his wife settled in Rambe, and Alang Pardoksi became aware of their presence when, one day, he saw a piece of hand-cut wood floating in the river. Alang Pardoksi, therefore, went upstream and found Si Namora's settlement. He asked Si Namora who he was and why he had settled there. Alang Pardoksi insisted that, according to *adat*, Si Namora should pay tribute to him if he wanted to live there. Si Namora agreed to this and promised that he would present the head of any animals or fish he caught to Raja Alang Pardoksi.[8]

Si Namora's wife eventually had a child after she had eaten Rambai fruit.[9] Alang Pardoksi presented the family with gifts of cloth on the birth of this son, whose name was Si Purbah Uluan and who later became Alang Pardoksi's son-in-law. After his marriage Si Purbah decided to challenge the tribute relationship existing between the two families. He carried out this intention by means of a trick played on Alang Pardoksi. For this purpose it was necessary for him to return to his father's *kampung* in Toba to collect his family's wealth in cloth and heirlooms. When he returned to Rambe many of the inhabitants of Toba accompanied him. Si Purbah then made a formidable looking deer out of the cloth and presented its head to Alang Pardoksi as tribute. Alang Pardoksi was so frightened by the animal that he refused the offering and released Si Purbah's family from the tribute.[10]

Having been tricked in this way, Alang Pardoksi detected a challenge to his position as Raja.

> If I have been swindled in this way by Si Purbah, my eldest son-in-law, then this Si Purbah is cunning. Eventually he will become Raja here and I will be killed by him.[11]

Raja Alang Pardoksi therefore moved and made another settlement in Si Pigembar. Si Purbah, however, resorted to treachery in order to attack this new *kampung*. A war

---

[6]Ibid.

[7]Ibid.

[8]Ibid., p. 4(55). "Dalam pada itu maka menjawab pula Raja Alang Pardoksi katanya, 'Kalau kamu mahu diam di sini ba'ik akan tetapi kamu mesti bari 'adat kepada aku.' Menjawab Raja Namora katanya, 'Apa tuan punya 'adat akan aku turut.'"

[9]Presumably this story was linked with the name of the region which was called Rambe. According to Wilkinson's *Malay English Dictionary* (1959) *rambai* is a "name covering a number of trees , the best-known of which is Baccaurea malayana that gives a good fruit (*buah rambai*)."

[10]Ibid., pp. 4(55)–7(52).

[11]Ibid., p. 7(52). "Kalau bagitu aku ini suda terkecoh oleh menantuku yang tuha bernama Si Purbah kalau bagitu cerdiknya Si Purbah ini akhirnya nanti kalau bagitu dia menjadi raja di sini aku dibunuhnya."

broke out and Alang Pardoksi moved once more, traveling further westwards with his people. He settled at a spot called Huta Ginjang.

This left Si Purbah in control of Kampung Tundang, and he became Raja there. Retribution followed when, under Si Purbah's leadership, the settlement was struck by famine. According to the advice of a *dukun*, the famine came about because of Si Purbah's treachery toward Alang Pardoksi.[12] As a remedy, Alang Pardoksi was invited to return. But he declined. He said that he did not want to return to the *kampung*, but that he would go back if Si Purbah built a house for him on the road at Guting. The house was to be, "in the middle of that road so that all the people will have to travel under my house."[13] The house was duly built and Alang Pardoksi moved back to Tundang with all his people. On his way he established *penghulubelang* in several of the districts through which he passed. According to Ypes' twentieth century ethnographic account, these *penghulubelang* were stone images which were indeed erected in Tukka Dolok and Tukka Holbung. Such images were regarded with awe, and only a datuk could approach them. Supplication was made to them for successful harvests, and they were also used for more aggressive purposes to mark out territory.[14] Raja Alang Padoksi also instituted arrangements for markets to be held (*onan*) and agreements which instituted *bongbong* or taxes.[15] His position at the intersection of important pathways gave Raja Alang Pardoksi great authority and he became, the chronicle records, the greatest of all the Rajas in the Batak lands.

His name was famous and supreme among the Rajas in *negeri* Batak.[16]

Raja Alang Pardoksi's story is recorded in Malay prose with many Minangkabau terms, but the process it describes is reminiscent of Batak social organization. The terms in which Alang Pardoksi's settlement of the intermediate regions between Toba and the coast are described here offer an insight into the way in which hinterland relations are conceptualized in the chronicle.

Alang Pardoksi's conflict with Si Namora served to confirm his authority over Rambe. At first he was prepared to allow Si Namora to live within Rambe, provided he acknowledged Alang Pardoksi as his overlord and offered tribute. Alang Pardoksi

---

[12]*Asal*, p. 9(50) "Adapun sebab maka demikian ini halnya tanam-tanaman tidak hidup karena Si Purbah telah suda kasi sumpah dan telah murka kepada Raja Alang Pardoksi."

[13]Ibid., p. 10(49). "Kalau masu' kembali kepada kampung aku itu aku tidak mahu tetapi jikalau Si Purbah mahu membikin satu [rumah] di jalan Gunting pada sama tengah itu jalan supaya segala orang jalan dari bawah rumahku, bagitu aku mahu."

[14]Ypes, *Bijdrage*, p. 505. In a more recent work Jean Paul Barbier describes *pangulubalang* as "magical statues" and discusses their origin and purpose, including the possibilities that they are considered as ancestor effigies or involve human sacrifice. Jean Paul Barbier, "The Megaliths of the Toba-Batak Country," in *Cultures and Societies of North Sumatra*, ed. Rainer Carle (Berlin and Hamburg: Reimer, 1987), pp. 48–49.

[15]*Asal*, p. 10(49). "Lamalah pula suda tinggal di sana maka ba'ik kembali itu negeri y-a-k-m-a-n di hulu dan serta dangan aturan dan perjanjian dan membikin onan dan membikin perjanjian dari bongbong pada masa itu." *Bongbong* is a Batak term to indicate "versperd"—an obstruction or something barred. See J. H. Meerwaldt, *Handleiding tot de Beofening der Bataksche Taal* (Leiden, 1904), p. 149. In this context it probably implies taxation arrangements.

[16]*Asal*, p. 11(48). "Dangan barapa lamanya masyhur namanya dan tertinggi daripada segala mereka itu raja-raja di dalam negeri Batak sebelah Dahiri di luar lua' Toba di sebelah rantau di luar tanah Toba pada masa itu sangat masyhurnya."

married his daughters to Si Namora's sons, and the two families co-existed until Si Purbah challenged the tribute relationship. Although Si Purbah's attacks on Alang Pardoksi were successful and Alang Pardoksi was forced to flee and found several new settlements, symbolically Alang Pardoksi's right to rule in Rambe was confirmed when famine struck Si Purbah's settlement. Guting, where Alang Pardoksi demanded his new house to be built, is situated on the border between Rambe and Tukka Dolok. The house, therefore, dominated an all important pathway on the route to the coast.[17] Alang Pardoksi is thus portrayed as having achieved authority (*perintah*) over Rambe and its border with Tukka Dolok and put himself in a position where he could control all movement between the two. Although the text does not state as much, a Barus reader or listener to this account would know that the movement which mattered was the passage of camphor and benzoin which, as we have already seen, had to be brought through Rambe and Tukka on its way down to the coast. Although the text uses the Minangkabau/Malay term *suku* to refer to the families from which Alang Pardoksi and Si Namora originated, the names used refer to specific Batak *marga* or clans. They are Pohan of the Toga Sobu group for Alang Pardoksi, and Simamora of the Toba Sumba grouping for Si Namora, both of the Sumba moiety.[18] What the chronicle appears to be describing here, then, is a social pattern which reproduces Batak clan relationships using Malay terminology. The settlement of an area by one *marga*, and its conflict with another *marga* to which it had married its daughters, are standard features of Batak clan relations. This is the relationship between the ruling *marga* in a territory and the members of the *boru na gadjong*, the indwelling *marga* with which it had marriage connections and which, in a long-established relationship, acquired an influential position.[19] The language of the text in these passages presents a combination of Minangkabau usage in expressions such as *barale'* or *baralek* (feast), *balun* (belum), and *baranti* (berhenti), and of Batak terms in the use, for instance, of the word *huta* in some instances instead of the Malay term *kampung*. The form of tribute paid to Alang Pardoksi by Si Namora, the heads of all animals and fish captured, appears to have been typically Batak. According to Ypes, such forms were still used in the first part of the twentieth century in many Batak areas in recognition of land rights.[20]

Raja Alang Pardoksi is thus established in the chronicle as the founder of a line which broke away from the heartland of Toba and began an expansion into the *rantau* or frontier lands. The process continued after his death, when his two sons, Pucaro Duan and Guru Marsakot, separated and moved in different directions. Pucaro Duan announced to his younger brother,

> Brother, it would be better if we each create our own *kampung*. Do not let us stay in one *kampung* together, (*satu kampung bedua*) and, moreover, we should not stay

---

[17]In the version of this story cited by Ypes, the name of the settlement is given as Gonting. Ypes, *Bijdrage*, p. 508. According to a nineteenth century Dutch report there was a narrow pass at Kampung Baringin on the border of Rambe and Tukka. In the past the people of Tukka Dolok are said to have erected a house over this pass and forced the people of Rambe to travel under, thus humiliating them. "Verslag van een reis van den Controleur van Baros," p. 198.

[18]J. C. Vergouwen, *The Social Organization and Customary Law of the Toba-Bataks of Northern Sumatra*, trans. Jeune Scott-Kemball (The Hague: Nijhoff, 1964), pp. 5–15.

[19]Ibid., pp. 50–54 and 122–23.

[20]Ypes, *Bijdrage*, p. 508.

here because our father is dead and later we may have trouble with Si Purbah. I will establish my *kampung* in another place.[21]

Pucaro Duan, therefore, moved a step closer to controlling the all important pathways in the hinterland of Barus by settling the area of Tukka which was, as we have seen, an important center for collecting supplies of camphor and benzoin. Guru Marsakot moved down to the coast itself, to a channel of water (*pancuran*)[22] on the sea shore where he met Tamils and Hindus (*orang ceti dan hindu*) who had been shipwrecked there.[23] Guru Marsakot challenged their right to have settled there and he asserted his own family's ownership over the land: "Why have you made a place here? I own this land."[24] The Tamils and Hindus explained that they had been unable to build a new ship because all of the wood there was rotten. Hence they had called the place Air Busuk (Rotten Water).[25] In time, they said, foreigners from many lands had arrived there and the settlement had developed into a *negeri*.

"Now," they said, "if it is true that you own this land very well, if you are willing, we will make you our Raja."[26]

Guru Marsakot thus became the ruler of Pancur[27] in Kampung Air Busuk and, according to the text, he was a famous Raja. The *negeri* is said to have become populous and the *adat* or custom used was unified (*bersebuahlah*). It was a combination of Tamil *adat* and Batak *adat* with the *adat* of Aceh and Melayu. Soon the settlement was moved to Lobo Tua. The people there became rich and much trade took place, it is said, with Indians, Arabs, and Acehnese.[28]

---

[21]*Asal*, p. 11(48). "Hai adi'ku ba'ik kita membikin kampung masing-masing, jangan kita suatu kampung bedua dan lagi jangan kita tinggal di sini sebab bapa' kita telah mati nanti lama-lama nanti barangkali kita dapat kasusahan jua sebab Si Purbah bikin melainkan aku bikin kampungku ka lain tempat."

[22]Ibid. "Suda barapa lamanya berjalan maka bertemu satu pincuran dia tinggal sedikit hari di sana dia kasi nama itu tempat Pancur."

[23]Pancur, or Fansur, as we have seen, was an early name given to the Barus region which was used frequently in Arab sources. Our knowledge of trading activity in Lobo Tua in earlier centuries depends upon archaeological sources. According to Deutz, archaeological excavations were first undertaken in Barus in the 1850s. Nilakanta Sastri identified the inscription on the Lobo Tua stone as Tamil in 1932, but the presence of Tamils and Hindus at Lobo Tua had long been part of local tradition. Deutz, "Baros," p. 159. In *Hobson-Jobson* "Chetty" is defined as "A member of any of the trading castes of S. India. . . ." H. Yule and A. C. Burnell, *Hobson-Jobson* (1886: London and New York: Routledge and Kegan Paul, 1968), p. 189. Iskandar describes *Ceti* as an Indian merchant from the Malabar or Coromandel coasts, T. Iskandar, *Kamus Dewan* (Kuala Lumpur: Dewan Bahasa dan Pustaka, 1970).

[24]*Asal*, p. 11(48). "Apa sebab kamu diam bikin tempat di sini adapun ini tanah aku punya?"

[25]Air Busuk is the present day for a swampy area near Lobo Tua.

[26]*Asal*, p. 12(47). "Sekarang pun kalau batul tuan yang punya ini tanah baiklah sekarang pun kalau tuan suka tuan kami bikin jadi kami punya raja di sini."

[27]Spelled Pangsur at this point in the chronicle.

[28]*Asal*, p. 12(47). "Pada masa itu Guru Marsakot dimasyhurkan jadi raja di tanah Pangsur dan maka dia tinggal di kampung Air Busu' lama dangan berkelama'an itu kampung Air Busu' pun bertambah menjadi ramai dalam pada itu maka bersebuahlah 'adat terpakai dalam negeri itu yaitu 'adat Ceti dangan 'adat Batak dan 'adat Aceh dan 'adat Melayu. Kemudian daripada itu suda barapa lamanya maka berpindah itu raja ka Lobo Tuha dangan segala ra'yatnya. Dalam pada itu suda barapa lamanya maka ramai pula Lobo Tuha sampai ka Sungai Macu

With God's grace, according to the chronicle, the Raja had two children, and when he died his son, Tuan Namora Raja, succeeded him. No explanation is given in the chronicle of the similarity of this name to that of Si Namora with whose family the Alang Pardoksi dynasty had come into conflict.

The narrative next moves, briefly, to the Tukka branch of the family. When Pucaro Duan died he was succeeded by his son, Raja Tutung. Raja Tutung became involved in a further dispute with the Simamora line. According to the text, the Raja of Rambe, who was Si Purbah's son, refused to obey Raja Tutung's orders (*menurut perintah Raja Tutung*).[29] Raja Tutung therefore traveled the coast in order to enlist the help of his cousin, Raja Lobo Tua, or Tuan Namora Raja. Together the two cousins traveled into the hulu, to Rambe, where they overcame all opposition. Henceforth, we are told, the Simamora line followed the old agreement between the two clans.[30]

Tuan Namora Raja returned to Lobo Tua where he had a son, who, in time, succeeded him. According to the text, "the succession changed many times" (*Raja berganti-ganti dalam kampung itu*) before the *negeri* accepted Islam.[31] A note in the margin of the manuscript states that the story of these events is not available.[32] These events took place in the time of a Raja called Tuan Kadir. No details are offered in the text concerning the conversion of the state to Islam, although the rulers' names change at this point from Batak to Malay/Islamic proper names. Tuan Kadir's son and successor was called Tuan Mualif, and in his reign Lobo Tua is said to have been attacked by *orang* Gergasi.[33] The inhabitants of Lobo Tua fled across the Aek Si Raha

---

dangan barapa banyak orang kaya-kaya pada masa itu ramai berniaga-berniaga dangan [kapal] Keling dan 'Arab dan Aceh."

Archaeological investigations undertaken both in the nineteenth century and in more recent years have produced numerous objects—beads, small pieces of gold and sherds which point to the existence of an early trading settlement in the Lobo Tua/Air Busuk area. See Deutz, "Baros," Nurhadi, "Laporan Penelitian Arkeologi Barus" Unpublished report of the Pusat Penelitian Arkeologi Nasional (Jakarta, 1985), and E. Edwards McKinnon, "A Note on the Discovery of Spur-marked Yueh-type Sherds," p. 43.

[29] *Asal*, p. 12(47).

[30] *Asal*, p. 13(46). "Dalam pada itu maka kembalilah itu raja parang pun baranti Si Purbah [sic] pun suda mengikut perjanjian seperti dahulu kala."

[31] Ibid.

[32] Ibid. The note states, "Tapi tidak dapat keterangannya." Such annotations are common in the manuscript.

[33] Gergasi may be a sanskrit word, and in Malay it is used for a tusked, man-eating ogre. Gergasi are mentioned in the *Hikayat Marong Mahawangsa*. See Wilkinson, *Malay-English Dictionary*, sv. *gergasi* and Low, trans., *Hikayat Marong Mahawangsa*, pp. 4 and 13.

The abrupt cut-off date for ceramic finds at Lobo Tua after the twelfth century indicates that the settlement was indeed abandoned as its name suggests. Different sources spell the name Lubok Tua, Lobu, or Lobo Tua. It was decided to romanize the *jawi* spelling of this name in the Barus chronicles as Lobo and this form has therefore been used here in the interests of consistency. Lobu or Lobo is a Batak term for a deserted settlement so Lobo Tua would be "old, deserted settlement." In Malay *lubok* means a cavity underwater in a river or pool which is not unlike the early name of Pancur: spring or conduit. Ceramic finds in Barus on the other side of the Aek Si Raha river appear to date from approximately the fourteenth century onwards. Archaeological investigations in Barus and Lobo Tua are still at a preliminary stage. However, the inferences drawn from the test digs which have been undertaken are that the Lobo Tua settlement was abandoned and that the centre of settlement and commerce in the region moved to Kota Barus, as in the chronicle. For a summary of archaeological investigations in Barus in 1978 see Nurhadi, "Laporan Penelitian Arkeologi Barus," also Lukman Nurhakim, "Makam Kuno di Daerah Barus."

river and created two new settlements in Kuala Barus; one was called Kampung Barus, and the other Kota Bariang. After some time the Gergasi died and peace was restored to the *negeri*. Tuan Mualif was succeeded by his son, Tuan Marah Pangsu, and it was in Tuan Marah Pangsu's reign that a party of Malays arrived from Tarusan.[34] Here, therefore, with the establishment of an Hulu settlement in Barus, the Hulu origin story can be considered to close. The actual meeting between the Hulu and Hilir families will be examined in Chapter Five.

In spite of the Malay language and terminology used in the text, the Batak features of this origin story are again apparent when one looks at the pattern of settlements which it describes. A distinctive feature of Batak custom is the tendency for land hunger or family disputes to force members of a family to split off and move away from the founding *kampung* of a *marga* in a particular territory, known as the *huta parserahan*, and to found offshoots which themselves might produce other new settlements.[35] This process is known as *pabidang panggagatan*, translated by Vergouwen as "unfolding the wings."[36] According to Vergouwen,

> the founding of a new village springs from the inclination of the Batak to provide living room in more than one village for a genealogical group that is growing in numbers and prestige.[37]

Various additional reasons have been listed by Vergouwen and others to explain why a Batak should seek to leave his "mother village" and found a new one. The expansion of living space is one, but protection against foes, dissension within a family, and a desire to split off from an extensive lineage are others.[38]

In the chronicle, family quarrels are an important reason for leaving home. Alang Pardoksi quarreled with his father and departed. Si Namora's wife quarreled with his brothers' wives and so they left. Alang Pardoksi's two sons, Guru Marsakot and Pucaro Duan, also decide to split off and found new *kampung*. The maintenance of links between mother *kampung* and offshoots is a notable feature of the splitting process, and at least once in the narrative such relations do occur, for example when Si Purbah returns to Si Namora's home *kampung* in Toba to collect his father's heirlooms (*pusaka*). Links between the branches of the Pardoksi family are also maintained when the Tukka and Lobo Tua settlements unite to defeat Si Purbah's descendants in Rambe. Pardoksi control over the hinterland is thus demonstrated, as is the network of Pardoksi settlements which had been created between Toba and the coast. Of course, the opening up of new territory by the founder of a new dynasty is a conventional theme which is not confined to Batak society. A Malay text from east Sumatra, the *Syair Perang Siak*, employs the same convention.[39] Nevertheless, the clan names

---

[34]*Asal*, p. 13(46).

[35]Vergouwen, *Social Organization*, pp. 121–22.

[36]Ibid., p. 121.

[37]Ibid., pp.121–22.

[38]Ibid. On village segmentation as part of the process of *merantau* in Minangkabau see Kato, *Matriliny and Migration*, pp. 111–12. Kato describes how in the *darek* this is regarded a process of maturation, which is expressed in a conception of "autochthonous metamorphosis."

[39]See Donald Goudie, "Syair Perang Siak: An Example of a Misunderstood but Rewarding Eighteenth Century Malay Text," *Archipel* 20 (1980): 244. See also Gullick, *Indigenous Political Systems*, p. 32.

used in the Hulu text, and the nature of the relationship between different branches of a clan and with other clans, appear to be identifiably Batak in style as well as content. These features are quite different, we shall see, from the Malay style origin story found in the Hilir text.

Batak society before colonial rule is said to have manifested a stateless quality when compared with Javanese or Malay notions of government.[40] Lance Castles has observed that, between the miniature world of the village (*huta*) and the much larger relationship of clan (*marga*), the links that bound Bataks and regulated their lives were changing and varied.

> The most important . . . were those which arose by dispersal of a mother village (*huta parserahan*) and those centering on a religious observance or sacrifice, the chief purpose of which was to assure fertility [*bius*].[41]

The process described in the story of Alang Pardoksi's family appears to represent the former of these. Not only does the text describe the settlement of Rambe by a particular *marga*, but it does so in a peculiarly Batak way. According to Ypes and Vergouwen, the *bius* structure of upper Barus was unusually highly organized.[42] The *bius* is a supra-*marga* grouping, the main purpose of which is religious and sacrificial.[43] However, in areas where a large number of parts of *marga* are grouped in one territory, the *bius* can also take on a political, legal, and economic character.[44] According to Ypes, this was the case in upper Barus, where the *bius* was important for the ordering of land rights and markets (*onan*).[45] The role of the *onan* in Batak society was to facilitate trade and intercourse between tribal groups. The "peace of the market," which held while the *onan* ran its course, allowed warring groups to meet and trade.[46] It is not surprising to find that in upper Barus the role of the *bius* should be extended from a purely religious function to the administration of intercourse between rival groups. The requirements of the camphor and benzoin trade meant that goods from the deep hinterland areas had to pass through various regions controlled by different groups before reaching Barus. As we have already seen, in these circumstances the opportunities for controlling trade through mastery of the pathways and traversable valleys were enormous. The hilly and inaccessible nature of the hinterland meant that only certain routes were practicable for the passage of goods, and among these the valleys of Rambe and Tukka Dolok were critical.[47]

The importance, stressed in the *Asal*, of controlling Rambe, Tukka, and the pathways down to Barus makes sense in the light of this information. The *marga* organization of upper Barus also reflects similar issues to those discussed in the *Asal*. Although the area was inhabited by a variety of *marga* and their offshoots, among the principal of these was the *marga* Pohan and its sub-branch, Pardosi. Ypes, who car-

---

[40]Lance Castles, "Statelessness and Stateforming Tendencies," passim.

[41]Ibid., p. 69.

[42]Vergouwen, *Social Organization*, pp. 125 and 108, and Ypes, *Bijdrage*, p. 504.

[43]Vergouwen, *Social Organization*, pp. 73–75.

[44]Ypes, *Bijdrage*, p. 407 and Vergouwen, *Social Organization*, p. 108.

[45]Ypes, *Bijdrage*, p. 497.

[46]Vergouwen, *Social Organization*, p. 107.

[47]See Chapter 1 above, p 15; also Chapter 2, pp. 33–35.

ried out the most thorough ethnographic work in this area, reported that the Pohan *marga* was represented in Tukka Dolok, Tukka Holbung, and Barus Mudik. Members of Pardosi inhabited Tukka Dolok.[48] Similarly, divisions of Si Purbah and Si Namora's *marga*, Simamora, lived in Rambe and included Purba among its subgroups. The *marga* claimed in the *Asal* for Alang Pardoksi (Pohan) and Si Namora (Simamora) were, then, represented in the same areas mentioned in the chronicle. Moreover, competition between these *marga* existed. The Pohan living in Tukka Dolok claimed, according to Ypes, the right to cultivate land between their respective areas on the basis of a *lobu*, a deserted settlement, in Rambe which they had vacated prior to the arrival of the Simamora, a right which was denied by the inhabitants of Rambe at the time when Ypes was writing.[49]

The movement of Alang Pardoksi's family from Toba to the coast, and the "wing spreading" process which it involved, is very different from the settled polity which they created in Barus. In subsequent episodes, as we shall see, the family remained in Barus, consolidated their authority, and instituted numerous regulations and governmental traditions. From the point where Guru Marsakot met Tamils on the coast, and his descendants accepted Islam and moved to Barus, the major issues with which the text is concerned are who should be Raja and what form of government should exist within this settled state. Although we shall see later that it might be feasible to compare the Hulu view of relations with the Hilir family in Barus with the treatment of the Simamora line as a *boru na gadjong*, an indwelling *marga*, the chronicle does, nevertheless, go on to describe an institutionalized kingdom which is more Malay in character. The kingdom has fixed borders, and a power structure and administration at the head of which is a Raja; it is a settled Malay-style polity in fact, and quite different from the unsettled and mobile situation that obtained when Alang Pardoksi was establishing his clan in the frontier area (*rantau*) and when every new generation was on the move, restlessly consolidating territory in the areas between Barus and Toba.

Reflecting upon the issue of statelessness and the generation of state-forming impulses among the Bataks, Castles has noted that "Only around the fringes of the Batak country do we detect a tendency towards state-forming under outside pressures and models."[50] The foundation of Barus, and the changes in style which occur within the text, may offer an illustration of the type of process these Toba Bataks underwent in establishing themselves in a more formal style of government on the coast. To some extent, perhaps, it is a process of "Malayization" that is being described here, and the extent to which the categories used in later stages of the Hulu text are typically Malay will be considered presently. The establishment of a secure hinterland was important, and we have seen that a need for more living space, and the desire to avert friction between family groups, provided an impulse for movement toward the coast. Doubtlessly, economic motives were also an important factor, but the chronicle makes little mention of trade. Reference to contact between the Bataks and foreigners in the chronicle offers, perhaps, a hint of the outside models mentioned by Castles. In the narrative, once the Pardoksi family had reached the coast it met, in quick succession, Tamils, Hindus, Arabs, and Acehnese; it participated in a prosperous trading settlement; it accepted Islam and came into contact

---

[48]Ypes, *Bijdrage*, p. 549.

[49]Ibid., p. 508.

[50]Castles, "Statelessness and State Forming Tendencies," p. 25.

with the Malay population. Jockeying for position with the Malay rulers from Tarusan may also have led to the adoption of new coastal style categories.

In the establishment of claims to authority in Barus, then, the chronicle invokes the Batak ancestors of the Hulu family. The non-Malay origins of the Raja di Hulu family are by no means disguised in the text. Central to its presentation of the Hulu family's right to settle in Barus is the development of its Batak *marga* network through strategically important areas of upper Barus. Territory is emphasized in this text and, in particular, the chronicle frequently mentions the ownership of land as the basis for the family's rights in the region. Alang Pardoksi defined the borders of the territory which he owned, and Guru Marsakot became ruler in Lobo Tua on the basis of his claim to own the land. The tribute offered by the Simamora clan was a traditional recognition of land ownership, and the Pardoksi family's opening up of land in Rambe is presented as giving them perpetual rights in the area.

We shall see that, while the Hilir origin account also involves a journey through the interior, the terms in which Hilir rights are established inland are very different.

SEJARAH (THE HILIR CHRONICLE)

The first six pages of this chronicle contain the Minangkabau royal seals to which reference has already been made. Page one is occupied by a doxology in Arabic and Malay. The doxology ends with a statement that this is the *kebasaran*, or insignia, of all the rulers who are descended from Pagaruyong in Minangkabau.[51] Page two lists items of the Minangkabau royal regalia which are set within circles on the page, as is the three-fold royal seal of Minangkabau on page three. Pages four to six list the Sumatran rulers who are said to be descended from Pagaruyung. In this fashion the rulers of Jambi, Palembang, Padang, Banten, Aceh, Siak, Indragiri, Sungai Paguh, Pariaman, and Inderapura are all mentioned.[52] Minangkabau and its royal family are thus connected with the beginnings of these coastal kingdoms, and the chronicle opens the narrative with a statement of the political and geographical world in which the story is set. The narrative commences on page seven, when Inderapura is reached. It concerns, we are told, Tuanku Sultan Muhammad Syah, who was the ruler of Tarusan in the kingdom of Inderapura, and who was the father of Sultan Ibrahim.[53]

Sultan Ibrahim is the name of the prince who left Tarusan and moved to Barus, where he founded the Hilir royal dynasty. Like Raja Alang Pardoksi, Ibrahim decided to leave his home because of a quarrel with his father. Here, however, the reason for a disagreement between father and son is drawn from a popular motif in

---

[51]*Sejarah*, p. 1. "Wa amma ba'du adapun kemudian daripada itu, maka inilah kebasaran dan kenyataan undang-undang asal keturunan sekalian raja-raja yang beketurunan yang berasal dari Minangkerbau bernama Kota Pagaruyung, maka dari sanalah asala kerajaan dan kemuliaan segala orang ber'adat yang memegang hukum syara' dan yang meramaikan segala Pulau Perca yang menarangi segala hukum pada tiap-tiap seorang raja-raja yang turun dari Minangkerbau Kota Pagaruyung."

[52]The formula is as follows with changes in name for different kingdoms and rulers "Inilah bab sultan dalam negeri Inderapura bernama Muhammad Syah anak yang dipertuan dalam negeri Pagaruyung melimpahkan 'adat dengan kemurahan kepada segala anak cucunya melimpahkan ka Moko-Moko ka Tarusan."

[53]*Sejarah*, p. 8. Muhammad Syah was the legendary first ruler of Inderapura. On the traditional links between the kingdom of Inderapura and the Minangkabau royal family, see Kathirithamby-Wells, "The Inderapura Sultanate," p. 66.

Malay literature. They quarreled as a result of an attack by swordfish (*todak*) on the kingdom. Confusion reigned because none of the warriors and ministers of state could find a satisfactory means of repelling the fish, which speared all who ventured near the beach. Eventually a young boy, Si Budak, beloved friend of the king's son suggested that banana tree trunks be used as shields upon which the long snouts of the fish would become impaled as they lunged. His solution worked. Soon the king became uneasy with the thought that such a clever youth might one day come to challenge his leadership. Si Budak was therefore put to death by the king's warriors. Sultan Ibrahim's grief and anger because his friend had died without committing a sin (*tiada dengan dosanya*) was intense and he determined to leave his father's home.[54] Before departing he collected a lump of earth and a container of water from his homeland, to take with him. He left with his wife and a thousand followers (*seribu orang*).[55]

Whereas Alang Pardoksi's origins were Toba Batak, Sultan Ibrahim's are clearly Malay. His father, Tuanku Sultan Muhammad Syah, is described in the chronicle as ruler of the Minangkabau-Malay coastal states of Inderapura and Tarusan. The story of a swordfish attack with which the chronicle opens is found elsewhere in Malay writings, and it may indicate that the authors of the text were familiar with the literature of the wider Malay world of the peninsula and east Sumatra. A. A. Cense has commented on the frequency with which certain story motifs recur within Malay literature, the swordfish attack being one of them.[56] It occurs, he notes, with only small variations, in the *Sejarah Melayu*[57] where the fish attack Singapore, in the *Hikayat Hang Tuah*, where they attack Inderapura, in the *Salasila of Berau*, and in the Barus chronicles.[58] There is also a Toba Batak version, forming part of the van der Tuuk collection. This version was found in Barus and is written in Toba Batak with some Dairi peculiarities. It seems likely that this otherwise apparently Malay motif found its way into Batak legend by way of a version of the Hilir story which itself was probably influenced by the classical Malay texts, the *Sejarah Melayu* and the *Hikayat Hang Tuah*.[59]

On his journey the prince (he is referred to as *baginda*, a royal title) stopped at each river mouth and weighed the water there, comparing it with the weight of the water from Tarusan and searching for a spot where they were equal and where, in

---

[54] *Sejarah*, p. 10. "Maka dengan takdir Allah subhanahu wa ta'ala [anaknya] seri paduka Sultan pun menengar khabarnya nan bahasa sahabatnya budak kecil sudah mati dibunuh oleh hulubalang sebab oleh titah seri maharaja bapanya mati sahabatnya tiada dengan dosanya. Maka baginda pun pergilah ka tapi air menangis budak itu karena sangat kasihnya kepada budak itu. . . . Maka datanglah ibu bapanya menurut ka tapi air memuju'-muju' membawa' pulang ka rumahnya maka anaknya itu pun sangat marahnya kepada ibu bapanya sebab membunuh oleh sahabatnya mati tiada dengan dosanya."

[55] Ibid., p. 12.

[56] A. A. Cense, *De Kroniek van Bandjarmasin* (Santpoort: Mees, 1928), pp. 174–75. See also P. E. de Josselin de Jong, "The Character of the *Malay Annals*," in *Malayan and Indonesian Studies*, ed. J. Bastin and R. Roolvink (Oxford: The Clarendon Press, 1964), pp. 235–36.

[57] C. C. Brown, trans., *The Sejarah Melayu; or, Malay Annals* (Kuala Lumpur: Oxford University Press, 1970), pp. 40–41 [80–82].

[58] Cense, *Kroniek van Bandjarmassin*, p. 175.

[59] Ibid. For mention of the Batak version of the tale see P. Voorhoeve, *Codices Batacici* (Leiden: Universitaire Pers, 1977), p. 192.

consequence, it would be right for him to settle.[60] At one spot his wife dropped a golden bathing bowl (*mundam*) into the water and the place was named Batu Mundam.[61] Here again is a motif which can be found elsewhere. In 1933, L.C. Westenenk reported a Minangkabau legend, in which one Mahardjo di Radjo was searching for a place to make a settlement. His method of choosing the appropriate spot was to weigh the earth at each possible place, comparing it with a stone of similar size.[62] The motif may have a link with the Tabut ceremony still practiced on Sumatra's west coast. Tabut, otherwise known as the Feast of Hasan and Husain, is a Shi'ite festival which mourns the defeat of the prophet's descendants on the field of Karbala.[63] The story of this defeat is known in the Malay world through the *Hikayat Muhammad Hanafiyyah*, which, according to the *Sejarah Melayu*, was read and listened to by Malays in the Melaka period.[64] West Sumatra is unusual as an area where the Asyura or Tabut celebration is still held in a long and complicated ceremony.[65] One aspect of the ritual is the carrying of earth: *ma'ambil tanah*.[66] This is thought to symbolize a handful of earth from the battlefield of Karbala which, according to the *Hikayat Muhammad Hanafiyyah*, was given to the prophet by Gabriel. It was to be kept in a bottle, and, when the deaths of Hasan and Husain were near, the earth would turn red.[67] In view of the important place the Tabut ceremony occupies in west Sumatran areas such as Bengkulu and Pariaman, a link between *ma'ambil tanah* and the earth/water weighing motif is possible.[68]

Sultan Ibrahim's route passed up the west coast as far as Batu Mundam and Kuala Batang Toru. On reaching the Batang Toru river, he went inland to begin a circumambulation of the Batak lands. Despite the contacts he made in these regions, and the many requests he received to become Raja of one place or another, Ibrahim did not test either water or earth inland. Only after he had returned to the sea shore some time later did he seek once more for an appropriate place to settle. It seems, therefore, that he had no intention of remaining in the interior. He looked, in the

---

[60]*Sejarah*, pp. 10–11.

[61]Ibid., p. 11 Batu Mundam is a place name on the west coast of Sumatra between Natal and Sibolga.

[62]L. C. Westenenk, "Opstellen over Minangkabau," *TBG* 56 (1913): 234 ff. Also cited by Cense, *De Kroniek van Bandjarmasin*, p. 125. John Bowen recounts a Gayo story in which a boy who cannot be circumcised is said to have fled from Lingë to Karoland, taking with him some earth from Lingë. See John Richard Bowen, "The History and Structure of Gayo Society: Variation and Change in the Highlands of Aceh" (Ph.D. dissertation, University of Chicago, 1984), p. 109.

[63]See the *Encyclopaedia van Nederlandsch-Indie*, vol. 2, sv. Hasan—Hoesain—or Taboet-Feest.

[64]See L. F. Brakel, *The Hikayat Muhammad Hanafiyyah*, 2 vols. (The Hague: Nijhoff, 1975), vol. 1, ch. 1, for background of the text, its importance in the Malay world, and its connections with the Tabut ceremony.

[65]See the *Encyclopaedia van Nederlandsch-Indie*; Brakel, *Hikayat*, vol. 1, p. 60; and M. Kartomi, "Minangkabau Musical Culture," in *What is Modern Indonesian Culture?*, ed. G. Davis (Athens, Ohio: Ohio University, Center for International Studies, 1979), p.26.

[66]Ph. S. Van Ronkel, "Nadere gegevens omtrent het Hasan-Hoesain feest," *TBG* 56 (1914): 336–37.

[67]*Encyclopaedia van Nederlandsch-Indie*, and van Ronkel, "Nadere gegevens," pp. 337–38 for an alternative suggestion.

[68]This connection was suggested to me by Dr. Margaret Kartomi of Monash University who has made an extensive study of west Sumatran musical culture and of rituals such as the Tabut festivities.

manner of other Malay Rajas, for a country that lay on a river mouth. His period in the Hulu was temporary, and his world remained that of the coast, not that of the mountains.

When Ibrahim turned inland, the areas he chose to visit were those which have obvious importance from the point of view of a Barus ruler. He first visited Silindung which, as we have already seen, was an important area for the passage and collection of resins from the hills further inland. Ibrahim's visits to various Batak regions are described in detail in the text. Much the same thing happened in each district, and elaborate language is used to describe his interaction with the Bataks, who all respected and honored him. In Silindung the Toba Bataks who lived there wanted him to become their Raja. The people are said to have presented themselves before Seri Paduka Sultan Ibrahim, as he is called here, morning and night without stopping. "Their desire was to keep Sultan Ibrahim there and make him Raja over all of Toba Silindung."[69] The Raja there attempted to restrain Sultan Ibrahim, but Ibrahim replied,

> Don't keep me here. God, may he be praised and exalted, has not decreed that I should stay here because I have not yet fulfilled my intention of finding water which weighs the same as that which I have brought.[70]

But Ibrahim told the Bataks that he would create four Penghulu in his place. The Empat Penghulu is a Silindung Batak institution which is mentioned in the ethnographic works on this area.[71] All the Batak Rajas then bowed down in adoration before his highness (*sujud sembah kebawah duli Sultan Ibrahim*).[72] They are said to have spoken to him with sweet words in order to soften his heart and make him stay, but they were unable to change his mind. Ibrahim, therefore, made an agreement (*perjanjian*) with the Rajas of Toba Silindung. Each side swore that they would not renounce the agreement and neither would their descendants.[73] "If we renounce the agreement," they promised, "our *padi* will become grass and our *gadung* [a tuberous plant] will become *akar kalimpanang* [roots] and all of our living things will die."[74] Sultan Ibrahim then instituted the *panghulu*, who were given Malay titles, to deputize for him. As a sign that Sultan Ibrahim had become the Raja of Silindung (*luhu'*

---

[69]*Sejarah*, p. 13. "Melainkan maksud segala orang Tobah henda' menahan Sultan Ibrahim di sana henda' menjadikan jadi raja pada sekalian antara Tobah Silindung."

[70]Ibid., p. 14. "Janganlah menahan hamba di sini karena Allah subhanahu wa ta'ala belum mentakdirkan hamba tinggal di sini karena maksud hamba belum sampai air yang hamba bawa' belum sama beratnya."

[71]Ibid. See Castles, "Statelessness and Stateforming Tendencies," pp. 68–69.

[72]*Sejarah*, p. 14. "Maka setelah sudah seri paduka Sultan berkata demikian buninya maka segala raja-raja Tobah pun sujud sembah ka bawah duli Sultan Ibrahim mengatakan kata yang manis-manis supaya terlunak hati baginda Sultan Ibrahim tinggal di tanah Tobah."

[73]Ibid. "Maka dilabuhlah perjanjian pada ketika itu melainkan sekalian luhak Silindung melainkan berbapa kepada Sultan Ibrahim melainkan Sultan Ibrahim menjadikan panghulu empat di sana jadi bersumpah bersaktilah kedua belah pihaknya Sultan Ibrahim dengan sekalian raja-raja Silindung basa tiada boleh mungkir-memungkiri berbapa kepada Sultan Ibrahim sampai kepada anak cucunya. Adapun sumpahnya tatkala itu, 'Jikalau kami mungkir berbapa tuan padi kami jadi hilalang gadung kami jadi akar kalimpanang hidup-hidupan kami habislah mati.'"

[74]Ibid. For *Akar Kalimpanang* see Iskandar, *Kamus Dewan*, sv. *Kalimpanang*.

Silindung beraja kepada Sultan Ibrahim) the four Penghulu would take tribute of a horse to Sultan Ibrahim.[75] This undertaking was also to apply to the descendants of each side up until the present. When all of this had been accomplished, Sultan Ibrahim took his leave of the people of Silindung and continued on his journey.[76]

In Silindung, therefore, Sultan Ibrahim was acclaimed as a Raja. Rather than con-quering territory, he was invited by the people to stay and rule over them. The Bataks addressed Ibrahim with respect, and they treated him as a great Raja. He is referred to here in the text as Sri Maharaja. Ibrahim traveled next to Bakara and his experience there was similar. When Ibrahim arrived in Bakara, the people there asked him from whence he had come and what he wanted. Ibrahim replied that there were many in his party "One thousand (*seribu*) people, men and women."[77] According to the text neither side understood what the other was saying,[78] presum-ably because of language differences, but conversation is nevertheless recorded. The Bataks replied, "If that is so then your *marga* is Pasaribu, we too are from the *marga* Pasaribu; will you stay here and become our Raja?"[79] Sultan Ibrahim did not reply to their question, but the next day the Bataks asked him again if he would become ruler since they did not have a Raja. In reply, Ibrahim suggested that the Bataks should enter Islam because that was his religion; then, he said, they would be one people (*satu bangsa*).[80] In that case it would be possible for him to remain. The Batak Rajas made obeisance to Sultan Ibrahim and said, "Pardon Tuanku Alam Syah [lord of the world], we do not want to enter Islam. Whatever else you order we will obey."[81] Sultan Ibrahim therefore asked that they build him a mosque. The Bataks are said to

---

[75]*Sejarah*, p. 14. "Demikianlah perjanjian tatkala itu dan adapun tandanya luhu' Silindung beraja kepada Sultan Ibrahim melainkan sekali atau di dalam dua tahun melainkan datang Panghulu Empat manjalang kepada Sultan Ibrahim membawa' kuda persembahan mengiring panghulu-panghulu yang empat dan segala anak buahnya menjalang seri paduka Sultan Ibrahim sampai kepada anak cucunya sebelah-menyebelah sampai sekarang kini."

[76]Ibid., pp. 14–15.

[77]Ibid., p. 15. "Maka sedemikian lakunya menengar kata yang demikian buninya seri paduka Sultan Ibrahim pun menyahut katanya, 'Kami ini banyaknya seribu orang laki-laki perempuan berjalan.' Demikian kata Sultan Ibrahim sebab tiada tahu bicara sebelah-menyebelah. Jadi Allah subhanahu wa ta'ala mentakdirkan raja Batak itu pun menyahut kata seri paduka Sultan Ibrahim, 'Jikalau begitu marga tuan Pasaribu, kami pun marga Pasaribu jikalau begitu di sini-lah tuan bertempat boleh kami jadikan jadi raja kami.' Baginda seri maharaja mendengar kata sambil tertawa serta menjawab kata sekalian raja-raja, 'Baiklah lain harinya kita bicara. Sekarang belum lagi senang karena kami sekalian payah-payah sebab oleh jauh jalanan.' Maka diperjamunya oleh Sultan Ibrahim makan kerbau dua tiga. Eso' harinya maka berbicaranya sekalian raja-raja dengan Sultan Ibrahim maka kata segala raja-raja kepada sultan, 'Di sinilah tuan bertempat boleh kami jadikan jadi raja kami karena negeri kami ini tida' beraja baru kematian raja.' Sultan menyahut kata sekalian raja-raja katanya, 'Janganlah saya tuan tahan di sini hanya jikalau tuan-tuan suka pada hamba dan saya masu'kanlah tuan-tuan jadi Islam karena agama kami agama Islam. Jikalau tuan-tuan masu' jadi Islam boleh kita satu bangsa boleh saya di sini diam. Apa tuan-tuan punya ma'alum?' Allah subhanahu wa ta'ala men-takdirkan mendengar kata yang demikian maka segala raja-raja pun menyahut lalu menyem-bah serta katanya, "Ampun tuanku Syah 'Alam jikalau masu' Islam kami sekaliannya kami tida' mahu kiranya barang apa perintah tuanku melainkan kami jujung atas batu kepala kami sekaliannya.'"

[78]Ibid.

[79]Ibid.

[80]Ibid., p. 15.

[81]Ibid.

have been pleased (*sukalah hati*)[82] to hear his request, and the mosque was duly built. When it was ready, Seri Maharaja Sultan Ibrahim, as he is called here, married the daughter of a Batak Raja. He stayed in Bakara for some time and ruled over all the people of Toba. Eventually Sultan Ibrahim decided once more to seek a place with water which was the same weight as his. He gathered the Batak Rajas together and told them of his intention. His wife was pregnant, Ibrahim informed them, and when the child was born they were to name it Si Singa Mangaraja. The sign that it was Sultan Ibrahim's child would be hair on the baby's tongue. The child would replace him, Ibrahim said, and would rule over all of the Bataks. Ibrahim then presented them with an umbrella base as a sign of *kerajaan*, or royal authority, in the *negeri* (*tanda kerajaan dalam negeri*). Again, the Batak Rajas are said to have all been pleased (*sukalah hati*) with this sign, and in polite and subservient language they asked Sultan Ibrahim where they would be able to find him.[83] Ibrahim replied in a gentle (*lemah lembut*) voice that he would inform them when he had established a settlement. The two sides then made an agreement (*perjanjian*) which was similar to that sworn in Silindung. They promised that it would not be broken (*tiada jadi rusak-merusakkan*)[84] Then incense was burnt, and the parties called upon God and upon their ancestors to witness the agreement. As in the previous agreement, made in Silindung, living things and crops would die, they said, if the agreement was broken, and tribute of a horse was to be taken to Sultan Ibrahim and his descendants.[85]

After Sultan Ibrahim had left Bakara his son was born, and the birth was accompanied by earth tremors and heavy rain. The child had hair on his tongue. They named him Si Singa Mangaraja, and he ruled over Bakara and all the Batak states.[86]

Sultan Ibrahim traveled next to the land of Pasaribu, where he was once again asked where he had come from and what his purpose was. Ibrahim replied, "My *negeri* is Bakara and my *suku* is Pasaribu." The Rajas of Pasaribu were pleased with Ibrahim's reply because it meant that they all belonged to "one *suku*," and they invited him to stay.[87] Again, Ibrahim made an agreement with the Bataks which each

---

[82]Ibid.

[83]*Sejarah*, p. 16. "Maka tatkala itu ada dibarinya payung sekaki akan tanda keraja'an di dalam negeri. Allah subhanahu wa ta'ala kiranya mentakdirkan mendengar kata yang demikian maka sukalah hati sekalian isi negeri menerima tanda daripada raja asali. Kemudian daripada itu maka raja-raja pun berkata pada seri paduka Sultan Ibrahim, 'Ampun tuanku beribu-ribu pengarapan di bawah jerpu yang maha mulia, jikalau tuanku seri maharaja akan berjalan dari sini ka manalah tuan hamba akan kami cari di manakah kita akan bertemu?'"

[84]Ibid. "Maka seri maharaja pun menjawab serta buninya yang lemah lembut kepada sekalian raja-raja yang menghadab itu katanya, 'Jikalau di mana saya sudah tentu membuat kota maka di sanalah tuan-tuan menurut saya.' Maka seri Paduka Sultan Ibrahim tatkala itu membuat perjanjian dengan segala raja-raja di sana membakar perasapan nan bahasa, 'Tida' jadi rusak-marusakkan sama menyebut nama Allah subhanahu wa ta'ala sama menyaru kepada arwah nenek moyang sebelah menyebelah. Dan apabila sudah tentu bertempat seri maharaja paduka Sultan Ibrahim melainkan datanglah semuanya kami mengantar persembahan kuda. Jikalau yang jauh-jauh melainkan sehingga ini saja tuan-tuan mahantarkan melainkan sudahlah sampai pada saya karena dianya pun anak cucu hamba juga inilah tandanya tuan-tuan beraja kepada saya. Kiranya jikalau tuan-tuan mungkir berbapa saya melainkan padi tuan-tuan menjadi hilalang gedung menjadi akar kalimpanang hidup-hidupan habislah mati semuanya.' Demikianlah persumpahan sekalian raja-raja Tobah semuhanya pada masa itu.'

[85]Ibid.

[86]Ibid., p. 17.

[87]Ibid. "Maka menjawab seri paduka Sultan Ibrahim, 'Negeri saya tanah Bakara suku saya Pasaribu.' Mendengar kata yang demikian buninya raja Pasaribu pun suka mendengar buni

side promised not to break (*rusak-merusakkan*). It was agreed that when Sultan Ibrahim had founded his own settlement then the Rajas of Pasaribu and their people would bring items of trade or food there. They sealed their bond with a promise that, if either side was lost, help would be given; and if either was adrift, or wandering, they would be taken in. They belonged to one *suku*, they assured each other.[88]

The version of this story which is cited in K. A. James's article is slightly different at this point, and the additional information in that version is worth noting here in view of the importance of the relationship which existed between the Pasaribu Bataks and the Hilir family. According to James's version, part of the agreement between Ibrahim and the Bataks provided for the establishment of a fixed market (*onan*) in Pasaribu Dolok, called *onan* Si Batu-Batu. The Toba people of Marbun would be obliged to exchange their resins at this market and would be forbidden to travel on to Barus. Otherwise they would be subject to tax (*bongbong*). As James points out, this provision would have given the inhabitants of Pasaribu Dolok a monopoly over the benzoin trade. Also in this version of the origin story, Ibrahim undertook to inform the Rajas of the *suku* Empat Pusaran (or of the four compass points) when a marriage or death feast was to take place. Each of his successors would travel to Pasaribu Dolok in order that all the *kampung* there should pay homage to him, and Ibrahim and his successors would also travel to Pasaribu, it was stated, to settle any disputes which could not be resolved by the Raja.[89] As we saw in Chapter 2, the Raja di Hilir of Barus and his retinue did indeed travel inland to Pasaribu in times of difficulty.

After he had lived in Pasaribu for some time, Ibrahim once more grew discontented and wanted to resume his search for a place where he would feel comfortable (*tempat kasenangan dalam hatinya*).[90] So he took leave of the Pasaribu Bataks, amidst assurances on each side of their unity and mutual interest. Four Rajas from the *suku* Empat Pusaran accompanied Raja Ibrahim on his journey. The first stop which they made was at a place called Pegaran Lampung, where they rested for the night. Here Ibrahim tested his water, but it was a little different in weight from that which he found in the river. At the next spot they came to, the party ate and Ibrahim once more tested the water, which again differed slightly from his. They went on and

---

seri paduka Sultan Ibrahim sebab sukunya raja nan datang suku Pasaribu satu suku dengan dianya. Maka sebentar itu juga raja Raba-Raba mengatakan kata demikian buninya, 'Jikalau Pasaribu suku tuan baiklah kita di sini tinggal karena kita sebuah suku.' Maka Allah subhanahu wa ta'ala pun mentakdirkan Sultan Ibrahim berhenti di sana."

[88]Ibid., p. 18. "Adapun tatkala berhenti di sana semalam-malam tidak tidur gila barunding jan berpapar Sultan Ibrahim dengan raja-raja Pasaribu membuat perjanjian tatkala itu: 'Tiada jadi rusak-marusakkan dan kalau siapa marusakkan demikian sumpah ka atas tiada berpucu' ka bawah tiada berurut.' Demikianlah perjanjian pada masa itu dan jikalau Allah subhanahu wa ta'ala sudah manentukan tempat seri maharaja Sultan Ibrahim maka datanglah sekalian raja-raja Pasaribu dengan anak buahnya membawa' barang perniaga'an atau makanan jikalau alang ditolongnya hanyut disambutnya seperti orang berdunsa[n]ak boleh habis-mahabiskan raja Batak Pasaribu dengan anak cucu tuanku Sultan Ibrahim sebab sukunya sudah sebuah. Demikianlah hal Sultan Ibrahim dengan raja-raja Pasaribu sekaliannya."

[89]James, "De Geboorte van Singa Maharadja," pp. 138–39. The most important clan group in Silindung is said to have been the Si Opat Pusaran clan or Empat Pasoran. Castles, "Statelessness and Stateforming Tendencies," p. 68. According to James, *empat pusaran* refers to the four quarters. In Malay *pusaran* indicates swirl or circle. The Malay word *suku* also means quarter so the *empat suku*, or *suku empat pusaran*, indicates the clans of the four quarters. On *empat suku*, the four original clans of Minangkabau, see de Josselin de Jong, *Minangkabau and Negeri Sembilan*, p. 12; and Marsden, *The History of Sumatra*, p. 330.

[90]*Sejarah*, p. 18.

came to another river mouth. There at last the water was the same weight as Ibrahim's. He was delighted. This, he told his followers was the proper (*patut*) place for them to stop and build a *kota*.[91] This was done, the region became populous and happy (*suka*), and Sultan Ibrahim was made Raja there with the title Tuanku Sultan Ibrahim Syah. He called the settlement *kampung* Barus, we are told, because this was the name of the *kampung* which he had left in Tarusan.[92] Sultan Ibrahim was thus established in Barus, by means of the magical correspondence of the water from his homeland with that of Barus and the Hilir origin story is brought to the point where we left the Hulu chronicle.

In the Hulu chronicle the Pardoksi family established hinterland supremacy in a practical fashion. They opened up new agricultural areas and established an exclusive network of settlements and their offshoots. Occasionally they met with opposition, but this was generally overcome because of their effective consolidation of an area. In time, therefore, the clan and its subgroupings came to exercise control over a large stretch of the hinterland of Barus. In the Hilir chronicle, however, Sultan Ibrahim's authority in the hinterland is portrayed more in moral than in practical terms. He is described in this text in a manner which emphasizes his qualities as a king. He is referred to as Baginda, a Malay term used to describe royalty, and by the similar expression, *maha-mulia* (most illustrious). When the Sultan meets the Batak chiefs of Silindung, they prostrate themselves before him and bow at his feet (*menyembah kebawa dulinya*), a phrase which is commonly used in Malay texts to describe the position of a Malay subject in relation to his Raja. The Bataks use sweet words in order to tempt Ibrahim to stay, and he speaks to them in gentle tones (*lemah lembut*). Graceful and charming behavior, including a soft and gentle voice, is among the qualities usually attributed to Rajas in Malay *hikayat*.[93] In the *Hikayat Deli*, for instance, a Raja is described as, "Truly a Raja, not a common man, because his manner and his words are gentle [*lemah lembut*]."[94] In Malay *hikayat* a ruler is expected to make his subjects happy (*bersuka*),[95] and in this chronicle Ibrahim's words and decisions are frequently described as having that effect on the Bataks (*sukalah hatinya*).

---

[91]Ibid., p. 19. In fact, the Malay states both that the water was the same weight and that it differed very slightly from that which Sultan Ibrahim had brought.

"Maka dengan takdir Allah subhanahu wa ta'ala maka samalah beratnya air dibawanya itu dengan air ditimbangnya tadi. Maka sukalah hati seri paduka maharaja Sultan Ibrahim sebab sudah sama beratnya air yang dibawanya dengan air muara yang didapati adalah kurang beratnya sedikit air yang dibawanya. Maka seri maharaja Sultan Ibrahim pun lalu berkata kepada sekalian leskarnya demikian buninya, 'Marilah sekalian tuan di ne'nek kaum hamba sekalian laki-laki dan perempuan kecil dan basar di sinilah kita berbuat kota karena air yang kita bawa sudah hamba timbang dengan air muara ini. Allah subhanahu wa ta'ala sudah mentakdirkan sama kiranya beratnya adalah kurang sedikit air kita bawa itu daripada air yang di sini. Maka patutlah kita tinggal di sini berbuat kota.'"

[92]Ibid., p. 20. "Maka Allah subhanahu wa ta'ala mentakdirkan kepada hambanya maka beberapa lama antaranya seri paduka seri maharaja Sultan Ibrahim dudu' di sana maka diangkat oranglah dianya jadi Tuanku Sultan Ibrahim serta dinamakan oleh tempat itu kampung Barus karena nama negeri yang ditinggalkan Barus itulah sebabnya maka dipindahkan ka negeri yang baharu Barus namanya. Maka tetaplah seri paduka baginda Sultan Ibrahim bersuka-suka'an dengan isterinya dan segala hamba ra'atnya di dalam negeri itu."

[93]See the *Hikayat Pahang*, p. 3, cited in Milner, *Kerajaan*, p. 41.

[94]*Hikayat Deli*, p. 7. Cited in Milner, *Kerajaan*, p.98.

[95]This point is made by Milner, *Kerajaan*, p. 24. He cites examples from the *Sejarah Melayu*, the *Hikayat Seri Rama*, and the *Hikayat Pahang*.

Such descriptions of a Raja's speech and behavior are typical of the qualities attributed to ideal rulers in many Malay texts. Ibrahim appears to possess the qualities of a Malay Raja and thereby to inspire loyalty and devotion.

In Bakara the same thing happens. He is invited to become Raja, and the existing Batak Rajas declare their wish that he do so because, they say, there is no Raja in Bakara, presumably meaning a raja greater than they, for they say that their own raja had just died.[96] The text refers to Sultan Ibrahim at this point as Seri Maharaja.

The chronicle's description of Sultan Ibrahim's response to these requests emphasizes that, while he declined to remain in the Batak lands, by linking himself with these people he emanated the qualities of Rajaship as it is understood in Malay *hikayat*. In Silindung he assigned deputies, and the people promised to send him tribute. In Bakara he attempted to spread Islam and had the people build a mosque for him. Before he left Bakara he presented the people with an umbrella base (a symbol of royalty), as a sign of *kerajaan* in the *negeri*, that is to say a sign that the *negeri* was part of a kingdom which possessed a Raja and was subject to the authority of a Malay Raja.

A distinction is clearly made in the chronicle between Sultan Ibrahim's identity as a Malay, and the Batak population he encountered. Not only did all the Batak Rajas submit to him and welcome him, recognizing his superior quality, but they also responded to him in a manner usually represented in Malay texts as characterizing a Malay subject's appreciation of a Raja. The people of Bakara, for instance, experienced satisfaction and joy when Raja Ibrahim ordered a prayer to be read.[97] When Sultan Ibrahim reached Bakara the people did not understand the language in which he spoke, and when he introduced Islam the Bataks of Bakara declined to change their religion, even though they promised to do all else that he might order. When he left Bakara they offered prayers, according to the chronicle, to the spirits of their ancestors. The difference between Batak and Malay ethnic identity is thus emphasized. In brief, all the qualities attributed to Sultan Ibrahim, and the Batak response to him, are described in the chronicle in the same fashion as the qualities of Rajas and their relationship with their subjects are dealt with in other Malay texts. The typical Malay Raja is described in terms of his sovereignty, his gracefulness, his piety, and his ability to inspire loyalty and devotion. The Bataks in this episode of the chronicle are shown as recognizing Sultan Ibrahim's qualities and submitting to his sovereignty. It is they who ask him to rule over them, and they act out with him the ruler/subject relationship as it is usually portrayed in Malay royal chronicles. Perhaps the most potent way in which the chronicle links this coastal Malay ruler with the Batak lands, and emphasizes his claims to authority there, is by connecting Ibrahim with the famous dynasty of Batak kings, the Si Singa Mangaraja. In the

---

[96]*Sejarah*, p. 15. "Di sinilah tuan bertempat boleh kami jadikan jadi raja kami karena negeri kami ini tida' beraja baru kematian raja." In Silindung he is also asked to become raja: "Melainkan maksud segala orang Tobah henda' menahan Sultan Ibrahim di sana henda' menjadikan jadi raja pada sekalian antara Tobah Silindung." (Ibid., p. 14.) In the Batak context, the word raja usually refers to village heads rather than, as in the Malay sense, to the ruler of a kingdom. See James, "De Geboorte van Singa Maharadja," p. 135 and Castles, "Statelessness and Stateforming Tendencies," p. 68.

[97]In the Hikayat Pahang a ruler is said to have been "clever at capturing their [men's] hearts" by "speaking sweetly." And, again, the inhabitants of Lingga are said to have been amazed, by a Raja, "to hear his speech disseminating both Islamic and customary law, and doing so in a manner which was both melodious and able to be understood." Both cited in Milner, *Kerajaan*, pp. 42 and 108.

chronicle, Sultan Ibrahim marries the daughter of the former chief of Bakara. He converts her to Islam and, through her, fathers the first of the dynasty of Si Singa Mangaraja kings.

In Batak legend, Bakara was the original home of the Si Singa Mangaraja. The date of the dynasty's foundation is not known, nor is the actual number of kings who claimed the title; but the last of the line is known to have died in upper Singkel during the Padri War. Heine-Geldern has pointed out that the Hilir account, cited by James, of Sultan Ibrahim's contact with the Batak lands, his special links with the Pasaribu *marga*, and his fathering of the first Si Singa Mangaraja king, is only one version of a legend which is found in various forms among the Batak people.[98] In the Batak version of the story, Sultan Ibrahim is not mentioned, but it is noted that tribute consisting of horses was sent in the past from Toba to Barus. Heine-Geldern explores, in his article on the subject, the history of the Si Singa Mangaraja rulers, the traditions surrounding them, and their historical relations with Barus, Aceh, and Minangkabau. Although his theories, built upon these various traditions, are complicated and ingenious, a proper consideration of them is out of place here. What is of direct relevance is his suggestion that the story of Raja Ibrahim's journey through the Batak lands is a Malay version of existing Batak beliefs, intended to legitimate the arrival of a Malay-Muslim ruling dynasty at Barus.[99] We shall see in later episodes of the Hilir chronicle that the relationship between the inland Bataks and the Hilir family is presented as much more than a question of legitimation. The Hilir relationship with these Batak regions was part of the essence of Hilir royal authority, and a key arena for the performance of a kingly role.

By linking Ibrahim so closely with the famous and important Si Singa Mangaraja dynasty, the text clearly emphasizes the relationship between the Hilir family and the Bataks of the Barus hinterland. Like the origin story in the Hulu text, Sultan Ibrahim's journey develops a picture of one family's royal authority in a particular region of the interior. In the case of the Hulu text, the areas in question are the important valleys of Rambe and Tukka which controlled the pathways along which resins had to pass, particularly from Dairi. In the case of the Hilir text, the important regions are the benzoin territories of Silindung, Pasaribu, and the hills which surround them. It is with these areas, as we have seen, that the Hilir family is frequently connected in VOC sources. Both texts use a similar basis for their story, and the motif of a journey undertaken by a prince or the founder of a new kingdom is not uncommon in Southeast Asian literatures. A well known Sumatran example is found in the *Hikayat Raja Pasai*, where Merah Silu's search for a kingdom took him into the interior. After a quarrel with his family, Merah Silu travels inland to the Hulu, where he is honored and proclaimed Raja, after which he leaves and founds the kingdom of Samudra on the coast.[100] Merah Silu's exploits inland are described much more briefly than those of the Barus royal families, but the structural similarities of the stories are clear. Like Merah Silu and like the Pohan clan, Sultan Ibrahim was recognized in the Hulu before staking his claim on the coast. In the Barus case, we have already seen not only that the hinterland was of vital economic and strategic impor-

---

[98]R. Heine-Geldern, "Le Pays de P'i-k'ien," p. 386.

[99]Ibid., pp. 387–88.

[100]A. H. Hill, trans. and ed., "The Hikayat Raja-Raja Pasai," *JMBRAS* 33, 2 (1960): 113–17 and 50–57. K. R. Hall has commented on this aspect of the Hikayat Raja Pasai in K. R. Hall, "Coming of Islam to the Archipelago," pp. 224–25.

tance for those who lived on the coast, but also that it appeared to have particular significance for the rulers of Barus. Lines of loyalty appear to have existed between each of the two royal families and the inhabitants of the interior. It is not surprising, then, that these special bonds with particular parts of the hinterland should be prominent in local perceptions of the past. Mutual protection and commerce between the coast and interior are mentioned in the local sources, just as in the VOC reports, but the origin stories in the texts suggest that the most important aspect of this hinterland relationship for the royal families may have been the substance this gave to their claims to royal authority on the coast.

What the origin stories most clearly reveal is the distinct concern of each chronicle with one of the two Barus families. The two texts, that is to say, appear to represent "Hulu" and "Hilir" versions of Barus's past, not only by dint of having belonged to each of the respective families, but also through their special concern with one family situation. They thus provide a remarkable opportunity to investigate two indigenous views of a single state.

5

A COMMON PAST: EPISODES ONE, TWO, AND THREE

The origin accounts in the two texts have been considered to end just before the point where each of the chronicles describes a meeting between the two families and from which, henceforth, characters and events mentioned in one are identifiable in the other. Despite their individual presentation of events, and the differences in emphasis between them, the two chronicles recount, from this point on, what can be described as a common past. In both, this past commences where the representatives of the two families meet in Barus for the first time and concludes with the war which broke out between them in the early nineteenth century. Within that framework, each text offers a history of the family which is its subject. Neither of these genealogically based narratives is entirely self-absorbed however. From the point at which the existence of two royal lineages is acknowledged in the manuscripts each recognizes the presence of the other family in Barus. Indeed, as this and subsequent chapters will suggest, an important concern in each chronicle is to explain the position of its family vis-à-vis the other, and to present a version of Barus' political history which suits its own self perception. The following chapters will explore the nature of that self perception. It will emerge, indeed, that these two versions of Barus' past constitute what might be called a discussion concerning political authority in Barus.

In order to illustrate this, it will be necessary to consider the two accounts side by side. In the following chapters the contents of each manuscript are divided into seven episodes. The episodes are not marked off as separate sections in the texts themselves. Rather, as with the origin stories, they are slices of the narrative which, in their respective ways, give an account of the same period or character. Not only will the Hulu and Hilir chronicles be compared with each other in the following pages, but they will also be considered in the context of similar works of Malay literature from other parts of the archipelago. Like any text, the Barus chronicles are open to a variety of readings and what follows is only one reading in which an attempt is made to confront the texts in their entirety. The episodic treatment offers an opportunity to consider terms and concepts which appear in the narrative of each in the context of the texts themselves, to consider, that is to say, the terms of discourse within and between the two texts. While we shall see that the two chronicles depict what is a recognizably common past in these seven episodes, it is frequently at the points where they part company and present the past differently that most can be learnt about their individual perspectives.

To explore the chronicles in this way requires that the two narratives be presented in considerable detail. Inescapably this will be a lengthy process. The stories presented, and the manner of their presentation, must be laid out if the reader is to become aware of the differences of style and content which distinguish the two perspectives. This chapter examines a section of the narrative in each chronicle in which similar events from the kingdom's past are described in three episodes. Here it is the way in which the events are depicted, rather than the events themselves, which is significant. The incidents described in the episodes are used differently in the two chronicles and form a basis for more fundamental differences in perspective which emerge later. Throughout this and the following chapter the method has been adopted of examining the *Asal* narrative first, followed by that of the *Sejarah*, and then considering the differences between them.

Episode One

In this first episode of the two texts, the Hulu and Hilir families, after both had arrived in Barus, meet and agree to co-exist. Although their mutual agreement does not last long, the events described by each chronicle form a basis for what happens later. The factual accounts presented in this episode are remarkably similar, but differences in emphasis reflect some of the themes which have already been identified in the origin accounts and which become even more apparent in subsequent episodes.

Asal

It was during the reign of Tuan Marah Pangsu that Sultan Ibrahim and his followers are said to have arrived in Barus.

> Sometime after Tuan Marah Pangsu had become Raja another person arrived called Sutan Ibrahim who was from Tarusan Seberang and was accompanied by many followers. They built a *kampung* in the jungle downstream and named the *kampung* Kampung Gugu'.[1]

A meeting between these two groups took place when Sutan Ibrahim noticed evidence of habitation upstream.

> By the decree of God, may He be exalted, one day Sutan Ibrahim walked downstream to the sea shore where he saw a mangosteen skin which had been peeled

---

[1] *Asal*, p. 13(46). "Barapa lama suda Tuan Marah Pangsu menjadi raja maka datang pula satu orang bernama Sutan Ibrahim dari Tarusan Seberang dangan banyak orang sertanya. Maka dia membikin kampung dalam rimbo di hilir kampung itu. Maka dinamainya kampung itu kampung Gugu'." The title *Sutan* is used for both Ibrahim and Marah Pangsu here; it appears frequently in both texts, and differs from *Sultan*. According to Wilkinson, *Sutan* is a Minangkabau form, "an honorific or title pronounced *sutan* or *selutan* and not implying sovereign authority." Both van der Toorn and Pamoentjak offer detailed definitions of this title. According to van der Toorn, the titles *sutan, marah, bagindo,* and *saidi* apply to the son of a *puteri*, regardless of the father's status. *Sutan* also applies to a son born of the reigning king who is eligible for the throne only if his mother is a *puteri*. Pamoentjak details the variations of meaning this term has in different parts of the west coast, such as Padang and Pariaman. Wilkinson, *Malay-English Dictionary*, p. 1132. Van der Toorn, *Minangkabausch Woordenboek*, p. 225; and Pamoentjak, *Kamoes Minangkabau*, p. 230.

with a knife. He thought to himself, "If this is the case then I think there must be people in a *kampung* upstream from this one. If so we must try to find it."[2]

Traveling upstream to investigate he met a villager (*orang dusun*), who asked where he had come from. Ibrahim replied that he also was an inhabitant of that *negeri* (*aku orang negeri di sini juga*).[3] After Sutan Ibrahim had returned home, the villager reported to his Raja that someone had visited his village—a man whose appearance was different from that of the local people (*lain rupanya*) although he claimed to live in the *negeri*.

> I could see that he was not from here, but when I asked him he replied that he did live here. My opinion, however, is that perhaps a settlement has been established downstream from us, or at the river mouth.[4]

The chronicle, then, identifies the relative upstream-downstream distinction between these two settlements and a difference in the physical appearance of their inhabitants.

No details are provided concerning this difference and its implications for the ethnic origin of the two groups. It is possible however, that different styles of dress are what is meant here and, by implication, a distinction between Bataks and Malays. As we have seen, dress is one characteristic which distinguishes Bataks and Malays in Sumatra. The Hulu family is said, in this text, to have been Batak in origin and, although they accepted Islam during the reign of Tuan Khadir, there is no mention of a simultaneous acceptance of Malay customs and manners. Reference, then, to Sutan Ibrahim's different appearance in this chronicle may be a means of indicating that he was a Malay, in the same way that the different languages used by Ibrahim and the Pasaribu Bataks in the Hilir chronicle implied their distinct cultural and ethnic origins.

According to the *Asal*, after Sutan Marah Pangsu heard the news of Sutan Ibrahim's visit he ordered a search to be made downstream. His envoys found Sutan Ibrahim and, on behalf of their ruler, they asked him his name and why he had made a settlement there. Sutan Ibrahim replied that he had founded the settlement because the land there belonged to him.[5] When this response was reported to Sutan Marah Pangsu it made him angry. Ibrahim, his envoys explained, asked why Marah Pangsu should want to quarrel. Ibrahim himself wanted to "follow a straight road" (*aku mahu manurut jalan yang lurus*),[6] and he suggested that he might demonstrate this by making an oath. Marah Pangsu consented and the next day he traveled downstream to Kota Gugu' to hear the oath in which Sultan Ibrahim swore that he alone owned the

---

[2]*Asal*, p. 13(46). "Hatta dangan takdir Allah ta'ala pada suatu hari Sutan Ibrahim berjalan-jalan ka hilir ka tepi laut dalam pada itu maka kelihatan olehnya satu kulit buah banggis yang terkupas dangan pisau. Dalam pada itu maka terpikir dalam hatinya, 'Kalau bagitu aku rasa ada orang punya kampung di mudik kampung ini kalau bagitu kita coba cari.'"

[3]Ibid., p. 14(45).

[4]Ibid. "Tetapi aku lihat bukan orang dari sini tetapi aku tanya dia menjawab katanya dia orang dari sini juga tetapi rasa hatiku itu orang barangkali ada bikin tempat dalam rimbo di hilir kampung ini atau di muara."

[5]Ibid. "Aku yang bernama Sutan Ibrahim serta dangan ra'yatku membikin kampung di sini di atas aku punya tanah sendiri."

[6]Ibid.

land where he had settled and the water which he then drank. If the oath was false, he declared, then God would destroy them all.[7]

Sutan Marah Pangsu accepted the oath, and, according to the chronicle, Ibrahim's authority over his *kampung* in the Hilir was thereby confirmed (*Setelah suda bersumpah perkara pun habis itu kampung tetaplah dia punya kuasa*).[8] *Kuasa*, the word used here to signify power or authority, is often employed in this chronicle to represent the authority of a ruler.

The chronicle then relates that Sutan Marah Pangsu returned to his *kampung* upstream. At this point, the text offers some information which is external to the narrative: a statement concerning the names which came into use at that time. These were the title "Tuanku Mudik" for Sutan Marah Pangsu and his successors—because his settlement was upstream (*mudik*)—and the name Barus, which according to the chronicle replaced the old name of Pancur and was derived from the arrival of newcomers (*orang baru*).[9] This naming process in the chronicle implies a recognition that new circumstances obtained. The definition here of names and their meaning constitutes a brief hiatus in the narrative and may be considered as a rhetorical device employed to illustrate a significant point. The establishment of dual authority in Barus and the acceptance of Ibrahim's oath is thus emphasized.

The account of this important meeting between the Hulu and Hilir settlements and of Ibrahim's oath is related in the Hulu chronicle in a straightforward, factual style. It occupies little space, and, with the exception of the brief departure from narrative just mentioned, there is little room for reflective or descriptive passages in the text. The word pictures evoked by the narrative here are all concerned with action and with the unfolding of events. This same episode of the Hilir text, however, is lengthier; a more descriptive style is used in the dialogue and causal statements are more common.

Sejarah

According to the Hilir story of origin, discussed in Chapter Three, Sultan Ibrahim chose to remain in Barus because (*sebab*) the water and earth which he had brought with him from Tarusan weighed the same as those which he found in Barus. In this

---

[7]*Asal.*, p. 15(44). "Hatta dangan takdir Allah ta'ala pada masa itu Sutan Ibrahim bersumpah di atas kampungnya duduk di atas tilam pende' dan serta dipegangnya air satu gelas serta diangkatnya sumpah demikian buninya, 'Sekarang aku bersumpah dari sebab aku membikin kampung di sini yang aku keduduki ini aku punya tanah sendiri kiranya jikalau tidak batul dangan sasungguhnya aku punya ini tanah yang aku duduki ini, maka diminumnya pula air dalam gelas yang dipegangnya itu, ini air aku minum, kalau tidak batul aku punya ini air yang aku minum ini, maka bagitulah Allah Taala membari la'anat dan membari bahaya atas aku dan kepada kami semuha selama-lamanya.'" According to Winstedt, "In Siam and Cambodia princes, courtiers, and officials drink twice a year water of allegiance in which the court Brahmins have dipped the State Sword and other royal weapons." Winstedt, "Kingship and Enthronement in Malaya," p. 136. Marsden also describes the use of drinking oaths in Sumatra, *History of Sumatra*, p. 242. See also J. G. de Casparis, *Selected Inscriptions from the 7th to 9th Century A.D.* (Bandung: Masa Baru, 1956), p. 7.

[8]*Asal.*, p. 15(44).

[9]Ibid. "Sutan Marah Pangsu pun kembalilah pulang ka kampungnya ka mudi', itu sebab bernama Tuanku Mudi' selamanya sampai sekarang pun tatkala itu juga bernama Barus kalau tidak dahulu bernama Pangsur. Adapun sebabnya maka bernama baru karena orang baru bikin negeri tatkala Lobo Tuha suda tinggal dahulu daripada namanya Pangsur. Adapun ertinya Pancur itu saluran air."

version of the story, Ibrahim and his followers called the new settlement Barus because (*karena*) that was the name of the *negeri* they had left behind.[10] Sultan Ibrahim
was made ruler over the new settlement. Here, too, an account is given of Ibrahim's
walk along the river, his sighting of the cut mangosteen skin, and his conclusion that
there must be a settlement upstream. The account presented here is similar to that
found in the Hulu chronicle. Discrepancies between the two accounts occur, however, when Ibrahim goes upstream. Instead of simply meeting a villager, a larger
settlement, a *kota*, is mentioned, and Ibrahim entered this *kota* through the main gates
(*pintu kota*). There the inhabitants questioned Ibrahim,

> "Where have you come from, on your own with no followers? Are you being
> pursued by anyone? In what *negeri* do you live and where are you going?"[11]

Sultan Ibrahim replied,

> "You people who question me. If you want to know what *negeri* I come from,
> then our *negeri* are close. I am also a person from hereabouts. 'Separate, but not
> far away: Close, but not touching.' That is how it is with our *negeri*."[12]

This encapsulation of the problem by Sultan Ibrahim in an oppositional formula, in
which far and near are juxtaposed, is typical of the style of exposition used in this
chronicle when difficult or incompatible ideas are considered. Oppositional formulae
of this type are not uncommon in Malay literature and are frequently used in the
articulation of Minangkabau concepts.[13]

The people of the *kota* then asked Sultan Ibrahim to go home, and he returned
downstream where he entered his *istana*, the text states, and seated himself surrounded by his *penghulu* and servants. In the Hulu, people agreed (*mupakatlah*) to see
this new settlement for themselves, and an armed party traveled down river and
came upon a large *kota*. In this account, unlike that found in the *Asal*, the size of the
settlement, as well as its vegetation, livestock, and defenses are described.

> Then they saw from afar a *kota* which looked very large. The vegetation was
> extremely plentiful and so were the animals; buffalo, cattle, and also goats. The
> *negeri* was encircled by bamboo spikes and a moat which stretched out around it.

---

[10]*Sejarah*, p. 20.

[11]Ibid. "Dari mana tuan berjalan seorang tida' berkawan adakah tuan dikejar orang, negeri
mana tempat diam kampung mana nan dijelang maka tuan sedemikian rupanya?"

[12]Ibid. "Ya tuan-tuan orang negeri ini yang bertanya kepada hamba, jikalau negeri tuan
tanyakan berdekat juga negeri kita saya pun orang di sini juga, jauh nan tiada ada antara dekat
nan tiada bersuatu. Demikianlah hal negeri kita ini."

[13]For examples of similar *jauh/dekat* opposition see Iskandar, *Kamus Dewan*, where he cites,
"nan jauh tiada terjelang, nan dekat tak tertandangi"; and K. St. Pamuntjak et al., *Peribahasa*
(Jakarta: Balai Pustaka, 1983), where this and other *jauh/dekat* pairings are quoted. Pamoentjak
M. Thaib gl. St. Pamoentjak, *Kamoes Bahasa Minangkabau—Bahasa Melajoe-Riau* (Batavia: Balai
Poestaka, 1935), cites "Djaoeeh tiada berdekat tentangan kediaman atau tentangan
perkariban."

The people were numerous, men and women, young and old. The party which had arrived there were astonished to see things thus.[14]

The Hulu party entered the *kota* and, after announcing that they had come on a mission for their Raja, they asked to meet the Raja and the *penghulu* of the *negeri*. Quickly they were taken into the presence of Sultan Ibrahim who is described here with the royal title, Seri Paduka Seri Maharaja Tuanku Sultan Ibrahim, and they paid homage to him (*dari jauh menjujung duli kalau dekat mengangkat sembah*).[15] Sultan Ibrahim asked the envoys from whence they had come and what their mission was. They replied:

"The mission from our Raja in the Hulu is to ask you, Seri Paduka, why you have made a *kota* here and from whom you requested the land, since (*karena*) we own this land."[16]

In this version of the meeting between Ibrahim and the people of the *Hulu*, then, Ibrahim and his settlement are idealized in a fashion which differs from the *Asal* narrative. Not only is the Hilir *kampung* described in glowing terms, but Ibrahim himself is given an honorific title; the Hulu people make obeisance to him and he is addressed in polite language which is typical of Malay courtly expression.

Instead of answering the Hulu people's question directly, Ibrahim called upon the four Rajas from Pasaribu who, as we saw in Chapter Four, had accompanied him to Barus. He asked them to answer for him, and the Raja Empat Pusaran complied saying:

"Why do you speak thus? It is not you who owns this land, but we."[17]

After this speech by the Rajas of Pasaribu a quarrel started, one person announcing that he owned the land and another that it was he who possessed it.[18] Presently, even though the dispute had not been settled, the Hulu envoys went home to explain the problem to their Raja. The Raja's name is not used in this chronicle. He is simply referred to as the Raja in the Hulu. According to the chronicle, when he heard their story he was extremely angry and gave orders to all his followers (*anak buah*) that the next day they travel downstream carrying firearms.[19]

After the war party arrived and entered the *kota* downstream, the Raja Hulu went up to the hall of assembly (*balai balairong*) and met with the Sultan. They took each

---

[14]*Sejarah*, p. 21. "Maka kelihatanlah dari jauh kota terlalu basar beberapa tanam-tanaman terlalu banyak serta dengan hidup-hidupan kerbau dan jawi dan kambing dan negerinya berlingkar dengan aur duri paritnya rantang berkuliling hamba ra'yat banyak laki-laki perempuan tuha dan muda. Maka heranlah tercengang orang yang datang itu sebab melihat yang demikian."

[15]Ibid.

[16]Ibid. "Perhamba ini utusan dari raja kami di hulu bertanyakan kepada seri paduka mengapa di sini membuat kota, dari siapa tuan meminta tanah karena tanah ini kami empunya?"

[17]*Sejarah*, p. 21. "Mengapa tuan-tuan berkata sedemikian buninya dan bukan kamu yang punya tanah ini melainkan kami empunya tanah?"

[18]Ibid., pp. 21–22. "Lalu bertengkar-tengkar pada masa itu seorang mengatakan dia yang punya tanah seorang dia mengatakan dia empunya tanah."

[19]Ibid., p. 22.

other's hands in greeting (*lalu berjawat salam kedua belah pihak tuanku Sultan Ibrahim dengan Raja dari Hulu itu*).[20] The Raja from the Hulu then put his question to Sultan Ibrahim:

> "Why have you made a *kota* here? From whom did you request the land and why did you dare to make a *kota* like this?"[21]

Sultan Ibrahim replied:

> "Why do you speak in this way? Regarding the land and the water it is I who own them. Of whom should I ask permission, since the water and land are mine?"[22]

The Hulu Raja said:

> "If it is true that you own the water and land, do you want to swear an oath? When you have made an oath it will certainly be true that you own the water and land."[23]

In response to this, Sultan Ibrahim called for the water and the earth that he had brought with him from Tarusan. He then declared:

> "If I do not own this land upon which I sit and this water which I hold then let God destroy us all. But if this is truly my water and my earth upon which I am seated, then may God keep us all safely."[24]

According to the chronicle,

> This was the oath sworn by Seri Paduka Tuanku Sultan Ibrahim, as for what he was sitting on (*dikedudukinya*) it was the earth which he had brought with him, what he held was the water which he had brought.[25]

---

[20]Ibid.

[21]Ibid. "Apa sebabnya maka tuan-tuan berbuat kota di sini. Dari mana tuan-tuan meminta tanah? Maka tuan berani membuat kota sedemikian rupanya."

[22]Ibid. "Mengapa tuan berkata yang demikian? Adapun tanah dan air hamba yang punya kepada siapa aku meminta karena air dan tanah aku empunya?"

[23]Ibid. "Jikalau sungguh engkau empunya air dan tanah mahukah engkau bersumpah. Apabila tuanku sudah bersumpah banarlah sungguh tuanku empunya air dan tanah."

[24]Ibid. "Jikalau tiada hamba empunya tanah yang hamba keduduki ini dan air yang hamba kako' ini melainkan dibinasakan Allah sekalian kami. Tetapi jikalau sungguh air hamba dan tanah hamba yang hamba keduduki ini melainkan diselamatkan Allah sekaliannya kami."

[25]Ibid. Demikianlah persumpahan seri paduka tuanku Sultan Ibrahim pada tatkala itu. Adapun yang dikedudukinya itu tanah yang dibawa'nya yang dikako'nya itu air yang dibawa'nya. *Dikeduduki* could also be read as "inhabited" here and in the earlier translations of Sultan Ibrahim's oath.

When the Hulu Raja had heard Ibrahim's oath (*sumpah*) he announced that the land and water must truly belong to Ibrahim and that the *kota*, too, was his.[26]

According to the chronicle this statement made both sides very happy (*serta bersuka-suka'anlah kedua belah pihaknya*), and they swore an oath of mutual loyalty (*bersumpah bersatia*).[27] They promised not to oppress each other (*nianya-menianya*) and the oath was sealed with a proverb, *terendam sama basah, tarampai sama kering*, the implication of which is that when in the water they would both be equally wet and when out of it they would be equally dry.[28] This would apply, they said, to their descendants (*hingga sampai kepada anak cucu kita*).[29] The two rulers then touched hands, the chronicle relates, and again we are told that this made the two sides happy (*baik pada hati kedua belah pihak*).[30] In the Hulu chronicle, the text mentioned simply that Ibrahim's authority (*kuasa*) was confirmed by the oath. Here, however, the two parties are described as taking pleasure in their mutual acknowledgement and forging a strong bond of loyalty expressed in a further oath, the *bersumpah bersatia*. This feeling of mutual harmony described by the text is encapsulated in the use of the proverb, which acts as a metaphor for their peaceful and united co-existence. In the *Sejarah* such expressions of harmony and consensus are frequently depicted as producing a feeling of joy and satisfaction among the participants. Consensus and agreement, we shall see, are important themes which recur throughout the chronicle.

In the *Asal* account of Ibrahim's oath and the events surrounding it, we saw that there was a break in the narrative immediately after the oath-taking ceremony, and it was suggested that the statement of place names and titles which occurs at that point acted as an emphatic device. In the Hilir text the departure of the Raja di Hulu is followed not by a statement of names but by the renewed agreement (*perjanjian*) of loyalty between Raja Ibrahim and the Raja Empat Pusaran of Pasaribu. This fresh agreement may act as a reminder, immediately after his acknowledgement by the Hulu Raja, of Ibrahim's support in the interior. It would also appear to reinforce the importance of agreements of loyalty as an ingredient in Hilir political thinking. The new agreement with the Pasaribu ensured that, if enemies came by sea, then the Malays (*anak Melayuh*) would resist them, and that, if enemies came from the interior, then the Bataks (*anak Batak*) would oppose them.[31] The agreement would apply to their descendants on both sides (*sampai kepada anak cucu sebelah-menyebelah*). This statement of Hilir relations with the groups surrounding their settlement functions, perhaps, as a different type of emphatic device from that found in the Hulu chronicle. The importance of Ibrahim's new position in Barus is implied in a manner which, at the same time, reveals consensus to be an essential element in the Hilir presentation of political authority. The description of these alliances, in other words, may be a

---

[26]Ibid. "Jikalau demikian rupanya sungguhlah tuanku empunya tanah dan air tuankulah empunya kota ini."

[27]Ibid.

[28]Ibid. See Iskandar, *Kamus Dewan*, s.v. Rendam. Pamuntjak et al. refer to the feelings of mutuality which this *perpateh* is intended to express and equate it with other Malay and Minangkabau sayings which have a similar, oppositional, structure. *Peribahasa*, p. 434. The proverb is also cited in Pamuntjak's Minangkabau dictionary, *Kamoes Bahasa Minangkabau*, p. 194.

[29]*Sejarah*, p. 22.

[30]Ibid., p. 23.

[31]Ibid.

Hilir way of making the same statement found in the Hulu text, that Ibrahim's authority was confirmed (*tetaplah dia punya kuasa*).

* * *

What is immediately striking about these two versions of Episode One is that there are no significant factual discrepancies between the two accounts. Indeed the stories are very similar, and they use the same motif in the story of the cut peel which Ibrahim sights floating downstream. A similar image was used in the Hulu origin story, when Alang Pardoksi became aware of Si Namura's settlement upstream because of the hand cut wood he saw floating downstream.[32] It is important, we shall see later, that the chronicles agree that it was the question of land ownership which was the basis of the Hulu challenge. The matter which had to be decided was whether or not Ibrahim actually owned the land he claimed. Both texts agree that the oath gave Ibrahim that right.[33]

The differences between the two chronicles are obviously in part a matter of perspective. It is not surprising, for instance, that Ibrahim is viewed as a stranger by the Hulu people, nor that the Hilir text devotes more praise to Ibrahim's settlement than does the Hulu chronicle. But the difference is also a matter of style. The Hulu chronicle gives little detail even of the Hulu settlement itself and, in fact, is generally less descriptive and elaborate. This episode also offers insights into the way in which issues of ethnic identity are handled in each of the chronicles. In the Hulu text, differences between the two families are hinted at. The text refers to Sultan Ibrahim's different appearance, but the terms Batak and Malay are not used. Only where the mixed *adat* of Pancur is mentioned in the Hulu origin story is the term Melayu used. In the Hilir text, by contrast, a clear distinction is made between the Bataks of the interior and the Tarusan Malays. The term Batak is used and also the Batak word *marga*, rather than the Minangkabau Malay term *suku* which occurs in the Hulu chronicle. Later when the oath is affirmed between Sultan Ibrahim and the Raja Pasaribu, the terms *anak Batak* and *anak Melayu* are central to the affirmations of loyalty made between these distinct groups. The term Batak, however, is not used for the existing settlers in Barus. The ruler is merely referred to as the Raja in the Hulu.

---

[32]Hooker cites a traditional history of Luak Gemencheh, in Negeri Sembilan, in which a migrant couple from Minangkabau settle there and clear the jungle. One day when they are fishing, the couple see signs (unspecified) of habitation upstream. They find that a family of aborigines live in the Hulu. "The two families agree to cooperate in opening up the area and agree to live in peace." Eventually they discuss the government of the area and decide to establish an *adat mufakat* according to which the aborigine was made *penghulu* and the Malay was made Dato' Pawang. According to Hooker's informants *pawang* had a higher status. See Hooker, *Adat Laws in Modern Malaya*, p. 185. The parallels with the Barus foundation stories are obvious, including the Minangkabau origins of the migrants.

[33]Sultan Ibrahim's oath based upon the earth and water which he brought with him from Tarusan has a parallel in a Gayo story related by John Bowen, in which incomers resort to trickery in order to become rulers over the original inhabitants of a settlement. In this instance, the earth was brought from their original settlement but the newcomers pretended they had always been there. The Sultan of Aceh was asked to adjudicate and, "The leader of Bukit sat down on the ground, on a spot where he had previously placed some of the Serule earth, and said: 'If this is not my original earth let me die right here and now.' Of course, it was, so nothing happened. And so, the Sultan of Aceh made the Bukit people the rulers of Kebayakan." Bowen, *History and Structure of Gayo Society*, p. 162.

What is particularly important, however, in the light of what follows in the two texts, is the way in which, in Episode One, as in the foundation stories, the texts diverge from one another in their description of authority. In this episode of the Hulu text, authority is presented in a straightforward fashion in terms of the possession of *kuasa*. In the Hilir text, there is an emphasis on consensus and harmony and a preoccupation with the titles and ceremonial which accompany claims to leadership.

EPISODE TWO

In Episode Two, which takes up the narrative immediately after the Hulu Raja had returned to his *kampung*, the two chronicles do differ from each other in their presentation of events, though the broad outlines of the narrative are the same. Hostility between the two families begins to emerge, and difficulties in their relations result in an attack by the Raja of Aceh on Sultan Ibrahim's *kampung*. As in Episode One, the Hulu account is the briefer of the two, and other differences are apparent which throw light on the distinct approaches of the two chronicles.

ASAL

In this episode Sutan Ibrahim is depicted as betraying the Hulu family with which he had established marriage relations. This betrayal, it emerges, justifies later Hulu hostility towards him. The story is taken up immediately after the oath sworn by Ibrahim and Sutan Marah Pangsu's acknowledgment of his right to found the Hilir settlement.

After Sutan Marah Pangsu had returned upstream to his *kampung* under his new name of Tuanku Mudik, the chronicle states that he moved his settlement to Pintu Ria. After that, Sutan Ibrahim was married (*semando*) to Marah Pangsu's daughter.[34] Sutan Ibrahim then moved his settlement to Ujung Tanah where he made a *kampung*.[35] Then Sutan Marah Pangsu died. The chronicle offers a date for this event, which is unclear, but may be read as 707 H, which is the Islamic equivalent of AD 1307.[36]

Sutan Marah Pangsu left behind three young sons and Sutan Ibrahim, since he was now their brother-in-law, acted as their regent or representative (*wakil*) in governing Sutan Marah Pangsu's *kampung*.[37] But Sutan Ibrahim was not trustworthy. According to the chronicle, he thought "It would be best if I kill my three brothers-in-law so that I may become the only Raja here."[38] The *Asal*, therefore attributes to

---

[34]*Semando* is one of several Minangkabau terms for marriage. *Semando* or *semendo* marriage usually implies a matrilocal form, in which the man marries into the woman's family. Finer distinctions within the *semando* class of marriage are also possible. See Wilkinson, *Malay-English Dictionary* (1959), and for two modern discussions of marriage forms in west Sumatra, M. A. Jaspan, "From Patriliny to Matriliny. Structural Change among the Redjang of Southwest Sumatra" (PhD dissertation, Australian National University, 1964), and J. J. J. M. Wuisman, *Sociale Verandering in Bengkulu: Een Cultuur-Sociologische Analyse* (Dordrecht/Cinnaminson: Foris Publications, 1985).

[35]*Asal*, p. 15(44). "Ujong Tanah" is mentioned in VOC records as the location of one of the Raja di Hilir's settlements in the seventeenth century.

[36]This is an early date in view of the chronicle's assertions concerning the ruler of Aceh, but not an impossible one for the abandonment of Lobo Tua as Chapter 2 has shown.

[37]*Asal*, p. 15(44).

[38]Ibid. "Kemudian dari itu berpikir Sutan Ibrahim, 'Itu ipar aku yang tiga laki-laki baik aku bunuh supaya dapat akan diakui menjadi raja sendiri aku di sini.'"

Ibrahim the motive of desiring to become the sole Raja of Barus (*raja sendiri*). In due course Sutan Ibrahim took the three children into the jungle and killed them. When his wife, their sister, heard what he had done she took her own life, thus underlining the horror of Ibrahim's crime. She left Ibrahim with one son, named Sutan Usuf.[39]

The Hulu line was not, however, obliterated. Two of Sutan Marah Pangsu's brothers remained, and one of these had a son called Sutan Marah Sifat, who now became the Hulu ruler. With Sutan Ibrahim in control of the Hulu *kampung*, the text implies, Marah Sifat now moved downstream to a spot near Batu Berdinding.[40] Many of the people who had lived in Pintu Ria, the former Hulu *kampung*, joined him there, and the new settlement became populous (*maka ramailah kampung itu*).[41] After some time, however, Sutan Ibrahim's aggression caused Sutan Marah Sifat to move again. The date for this move is 710 H (AD 1310). After this second move many people became ill and died, so they shifted a third time to a new *kampung* in Si Antomas. They called the settlement they had vacated Si Tiga Bulan because they had only been there for three months. More people moved from Pintu Ria to Si Antomas and the settlement now grew to such a size that a new one was made nearby in Simugari. Sutan Ibrahim's hostility continued, however, and the text explains that he "continually wished to quarrel."[42]

Faced with this determined enmity, Marah Sifat sent a secret envoy to appeal for help to the Raja of Aceh. In reply, the ruler of Aceh sent his own envoy to Sutan Ibrahim with the order that Ibrahim should follow his commands (*mengikut perintah Raja Aceh*). Ibrahim defied the order.

> "No more will I bow towards the Raja of Aceh. If the smoke from my fire leans towards Aceh I will fan it. If my cock crows towards Aceh I will kill it." Those were Sutan Ibrahim's words to the envoy.[43]

When the Raja of Aceh, who is referred to in the text by an honorific Malay title, *Yang Maha Mulia Daulat Raja Aceh*, heard about Ibrahim's defiance, he "shook with anger."[44] He ordered a ship to set sail with his war leaders (*dubalang*)[45] and officers (*panglima*). Their instructions were to capture Ibrahim. In a brief and straightforward manner, the text states that the force arrived in Barus and went straight to Ujung

---

[39]Ibid.

[40]*Asal*, p. 16(43). "Adapun Sutan Marah Sifat tatkala suda mati raja yang bernama Marah Pangsu maka dianya berpindah tempat ka hilir tiga bulan membikin kampung dekat dangan Batu Berdinding."

[41]Ibid.

[42]Ibid. "Kemudian dari itu maka datang pula sangketo dari Sutan Ibrahim kepada Sutan Marah Sifat berkelahi sentiasa."

[43]Ibid., p. 16(43). "Jangan lagi aku akan tundu' kepada Raja Aceh. Jikalau asap apiku saja condong mengadap ka Aceh aku kipas. Jikalau ayamku berkoko' mengadap ka Aceh aku potong.' Bagitu kata Sutan Ibrahim kepada utusan itu."

[44]Ibid. "Demi didangar oleh yang maha mulia daulat Raja Aceh jawab Sutan Ibrahim itu maka sangat marahnya serta terketar-ketar."

[45]*Dubalang* is a Minangkabau equivalent of Malay *hulubalang*. See Yunus St. Majolelo, *Kamus Kecil Bahasa Minangkabau* (Jakarta: Mutuara, 1983); Wilkinson, *Malay-English Dictionary* (1959) and Pamoentjak, *Kamoes Bahasa Minangkabau*.

Tanah, where it attacked and seized Ibrahim. His head was cut off and carried back to Aceh.[46]

In this very short Hulu account of relations between the two families several points are made. A marriage relationship and, by implication, a situation of trust is established between the two sides. That trust is betrayed when Ibrahim murders his three brothers in law. Morally, then, Ibrahim is portrayed in a bad light in this chronicle. The motive that the text attributes for his crime is the desire for sole power (*didakui menjadi raja sendiri aku di sini*) in Barus. When this proves to be unobtainable because of the existence of a further branch of the Hulu family, Ibrahim responds with continued hostility, chasing his rival from place to place and preventing Marah Sifat from governing his subjects in peace. By implication, the ruler of Aceh is treated as an overlord. Marah Sifat appeals to him for help, Raja Aceh has an elaborate Malay title, and a tributary relationship is indicated by the statement that Ibrahim refused to bow (*tunduk*) towards Aceh. Another authority word is introduced in this Hulu version of the episode, *perintah*, which indicates government, jurisdiction, rule, or command.[47] This word is used of Ibrahim's refusal to follow the orders of the ruler of Aceh, and of his assumption of authority in Sutan Marah Pangsu's *kampung*. We shall see that, like *kuasa*, *perintah* is a term which recurs frequently in this text.

Although the broad outline of these events is also present in the *Sejarah* Tuanku Batu Badan account, where considerable movement of settlements takes place, and where the Acehnese attack Sutan Ibrahim's *kampung*, the Hilir version of this episode differs in detail and in moral emphasis.

SEJARAH

In this version of the episode, once the Rajas of Pasaribu had returned home, the story focuses on the Raja di Hulu, who is said to have been resentful towards Seri Maharaja Sultan Ibrahim. This was because Sultan Ibrahim was a person of great *akal*, and because his subjects were numerous and his *hulubelang* strong.[48] Sultan Ibrahim's superiority thus continues to be emphasized in the *Sejarah*. "It would be best," the Hulu Raja is said to have thought, "to get away from here because (*karena*)

---

[46]*Asal*, pp. 16(43)–17(42). "Pada seketika itu Raja Aceh suruh satu kapal dangan dubalang dan panglimanya mendapatkan Sutan Ibrahim. Lamanya pula antaranya itu kapal Raja Aceh sampailah ka negeri Sutan Ibrahim maka turunlah ka darat panglima dan segala lesykarnya lantas dilanggarnya kampung Sutan Ibrahim di Hujung Tanah. Dalam pada itu pecahlah parang pada seketika itu. Hatta dangan takdir Allah ta'ala maka terpenggallah kepala Sutan Ibrahim itu dubalang Aceh penggal dan serta dibawa'nya ka kapal kemudian dari itu maka itu kapal balayar ka Aceh. Lamalah suda antaranya itu kapal pun sampai di negeri Aceh dan serta dipersembahkan itu kepala Raja Aceh."

[47]See, for instance, Wilkinson, *Malay-English Dictionary*, sv. *perentah*; and W. Marsden, *Malay-English Dictionary* (1812; Reprint, Singapore: Oxford University Press, 1984), vol. 1.

[48]*Sejarah*, p. 23. "Maka dengan takdir Allah subhanahu wa ta'ala berpindah carita kepada raja di hulu. Allah subhanahu wa ta'ala mentakdirkan sakit hatinya kepada seri maharaja Tuanku Sultan Ibrahim, adapun Tuanku Sultan Ibrahim 'akalnya panjang dan ra'yatnya banyak hulubalangnya gagah."
Where the name Raja di Hulu appears in the manuscript, the word Batak has been crossed out and Hulu inserted. The word *akal*, used to describe Sultan Ibrahim, can be translated as cleverness or intelligence, as in *akalnya panjang*. More broadly, however, it indicates rationality. It is an important term with special implications in Minangkabau society. See Wilkinson, *Malay-English Dictionary*; Taufik Abdullah, "Some Notes on the Kaba Tjindua Mato: An Example of Minangkabau Traditional Literature," *Indonesia* 9 (1970): 14–15; and James Siegel, *The Rope of God* (Berkeley and Los Angeles: University of California Press, 1969).

he is a person with *akal*."[49] The Raja duly conferred with his people, and it was decided (*mupakatlah*) that they should move. A settlement was built in Si Tiga Bulan and, when it was ready, the subjects of the Raja di Hulu moved there.

When Sultan Ibrahim heard that the Hulu Raja had moved, he agreed (*berpakat*) with his ministers and his subjects that they should move their own *kota* in order to reach the Raja di Hulu and be close to his settlement again.[50] Ibrahim and his subjects were all very joyful and laughed when they heard that the Raja di Hulu had run away for fear of Ibrahim (*sebab oleh takut*). They moved their settlement from Koto Guguk to Ujung Tanah, therefore, and the text describes the strength and defense works surrounding the new *kota*:

> Then, by the decree of God, may He be praised and exalted, the *negeri* was ready with its moat stretching around it, implanted with bamboo stakes and fenced with projecting wood and bounded by stakes which stuck out of the ground of the *kampung*. They would not die like rats: their guard was constant, day and night.[51]

This, according to the chronicle, was the situation of Sultan Ibrahim's settlement, and his ministers, warriors, and subjects multiplied, as did the merchants who came bringing trade in fine things. Then Seri Maharaja Tuanku Sultan Ibrahim's fame (*masyhurnya*) increased, and the news spread of his good government.[52] Such expressions of his prestige are made here in the familiar idiom of Malay *hikayat*, where the fame of a ruler and his good government are often described as spreading to foreign lands.[53] The *Sejarah* text thus advances the theme of praise for Sultan Ibrahim and his settlement which was identified in the previous episode.

Next, suddenly, and, according to the text, without provocation, an unidentified person is said to have acted treacherously towards Sultan Ibrahim (*maka datanglah fitnah orang yang khianat kepada Tuanku Sultan Ibrahim*). This person is said to have incited the Raja of Aceh (who here, as in the *Asal*, is given an honorific title, *Daulat Yang Dipertuan*), to whom he announces that Sultan Ibrahim is extremely obstinate (*terlalu keras*), that he does not want to pay homage and give land rent to the Raja of

---

[49]*Sejarah*, p. 23. "Jadi berpikir dalam hatinya, 'Baiklah dijauhi dari sini karena dianya orang ber'akal.'"

[50]Ibid. "Allah subhanahu wa ta'ala mentakdirkan Tuanku Sultan Ibrahim pun menengar khabar nan bahasa raja di hulu sudah berpindah kota maka dengan takdir Allah subhanahu wa ta'ala dianya pun berpakat dengan segala menteri dan hulubalangnya dan sekalian ra'yatnya bahasa henda' berpindah kota mendapatkan raja nan di hulu supaya berdekat juga."

[51]Ibid., p. 24. "Maka dengan takdir Allah subhanahu wa ta'ala negeri itu pun sudah sedia serta dengan paritnya rentang berkuliling bertanam dengan aur duri serta berpagar dengan kayu dan jungurnya dan ranjaunya sigap kampungnya, bukan seperti tikus lalu pun mati juga sebab oleh keras jaganya pada siang dan malam tiada berhenti-henti."

[52]Ibid. "Demikianlah halnya tuanku Sultan Ibrahim sehari-hari dihadap oleh segala menteri dan hulubalang dan ra'yatnya negeri itu pun bertambah-tambah ramai juga anak dagang pun banyak datang membawa' perniaga'an selangkapnya yang indah rupanya. Maka dengan takdir Allah subhanahu wa ta'ala seri maharaja Tuanku Sultan Ibrahim pun bertambah-tambah mashurnya ka negeri asing bahasa Tuanku Sultan Ibrahim hukumnya baik." (Masyhurnya is spelt with *s* at this point in the MS, rather than *sy*.)

[53]Ibid. See, for instance, the *Hikayat Patani*, where the people of Patani are said to be tranquil and contented and the name of the king was famous in other countries. A. Teeuw and D. K. Wyatt, eds., *Hikayat Patani: The Story of Patani*, 2 vols. (The Hague: Nijhoff, 1970), 1: 131.

Aceh. If Ibrahim's cock crows in the direction of Aceh, it is said, he kills it; if the smoke from his fire inclines towards Aceh he fans it the other way, and if any of his trees leans towards Aceh he cuts them down. Such, according to the chronicle, was the slander (*fitnah*) that was reported to the Sultan of Aceh concerning Sultan Ibrahim.[54]

This description of Sultan Ibrahim's attitude towards Aceh is, of course, very similar to that offered in the *Asal;* but here it is depicted as slander, not as fact.

Like the Hulu chronicle, the *Sejarah* now proceeds to relate that the ruler of Aceh, hearing of Ibrahim's rebelliousness, was furious (*berang bangis*).[55] He ordered his officers to prepare a ship in order to make war on Barus and to kill Sultan Ibrahim. Ujung Tanah is attacked, but in this version we are told that, by God's decree, the Acehnese were not at first able to defeat the settlement. Whereas in the Hulu account the Acehnese are crisply described arriving in Barus, where they attacked the settlement and immediately decapitated Sultan Ibrahim, here Sultan Ibrahim and his subjects are shown as bravely resisting the invaders. The Acehnese retreated home, where they presented themselves to their Raja and explained that they had been unable to defeat Sultan Ibrahim's settlement because of its strength and large population.[56] The warriors counseled their ruler to postpone a renewed attack upon Barus. Although the Raja of Aceh was troubled by the news they brought him, he decided that it would be best to accept their advice and wait until the idea of an attack had faded in Barus.

It will be noticed, even from this summary of the narrative, that more space is devoted to Aceh's attack on Sultan Ibrahim's settlement than in the Hulu story. Eventually the Acehnese returned and succeeded in taking Hujung Tanah by surprise. Ibrahim was found and decapitated (*nyawanya pun sudah hilang kepalanya pun dikerat oleh Aceh*).[57] The pathos of his death is highlighted in the chronicle by a description of his daughter's suicide. When she saw that her father had been killed without having sinned, she threw herself from the palace. The word used for sin (*dosa*) signifies an offence against the laws of God and of religion. Its use here, and its subsequent repetition in the chronicles, seems to emphasize Ibrahim's purity and the wrongful nature of his execution.

After describing the death of Ibrahim, the chronicle relates that his son, Sultan Raja Usuf, fled into the forest with all his people, while Sultan Ibrahim's head was conveyed to Aceh.

*   *   *

---

[54]*Sejarah*, p. 24.

[55]Ibid.

[56]Ibid., p. 25. "Maka segala hulubalang Aceh itu pun larilah dari negeri itu pulang ka bandar Aceh lalu menyembah segala hulubalang demikian buninya, 'Ya Allah ya mulia daulat marhum seri paduka, kami jujung atas batu kepala patik. Adapun negeri Barus Tuanku Sultan Ibrahim tiada mahu kalah oleh kami karena ra'yatnya dan hulubalangnya sampai banyak negerinya itu pun sigabnya tiada seperti aurnya tebal berkuliling paritnya rantang berkuliling. Jikalau semuhanya sekalipun isi negeri ini pergi memarangi tiada juga akan dapat kami ini sekalian hampir mati dibunuhnya, jikalau tiada segera kami lari niscahaya kami mati semuhanya.'"

[57]Ibid.

A comparison of these versions of Episode Two reveals different perspectives on the same events. The Hulu text portrays Sultan Ibrahim in an unfavorable moral light. He was a murderer, we learn, and he oppressed the Hulu Raja and his people. In the Hilir version Ibrahim was wrongfully accused, he is slandered and he dies without having committed any sin. Evidence of this is seen in the use of the serious and powerful Malay words *khianat* (treachery) and *fitnah* (calumny).[58] In the Hilir text, Ibrahim is innocent and his death is unjustified. Here the Hulu people are portrayed as cowards, who are mocked by Ibrahim and his subjects. Ibrahim, by contrast, is praised as a person of *akal*. The Hilir *kampung* is also eulogized, and these expressions of praise for the Hilir ruler and his settlement are made in terms which belong to the conventions of traditional Malay *hikayat* as, for instance, when Ibrahim's good government is praised, and the text mentions his fame in foreign lands. An intriguing parallel between the two versions of this episode are the two female suicides. In the *Asal* Marah Pangsu's daughter kills herself from grief, in the *Sejarah* it is the daughter of Sultan Ibrahim. The structural analogies between the two chronicles are thus maintained even when the import of the narrative differs.

Underlying these differences in perspective, other more subtle disparities exist which may help to illuminate intrinsic concepts of political authority and world view in the two chronicles. An important statement of motivation is made, for example, in the Hulu text, when it is stated that Ibrahim decided to kill his wife's brothers in order to become the sole ruler. Although attributed to Ibrahim and not to a member of the Hulu family, the suggestion that one might act in order to rule alone reflects, as we shall see, a view of political authority which is peculiar to the Hulu chronicle. Further insight into a Hulu perception of authority can be gleaned from the use of the word *perintah* to characterize authority. *Perintah*, which implies government and command, is used twice in this episode, to refer to the Raja of Aceh's commands and to Ibrahim's control over the Hulu settlement. In the *Asal*, command words such as *perintah* and *kuasa* are used to typify the ruler's role. In this episode of the Hilir text, by contrast, the word *pakat*, to confer or agree, is used to describe both the Hulu and Hilir Rajas' relations with their subjects. The emphasis on consensus and harmony, which was observed in Episode One of this chronicle, is thus continued.

EPISODE THREE

In this episode, both chronicles concentrate on the fate of Sultan Ibrahim's head in Aceh. The head is revealed to possess special properties which embody Sultan Ibrahim's sovereignty, and which even the Raja of Aceh is forced to recognize. Briefly, the head is taken before the Raja of Aceh, who insults it by kicking it. The Raja then becomes ill and, simultaneously, Aceh is flooded. The Raja attributes these misfortunes to the insult he offered to Ibrahim's head, and he declares that the head must be sent back to Barus accompanied by royal honours. The sickness and flood abate, and the Raja duly sends Ibrahim's head back to Barus, accompanied by regalia and numerous royal honors. Like the other particularly colorful aspects of Sultan Ibrahim's story, such as the words of his defiance of Aceh and the mangosteen skin story, the descriptions of this incident are similar in both chronicles. Whatever other

---

[58]Virginia Matheson refers to the "destructive force" of *fitnah*, or "calumny," as it is depicted in the *Tuhfat al Nafis*, in "Concepts of State in the *Tuhfat al Nafis*," in *Pre-Colonial State Systems*, ed. Reid and Castles, pp. 18–19; and Wilkinson, *Malay-English Dictionary*, refers to the use of *khianat* or "treachery" in several well-known Malay texts.

discrepancies exist between the two chronicles, these vignettes seem to have a special appeal, as if they were well known and established features of Barus tradition.

The chronicles differ, however, in the space allotted to these events and the manner in which they are described. In the *Asal*, the entire sequence takes only a page to relate, whereas the *Sejarah* account of the departure of Sultan Ibrahim's head until its return to Barus covers four-and-a-half pages of manuscript. What adds space to the Hilir account is the detail with which ceremonial features of the head's return to Barus are described. Simultaneously, more emphasis is placed on Ibrahim's royal status. Differences of this sort are not superficial. Discrepancies in the language and descriptive style of the texts bear on their overall concerns and their portrayal of the character of political authority in Barus.

ASAL

After Sultan Ibrahim's head had been carried to Aceh by the Raja's warriors, the Raja ordered that it should be put away for three days. After that period, the head was brought to the audience hall (*balai penghadapan*) and presented before the ruler. He accused the head of doing him wrong by defying him, and he then kicked and trod on the head, which rolled over.[59] The Raja of Aceh then returned to his dwelling.

That evening, with God's will according to the chronicle, the sea flooded and the Raja became sick. His leg swelled up with a boil which was like a snake bite.[60] The Raja then realized that the cause of his illness was the insult he had given to Sultan Ibrahim's head.

> The Raja of Aceh vowed to himself: "If the reason that I am sick is that I kicked that head, then I ask the pardon of the Raja whose head it is and when my sickness has healed then I will order that the head be conveyed back to its country and I will give it every honor."[61]

Then, by God's decree, the Raja's sickness was cured and the floodwaters abated. He duly ordered that Sultan Ibrahim's head be conveyed back to Negeri Pancur (as Barus is called at this point in the chronicle) with many honors for the raja of *negeri* Pancur (*dengan berapa hormat dikurniainya kepada raja ka negeri Pancur*). These included the *nobat*, the traditional Malay royal orchestra, which was a symbol of sovereignty.[62] To the Raja of Pancur the ruler of Aceh also granted the title Raja, together with

---

[59]*Asal*, p. 17(42). "Kemudian daripada itu pada satu hari maka dibawa' itu kepala ka balai penghadapan pada ketika maka bersabda raja katanya, 'Ini malah kiranya kepala orang yang sangat gagah melawan aku.' Dan serta disepa'nya kepala itu serta diinja'-inja'nya dan diguling-gulingnya kepala itu. Kemudian dari itu maka kembali Raja Aceh ka rumahnya." Wilkinson, *Malay-English Dictionary* (1959) identifies *injak*, "to step; to tread" as having a Minangkabau origin.

[60]*Asal*, p. 17(42). "Haripun malam dangan takdir Allah ta'ala maka gadanglah air melaut-laut dan lagi Raja Aceh pun sakitlah bengka' kakinya seperti biso na'ik pada kakinya seperti di putu' ular biso."

[61]Ibid. "Dalam pada itu maka berniatlah Raja Aceh dalam hatinya katanya, 'Kalau sebab dari aku inja' kepala itu maka jadi sakitku ini maka minta' ma'aflah aku kepada raja yang punya kepala itu dan apabila sakitku suda sembuh maka aku suruh hantarkan itu kepala ka negerinya dangan segala hormat aku bari kepadanya.'"

[62]Ibid. The role of *nobat* in Malay royal ceremonial is described in R. O. Winstedt, "Kingship and Enthronement in Malaya," pp. 129–40. The closing pages of the *Hikayat Patani* list the instruments and melodies of the Patani *nobat*. Teeuw and Wyatt, eds., *Hikayat Patani*, 1: 140–45.

permission to use the *nobat*. A grant of *nobat* and a royal title was convincing recognition of the independent royal status of Barus.[63]

During the journey, as Sultan Ibrahim's head was conveyed home to Barus, cannon shots were fired ceaselessly, the *nobat* played laments, and servants attended. Black and red pennants were used and flowers surrounded the Raja. All these marks of honor are symbols of royalty often mentioned in Malay *hikayat*.[64] These honors are not described at length in the *Asal*. What is significant about this account, however, is that it was to Sultan Marah Sifat, the Hulu prince who had complained about Ibrahim, that the head and honors were given. No mention is made here of Ibrahim's own son, Sultan Usuf.

> Then after some time had passed the head arrived at *negeri* Pancur and cannon shots were sounded with much honor towards Raja Sultan Marah Sifat because the head of Sultan Ibrahim had been brought back to him. And the head was given to Sultan Marah Sifat, together with all the regalia and a letter from the Raja of Aceh.[65]

After these had been received by Sultan Marah Sifat, the chronicle relates the contents of Raja Aceh's letter. It stated that Pancur was to be released from paying tax or tribute to Aceh, and was also granted all of the regalia because of the Raja's regret at the beheading of Sultan Ibrahim.[66]

The Hulu account of Ibrahim's head concludes here and is accomplished in just thirty two lines. We shall see that this description of the honor and respect shown to the severed head is a fraction of that found in the Hilir text.

SEJARAH

According to the version of events recorded here, after the battle in Barus, Sultan Ibrahim's head was taken back to Aceh, where gun shots were sounded to mark the Acehnese victory. In the *Sejarah*, when the head was presented to the Acehnese ruler, it actually defied him by revolving to turn away from him. The head, we are told, had been placed on a silver tray. It was like a cempaka flower in bloom and had no odor.[67] It was in response to this defiance that the Raja of Aceh kicked Ibrahim's

---

[63]*Asal*, p. 17(42). "Dan serta dibarinya gelar raja di Pancur Sultan kedua boleh memakai nobat." The wording of this passage is obscure. The words "di Pancur Sultan kedua boleh," might suggest that the title was granted to both a Raja and a Sultan, or to two rulers "Sultan kedua." Subsequent events in the narrative make it clear, however, that this is not intended. There is also a space in the MS between the words Sultan and *kedua* which may suggest punctuation, as in "Sultan, kedua boleh memakai nobat."

[64]Ibid. The *Sejarah Melayu* contains a description of the honors which were used when a Raja traveled. Brown, trans., *Sejarah Melayu*, p. 47[786–87].

[65]*Asal*, p. 17(42). "Kemudian daripada itu lama pula antaranya sampailah kepala itu ka negeri Pancur dan serta melapaskan meriam dangan barapa banyak hormat kepada raja Sultan Marah Sifat sebab membawa' kepala Sutan Ibrahim akan di kembalikan kepadanya dan serta membawa' kepala itu kepada Sultan Marah Sifat dan serta sekalian kebesar[an] dan serta surat dari Raja Aceh itu semuhanya diterimakannya kepada Sultan Marah Sifat."

[66]Ibid. "Bahwa maka adalah tersebut di dalam surat Raja Aceh dari melapaskan negeri Pancur daripada wasil kedua dari membari kurnia dari itu segala kebesaran yang dikurnianya sebab dari menyesal memenggal kepala Sutan Ibrahim."

[67]*Sejarah*, p. 26. "Seperti bunga cempaka kembang sedikit tiada berbaunya."

head and subsequently became ill. In this version, thunder and lightning accompany the flood and the Raja's swollen leg.

The language used in this account is more elaborate and the expression more vivid. Here, when the Raja realizes his mistake, he recognizes Raja Ibrahim as an original Raja, *Raja asal*.

> God, may He be praised and exalted, predestined that the Sultan realized his sin (*dosa*). Then he said to himself "If it is true that Tuanku Sultan Ibrahim is an original Raja descended from his ancestors, then if God removes this sickness of mine which I can no longer endure, then I will convey the head back to Bandar Barus. I will order honors along the way. I repent towards Sultan Ibrahim and now make him my brother, and this will apply to the descendants of each of us, I will no longer make war on Barus."[68]

Once this decision had been taken, the Raja's sickness disappeared and the flood abated. He left his palace and went down to the *Balai Gadang*. There he ordered that the royal white elephant be brought, dressed in its gold finery. Sultan Ibrahim's head was respectfully wrapped in a gold winding sheet as befitted a Raja, placed on a golden tray, and lifted on to the white elephant, which also carried open umbrellas. Musical instruments were played, notably the *serunai* (a type of clarinet), gongs, and the royal orchestra, the *nobat*. In this fashion, Ibrahim's head was escorted to the sea shore on the elephant's back.[69]

These ritual items convey the respect (*hormat*) shown towards Ibrahim's head. White elephants, the use of gold cloth, umbrellas, and the *nobat* are dignities reserved for the use of a true Raja. They mark his exalted position and his sovereignty (*daulat*), setting him apart from mere mortals. While the Barus chronicles are less courtly in their style than many works of Malay literature, here, in the description of royal honors accorded to Sultan Ibrahim's head, the Hilir, and to a lesser extent the Hulu, chronicle echoes the descriptive style of the *hikayat*.[70]

A similar concern with ceremonial is shown as Ibrahim's head is lifted from the elephant on to the royal vessel, a *perahu raja*, which henceforth is described as a *gurab* (a vessel of Arab type), and the Raja of Aceh gave orders to the *hulubelang* that they should convey the head to Barus and that the *nobat* should play all the way. He instructed them not to fall short in their task, because he and Sultan Ibrahim were now brothers (*kami sudah bersaudara*) and there would no longer be any differences between Aceh and Barus, a condition which would extend to the descendants of

---

[68]Ibid. "Allah subhanahu wa ta'ala mentakdirkan Sultan pun pikir di dalam hatinya tahulah ia akan dosanya lalu bertitah di dalam hatinya, 'Jikalau sungguh bertuah Tuanku Sultan Ibrahim raja asal berasal dari nenek moyangnya hingga kepadanya maka disurutkan Allah lah penyakitku ini tiada lagi tertahan oleh aku sakitnya ini. Jikalau surut penyakitku ini aku hantarkan pulang kepala itu ka bandar Barus kusuruh hormati sepanjang jalan taubatlah aku kepada Sultan Ibrahim aku buatkanlah dianya jadi saudaraku sekalian kegadangku aku barikan kepadanya sehingga sampai ka anak ka cucu kami dan ka Barus tiada kuperang lagi,' titahnya sampai pada masa itu."

[69]Ibid., p. 27.

[70]A description of the use of a royal elephant and the restricted use of gold and yellow cloth by a ruler can be found in the *Sejarah Melayu*. (Brown, trans., *Sejarah Melayu*, pp. 44–49[83–88].) For a list of items which were reserved for the use of rulers, see Hadidjaja Tardjan, *Adat Raja-Raja Melayu* (Kuala Lumpur: Pustaka Antara, 1964), pp. 78–80.

each. The ruler released Barus from tribute and ordered that these instructions were never to be altered.[71] These expressions of warmth and mutuality towards Sultan Ibrahim and towards Barus echo the language of consensus and agreement which has already been identified in earlier parts of this chronicle and which is given even greater emphasis in subsequent episodes. The guarantee (*menanggung*) of the ruler of Aceh has the flavor of earlier agreements (*perjanjian*) and oaths (*sumpah*) mentioned in the text.

After Sultan Ibrahim's head had been placed in the *gurab*, prayers were read for the safety of the voyage and gun and cannon shots marked the departure of the vessel, which sailed for five days and five nights. According to the text, when it arrived at Barus the people recognized it as the vessel of a Raja, and they ran to tell their own Raja that it had come.[72]

The reception of the head in Barus, and the procession in which it was carried to the *istana* and subsequently buried, is described again in detail and with attention to ceremony. What astonished the people most was that the appearance of Sultan Ibrahim's head was unchanged, even though it had been separated from his body for a long time. It was like an open cempaka flower and had no odor. Its color was yellow like tumeric (*kuning seperti kunyit*). The people were filled with sorrow to see this and wept. Then they wrapped the head in a new cloth which had camphor in it, and took the head in procession to the place of burial (*tempat kuburan*).[73]

The burial of Sultan Ibrahim's head is described. It was escorted to the *tempat kuburan* in a procession, with many honors along the way. A *malim* conducted the service (*sembahyang*), then the people opened the grave of Seri Maharaja Sultan Ibrahim. When they came to the trunk of his body it was the color of a ripe banana (*seperti pisang dalam peraman*), and it too reminded the people of a flower in bloom. When they placed the head inside the grave, the head and body were joined (*kepala dan badan pun lantas bertemu*) and there was no mark to show that they had ever been separated. The Acehnese who observed this were astonished and frightened and quickly returned to their ship. Ibrahim's tomb was closed, and the *imam* read the burial prayers (*talkin*). Then the people of Barus all returned to their houses and the Acehnese went home.[74]

When the ceremony had been completed, the people of the *negeri* agreed (*pakat*) to make Sultan Raja Usuf Raja in his father's place (*Sultan Raja Usuf akan menggantikan bapanya jadi kerajaan ayahnya itu*). In this version of the episode, no mention is made of a particular Raja receiving the head or of the royal honors from Aceh. Indeed, no letter from the Raja of Aceh is mentioned here and no title or *nobat*. Barus

---

[71]*Sejarah*, p. 27. "Bicara hamba sudah terdorong itulah sebab aku menanggung dengar dituan sekalian rata-rata umanatku nan jangan tuan ubahi ka Barus tida' diperang lagi sampai ka anak ka cucu kami wasil nan tida' dibarinya lagi. Barang siapa ubahikan janji hamba sampai habis sekalian Allah dan nabi membinasakan umanatku nan jangan tuan ubahi."

[72]Ibid., pp. 27–28.

[73]Ibid., p. 29. "Maka dengan takdir Allah subhanahu wa ta'ala maka orang pun membuka tungkus kepala itu dilihat orang warna mukanya seri paduka Tuanku Sultan Ibrahim sedikit tiada ada berubah. Allah subhanahu wa ta'ala mentakdirkan bertambah manis warnanya muka kuning seperti kunit dipatah sedikit tiada ada beruba tuanku Sultan Ibrahim. Heranlah orang habis memandang melihat laku kepala Sultan bercarei sudah beberapa lamanya sedikit tiada ada berubah selama orang berkata yang demikian buninya kepada kepala itu pun diganti orang tatkala itu dimasu'kan lalu dengan kapurnya."

[74]Ibid., pp. 29–30.

is simply said to be free from tribute. In this text the marks of respect are concentrated on the head itself. We are not told who ruled Barus before Raja Usuf's appointment; but a Raja did exist since the people are said to have informed the Raja when the Acehnese ship arrived. The implication here is that two rulers, in fact, existed—Raja Usuf and the Raja di Hulu.

* * *

In Malay culture the head is considered to be a most sacred part of the body, and this applies especially to the head of a ruler.[75] Sultan Ibrahim's head, therefore, appropriately embodies his royal status. Ibrahim's sovereignty is recognized even by one so powerful as the Raja of Aceh, and the narrative recounted here in both Barus chronicles therefore makes an important statement concerning relations between Barus and Aceh. As we have seen, this early part of Hilir history appears to have been a significant and popular story in Barus which was transcribed in other, shorter, versions.

Both chronicles use the Ibrahim story in their narrative, but they direct the implications of events in different ways. In the *Asal* text, the ceremony and the royal honors from Aceh center on a single, Hulu, Raja, whereas in the *Sejarah* Sultan Ibrahim's royal status is emphasized, and two rulers appear to have existed. The differences in length and style in the two chronicles also bear on the way in which authority itself is depicted. In the *Sejarah* account, more emphasis is given to describing authority in terms of its ritual and ceremonial characteristics. Recent work on Malay political culture has highlighted the ceremonial functions of a Malay Raja. It has been suggested that these ceremonial aspects of rulership, rather than being the mere trappings of power, represent the essence of the ruler's role in traditional Malay kingdoms.[76] In this episode of the Hilir text, many of the conventional ceremonial attributes of Malay kingship are used to make the point that Raja Ibrahim was an original or true Raja, *Raja asal berasal*. The terms *asal* and *berasal* are used in several well known Malay texts to convey the supernatural origins of rulers who trace their descent to Bukit Seguntang.[77] Linked to this emphasis on ceremony in the narrative are the spiritual and magical aspects of the story of Ibrahim's head, which suggest his special qualities, his martyrdom, and his sanctity (a mortal body which does not decay), qualities which are recognized by another great Raja, the Raja of Aceh. In this episode of the *Sejarah*, where Raja Ibrahim's qualities and the tragedy of his death are elaborated, the chronicle employs a language of sovereignty which is familiar from *hikayat* of the Melaka Straits tradition.

Much less detailed attention is paid to these matters in the Hulu chronicle, where the *kebesaran* are described as "*nobat* and so forth" (*nobat dan lain-lainnya*). The Hulu chronicle concentrates to a greater extent on the practical issue of Sultan Marah Sifat's release from tribute, whereas, in the Hilir text, consensus and mutuality are again emphasized in the words of the guarantee of the ruler of Aceh to Ibrahim and his descendants.

---

[75]See for instance W. W. Skeat, *Malay Magic* (London: Macmillan, 1900), pp. 43–45.

[76]Milner, *Kerajaan*, passim. See also Clifford Geertz, *Negara: The Theatre State in Nineteenth Century Bali* (Princeton: Princeton University Press, 1980).

[77]Virginia Matheson, "Concepts of Malay Ethos in Indigenous Malay Writings," *JSEAS* 10, 2 (1979): 365.

* * *

In these three episodes, the narrative in each chronicle moves from relating the separate, early, history of the two royal families of Barus to a discussion of their first meeting and accommodation in Barus. The differences between the chronicles in these three episodes hinge on their different presentation of the past, rather than upon the choice of events narrated. The story of Sultan Ibrahim's head and of the symbolic meeting and accommodation between the families appears to have been a potent and important chapter of Barus history which belonged to the past of both royal houses. In the next four episodes, however, the differences of presentation and interpretation, which have begun to emerge between the chronicles, deepen and become more clearly defined. Gradually the two narratives begin to diverge not only in the telling of their stories, but in the facts of those stories themselves. These differences are explored in the following chapter.

6

A DUAL SETTLEMENT:
EPISODES FOUR AND FIVE

Episode Four concerns events in Barus after the return of Sultan Ibrahim's head from Aceh. Both chronicles depict a unification of the two Barus settlements brought about in order to protect Barus from enemy attack. They portray the character of this alliance differently, however. In the *Asal*, there is said to be only one ruler drawn from the Hulu family, whereas in the *Sejarah*, an agreement between equals is reached. There is a discrepancy in the space the two texts devote to the events of this episode and, while the Hulu account is again brief and presented in a straightforward, matter of fact, style, the Hilir chronicle is lengthier, more complicated, and includes extended passages of involved dialogue. Different explanations of events are offered which coincide with the opposing interests of Hulu and Hilir views, and different concepts of authority emerge more clearly in this episode. Two theories of political authority are enunciated in a discussion which involves a questioning of basic assumptions about Malay kingship.

ASAL

In the Hulu text, Episode Four occupies merely one page of the manuscript. Events are stated in a bald and jerky style. Event follows event in phrases piled one on top of another. There is little apparent emphasis in the narrative, and statements are only rarely connected to one another in a causal fashion.

According to the narrative, after the Acehnese had presented Sutan Ibrahim's head to Sultan Marah Sifat and bestowed upon Marah Sifat his new title and honors, they went home. Marah Sifat then assembled the inhabitants of Sutan Ibrahim's *kampung* and took them to a united *kampung* (or a *kampung* which had been "made one"—*kampung bersebuah*) in Simugari.[1] The chronicle then mentions Sutan Ibrahim's son, Sutan Usuf. He too was taken (*dibawa'nya*) to Simugari. We know that Usuf is considered to be a child in this chronicle, since the text also states that later, when Sutan Usuf grew up (*pun suda gadang sampai*), he married and had a child called

---

[1] *Asal*, p. 18(41). "Alkisah maka tersebutlah perkata'an kepada Sultan Marah Sifat tatkala Sultan Ibrahim suda terpenggal maka dikumpulnya sekalian orang yang ada pada kampung Sutan Ibrahim dibawa'nya ka kampungnya bersebuah di Simugari pada kira dalam tahun 700." The date offered for this event is, unfortunately, obscured by an ink blot on the MS. Kampung Simugari, as we have seen, was was mentioned in VOC sources, it is a name for the upriver settlement and henceforth in this text it appears to be synonymous with Kampung Mudik.

Sutan Alam Syah.[2] Even after Sutan Usuf became an adult, however, he still remained in Marah Sifat's *kampung,* and when Marah Sifat moved to a new settlement and took all his subjects Sutan Usuf went too.[3] The Hilir family, therefore, are not depicted here in a settlement of their own, with their own subjects; they and their people are subsumed, rather, under the authority of the Raja di Hulu. The Hilir family is presented passively here, in contrast to Marah Sifat's control of the situation.

After a lengthy period had elapsed, Sutan Usuf received a command from the Raja of Aceh, who ordered him to go to Aceh. Sutan Usuf duly departed and, the text states, he left his son, Alam Syah, behind with Sultan Marah Sifat, because (*karena*) Marah Sifat was his uncle (*mamak*).[4] Here, then, for a second time, the Hulu text mentions a marriage relationship between the two families. In Episode Two of the *Asal,* Sultan Ibrahim is said to have married into (*semando*) the Hulu family by marrying Marah Pangsu's daughter. No such marriage is mentioned in Episodes Two and Three of the *Sejarah,* and the Hulu chronicle appears to be implying here the absorption of the Hilir family by the Hulu line. Once he arrived in Aceh, Sutan Usuf married the Raja of Aceh's daughter. Not long afterwards he murdered his wife and was, himself, put to death by the Acehnese.[5] It takes just twenty lines to recount this story, and no explanation is offered of these events.

The chronicle then rapidly relates that, when Sultan Marah Sifat died, his son, Sutan Raja Bongsu, became Raja and assumed the title Sultan Maharaja Bongsu.[6] Usuf's son, Alam Syah, also died and left behind two sons. The elder of these was called Marah Sutan and the other was named Sutan nan Bagonjong. The chronicle subsequently refers to this prince both as Sutan Bagonjong and Bergonjong, I have used Bagonjong except in quotations from the Malay. Like their father and their grandfather, these Hilir princes are not referred to as Raja, and they appear to have no authority in the Hulu *kampung.* This point is developed in the next lines of the text. After the two had grown up, and when Maharaja Bongsu had become Raja, Sutan Bagonjong left Barus with a feeling of bitterness (*dengan merajok*) because he was not permitted to have authority there (*sebab dia tidak boleh kuasa di sini*). This is stated even more firmly with the declaration, "There was always only one person in authority (*selamanya [se?]orang saja yang kuasa*)."[7] These, we are told, were the circumstances in which Sutan Bagonjong was bitter and left Barus. No mention is made

---

[2]Ibid. "Lamalah pula antaranya itu Sutan Usuf pun suda gadang sampai suda berkawin dan suda beroleh anak laki-laki bernama Sutan 'Alam Syah."

[3]Ibid. "Sultan Marah Sifat pun berpindah ka Lobo Dalam dangan segala orang isi kampungnya dan serta Sutan Usuf juga."

[4]Ibid. *Mamak* indicates maternal uncle. Mothers' brothers have a particularly important role in Minangkabau society and, in a west Sumatran context the use of this term might imply a relationship of supervision. On the role of *mamak* in Minangkabau social structure see G. D. Willinck, *Het Rechtsleven bij de Minangkabausche Maleiers* (Leiden: Brill, 1909), pp. 6–7.

[5]*Asal,* p. 18(41).

[6]Ibid.

[7]Ibid., pp. 18(41)–19(40). "Hatta maka tersebut perkata'an kepada Marah Sutan dan Sutan Bergonjong telah suda gadang keduanya dalam pada itu maka itu Sutan Bergonjong berjalan dangan merajok membawa' dirinya sebab dia tidak boleh kuasa di sini selamanya orang saja yang kuasa. Dalam pada itu maka itu Sutan Bergonjong berjalan dangan merajok tidak tentu penjalangannya melainkan berjalan seperti orang risau saja sampai barapa lama Sutan Bergonjong berjalan sama kuliling Pulau Perca lalu pula ka negeri Jawa dan kepada lain-lain negeri Sutan Bergonjong mencari 'ilmu adanya."

of his elder brother, Marah Sutan, and the statement concludes Episode Four of the *Asal*.

Here, then, earlier indications that the Hulu version of this period was presented in terms of single rule by the Hulu family are confirmed by an explicit statement that the Hilir family held no position of authority. Not only are all the members of the Hilir family who are mentioned in this episode represented in the text as subordinate to the Hulu rulers, but the text makes a firm statement of principle in declaring that there was only one person in authority. The manner in which authority is described is also familiar from earlier episodes of the text. The word *kuasa* is used with the implication that authority was a simple case of either having or not having *kuasa*, or power. In this part of the Hilir text, however, we shall see that political authority is defined in more complex terms, consistent with that chronicle's altogether more involved and unconventional presentation of political life in Barus.

Sejarah

In contrast to the brief statement of events in the Hulu text, the Hilir version of Barus's past, between the return of Ibrahim's head and the departure of Sultan Bagonjong, occupies six pages of the manuscript. Here the people of Hulu and Hilir also come together, but in a different way. In this text, not one, but two, rulers are said to exist, and they make an agreement to ally for their mutual protection.

As in other episodes of this chronicle, consensus and mutual agreement are shown to characterize a ruler's relations with his subjects and also relations between rulers. At the end of Episode Three, we saw that the people agreed (*berpakat*) to make Raja Usuf ruler in his father's place. The word *pakat*, which indicates agreement and general consensus, is also used to describe their decision to make an alliance with the upriver settlement. The chronicle records that,

> After the appointment of the raja had been accomplished, the people agreed (*mupakatlah*) to unite with the *kota* upstream, and to go to the Hulu, to Simugari.[8]

They made an agreement (*perjanjian*) with the Raja in the Hulu. Frequent reference to the making of *perjanjian* has been noted in earlier episodes of the Hilir chronicle, and here, in Episode Four, *perjanjian* play an important role in the Hilir presentation of relations between the two families, and in Hilir political thinking generally. In this episode, it will be necessary to look closely at the way in which these agreements are described, in order to appreciate their function in the chronicle's presentation of the past.

According to the text, Hilir envoys were sent upstream in order to secure an alliance with the Raja in Simugari. They delivered this message:

> Pardon Tuanku, this is our submission. We have been commanded by our Raja to bring word here. He desires an agreement because he fears a war with Aceh. When an agreement exists it will be possible to resist foes who come here.[9]

---

[8]*Sejarah*, p. 30. "Setelah selesai daripada mengangkat raja maka mupakatlah orang henda' bersebuah kota mudik ka hulu ka Simugari."

[9]Ibid. "'Ampun Tuanku sembahnya saya kami disuruh raja kami membawa' kata datang kemari dianya henda' sebuah pakat takutlah ia diparang Aceh apabila sudah sebuah pakat melawan musuh barang yang datang.' Mendengar kata orang yang datang serta katanya, 'Insya Allah baiklah itu karena kami berdua di negeri ini jikalau sudah satu bicara kami bukan

When the Raja di Hulu, who is given no proper name in this text, heard the submission he agreed, "because we are together in this *negeri*" (*karena kami berdua di negeri ini*), that they should have one opinion (*satu bicara*).[10] The envoys returned downstream and reported to their ruler.

Concerning the words of the Tuanku which your slaves bring.Our need is met.[11]

So the next day the Sultan with his *penghulu* and all his subjects went upstream to Simugari. They were greeted outside the *kampung*, and a hundred guns were sounded. Then Raja Usuf entered the royal palace and they were entertained. They ate buffalo meat and there was general rejoicing (*serta bersuka-suka'an*).

All of the gongs and drums were beaten because (*karena*) the two Rajas had become one (*raja yang dua sudah bersuatu*).[12]

When the music and the general rejoicing had finished, the two rulers made an agreement (*mupakatlah*) and swore an oath of mutual loyalty (*bersumpah bersatia*) not to harm one another (*tiada jadi rusak-merusakkan*).[13] Once this agreement had been completed, Raja Usuf returned home to Ujong Tanah, and the populace was once more happy (*sukalah semuanya hamba ra'yat*) because the two *negeri* were joined (*negeri dua sudah bersuatu*).[14]

Here, then, as in the Hulu account, the people of the Hilir go upstream to Simugari, but in this version they are not taken there by the Hulu Raja; rather they accompany their own Raja, who has made a formal approach and reached an agreement with the ruler upstream. In contrast to the Hulu account, two rulers are said to exist simultaneously. The presence of two sources of authority is made plain through the words of the Hulu Raja ("because we are together in this *negeri*") and by means of the chronicle's description of events.

The Hilir text offers, therefore, a very different picture of unity between the two settlements from that found in the Hulu chronicle, where monarchy is presented as

---

sudah banyak negeri ini.' Demikianlah kata raja yang dudu' di sana. Mendengar kata yang demikian buninya utusan tadi pun pulang ka Hujung Tanah lalu dipersembahkannya katanya demikian buninya, 'Tentangan daripada titah tuanku yang patik bawa' sudahlah bertemu apa hajat kita. Bareso' hari Tuanku bertemu mudik ka hulu ka Simugari di sanalah dianya hadir mananti.' Dengan takdir Allah subhanahu wa ta'ala hari bareso'nya berkemas Sultan serta dengan penghulunya dan segala ra'yatnya henda' ka hulu ka Simugari. Maka dengan takdir Allah subhanahu wa ta'ala Sultan pun sampai ka Simugari maka disongsong oranglah keluar kampung serta dipasangkan orang bedil selatus serta naik lalu ka istana. Maka diperjamu orang makan kerbau serta bersuka-suka'an pada masa itu berapa buni-bunian pun diperusuh orang agung dan canang dan agung semuanya itu dipalu orang karena raja yang dua sudah bersuatu. Setelah selesai daripada itu mupakatlah raja-raja yang dua serta bersumpah bersatia bahasa tiada jadi rusak-marusakkan. Demikianlah halnya tatkala itu."

[10]Ibid.

[11]Ibid.

[12]Ibid.

[13]Ibid.

[14]Ibid. p. 31. "Maka dengan takdir Allah subhanahu wa ta'ala habislah bicara tatkala itu tuanku pun pulang ka Hujung Tanah maka sukalah semuanya hamba ra'yat dalam negeri sebab negeri dua sudah bersuatu."

the only conceivable form of authority. Here, by contrast, two rulers can live together in harmony and are depicted making an alliance for mutual protection. They "become one"; they have one opinion," and they rule over a kingdom which is united (*negeri dua sudah bersuatu*).

The chronicle continues with the account of Sultan Usuf's reign. After Usuf returned to Hujong Tanah, a letter came from the Raja of Aceh requesting that he go to Aceh. Usuf decided to comply, thinking to himself:

> "It is best that I comply with this letter because I wish to go to Aceh in any case. I wish to ask for compassion for my father who died without committing a sin."[15]

His subjects did not want to let Raja Usuf leave, but they were unable to restrain him because his resolve was firm. Instead, he gave the people his instructions.

> "These are my instructions to you all. My child remains with you and will be my replacement. Sultan Adil will become Raja to rule and make decisions. When I have left, go upstream—all of you."[16]

Then Raja Usuf traveled down to the river mouth, where a hundred gun shots were sounded and the royal drum (*tabuh*) was beaten as a sign that a Raja was taking his leave. When the party reached the estuary, Raja Usuf spoke to the *penghulu* and to all of his subjects. He instructed them to protect the *kampung* and its grounds and to pray for his safety. The Imam read a prayer, and the subjects wept (*orang pun menanggis sekaliannya*). [17]

This elaborate account of the Raja's departure, the marks of honor shown to him, and his people's sorrow when he leaves are characteristic of the style of description found in other Malay *hikayat*, where a Raja's comings and goings are the subjects of minute description and where the passionate loyalty of his subjects is emphasized.[18]

The kingly qualities of Raja Usuf continue to be enumerated after his arrival in Aceh. When his vessel arrived, cannon shots were sounded from on board, and these were answered from within the *kota*. Then the people of Aceh came down to greet Sultan Usuf and pay their respects to him. They came with instructions from the Raja of Aceh to convey him to the *kota*. When he arrived at the audience hall, the chronicle states that the Raja of Aceh accepted him as his son-in-law because he was pleased by his handsome appearance (*rupanya bagus*).[19] Personal beauty is kingly quality in Malay literature,[20] and the Raja of Aceh thus considered that Usuf was an appropri-

---

[15]Ibid. "'Baiklah aku turut sepanjang perkhabaran surat ini karena aku pun henda' pergi juga ka negeri Aceh meminta belas bela bapahanda saya karena dianya mati tiada dengan dosanya.'"

[16]Ibid. "'Nan mana hanya umanat hamba kepada tuan-tuan sekalian, anak hamba tinggal kepada tuan-tuan akan ganti hamba kepada tuan-tuan. Dengarkanlah tuan sekaliannya raja Sultan 'Adil jadikan raja akan mehukum buat bicara. Jikalau hamba sudah berjalan tuan-tuan mudik habis sekalian,' katanya."

[17]Ibid., pp. 31–32.

[18]See, for instance, Milner, *Kerajaan*, pp. 94–95.

[19]*Sejarah*, p. 32.

[20]See, for instance, Low, trans., *Hikayat Marong Mahawangsa*, p. 70, and Milner, *Kerajaan*, p. 42, on the *Hikayat Pahang*. According to a Minangkabau legal digest, good looks were the first of

ate (*patutlah*, which conveys the proper order of things) person to become Raja.[21] The royal attributes of Sultan Ibrahim's family are, therefore, emphasized again in the Hilir text.

The narrative continues with an account of what happened to Sultan Usuf in Aceh. After he had been there for a period, we are told, the "unhappiness in his heart" led him to resolve to kill his father-in-law.[22] But since he was unable to accomplish this, he killed his own wife—the Raja's daughter—instead. The chronicle explains Usuf's act by stating that the devil had arisen within him.[23] In response to the crime, the royal guards of Aceh put Usuf to death and the Raja of Aceh sent a letter to Barus to inform Raja Adil that his father was dead. The letter attributed Usuf's behavior to his impaired reason (*akalnya bersalahan*).[24]

After Sultan Usuf is removed from the scene, the thread of the narrative returns to Barus. Once more the question of two rulers within a single kingdom is discussed, as Usuf's son, Raja Adil, implements his father's agreement with the Hulu Raja. Much of the language which was used to describe that alliance is reiterated here as the terms of the agreement are acted upon.

Sultan Adil wept when he read the Acehnese letter and had a buffalo slaughtered for a ceremonial feast (*kenduri memotong kerbau*) to honor his father. Then he ordered an envoy to go to Simugari, with the task of bringing about an agreement to make a single state (*henda' mupakat satu negeri*).[25] As on other occasions when this chronicle records important decisions and events, the text turns from continuous narrative to dialogue. Extended dialogue rarely features in the *Asal*, but in this text it appears to function as a means of highlighting and exploring important issues.

When Sultan Adil's envoy reached Simugari, he informed the Tuanku Mudik that he had come on Sultan Adil's behalf because his father had died in Aceh. Sultan Usuf, he said, had left behind instructions that his son should go upstream to the Tuanku. The Raja of Simugari replied with deliberation:

"If he left the instruction then all of you come upstream. Go back now all of you."[26]

---

the eight attributes of a prince. R. O. Winstedt, "An Old Minangkabau Legal Digest from Perak," *JMBRAS* 26 (1953): 4.

[21] *Sejarah*, p. 32. On the emphasis given to *patut* behavior in Malay writing, see Milner, *Kerajaan*, passim.

[22] *Sejarah*, p. 32. "Karena tiada juga senang di dalam hatinya."

[23] Ibid. "Tumbuhlah setan pada Sultan."

[24] Ibid., p. 33.

[25] Ibid.

[26] Ibid. "Maka kenduri pun sudah habis maka dengan takdir Allah subhanahu wa ta'ala maka Sultan 'Adil pun menyuruh utusan pergi ka Simugari henda' mupakat satu negeri. 'Ampun tuanku saya ka sini hamba disuruh Tuanku Sultan 'Adil sebab ayahnya tiada di sini dianya terpanggil ka bandar Aceh. Raja berpasan sepertilah kasih jadi diturut ka bandar Aceh maksud henda' meminta belas ditahan tiada lagi tertahan hatinya sudah dirasa berjalan itulah dianya bertinggal pasan manyampaikan anaknya kepada tuan.' Raja menyahut dengan perlahan, 'Jikalau dianya bertinggal pasan mudiklah tuan habis sekalian. Pulanglah tuan habis sekalian.' Katakan kata sudah menjadi utusan hilir ka Hujung Tanah dipersembahkan lalu pada Sultan 'Adil, 'Tuanku ampun sembahnya saya bicara baik tida' mengapa bareso' pagi bongkarlah kita.' Orang bepakat semata-mata henda' berbongkar berpindah kota mudik ka hulu ka Simugari, bareso' hari orang pun pergi mudik ka hulu ka Simugari. Setelah sampai ka Simugari disongsong orang dengan bedil dan canang diperjamu orang habis sekalian. Setelah

The envoy duly left and traveled downstream. There he presented himself before Sultan Adil and said:

> "Pardon my lord, I have negotiated successfully. Tomorrow morning we may leave."[27]

Then all the people agreed (*berpakat*) to move upstream to Simugari. As on the previous occasion when Sultan Usuf had traveled upstream they were welcomed with gunshots and gongs. Everyone was entertained and, having eaten and drunk together, the Raja sat with the Sultan (*duduklah raja dengan sultan*).[28] The text states that,

> There was no dissension between them and no injury divided them, such was the agreement at that time.[29]

These words echo those of the original agreement made between the Hulu Raja and Sultan Usuf, and also those of other *perjanjian* recorded in the chronicle, where no harm was to be done by either party. The people who saw this harmony between the two rulers were happy (*sukalah hati*). A dwelling place was made for the Sultan and, during the period in which he lived there, no dissension occurred (*turut menurut tiada bersalahan*).[30]

We saw that, in the Hulu chronicle, a unified settlement was formed in Simugari. There is no mention, however, of mutual agreement or consensus with the inhabitants of the Hilir in that version. According to the Hulu text, only one ruler existed, Sultan Marah Sifat, who simply assembled the people of the Hilir *kampung*, including Raja Usuf, and took them upstream. Far from declaring the existence of two Rajas, the Hulu text states that there was always only one ruler, and that this position was held by a member of the Hulu family.

The Hilir text by contrast presents a more elaborate account. Here, too, the story is of the formation of a united settlement, but this time under the authority of two rulers living together harmoniously. The narrative and dialogue through which these events unfold is hesitant and repetitive, perhaps because the issue in question is complex and not easily stated: Ibrahim dies and an approach is made to the inhabitants upstream; the Hilir folk return downstream; Usuf leaves and when he is murdered the Hilir people once more make an approach to the people of the Hulu, who honor the previous agreement; again the inhabitants of the Hilir travel upstream, to dwell in a united settlement where two rulers live together in harmony. Instead of one kingdom under one ruler, the Hilir text establishes grounds for duality, for two in one.

---

sudah makan dan minum duduklah raja dengan sultan turut-menurut tida' bersalahan tida'lah jadi rusak-marusa'kan. Demikianlah perjanjian tatkala itu. Sukalah hati orang memandang diparusaha orang tempatnya Sultan seketika dianya diam di sanan turut menurut tiada bersalahan."

[27] Ibid.
[28] Ibid.
[29] Ibid.
[30] Ibid.

The language in which duality is developed in the chronicle is, however, tentative. In keeping with the more elaborate and complex style of the *Sejarah*, this language may also be an indication of the difficulties inherent in establishing duality, difficulties of a theoretical as well as a practical nature. The language used in the Hulu version of Episode Four is plain, assertive, and somewhat jerky. This is a common style in Malay literary expression, which is known as "paratactic" rather than syntactic language. In a paratactic style of exposition, it has been suggested, ideas are linked by "juxtaposition rather than by conjunction, and therefore words such as 'because' and 'as a result of' are unnecessary."[31] In the Hulu text, we have seen that causal statements do occur, but these are more rare than in the Hilir chronicle where, in this episode in particular, the words *sebab* and *karena* abound. The development of a causal, as distinct from a paratactic, style in Malay writing had been considered to be evidence of modern, Islamic, and European-influenced, syntactical structures.[32] This suggestion fails, however, fully to explain the differences in style between these two nineteenth century Barus chronicles. An alternative suggestion, that does throw light on the stylistic differences between these two texts, is that parataxis also occurs in situations where common assumptions exist.[33] A departure from this style may reflect not just modern influence, but circumstances where it is necessary to make explicit connections which usually remain implicit. Causal notions, therefore, may be more likely to be introduced where new and uncertain ideas and connections are under consideration.

The frequent use, in the Malay passages quoted here, of explanatory expressions such as *sebab* and *karena* (because, owing to, by reason of) and other tentative words, like *jikalau* (if, supposing that), may be attributable, then, to the sensitive nature of the ideas being presented, and the difficulties involved in presenting a context in which *raja yang dua sudah bersuatu*.[34] The repetitive and elaborate fashion in which the chronicle describes the establishment of duality also suggests that this is a concept which requires reinforcement, as does the presence of numerous conventional ceremonial expressions of Malay political behavior. The Hilir text, then, not only depicts a situation in which two rulers co-existed in a single state during this period, but, by explaining the position with such care, it appears to defend and elaborate a situation in which this was possible.

There are other features in the passage just cited, some of which have already been identified in earlier episodes, which also contribute to the Hilir text's presentation of a world in which two Rajas might rule together. The importance of solemn contracts and agreements is evident, as is the general emphasis placed on consensus. In Episode One we saw that the establishment of mutual relations between the two families was based upon Sultan Ibrahim's oath (*sumpah*). An agreement of mutual loyalty (*bersumpah bersatia*) was also made between the two families and between

---

[31]Milner, *Kerajaan*, p. 113; see also Shelly Errington, "Some Comments on Style in the Meanings of the Past," *JAS* 38, 2 (1979): 232–44; and Sweeney, *Full Hearing*, pp. 209–10 and passim on parataxis as evidence of an "oral orientation" in both oral and written composition.

[32]C. Skinner, "The Influence of Arabic upon Modern Malay," *Intisari* 2, 1 (nd): 34–47.

[33]I am indebted for this suggestion to A. C. Milner.

[34]On the use of causal and conditional language in Malay composition see Sweeney, *Full Hearing*, pp. 213, 224, 250, and 264. Sweeney finds that causal constructions are more likely to be used in dialogue than in plain narrative contexts.

Ibrahim and the Rajas of Pasaribu.[35] A guarantee (*menanggung*) of good and peaceful relations was given in Episode Three by the Raja of Aceh to Sultan Ibrahim's descendants in Barus.[36] Here again, in Episode Four, a further agreement of unity and mutual protection is made between the Hulu and Hilir settlements in Barus. Furthermore, in this instance the *perjanjian* is depicted being implemented in time of need, when the Hilir Raja moved upstream to join his Hulu counterpart. Oaths and agreements would seem, therefore, to have a significant place in the political thinking which informs this Hilir chronicle.

Harmony achieved through a formal pledge is a reason for happiness in the chronicle, and a cause for celebration. For instance, after the Hulu Raja accepted Ibrahim's oath in Episode One, both sides were said to have rejoiced (*serta bersuka-sukaanlah kedua belah pehaknya*).[37] And in this episode the people are said on two occasions to have been made "happy," as a result of harmony and mutual agreement between the Rajas of Hulu and Hilir. The wording used on these occasions is similar to that in Episode One. The word *suka,* to indicate happiness or pleasure, is used in both instances: *maka suka semuanya hamba rakyat*[38] and *sukalah hati orang.*[39]

There is a similarly repetitive character about the wording used here to describe promises of agreement, both generally and between the two ruling families. In Episode One, the Hulu and Hilir Rajas undertook not to oppress each other and this was an agreement which would also apply to their descendants (*anianya-menianya . . . hingga sampai kepada anak cucu kita*).[40] Later in the same episode, after the agreement between Ibrahim and the Pasaribu Bataks, the bond was also said to apply to their descendants on both sides (*sampai kepada anak cucu kita sebelah-menyebelah*).[41] The Raja of Aceh, in Episode Three, also promised that there would be no difference between himself and Barus, and that this would apply to their descendants (*tiada berlain sampai kepada anak cucu kita*).[42] Here, in Episode Four, it is emphasized in the agreements that the two sides will not harm each other (*tiada jadi rusak-merusakkan*)[43]—and again that they will proceed together, doing each other no wrong and not harming each other (*turut-menurut tiada bersalahan tiadalah jadi rusak-merusakkan*).[44] The repetitive construction used here, in the expressions *anianya-menianya, sebelah-menyebelah, rusak-merusakkan*, and *turut-menurut*, serves to intensify the terms used, and the presence of partial reduplication conveys the reciprocity and also the plurality and continuity of the promises made.[45]

The reiteration of words and phrases which imply lasting mutual agreement, and people's pleasure at this, reinforces these ideas in the text. Not only are such phrases frequently reiterated; they also appear in association. *Pakat* and *suka* often appear side

---

[35]*Sejarah*, pp. 22–23.

[36]Ibid., p. 27.

[37]Ibid., p. 22.

[38]Ibid., p. 30.

[39]Ibid., p. 33.

[40]Ibid., p. 22 .

[41]Ibid., p. 23.

[42]Ibid., p. 27.

[43]Ibid., p. 30.

[44]Ibid., p. 33.

[45]See R. O. Winstedt, *Malay Grammar* (Oxford: The Clarendon Press, 1927), pp. 84, 94, and 102.

by side, and when they occur in association they are generally related to the establishment of group unity. That is to say, whenever the creation of one state or settlement (*sebuah kota, sebuah negeri*) is proposed in the text, it is accompanied by the associated notions of *pakat* and *suka*. *Pakat* and *suka* appear as equivalences of *sebuah*. The specific relationship between these concepts and its consistency in the text creates a pattern, or a paradigm, for good, and thus unified, government. A model is thereby developed in the text, in which duality can be established successfully without challenging the existence of good and peaceful government.

Consensus, therefore, is a key element in the Hilir text's presentation of relations between the Hulu and Hilir families. The significance of this concept to a Hilir world view is not limited, however, to the issue of relations between the royal families. It appears in Hilir relations with Aceh and with the Pasaribu Bataks, and also in internal political decisions and the relations between ruler and subjects. Decisions are often said, in this chronicle, to be the result of deliberation and agreement (*pakat* and *mupakat*). For instance, in Episode One, after Sultan Ibrahim has discovered the *kampung* upstream and returned home, the inhabitants of that settlement are said to have agreed (*mupakat*) to go and see Ibrahim's settlement.[46] In Episode Four, Sultan Ibrahim's subjects agreed (*berpakat*), after his death, to make Sultan Usuf Raja. They also made a general agreement (*mupakat*) to approach the Hulu Raja in Simugari.[47] After Usuf's death, Sultan Adil sent his envoy to Simugari to bring about an agreement (*mupakat*) to make one state.[48] When the envoy returned with the news that all was well, the inhabitants of the settlement, we are told, agreed (*berpakat*) once more to go upstream.[49] Considerable respect, therefore, appears to be paid in this chronicle to the views of the general population, and consensus is depicted as an essential component of political life in the *negeri*. As we shall, see an emphasis on deliberations which achieve *mupakat* is an important element in Minangkabau thought which appears to influence the Hilir perspective.

The remaining pages of Episode Four in the Hilir text contain an important and complex presentation of the issue of dual government. Not only do themes which have already been identified recur here, but elements are introduced which add dimension to the chronicle's presentation of dual Rajaship.

After Sultan Adil moves to Simugari, he lives there for a period during which there is no discord. Then the Hulu Raja is said to have died.[50] A decision is taken by the *menteri* and the people formally to institute dual Rajaship. Although we have al-

---

[46]*Sejarah*, p. 21.

[47]Ibid., p. 30.

[48]Ibid., p. 33.

[49]Ibid.

[50]*Sejarah*, p. 34. "Setahun sudah lamanya tinggal di sana raja yang tuha matilah sudah susahlah orang dalam negeri karena tida' lagi akan mehukum orang membawa' kahendak hati berpakatlah orang yang tuha-tuha anak raja tida' dibari serta berkumpullah orang keluar kampung. Yang tuha-tuha bertanya kepada sekaliannya orang, 'Dengarkan kata hamba bertanya, dengarkan tuan sekalian rata, raja kita nan sudah meninggalkan kita. Siapa dibuat mehukum kita? Tuan menyahut habis semata, nan mana kita buatkan raja? Setahun sudah Raja berpulang. Kusutlah sudah lakunya orang jikalau musuh garangan datang siapalah dapat akan mahatur orang?' Demikianlah kata orang yang tuha disuruhnya menyahut orang semata menyahut orang mendengar kata. 'Janganlah kami tuan tanyakan, basarnya orang sudahlah sama, bagaimanalah kita maubahkannya berdua dengan Sultan yang datang? Itulah orang akan memegang supaya tida' bencana datang.' Itulah pakat orang semata."

ready seen that the Hulu and Hilir settlements had "become one" and their rulers also were "united," the formal inauguration of two rulers is presented in the text as a further, more serious, step. In the discussion leading to this decision, dual government is treated as a problematic issue, which the people and the rulers of Barus resolve together to their satisfaction. At this crucial stage, the language of the chronicle is more ambiguous and involved than in other places. Much of what follows consists of dialogue in which the identity of the participants is only loosely indicated, and between whom it is difficult to distinguish. The later context of these discussions does clarify these matters, and the participants have, therefore, been identified in the translations offered below. Where ambiguities exist this is indicated in footnotes.

After the death of the Raja di Hulu, the inhabitants of Simugari were troubled (*susahlah*), because there was no-one to give judgments and to whom they could submit their wishes.[51] Despite the presence of Sultan Adil, the Hilir Raja, the people felt themselves to be without a Raja, and this statement may therefore apply particularly to the subjects of the Hulu Raja who were, it will be remembered, the original inhabitants of Simugari.

The elders of the community decided not to include the Raja di Hulu's son in their discussions,[52] and they gathered all the inhabitants outside the *kampung*. The elders then addressed the people:

Hear the words of my question. Listen all of you. Our Raja has left us. Who will rule us? Answer all of you, whom should we make Raja? It is a year since the Raja's death and the behavior of the people is confused (*kusutlah*). If an enemy should come, who would give orders?[53]

The people of the *negeri* appear, then, to be confronted with a problem concerning who should now be considered their Raja. People in the *negeri* were confused, we are told, and the implication here is that there is a choice as to who should be made Raja.

The people answer,

"Don't ask us—their greatness is already the same. How can we alter things to include the Sultan who has come? That is a person who should be in position of command so that disaster cannot strike."[54]

---

[51]Ibid. As we saw in Chapter 1, such a statement of disquiet or despair among subjects who are without a Raja is not uncommon in Malay literature, and these consequences of "Rajalessness" help to emphasize the centrality of the Raja in Malay political thinking. This point is made by Milner, who draws on the example of the *Hikayat Deli, Kerajaan*, pp. 94 and 109. Other examples of Rajalessness can be found in Teeuw and Wyatt, eds., *Hikayat Patani*, l: 131 and in Low, ed., *Hikayat Marong Mahawangsa*, p. 124.

[52]*Sejarah*, p. 34. What the Malay says is "anak raja tida' dibari serta berkumpullah orang keluar kampung." The identity of this "anak raja" is not explained in the text, but in view of the fact that a new Raja di Hulu is mentioned later in the episode, it is assumed here that the "anak raja" is, in fact, the dead Raja's son. An alternative reading of the phrase "anak raja tida' dibari" would be that the Raja had not left a child. But, as we shall see below, that reading of the passage would leave the identity of the new Raja di Hulu unexplained.

[53]See footnote 50 above.

[54]*Sejarah*, p. 34.

There is seen to be a need, despite the previous agreement made between the Hulu Raja and Sultan Adil, to find a new way of dealing with the existence of two Rajas. The Raja di Hulu's death provides, in the text, an opportunity for a further definition and formalization of dual government.

Having decided (*pakat*) that Sultan Adil should be included in the government, the people and elders returned to the *kota*.[55] They reassembled at the hall of audience and made their wishes known. They addressed the two princes—the Raja di Hulu's son and Sultan Adil:[56]

> Pardon Tuanku, we submit to you that we are in difficulties without a raja. The law has no definition and there is nowhere for us to take our complaints. Therefore, if God should make it possible, then concerning the question of a ruler, we may give both of you the quality of sovereignty (*daulat*) in order to rule over all of us and we are not doing anything which is prohibited.[57]

Here, then, the people suggest that both princes should rule. Sultan Adil, however, replied that they did not want to be Raja together.

> "We (*kami*) do not want to be raja."[58]

The people, through their representatives, the *menteri*, then attempted to persuade the princes to accede to their wishes.

> "Pardon my Lords, our desire is you should become Raja together (*tuanku berdua jadikan raja*). Whatever wishes of yours you make known to us, we will not fail you in them. If you do not believe this, then truly we will swear it in an oath."[59]

---

[55]Ibid. "Itulah pakat orang semata. Orang pun pulang sekalian rata berkumpul orang ka Balai Gadang orang manyembah habis semata, 'Ampun tuanku sembahnya saya susahlah kami tida' beraja, hukum nan tida' ada bertentu berjaga nan tiada tempat mengadu dan jikalau dimudahkan Allah kiranya hati daulat yang dipertuan melainkan tuanku berdualah yang akan kami daulat akan mahukum kami sekaliannya pantangan tiada kami lalui.' Sultan menyahut mendengar kata, 'Kami nan tida' mahukan raja.' Menteri menyahut mendengar kata, 'Ampun tuanku sembahnya saya tuanku berdua jadikan raja, barang kehendak tuanku katakan kehendak tiada kami salahi. Kalau tuanku tiada percaya biar bersumpah kami semata.' Senanglah hati Raja mendengar disahut dengan bicara benar, 'Dengar dituan habis semata, jikalau sungguh menurut kata apakala ubahan kamikan raja.' Menyahut orang semata-mata, 'Apa kehenda' tuanku katakan janjian tiada kami ubahi sampai ka anak ka cucu kami.' Raja menyahut mendengar kata pikir sasa'at sekejap mata maka diulang pula bicara raja bicara kepada Sultan, 'Apa bicara kita nan tuan bicara orang itu rupanya?' Sultan menyahut mendengar kata tuan menjawab, 'Tiada mengapa karena orang sudah mupakat di mana boleh kita salahi barang kehendak kita turutkan?' Setelah sudah berpadu padan dianya pun manitah kepada sekalian kehendak hati boleh dekat seperti takhta keraja'an raja."

[56]The text does not specify that these are the identities of the two Tuanku whom the people address, but this is made clear in the subsequent discussion.

[57]See above, footnote 55. The phrase "tuanku berdualah yang akan kami daulat akan mahukum" is difficult to translate. It seems to imply that the people bestow *daulat* upon their rulers, but this would be very unusual. An alternative reading might be that the two rulers were considered to possess the necessary *daulat* already.

[58]See above, footnote 55.

[59]*Sejarah*, p. 34.

The princes were gratified (*senanglah hati Raja*) to hear this good council (*bicara benar*), and they announced that they would consent to become Raja.

> "Listen to this all of you, if it is really as you say, when things are altered then we (*kami*) will become Raja."[60]

The people, therefore, responded with their oath.

> "Whatever wishes you make known to us, we will not alter this undertaking (*perjanjian*) and neither will our descendants."[61]

This assertion of continued loyalty by the inhabitants of the *negeri* did not conclude the matter, however, since the two princes now turned to each other and discussed the situation together. Their words reflected an acknowledgment, which was also evident in the earlier discussion between people and elders, of the difficulties inherent in the establishment of a dual Rajaship. According to the chronicle, the Raja (son of the Raja di Hulu) spoke to Sultan Adil. He said:

> "What is our response to this submission by the people?"[62]

The Sultan (Sultan Adil) replied:

> "There is no difficulty, since the people have agreed (*mupakat*), how can we go against it? Whatever they desire we will follow."[63]

The two princes thus consented to the wishes of their subjects and agreed to rule together. Not only are the wishes of the people presented in the chronicle as a means of establishing duality, but the important role of the people in choosing their rulers is illustrated. The authority of the assembled people in choosing those to rule over them, in this and other episodes of the *Sejarah*, is much more reminiscent of Minangkabau patterns of government than those which are usually expressed in Malay *hikayat*.

The chronicle then proceeds to relate that, after the rulers had been united, they issued instructions concerning the arrangements of their government. These dealt with the regalia and objects of display to be used, the *adat* (custom) to be employed, and the *penghulu* who were to be appointed by the rulers. According to the text, after they had been united (*berpadu padan*), they spoke to everyone and told them their wishes concerning the excercise of their sovereignty.[64] An announcement was made concerning the nature of the royal array (*angkatan*)[65] to be used by the two Rajas.

---

[60]Ibid.

[61]Ibid.

[62]Ibid.

[63]Ibid.

[64]Ibid. "kehendak hati boleh dekat seperti takhta keraja'an raja."

[65]The word *angkatan* is more commonly used in the sense of an armed force or expedition. Such a definition is inappropriate in the present context, however, and *angkatan* here appears to be used in the sense mentioned by Marsden, i.e., an array or procession. See Marsden, *Malay-English Dictionary*, s.v. angkatan.

At this crucial point in the text, where two rulers have been formally appointed, the theme of duality and the possibility of "two in one" is reiterated. The important symbols of royal authority in Barus go "in twos," but are at the same time united. Sultan Adil makes a statement which suggests that the array of the princes must not be separate.[66]

"This is the array of we two together. The *adat* which we will use has two sources, first from Minangkabau and second from Aceh. Concerning the array which comes from Aceh, it includes *binas*[67] and a single open umbrella and other things besides which the sovereign Raja Aceh gave to my grandfather, Tuanku Sultan Ibrahim. The marks of greatness that came from Raja Aceh are mentioned in this letter. That which comes from the sovereign of Pagaruyung contained all the laws which have come down to me from my ancestors and which are still in use. I cannot mention all of these since they are so numerous. That is the situation with my array. But, because we have been united with the Raja here, now our array will be the same."[68]

When the assembled people heard this announcement, they made obeisance to the Rajas and declared that they were pleased with it (*sukalah kami tentangan itu*).[69] Sultan Adil then proclaimed the Raja's intention to appoint four *penghulu* to govern the *kampung*. These were named, and the *penghulu* promised (*bersumpah*) the gathering that they would not act individually or of their own accord.[70] Once this was settled the two rulers were enthroned together.

By the decree of God, may He be praised and exalted, the people elevated the two rulers. They made ready the coronation regalia which it was used at that time and then all the people stood and prostrated themselves before the royal presence of their two royal lords.[71]

---

[66]See the first sentence of footnote 68 below. The passage is difficult to translate directly into English.

[67]I have been unable to identify this word. The third of the romanizations of this text which are kept in the Korn Collection has *bangsi* or "flute" here.

[68]*Sejarah*, p. 35. "Tida' boleh tuan semata seperti angkatan kami berdua dengar dituan habis semata, angkatan kami hamba khabarkan barang memakai kami salahkan. Demikianlah angkatan kami berdua adapun 'adat yang kita pakai dua perkara pertamo turun dari Minangkabau kedua turun dari Aceh. Adapun angkatan dari Aceh seperti binas dan tunggul payung bertelanjang dan lain-lainnya sebab daulat Raja Aceh sudah membarikan kepada nenek saya Tuanku Sultan Ibrahim. Demikianlah kegadangan dari Raja Aceh seperti yang tersebut atas surat ini dan angkatan dari daulat Pagaruyung ialah yang sepanjang undang turun tumurun dari nenek saya hingga sampai kepada saya yang telah sudah kita pakai pada zaman sekarang kini dan tida' boleh hamba sebutkan semuanya karena sangat banyak rupanya. Demikianlah angkatan saya akan tetapi sebab kami sudah bersebuah dengan raja di sini melainkan samalah angkatan kami karena sangat sukar membejakannya. Demikianlah hal kegadangan kami kedua."

[69]Ibid.

[70]Ibid. "Setelah selesai penghulu empat bersumpah orang sekalian rapat jangan diturut masing-masing pendapat penghulu empat akan merapat sudah sepakat satu bicara diangkat takhta raja yang ghani Allah subhanahu wa ta'ala sudah menolong kepadanya sampai kehendaknya jadi raja keduanya."

[71]Ibid. "Dengan takdir Allah subhanahu wa ta'ala orang pun mengangkat raja keduanya serta disediakan oranglah halat angkatan raja-raja yang telah biasa terpakai pada zaman itu. Maka

Some of the elements of the ceremony are then mentioned in the text. These are consistent with the type of ceremonial often described in Malay *hikayat* in connection with royal occasions. They include the use of royal umbrellas, the color yellow, gun shots, and the sound of numerous musical instruments including the beat of a special state drum (*Taboh Larangan*) and the mosque drum (*Taboh Juma'at*).[72] When the ceremony was at an end, the Khatib read a prayer requesting God's blessing so that there would be uninterrupted loyalty and perfect understanding. Then Sultan Adil spoke to the people once more.

> "We have a joint government and our four *penghulu* are divided in two: Setia Lela and Maharaja Muda are the *penghulu* of the Raja of the Hilir and Orang Kaya Balai and Raja Setia Muda are the *penghulu* of the Raja in the Hulu."[73]

Sultan Adil also defined the status of the *penghulu* by means of declaring which honors and emblems of authority they were entitled to use. The *penghulu* replied deferentially, and the assembled people were pleased at the honor which had been shown to the *penghulu*.[74]

Not only was the array or *angkatan* of the two rulers "the same," then, according to the chronicle, but their government (*kerajaan*) is also said to be "joint" or the "same" (*sama*). They appointed four *penghulu*, but these officers, like the *angkatan*, were in two parts (*perdua*) and thus reflect the dual sources of royal authority in the *kerajaan*. In these passages, the Hilir text depicts a situation which might best be described as representing the idea of "two in one." These new arrangements, announced by Sultan Adil, serve to emphasize the significance of the decision which had just been taken. The two new rulers immediately exercise an essential royal prerogative by appointing the *penghulu* and investing them with authority.

In the ideal model of the *kerajaan*, the bestowal of titles and the investiture of chiefs and other subordinates were among the most important duties of the ceremonial Malay ruler.[75] In this manner the two Barus Rajas establish their role and immediately activate the *kerajaan*. In Episode One, it was suggested that the foundation of Barus and the first meeting between the Hulu and Hilir Rajas was highlighted by a redefinition of place names in one text, and of existing alliances in the other. Here, in Episode Four of the Hilir chronicle, the appointment of two rulers is solemnized and emphasized, it seems, by a statement of the ceremonial aspects of their authority both in relation to the rulers themselves and to their officers, the *penghulu*. In this particular case, the court which they establish and the officers whom they appoint are said to have two components, and they thus also serve to reflect the dual nature of the *kerajaan* itself.

---

orang pun berdiri semuanya menjungjung duli ka bawah hadrat seri paduka tuanku keduanya."

[72]Ibid., p. 36.

[73]Ibid. "Hai tuan-tuan sekaliannya rata dengar dituan hamba berkata keraja'an kami sudahlah sama, penghulu empat kami perdua; Setia Lela dan Maharaja Muda itulah panghulu Raja di Hilir; Orangkaya Balai dan Raja Setia Muda itulah panghulu Raja di Hulu."

[74]Ibid.

[75]See, for instance, Milner, *Kerajaan*, passim.

Despite the assertion of duality made here, it is Sultan Adil, the Hilir Raja, who proclaims the new arrangements. Just as the Hulu Raja is given no name, and is thereby denied an all-important title or *nama*, he is also denied a voice at this point in the narrative. Although the Hilir chronicle presents a case for duality in the political life of the *negeri*, it is a dual situation in which the Hilir family is depicted, in this episode at least, as having the dominant role.

The concluding passages of this episode of the Hilir text describe the happy and peaceful situation which resulted from the installation of two rulers and the perpetuation of dual government by their successors.

At the end of the day, the people requested leave to go home. Then, according to the chronicle, after the *kerajaan* had been in existence for some time, the desires of the two Tuanku were fulfilled. Simugari was ". . . happy (*suka*) and populous, husked and unhusked rice was plentiful, and the *kerajaan* was uninterrupted from day to day and from month to month."[76] Once again, general happiness is said to result from a situation of unity and mutual agreement between the Hulu and Hilir families. The description of a happy and populous state, in which rice was plentiful and nothing interrupted the government, is a convention of traditional Malay writing. Duality, it is implied here, and the existence of two rulers, is synonymous with happiness and prosperity, an association of ideas which was also observed in earlier parts of the episode.

The descendants of the two rulers are then mentioned. When the Raja di Hulu died, he left male and female children whose names are not given. Tuanku Raja Adil also "returned to God's mercy," and he left two sons, the eldest of whom was entitled Tuanku Sultan and the younger, Tuanku Sultan Marah Laut.[77] These princes, the great grandsons of Sultan Ibrahim, are the same two sons of Alam Syah who were mentioned in the Hulu text and who are also said to be Ibrahim's great grandchildren. In that text, their father's name is Sultan Alam Syah, whereas here it is Sultan Adil and the two are called Tuanku Sultan and Sultan Bagonjong. Not only is Tuanku Sultan Marah Laut recognizable as Sultan Bagonjong by his ancestry, but, as we shall see, his exploits identify him and, at a later stage of this chronicle, Marah Laut's name is actually changed to Bagonjong in the text.

> "Concerning Tuanku Sultan he was raised by the people to become ruler replacing his father. Those were the circumstances. God ordained that Tuanku Sultan had male and female children. Tuanku Sultan was then confirmed as ruler in Simugari together with the Raja di Mudik."[78]

The new generation thus inherits the union of its parents and two Rajas continue to rule together in Simugari. The text continues in its policy of not naming the Hulu Raja and provides titles only for its main protagonists, the descendants of Sultan Ibrahim. It records that the younger of Ibrahim's great grandsons, Marah Laut

---

[76]*Sejarah*, p. 36. "Habislah sudah sehari itu orang memohon meminta kembali tinggallah raja dudu' sendiri. Lamalah sudah jadi keraja'an pikir tuanku dua kedudukan maksud hati henda' masu' bermasukan suka dan ramai di Simugari baras dan padi banyak menjadi keraja'an tiada berkeputusan sepanjang hari segenap bulan."

[77]Ibid., p. 37.

[78]Ibid. "Adapun Tuanku Sultan diangkat orang jadi keraja'an menggantikan ayahnya demikianlah halnya. Maka dengan takdir Allah Tuanku Sultan pun beranak laki-laki perempuan maka tetaplah Tuanku Sultan jadi keraja'an di Simugari bedua dengan raja di mudik."

(Bagonjong), left the kingdom and traveled to the Batak states in the east. No reason for his departure is offered in the text.[79]

This event brings the Hilir account to the point where Episode Four of the Hulu text concluded, the departure of Sultan Bagonjong (Marah Laut). In the Hulu chronicle, however, an important reason was given for Bagonjong's departure: the fact that only one Raja, drawn from the Hulu line, held authority in Barus. No such reason is offered in the Hilir version. There is no need. According to the Hilir view, the two families ruled together.

* * *

It is now possible to compare these two very different versions of Episode Four. The discrepancy between them is considerable. In length alone there is a large variation, and, although both describe a form of unification between the two Barus settlements, they depict it differently. In the *Asal* there was no hesitation involved in the issue of kingship. One ruler existed. He was drawn from the Hulu family. The existence of Sultan Ibrahim's descendants is acknowledged in the text, but, since the death of Ibrahim himself, they are presented merely as poor relations of the ruling family who are denied access to power (*kuasa*). In the *Sejarah* a much more complex situation is portrayed. There, by means of an involved series of alliances and agreements, the Hilir and Hulu settlements unite on equal terms. This bonding, initially brought about on the grounds of mutual protection, subsequently develops into a formal commitment to dual government which is portrayed in ideal terms. In the *Asal*, the episode concludes with a sorrowful Bagonjong departing from a Barus which is firmly under the authority of a Hulu ruler. The *Sejarah* episode closes with enthusiastic praise for the institution of dual government in Barus and its transmission to the descendants of the two royal families. This subtle and complicated elaboration is in sharp contrast with the spare story presented in the Hulu text.

In their discussion of relations between the ruling dynasties, these chronicles touch on the theoretical aspects of royal authority and the appropriate form for government to take. It is in this respect that Episode Four offers most to the reader interested in how the particular problems of Barus were perceived within the kingdom itself. The Hulu approach is clear. Authority is *kuasa*, which is held by one person only. As far as it goes, this single Raja philosophy is a conventional view. The Hilir presentation, however, is more complex; not only is it quite different from the Hulu perspective, but the language and style of the text suggests an awareness of the problematic nature of dual kingship. The *pakat—suka—sebuah* paradigm is presented as one means of resolving the difficulty. The tentative nature of the dialogue in these passages may be due to an awareness of the conceptual difficulties inherent in the business of formally appointing two kings. It is by no means a clear cut decision in the text. When the *menteri* ask the assembled people who should be made Raja, they indicate that there is a problem. As the subsequent discussion shows, there was more than one possible king. But the populace desire a change in the existing arrangement of government. Despite the alliance already made between Hilir and Hulu Barus, and the assertion made earlier in this episode that the two rulers had "become one," the

---

[79]Ibid. "Dengan takdir Allah subhanahu wa ta'ala Tuanku Sultan Marah Laut pun berjalan ka negeri Batak lua' Segala Limbong sehingga sampai ka timur ka negeri Doli."

appointment of two Rajas is still a weighty matter. Things must be changed to make it possible.

Further, when it comes to asking the two Tuanku to rule together, the people's request is couched in involved and tentative language.

> "... if God should make it possible, then concerning the question of a ruler, we may give both of you the quality of sovereignty in order to rule over all of us."[80]

Clearly, it is understood in the text that there is reason to doubt that two princes can, properly, be made ruler together. The Tuanku confirm this when they refuse:

> "We do not want to be Raja."[81]

And again, when they discuss the issue together and decide that it is permissible to go ahead with the plan, the Tuankus' dismissal of the problem inherent in the project testifies to their appreciation of its existence:

> "There is no difficulty. Since the people are agreed, how can we go against it?"[82]

Acceptance of the people's wishes did, therefore, involve doubt and the possibility of a false move. The caution, which is expressed here in connection with the formal establishment of a dual kingship, strongly suggests an awareness in the chronicle that the appointment of two rulers was not an ordinary occurrence.

Not only is the inherent difficulty of dual kingship apparently recognized in the Hilir text; the chronicle also presents solutions to the problem. There are a variety of means in these latter passages of Episode Four by which dual government is, apparently, justified and a coherent presentation of duality made possible. The will of the people is one means by which the situation is validated. It is the people, for instance, who tell the elders of their desire to "include" the newly arrived Sultan. "That was their decision,"[83] the text tells us. Moreover, when the Rajas discuss the problem, they place the moral burden of the choice upon their subjects and, apparently, also recognize the right of their subjects to determine the situation and choose the type of government they desire.[84]

A further means by which the new arrangement is made tenable in the text is the oath sworn by the people to the two Rajas.[85] We have already seen that oaths and alliances form part of the pattern of political life in Barus, as it is presented in the Hilir text, and may be considered to be part of the ideological apparatus of the Hilir world view. Oaths between rulers and between Malays and Bataks have already been encountered. Here, though, is an oath between rulers and people, and it is this which clinches the deal between the subjects and their two new kings.

---

[80]*Sejarah*, p. 34.

[81]Ibid.

[82]Ibid.

[83]Ibid. "Itulah pakat orang semata."

[84]Ibid. "Tiada mengapa karena orang sudah mupakat di mana boleh kita salahi barang kehendak kita turutkan?"

[85]Ibid.

The language of this undertaking, which is not to be altered and which is said to apply to the descendants of those who made it, links this agreement to all of the others which appear throughout this text and which are made in similar terms. Such a bond between rulers and subjects is also reminiscent of the so-called pact in the *Sejarah Melayu* where Sri Tri Buana promised never to shame Malay subjects and Demang Lebar Duan undertook in response that Malays would never be disloyal to their ruler.[86] This covenant, like that in the *Sejarah Tuanku Batu Badan*, was intended to apply to the descendants of those who made the oath and, like the Barus text, it had a special relevance to one issue with which the text is concerned. In the case of the Melaka text, this issue was loyalty between ruler and subjects, but in the *Sejarah Tuanku Batu Badan* the oath refers to the dominant concern of appointing two kings. Inscriptions in old Malay from the empire of Srivijaya indicate that oaths (*sumpah*) have long been important in Malay thinking,[87] and the use of such a solemn contract in the Barus text thus helps to justify the establishment of a dual kingship.

A further means by which the new situation is sanctified is through an appeal to God. In the text, Islam sanctions the appointment of two rulers. When the people first broach the question of duality with the Tuankus they explain that they are without a ruler, and add: "if God should make it possible, then concerning the question of a ruler."[88] Later, when they came to enthrone the two Rajas, we are told that: "God, may He be praised and exalted, assisted them in their desire to become Raja together."[89] And it was by "the decree of God" that the ceremony took pace. Later still, the Khatib read a prayer to God in which it was asked that nothing should damage the alliance.[90]

Although to a certain extent such appeals to God are a standard feature of this type of Malay literature, and they occur frequently in this chronicle, God's support is mentioned more often here than in other less important parts of the story. As in the early passage where Sultan Ibrahim appealed to God to prove the sincerity of his claim to own the water and earth he found at Barus, God is invoked in the decision to appoint two kings. He assisted the Rajas to achieve joint rule, and His name helps to consecrate the institution of duality with which this episode is concerned.

The language of numbers permeates the text. The words for one and two appear constantly in different forms. An example of this occurs early in the episode when the Hulu Raja is made to say, "we are two here" (*kami berdua*) and to suggest that they should be of "one opinion" (*satu bicara kami*). The two Raja, we are told, therefore became one (*Raja yang dua sudah bersatu*) and the the two *negeri* were joined or made one (*negeri dua sudah bersuatu*). Later Sultan Adil agreed, with the Hulu Raja, to create a single state (*mupakat satu negeri*). The people in Simugari also wanted to alter things to include the Sultan who had arrived there (*kita mengubahkannya berdua dengan Sultan yang datang*). And, they announce, they want both princes to act as Raja (*Tuanku berdua jadikan Raja*). Not only are the rulers and the state described in ones and twos, but the *angkatan*, the *adat*, and the *penghulu* are similarly identified in the

---

[86]Brown, trans., *Sejarah Melayu*, pp. 16–17.

[87]J. G. de Casparis, *Selected Inscriptions From the 7th to the 9th Century A.D.* (Bandung: Masa Baru, 1956), pp. 1–36; and J. Miksic, "Classical Archaeology," pp. 50–54.

[88]*Sejarah*, p. 34.

[89]Ibid., p. 35. "Allah subhanahu wa ta'ala sudah menolong kepadanya sampai kehendaknya jadi raja keduanya."

[90]Ibid., p. 36.

text. Like the rulers and, indeed, the state itself, these royal appendages are all considered to be dual components of a unified whole.

In this episode the Hilir text declares itself. In earlier parts of the chronicle, duality and the significance of harmony and consensus are hinted at: here they are elaborated in a consistent pattern. A network of related ideas begins to emerge in this episode within which dual government is a coherent and understandable part.

The urgent concern, displayed in this episode, with a dual alternative, the anxieties expressed concerning duality, and the elaboration of ways in which such a situation might come about are sustained in the episode which follows.

EPISODE FIVE

In the previous episodes differences were identified between the Hulu and Hilir texts at three levels: each displays a bias in favor of its own ruling family; each presents rulership in Barus in its own distinctive fashion; and, underlying their disagreement concerning the organization of political life in the *negeri*, each text also presents what is emerging as an individual and coherent conception of political authority. These differences are developed in Episode Five.

The episode concerns Sultan Adil's younger son, Sultan Bagonjong or Sutan Baganjong as he is called in the *Asal*. The outline of his story is similar in both texts, but, as with other episodes, significant differences of emphasis occur. These differences bear on the developing perspectives of the two chronicles. We shall see that each text uses Bagonjong's story in order to pursue its own concerns. There are surprises, however, in the way that the Hulu chronicle handles this story. For a while, the Hulu chronicle seems to lose confidence in its presentation of Hulu dominance, and this temporary hesitation needs careful exploration. It reveals itself in the treatment of Sultan Bagonjong himself.

Bagonjong's presence forms a common thread in the two accounts, and he comes through in both texts as a person of stature. Unlike many of the figures in these texts, who are credited with few personal attributes and who feature purely on account of their place in the genealogical tables, Bagonjong stands out. He is not a personality: Malay *hikayat* rarely develop the character and individual thought processes of their *dramatis personae*,[91] and in this respect Sultan Bagonjong is no exception. He is, however, a person of unusual stature in both chronicles and might be described as a "man of prowess."[92] This treatment of Bagonjong, a Hilir prince, in the *Asal* is an unusual departure for that chronicle. In this episode, the possibility of a Hilir challenge to Hulu authority is acknowledged. Representatives of the two dynasties are actually portrayed in hand-to-hand combat, as individual princes battle out the authority dispute in Barus. In a sense, the struggle between the two dynasties which, hitherto, was only hinted at in the Hulu text, comes more to the fore. Yet, in another sense, the whole situation is less well defined, and the issue of authority is more ambiguous than in other episodes of the *Asal*. The sure voice of earlier sections falters

[91]For comments on the absence of a "personality base" in Malay *hikayat*, see, J. Bastin, "Problems of Personality in the Reinterpretation of Modern Malaysian History," in *Malaysian and Indonesian Studies*, ed. J. Bastin and R. Roolvink (Oxford: Clarendon Press, 1964), pp. 141–55. Also Milner, *Kerajaan*, pp. 100–101 and p. 155, n. 17.

[92]See O. W. Wolters, *History, Culture and Region in Southeast Asian Perspectives* (Singapore: Institute of Southeast Asian Studies, 1982), pp. 5–6.

briefly. Before the episode closes, however, these doubts disappear, and the chronicle deals decisively and masterfully with Hilir pretensions to royal status.

In the *Sejarah*, duality, the dominant theme of Episode Four, is further explored in the context of the possibility of dual government. As with Episode Four, it is less the competing claims to royal status *per se* which are of interest, than the way in which each chronicle advances its claim. The language of political experience employed in these texts can usefully be compared with what we know of Sumatran and Malay States elsewhere, in order to establish the local and individual Barus statements.

ASAL

According to this version of events, at the end of Episode Four Sutan Bagonjong left Barus with a feeling of bitterness. The Hulu Raja, Raja Bongsu, is presented as the sole ruler, and Barus is described as a kingdom within which only one person held authority (*kuasa*). Because Bagonjong and his elder brother, Marah Sutan, were excluded from authority, Bagonjong left.

> In the meantime Sutan Bagonjong traveled with a feeling of bitterness. The direction in which he traveled was not certain; rather, like a restless person he traveled for some time all around Pulau Perca [Sumatra] and also to Java and to other countries. Sutan Bagonjong went in search of knowledge (*ilmu*).[93]

Raja Bongsu was left in sole control over Barus, but, according to the text, shortly after he became Raja the kingdom was attacked by Acehnese.

> These Acehnese, however, did not come from their homeland, rather they were Acehnese of the outlying districts (*rantau*), who were trespassing and had made a small *kampung* near to the *kampung* of Sultan Maharaja Bongsu in Lobo Dalam. They fought continuously for a long time and were not defeated.[94]

It was then that Sutan Bagonjong returned from his travels. He came from the kingdom of Deli in east Sumatra, where he had married. On his return journey, he traveled through the Batak state of Toba Limbong and there, according to the text, he married again, to the Raja's daughter.[95] These new connections of Sutan Bagonjong

---

[93]*Asal*, p. 19(40). "Dalam pada itu maka itu Sutan Bergonjong berjalan dangan merajok tidak tentu penjalangannya melainkan berjalan seperti oraŋ risau saja sampai barapa lama Sutan Bergonjong berjalan sama kuliling Pulau Perca lalu pula ka negeri Jawa dan kepada lain-lain negeri Sutan Bergonjong mencari 'ilmu adanya." The departure of a prince in search of *ilmu* is a convention which is often employed in Malay texts. In the *Siak Chronicles*, Raja Kecil is said to have left Pagaruyung to "*mencari 'ilmu*," L. Andaya, *The Kingdom of Johor*, p. 260. The *Riwajat Hamperan Perak*, a text from Deli, on the east coast of Sumatra, also mentions a character who left Sumatra for Java in search of *ilmu*. Copy in the possession of A. C. Milner.

[94]*Asal*, p. 19(40). "Tetapi itu Aceh bukan orang datang dari negerinya melainkan Aceh dari rantau yang melanggar dan serta suda membikin kampung kecil dakat kampung Sultan Maharaja Bongsu di Lobo Dalam dan serta berparang sentiasa tidak berkeputusan telah suda barapa lamanya berparang itu dan tidak juga berkalahan."

[95]Ibid. According to Ypes, Limbong is a *marga* and *bius* grouping which is found principally on the island of Samosir. In the Hilir version of Bagonjong's story, the area he visited is referred to as Segala Limbong. Segala is a similar grouping also found on Samosir. Possibly the Laut in the name Laut Segala Limbòng is derived from Laka Toba. Some members of Limbong were

receive some attention in the text, which records the names of those to whom he was now related. His wife, for instance, is said to be the daughter of Raja Buma-Buma and the sister-in-law of Jongi Mali.[96] Raja Bagonjong's travels, and perhaps his new relations in the east, appear to have added to his prestige. When he arrived in Barus, he made a strong impression. He made straight for the field of battle:

> Tuanku Bagonjong went into the midst of the fighting between the two sides. There he rose up on his horse and held up his hand, calling upon them to stop fighting immediately.

The fighting stopped

> . . . because those on both sides saw Sutan Bagonjong strong and standing, having the appearance of a man of quality, a Raja.[97]

Bagonjong's appearance was, therefore, a significant factor in his effect on the two armies. Like his ancestors, Sutan Ibrahim and Raja Yusuf, the way he looked, his presence (*tampannya*),[98] was an indication of his royal status.

The contestants agreed to listen to Sutan Bagonjong's opinion of their dispute. Bagonjong found that the Acehnese were at fault and, when they refused to accept his decision, he joined the fighting against them. The Acehnese soon became frightened and fled. Peace was restored, and Sutan Bagonjong stayed in Barus although he had not yet been recognized by the inhabitants (*balun orang kenal kepadanya*).[99]

Bagonjong had left Barus as a outsider but came back with the aura of a superior person who looked like a Raja. His travels around Sumatra and other countries, his search for *ilmu*, and his marriages in the East, appear to have acted as rites of passage which transformed him. On his return, he commanded sufficient prestige to intervene in the war without being recognized. It is also implied that his presence on Sultan Bongsu's side contributed to the defeat of the Acehnese. Sutan Bagonjong's increased standing becomes more apparent when the people of Barus learned of his true identity.

> Then, after some time had passed, people recognized that Sutan Bagonjong was the younger brother of Marah Sutan, son of Sutan Alam Syah, and Sutan Usuf's grandson who was descended from Sutan Ibrahim. In those circumstances the

---

represented in Barus Mudik, according to Ypes, and also in Pasaribu Dolok and Dairi. See Ypes, *Bijdrage*, pp. 39, 538, and 549.

[96]*Asal*, p. 19(40).

[97]Ibid. "Dalam pada itu maka Tuanku Berganjong masu' ka tengah-tengah peparangan antara kedua belah pihak di sanalah dia berdiri dangan kudanya dan serta mahangkat tangan kepada kedua belah pihaknya meminta' dibarantikan seketika itu parang. Dalam pada itu maka baranti itu parang sebab dilihat orang kedua belah pihaknya itu kepada Sutan Bagonjong ada kekar bangunnya dan lagi tampannya seperti orang ba'ik-ba'ik juga atau raja kepada pikiran."

[98]*Tampan* is defined by Wilkinson as ". . . looking the part; having a suitable presence. Of a king looking royal," Wilkinson, *Malay-English Dictionary*.

[99]*Asal*, p. 20(39).

people respected him. They thought of him as a leader because of his strength and, moreover, he was mindful of his *bangsa*.[100]

This respect paid to Sutan Bagonjong quickly led to conflict between Bagonjong and Maharaja Bongsu.

> After that, and after some time had passed, Maharaja Bongsu confronted Tuanku Bagonjong because Tuanku Bagonjong was accumulating authority (*kuasa*) in the *negeri* as if he had become Raja.[101]

So Tuanku Bagonjong left with his brother and moved to a place called Antomas.[102] There was a war between the two settlements and many of the inhabitants fled, running to Singkel, Sorkam, Korlang, and elsewhere.[103]

Here then, for the first time in the Hulu chronicle since the arrival of Sultan Ibrahim, a member of the Hilir family is portrayed as a serious challenge to the authority of the Hulu line. The *negeri* was split by the conflict between the two families, and it is admitted in the text that Sutan Bagonjong was regarded by the people as a Raja. That Bagonjong also behaved as if he were a Raja is expressed in the text in terms of his accumulation of *kuasa*, the term repeatedly used in the Hulu text to describe royal authority, which is presented in terms of the possession or absence of *kuasa* itself. In the text, Bagonjong appears to have achieved this *kuasa* by means of his prowess. Bagonjong's strength is mentioned twice, and his fine appearance is also stressed. He achieved *kuasa*, in short, because of his special qualities, and it may be that these individual qualities are what makes it possible for Bagonjong's status to be acknowledged in the Hulu chronicle.

In the account which follows, the friction between the Hulu and Hilir families resulting from Bagonjong's behavior is graphically described. According to the text, a Syekh arrived from Singkel. He had heard about the war, and he brought with him some of the people who had run to Singkel. This Syekh asked both sides to stop fighting which they declined to do. The Syekh then responded:

> "If you do not want to do so, then I command that you stop. I order you to make war with every effort for one day only. Whoever is right will win on that day. If both are right, both will win."[104]

---

[100]Ibid. "Hatta dangan barapa lamanya maka orang dapat tahu bahasa itu Sutan Bergonjong adi' Marah Sutan anak Sutan 'Alam Syah cucu Sutan Usuf turunan Sutan Ibrahim. Dalam pada itu maka dihormati oranglah kepadanya disangka orang seperti satu kepala juga kepadanya karena dia ada kakar dan lagi dia ingat dari bangsanya."

[101]Ibid. "Kemudian dari itu lama dangan berkelama'an maka bergaduh pula Maharaja Bongsu dangan Tuanku nan Bergonjong karena itu Tuanku nan Bergonjong suda membikin bagaimana kuasa dalam negeri itu seperti dia suda jadi raja."

[102]Sintuamas was mentioned in Chapter Two, and a reference to the establishment of Si Antomas occurs in Episode Two of the *Asal*.

[103]*Asal*, p. 39.

[104]*Asal*, p. 20(39). "Jikalau tidak engkau mahu aku suruh baranti melainkan sekarang aku suruh engkau berparang dangan bersungguh-sungguh pada satu hari saja kiranya jikalau siapa yang benar dalam itu hari dia menang jikalau sama benar sama menang."

These instructions were followed, and the two sides made war energetically for a whole day. They each used all their skills without defeating the other. So then with equal valor Tuanku Bagonjong and Maharaja Bongsu engaged in individual combat.[105]

Since there was no clear winner to this contest, the Syekh came and took their hands which he held together (*diperjawat salamkan*) "Tuanku Bagonjong and Sultan Maharaja Bongsu, follower with follower."[106] The two sides were reconciled, the war stopped, and, according to the text, "things returned to the way they had been before."[107]

The status quo to which the text is referring here is not specified. The struggle appears to have been inconclusive. The implication is that the contestants were equally matched. This conclusion is at odds with the "dominant Hulu" theme discernable in previous episodes of the text, and appears to be much closer to the "evenly matched" message of the Hilir text. This is a surprising twist in the Hulu chronicle's view of things. It might be said that the text falters at this point. We shall see, however, that in the following pages a firm restatement of single, Hulu, royal authority is made. The challenge represented by Sutan Bagonjong appears to be accommodated in the narrative, and it may be that this is possible because Bagonjong's *kuasa* is presented in terms of his prowess and unusual stature, rather than as an automatic right, as an Hilir prince, to a position of royal authority in Barus.

According to the chronicle, after the war was over and the kingdom was once more peaceful, the Dutch (*Olanda*)[108] arrived, and also a prince who is referred to as Anak Daulat or simply as Daulat from Minangkabau.[109] These outsiders play a role in arbitrating between the two families, which leads to a settlement of the question of who, rightfully, was ruler.

> Then, by the decree of God, may He be exalted, at that time Tuanku Bagonjong with Tuanku Marah Sutan [his brother] presented their cause before Daulat and Olanda to ask for their help in recovering the *pusaka* of their ancestors from former times.[110]

---

[105]Ibid.

[106]Ibid.

[107]Ibid.

[108]*Asal*, p. 22(38). According to the chronicle the Dutch (*Olanda*) arrived in 1050 H (AD 1640) and made a trading settlement in Barus. According to VOC records, the first Company settlement in Barus was established in 1668.

[109]Ibid. The identity and status of this Anak Daulat is never fully explained in either text—he is mentioned in both. He is said to have come from Pagaruyung which was the old royal capital of Minangkabau. *Daulat* refers, in Malay, to the essence of sovereignty, and, in particular to its divine element. Anak Daulat, then, is most probably a means of referring to a scion of the Minangkabau royal family, a son or other relation of the ruler. We have seen that it was by no means uncommon for princes from the Minangkabau highlands to visit the coastal areas on the east and west which fell under the loose authority of the Kingdom of Minangkabau in its largest sense. The Anak Daulat mentioned here is a person of status and henceforth he is referred to in the text simply as Daulat.

[110]*Asal*, p. 21(38). "Hatta dangan takdir Allah ta'ala pada masa itu Tuanku Bergonjong dangan Tuanku Marah Sutan kasi masu' pengaduan kepada Daulat dan kepada Olanda minta ditolong dia dari mengambilkan pusaka nene'nya dari dahulu-dahulu."

The meaning of the term *pusaka* in this context is not immediately clear. Usually, the word is used is to indicate an heirloom. No reference, however, occurs in the chronicle to the removal of any objects belonging to the Hilir line. Neither is property mentioned later in the text in connection with this lost *pusaka* of the Hilir princes. It may be, then, that *pusaka* at this point refers to the rights and heritage of the Hilir princes in a general sense—to their royal status within Barus—rather than to any specific objects.[111] Throughout each of the two texts, the *pusaka* of both families is portrayed as an important ingredient of their legitimate authority and sovereignty.

This impression is strengthened by the text's description of the Dutch response to the families' request which addresses itself, not to the retrieval of specific objects, but to the re-arrangement of political life in the kingdom. According to the chronicle, Daulat helped the two Hilir princes by giving the Dutch his opinion:

> ... arranging it so that the *pusaka* of Tuanku Bagonjong and Tuanku Marah Sutan's ancestors should be restored. After that, the Dutch Company (*Kompeni Olanda*) agreed with Daulat and asked Tuanku Sultan Maharaja Bongsu to give good council in the *negeri* in order to make life pleasant there. This took place in the Hijrah year 1054 [AD 1644].[112]

This euphemistically phrased request produced a ruling from Maharaja Bongsu, which dealt with the question of who was ruler: Bongsu made Tuanku Marah Sutan his *Bendahara*.[113] The eldest Hilir prince was thus given an official non-royal position under (*di bawah*) the Hulu Raja which was sanctioned, apparently, by the role of two outside participants—Daulat and the Dutch.

This appointment is a new and significant development in the Hulu text which quite dispels the doubt and hesitation apparent earlier in the episode. The position of *Bendahara* often carried with it considerable authority and prestige in Malay kingdoms but usually the *Bendahara* is not, himself, regarded as having been of royal blood.[114] The *Bendahara* family, on the other hand, has been described in the Melaka case as having the role of a complementary lineage which provided the royal lineage with brides. As we have seen, John Bowen describes the role of the *Bendahara*, as it is portrayed in the Shellabear version of *Sejarah Melayu*, as having been that of "junior

---

[111]Wilkinson suggests that, in addition to its use in connection with property, the word *pusaka* may convey heritage. Wilkinson, *Malay-English Dictionary* sv. *pesaka*.

[112]*Asal*, p. 21(38). "Dalam pada itu maka Daulat tolong kepadanya membawa' bicara kepada Olanda dan serta maaturkan perkata'an supaya dapat kembali itu pusaka nene' Tuanku Bergonjong dan Tuanku Sutan. Kemudian daripada itu maka bersepakatlah kompeni Olanda dangan Daulat dan serta mendapatkan Tuanku Sultan Maharaja Bongsu membari pikiran yang kebai'kan di dalam negeri supaya senang kehidupan adanya pada masa Hijrah 1054."

[113]Ibid. "Adapun aturan yang dibaginya itu bermula dibikin Tuanku Marah Sutan menjadi Tuanku Bendahara di bawah Sultan Maharaja Bongsu kedua dibikin pula penghulu salapan di bawah menteri yang barempat."

[114]This is evidenced by the exceptional situations in which a *Bendahara*, or *Bendahara* dynasty, ruled as Raja. In such cases, Malay writers appear to have felt the need to explain the circumstances and justify such a deviation from the ideal. See, for instance, Barbara Andaya, "Nature of the State in Eighteenth Century Perak," p. 34. Leonard Andaya has discussed the problems of legitimation which faced the *Bendahara* dynasty of Johor in the seventeenth and eighteenth centuries. Because they lacked the distinguished royal ancestry of the toppled Melaka dynasty, the *Bendahara* kings were deficient in the qualities of sovereignty represented by *Daulat*. Leonard Andaya, *Kingdom of Johor*, pp. 7, 191, 188, and 313–14.

royalty."[115] However ambiguous the *Asal* representation of the position of *Bendahara* may be in symbolic terms, it does seem that the appointment of Marah Sultan as *Bendahara* is used in the text as an overt denial of the Hilir family's royal claims. This is suggested in the text when, after documenting Bongsu's second ruling, which established that there should be eight *penghulu* who were to be below four ministers, the chronicle goes on to state:

As it was in the past, there was one Raja and his four *menteri*.[116]

This is a firm restatement of the "single Raja" philosophy which was displayed so unequivocally in Episode Four of the Hulu text. The technique of acknowledging the existence of the Hilir princes only to confine them to a subordinate position seems to deal decisively with their claims, while simultaneously emphasizing the exclusive rights to royal status enjoyed by the Hulu family. Although the existence of a Hilir challenge is acknowledged here, it is accommodated by means of the introduction of the *Bendahara* position. The subordinate role of the *Bendahara* is delineated in the detailed regulations which Maharaja Bongsu instituted. These emphasize that the Raja had ultimate authority: the *Penghulu*, it is said, were below (*di bawah*) the *menteri*, but it was the Raja who had authority (*kuasa*) over them.[117] All the officers of state lived in the Raja's *kampung*, which was divided into two (*dibagi dua*). This division was not equally weighted however: the Tuanku Bendahara lived in one half with two *penghulu* and the Raja in the other with the four *menteri* and two *penghulu*.[118] Decisions concerning regulations in the *negeri* were to be made by the *penghulu*, the *menteri* considered issues which could not be decided by the *penghulu* and those which they could not settle were taken to the Tuanku Bendahara. If the Tuanku Bendahara could not settle the matter, it was decided by the Raja in front of all the assembled officers.[119] Despite the involvement of the *Bendahara* in government, therefore, the Raja is presented as in a position of final authority. This statement of Hulu dominance also appears to be given added substance in the text by means of the implication of outsiders. After listing the names of the *menteri* and *penghulu* who were appointed, their duties, and where they were to live, the text announces that these were "the arrangements which were made widely known by the old Dutch Company and by Daulat....[120]

---

[115]Bowen, "Cultural Models," p. 171. See Chapter One, n. 110 above. A contemporary local history from the Johor-Riau area states that, in cases where a Sultan has no descendants, then he should be succeeded by the descendants of the Bendahara. For this reason, the *Bendahara* should himself be descended from a Raja. Virginia Matheson, "Strategies of Survival: The Malay Royal Line of Lingga-Riau," *JSEAS* 17, 1 (March 1986): 13.

[116]*Asal*, p. 21(38). "Adapun dari dahulu-dahulunya satu raja empat menterinya."

[117]Ibid.,p. 37. "Adapun penghulu yang baru diangkat empat orang demikian juga masing-masing memegang jabatannya di bawah menteri yang empat tetapi Raja yang boleh kuasa kepadanya."

[118]Ibid.

[119]Ibid.

[120]Ibid., p. 22(37). "Bagitu aturan yang di masyhurkan oleh kompeni Olanda yang dahulu dan serta dangan Daulat pada masa itu dangan segala hormat dan kebesaran dibaharui angkatan yang terdahulu itu dangan serta kebesarannya seperti yang tersebut dari dahulu-dahulu itu kebesaran yang terpakai kebesaran Raja Aceh dan kebesaran Raja Batak itu di membari oleh Daulat dangan kebesaran Raja Pagaruyung itu ketiganya di persembahkan dan lagi dari jabatan masing-masing ditentukan seperti yang tersebut di atas."

The array (*angkatan*) of the past is also said to have been renewed at the same time. The text states that the "marks of greatness" or *kebesaran* which were included in this court were those used by the Raja of Aceh, by Batak Rajas, and by the Raja of Pagaruyung (Minangkabau).[121] This is a similar statement to the one made in the Hilir version of Episode Four, when two rulers were appointed and Sultan Adil announced the composition of their court. Whereas the Hilir court was said to come from Aceh and Minangkabau, the Hulu text also includes the *kebesaran* which were used by Batak Rajas, although these are not specified individually.

The chronicle then embarks on a five page list of these *kebesaran* which are described as "*Kebesaran Raja*," in which the Raja is the central feature.[122] The list contains many of the conventional Malay royal honors used when a Raja goes out, when he dies, gives feasts, and so forth. It also includes what might be described as a definition of all the important offices, ceremonies, and attributes of state in the kingdom, and these are all presented in a way which reflects the central position of the ruler. The existence of Islamic officials (under the ruler's authority), a mosque, and *penghulu* are all mentioned under the heading of "*Kebesaran Negeri*."[123] The Raja's duties are spelt out as well as those of the *penghulu* and the marks of respect which all the officers of state could expect to receive. The Bendahara is not mentioned in these. In the text, the list itself is divided into subsections as follows: the *kebesaran* used when the Raja goes out; the *kebesaran* of the State; the *kebesaran* used for a feast (*bimbang*);[124] the *kebesaran* used when a Raja dies; the *kebesaran* used when people are summoned to a royal feast; the functions (*jabatan*) of the Raja; the signs of *kebesaran* and honors to be received by the Raja; the marks of honor given to the *penghulu;* and the function of religious officials.[125] The Raja is the focal point of these provisions, the majority of which are concerned with the marks of respect which were used to enhance his position.

In character, these *kebesaran* are typical of the honors and insignia which usually accompany sovereignty in the Malay World. They include items of regalia, such as the *nobat*, royal ceremonial umbrellas, swords, lances, pennants, gun salutes, and royal attendants. Among them is a lance, which is also listed among the royal regalia of Minangkabau.[126] The Raja's functions are said to involve giving orders (*memerintah*) to the *penghulu*, appointing and dismissing officials, making regulations

---

[121]Ibid.

[122]Ibid., pp. 22(37)–25(32).

[123]Ibid., p. 23(36).

[124]Van der Toorn, in his *Minangkabausche-Maleisch Nederlandsch Woordenboek*, p. 55, gives a secondary definition of *bimbang* as "*feest*."

[125]The references to Islam here include not only the presence of a mosque and religious officials in the *negeri*, but also some discussion of the ruler's role in relation to that of Islamic officials and their duties. *Adat* and Islam in Barus were said to be united (*dipasebuahkan*). And the phrase *Syarak yang bersendi Adat, Adat Bersendi Syarak* is used, which indicates that Islamic Law is based upon *adat*, and *adat*, in turn, is based upon Islamic Law. This phrase is often used in Minangkabau texts to describe the relationship betwen *Adat* and Islam. See Abdullah, "Some Notes on the Kaba Tjindua Mato," p. 12; see also Taufik Abdullah, "Adat and Islam: An Examination of Conflict in Minangkabau," *Indonesia* 2 (1966): 1–24.

[126]*Asal*, p. 23(36). This is the *Tombak Janggut Janggi*—a lance tipped with the beard of Janggi which in Persian indicates a negro, and specifically an Ethiopian. It is used in Malay of rare objects. It is also used in Persian for warrior. See Wilkinson's Dictionary s.v. Janggi. This item appears in the Minangkabau royal regalia and is mentioned in eighteenth century Minangkabau royal letters and seals. See Marsden, *The History of Sumatra*, p. 338.

for the improvement of conditions in the State, determining land ownership, and his own ownership over the jungle, sea, rivers, and islands.[127] Here, as in other parts of the Hulu chronicle, the giving of orders, the practical aspects of government and the ownership of land are given greater attention than in the Hilir chronicle.

It has already been noted that one of the differences, in earlier episodes, between these two texts is the relative absence of ceremonial description in the Hulu chronicle. Here, however, the ceremonial used in the kingdom of Barus is described at length. Unlike the *Sejarah*, however, which incorporates ceremonial behavior into the narrative, associating it with routine descriptions of the rulers activities, the *Asal* presents it in list form. The stylistic change here from narrative to a series of enumerative statements serves to separate the ceremonial listed from the narrative flow of the chronicle. It is marked off from the main body of the text and thus acts to punctuate the narrative itself. In this way, the five-page list of *kebesaran* which follows the announcement of single Rajaship by Sultan Maharaja Bongsu appears to function in the text as a means of emphasising the significance of that event. Not only does the style in which ceremonial is incorporated in this part of the Hulu text emphasize the single Raja point, but the contents of the list also symbolize the centrality and pre-eminence of the monarch.

In this episode of the Hulu chronicle, then, the point made at the end of Episode Four, when it was declared that there was "always only one Raja," is reiterated. Here, it is stated that, just "as it was in the past, there was one Raja." The existence of a Hilir challenge in the person of Sutan Bagonjong is acknowledged in the text, but apparently accommodated by means of depicting Bagonjong as an exceptional figure, a "man of prowess," and by introducing the role of *Bendahara* for the Hilir family. Powerful outsiders are implicated in this clear announcement that only one ruler existed, and the statement appears to be given added emphasis by means of the list of *kebesaran* and regulations which are then announced and which represent an affirmation of single rule.

SEJARAH

In the Hulu version of this episode the case for monarchical rule in Barus is developed further. The concept of single rule is given emphasis and theoretical support by means of a ceremonial language of kingship and by a compressed portrait of the kingdom with one ruler at its apex. In the Hilir version of Episode Five, however, Sultan Bagonjong's story is used in support of a quite different theoretical approach to kingship. Here the ideas concerning duality and unity in government, which were presented in the Hilir version of Episode Four, are placed in a wider context. This episode develops a portrait of a world in which dual government is depicted as an acceptable and realizable state of affairs. The text uses various means to reinforce its message and, in so doing, it adds perspective to our picture of local priorities and of political thought, as presented in this chronicle.

In this text, the *Sejarah*, Sultan Bagonjong had no reason for bitterness when he left Barus. The kingdom was jointly ruled by his brother, Marah Sutan, and the Raja di Hulu.[128] The episode follows Sultan Bagonjong/Marah Laut on his travels and

---

[127]*Asal*, p. 34.

[128]*Sejarah*, p. 37. "Maka dengan takdir Allah Tuanku Sultan pun beranak laki-laki perempuan maka tetaplah Tuanku Sultan jadi keraja'an di Simugari bedua dengan raja di mudik."

gives an account of his exploits, which are of interest since the things which happen to the Hilir prince outside the kingdom reflect circumstances within Barus.

According to the text,

> By the decree of God, may He be praised and exalted, Tuanku Sultan Marah Laut (Bagonjong) traveled to the Batak states in Segala Limbong. He went to the east as far as Negeri Doli [Dolok].[129]

Bagonjong/Marah Laut, we are told, married and had a son in Negeri Doli, after which he returned to Segala Limbong. There he became ruler of the Batak population. The text describes how this was brought about.

> Then by the decree of God, may He be praised and exalted, Tuanku Sultan Marah Laut was moved to subjugate all of the Bataks of Segala Limbong. Then by the decree of God, may He be praised and exalted, they all submitted to him since they were not able to resist him because Tuanku Sultan Marah Laut was extremely strong (*terlalu gagahnya*). Then the Bataks knelt in homage below his highness and they raised him to become their Raja there.[130]

The events described here, and the wording of the passage, are strongly reminiscent of an earlier part of the Hilir text where Bagonjong/Marah Laut's ancestor, Sultan Ibrahim, was recognized as a ruler by the Bataks of Pasaribu, Silindung, and Bakara. Like Bagonjong/Marah Laut, Sultan Ibrahim was the possessor of considerable prestige. Ibrahim's reception in the Bataklands, and his assumption of sovereignty over the population, was described in language which is usually used in Malay texts to indicate the reverence of Malay subjects towards their Raja. He was called *maha mulia*, most illustrious, and the Batak chiefs prostrated themselves before him (*menyembah ka bawah dulinya*). The same language is used to describe the assumption by Bagonjong/Marah Laut of sovereignty over the Bataks of Laut Segala Limbong. In this instance, the Bataks are said to kneel on the ground in front of his majesty (*maka Batak pun sujudlah menyembah ka bawah duli yang maha mulia*), before elevating him to become their Raja.

The use of Malay court vocabulary recurs again in the next passage, when Bagonjong became unhappy in Segala Limbong and decided to leave.

> For some time Tuanku Sultan Marah Laut remained there ruling (*mehukum*) over all of Toba Segala Limbong. God, may He be praised and exalted, then caused his majesty to become unhappy there because he was of a different descent (*bangsa berlainan*).[131]

---

[129]Ibid. "Dengan takdir Allah subhanahu wa ta'ala Tuanku Sultan Marah Laut pun berjalan ka negeri Batak lua' Segala Limbong sehingga sampai ka timur ka negeri Doli."

[130]Ibid. "Maka dengan takdir Allah subhanahu wa ta'ala pun sudah mengarangkan kepada hati Tuanku Sultan Marah Laut maka di taklu'kannyalah orang Batak Segala Limbong semuanya. Maka dengan takdir Allah subhanahu wa ta'ala sekalian Batak itu pun taklu'lah kepadanya karena tiada dapat melawannya karena Tuanku Sultan Marah Laut terlalu gagahnya. Maka Batak pun sujudlah menyembah ka bawah duli yang maha mulia serta diangkatnya jadi akan rajanya di sana."

[131]*Sejarah*, p. 37. "Maka beberapalah lamanya Tuanku Sultan Marah Laut tinggal di sana mehukum sekalian Tobah Segala Limbong. Allah subhanahu wa ta'ala pun mengarangkan

The word *bangsa,* we saw, was also used in connection with Sultan Bagonjong in the *Hulu* version of the story. There he was admired because of his *bangsa.* Here *bangsa* distinguishes Bagonjong from the Batak populations over which he ruled, and the text uses the word "Batak" to describe the population of Segala Limbong. In view of the association of the word *bangsa* with concepts of Malay identity,[132] it may be that the intention here is to emphasize Bagonjong's Malayness, and contrast this with the Bataks of Limbong. Whether or not *bangsa* is meant to be interpreted here as a specifically *Melayu* term or as a more general reference to ethnic identity, two things are clear from the passage cited above. Bagonjong felt himself to be different from the Batak population of the east, and this ethnic difference mattered to him. There are other instances in both chronicles where Bataks and Malays are portrayed as feeling and looking different from each other.

Bagonjong told the populace that he wished to go home to *negeri* Barus, since he had already been parted from his brother for a long time. He then made provision for a substitute authority to rule in his place. This appointment is significant since it reveals a further instance of duality in government and indicates the continued elaboration, in this text, of a reference world in which duality is acceptable. Marah Laut/Bagonjong spoke to the inhabitants of Segala Limbong:

"Now I shall appoint someone to represent me here while I am away. If I do not return then follow me to *negeri* Barus. If I am not there then there are many of my descendants in Barus. Take your tribute there."[133]

He then appointed two people to be his representatives (*wakilnya*), and it is at this point that his name in the text changes from Marah Laut to Tuanku Bagonjong. His representatives were Raja Jonggi Menawar and Raja Bunga Bunga. According to the text:

Those were the Raja who were to rule (*mehukum*) in Segala Limbong. That was the government (*kerajaan*) which was left behind by Tuanku Sultan Marah Laut.[134]

Tuanku Bagonjong, then, left a dual rajaship to act for him in Laut Segala Limbong. A connection with the Barus situation is made explicit in the next passage:

---

pada hati seri paduka yang maha mulia tiada senang di dalam hatinya tinggal di sana karena bangsa berlainan."

[132]See, for instance, Matheson, "Concepts of Malay Ethos," pp. 351–71.

[133]*Sejarah*, p. 37. "Sekarang pun hamba perbuatlah akan wakil saya di sini sementaranya hamba belum bale' kiranya jikalau tida' hamba berbale' kemari melainkan turut oleh tuan hamba ka negeri Barus. Jikalau hamba tida' ada melainkan anak cucu hamba banyak di Barus ka sanalah tuan-tuan mengantar persembahan."

[134]Ibid., p. 38. "Itulah raja akan mehukum di Segala Limbong supaya mengantar persembahan kepada Tuanku Bagonjong dan demikianlah perjanjian tatkala itu. 'Dalam satu tahun melainkan satu kali raja kedua itu mengantar persembah kuda satu akan tetapi apabila raja kedua itu membawa' kuda persembah melainkan menurut membawa' kambing jantan gadang seekor pembari kepada tuanku mudik karena kami sudah sebuah kota.'"

This was the agreement (*perjanjian*) at that time. In one year the two Rajas will bring tribute of a horse. But when the two Rajas bring the horse in tribute, then they must also bring one large male goat to give to Tuanku Mudik because we are already one *kota*.[135]

Barus and Limbong are thus linked by each possessing two rulers. The depiction of duality in Limbong reflects the situation in Barus. The Hilir prince Bagonjong is also portrayed as acting in the spirit of harmonious duality by considering the position of the Tuanku Mudik and ordering tribute for him.

In addition to offering a further example of duality, Episode Five displays other features which have already been identified as important elements in the world view of the Hilir text. The *perjanjian* which Bagonjong made with his subjects is one example. *Perjanjian* (agreements) and *sumpah* (oaths), it has been suggested, play a significant part in this text's presentation of government in Barus, both with regard to relations between the ruling groups and in relations with people of the interior. Like the *perjanjian* between Hulu and Hilir Barus, discussed in Episode Four, Bagonjong's agreement with the Bataks of Laut Segala Limbong is not only made, but also honored. This particular agreement is of interest for the light it throws on perceptions of Barus's relations with the inland, Batak, population.

After the Bataks had formalized their agreement with Bagonjong by making a solemn oath, Bagonjong left them to return home. Some time later the Bataks fulfilled their agreement by sending tribute to him at Barus. Jonggi Mawar, one of the two Rajas whom Bagonjong had left in charge of Segala Limbung, accompanied the tribute,[136] and the text gives an account of the route by which it was taken to Barus. The description provides in effect a map of the tribute route, and probably also the commercial route between Barus and the interior. The text names districts, such as Si Manulang and Rambe, through which the goods had to pass on their way to the coast, and lists the names of their Rajas. For the Barus listener or reader, this map must have represented a familiar network of relationships which were essential to Barus's survival.

The chronicle then moves to Sultan Bagonjong's return to Barus. In outline, this part of the story is similar to that in the Hulu version. Bagonjong returns to find Barus at war with Acehnese forces, and he intervenes successfully in the conflict. The manner in which these events are described differs significantly from the Hulu account. According to the *Sejarah*, when Bagonjong returned to Kampung Simugari, he found that it was under attack by a group of Acehnese. "Many had already been wounded and killed on both sides."[137] The Acehnese were strong, and Kampung Simugari was on the defensive. When Bagonjong arrived, he intervened in the fighting and asked the Acehnese to stop their attack. The Acehnese, however, defied him, saying:

"You who speak this way, we do not want to do as you say because this is already our *negeri* and we intend to put it to fire. Our intention is to kill its Raja and to imprison all the slaves and *rakyat*. We shall sell the women and children

---

[135]Ibid.

[136]Ibid., pp. 38–39.

[137]Ibid., p. 39. "hamba ra'yatnya pun sudah banyak luka dan mati sebelah-menyebelah."

and seize everything of value. We shall eat the buffalo and goats, because we have taken this *negeri* in war and have defeated all the inhabitants."[138]

Bagonjong was extremely angry to hear this speech and he attacked the Acehnese, who took fright and fled.[139] After they had gone, Bagonjong went in to Kampung Simugari, where he found that all the women had fled and had been taken to Kampung Si Antomas by Tuanku Raja Bongsu. In the narrative and dialogue which follows, this Hulu Raja is portrayed in a bad light, because he had fled into the jungle with the women and had left the Hilir Raja to defend the *kampung*. The Hilir Raja, who was Bagonjong's brother, Tuanku Sultan, had remained behind with the menfolk to resist the Acehnese.

Bagonjong addressed his brother:

"Oh my brother, concerning your Acehnese enemies, by the decree of God, may He be praised and exalted, I have fought them and defeated them and they have retreated to their boats. . . . Now I ask where has Raja Bongsu gone, since I see that none of his people are here?"[140]

Tuanku Sultan replied:

"If you are asking about Raja Bongsu, he has run into the jungle with his wife and children."[141]

Then,

Tuanku Bagonjong was silent for a while because of his anger at the desertion of the settlement.[142]

But, despite his anger over Raja Bongsu's cowardly behavior, Bagonjong did not attempt to exclude the Raja di Hulu. Bagonjong told his brother that it would be best if the Hulu Raja were recalled from the jungle since the enemy had fled. An envoy was duly sent into the jungle to find Raja Bongsu and inform him that the war was over. Raja Bongsu returned and, we are told, was once more "Established in the gov-

---

[138]Ibid. "Hai engkau yang berkata demikian, kata engkau itu tiadalah kami mahu karena negeri ini sudah dapat pada kami maksud kami henda kami bakar, rajanya henda' kami bunuh, hamba ra'yat kami tunggu perempuan dan anak-anak kami jual, harta benda akan rampasan kami, kerbau kambing makanan kami karena negeri ini sudah dapat perang oleh kami karena segala isi negeri ini sudah kalah oleh kami."

[139]Ibid.

[140]Ibid., p. 40. "Ya kakanda tentangan dari Aceh musuh kakanda, dengan takdir Allah subhanahu wa ta'ala sudahlah hamba perangi sudah kalah masing-masing membawa' dirinya pulang ka perahunya sekarang pun jangan kakanda terlalu gusar oleh itu Aceh. Sekarang hamba tanya ka mana pergi Raja Bongsu karena segala anak buahnya saya lihat tiada lagi di sini?"

[141]Ibid. "Maka Tuanku Sultan pun menyahut demikian buninya, 'Jikalau Tuanku Raja Bongsu adinda tanya dianya sudah lari masu' hutan belantara serta dengan anak isterinya.'"

[142]Ibid. "Maka seri paduka Tuanku Bagonjong pun diam sesa'at marahnya sebab maninggalkan kampung halamannya."

ernment of Simugari together with Tuanku Sultan."[143] Dual Rajaship, therefore, was confirmed, and the text emphasizes this by stating that "That was the situation with the two Raja."[144]

The Hilir chronicle thus continues to develop the premise that the kingdom was governed by two rulers. The credit for saving Barus from the Acehnese, however, is attributed entirely to the two Hilir brothers. The passage is reminiscent of Episode Two, where the Hulu Raja was made the object of ridicule for running away from Sultan Ibrahim. The impropriety of Raja Bongsu's retreat into the jungle is illustrated by the statement that Sultan Bagonjong was "silent for a while because of his anger." Bagonjong's brother, Marah Sutan, on the other hand, had remained behind with the people (*rakyat*) to fight off the Acehnese.

Despite such inappropriate and unkingly behavior on the part of Raja Bongsu, the Hilir family is shown as behaving honorably towards him. He was called back from his retreat and installed once more in the co-rulership of the kingdom. Hilir bravery and Hulu cowardice notwithstanding, the Hilir version continues to present dual rajaship as the norm.

After peace had been restored, Tuanku Bagonjong decided to leave and to find a place to make a *kampung* and a *negeri* of his own. He found an excellent place called Sawah Lagundi and settled there.[145] As was the case with Sultan Ibrahim's *kampung* in Episodes One and Two of the Hilir text, this is described in glowing terms and in the conventionally formulaic style used here, but not in the Hulu chronicle, to describe an ideal Malay settlement:

By the decree of God, may He be praised and exalted,the Tuanku established a *kota* there in Sawah Lagundi. Its moat stretched out all round it and bamboo stakes were planted all round. Then God, may He be praised and elevated, ordained that the negeri became more and more populous. Tuanku Bagonjong became famous in other countries. The Hulubelang were in agreement and the menteri were of one judgment (*satu hukum*). The people (*rakyat*) were many all round, and their Raja was exceptionally forceful. Such was the situation with Tuanku Bagonjong in Kampung Barus.[146]

After some time had passed, Tuanku Bagonjong asked his brother, Tuanku Sultan, to come to Kampung Simugari, with the aim of making an agreement (*hendak sepakat*).[147] Tuanku Sultan duly came with his wife, and together the two brothers

---

[143]Ibid., pp. 40–41. "Maka tetaplah dianya di kampung Simugari jadi keraja'an bedua dengan Tuanku Sultan."

[144]Ibid., p. 41. "Demikianlah halnya Raja kedua itu."

[145]Ibid.

[146]Ibid. "Maka dengan takdir Allah subhanahu wa ta'ala tuanku pun lalu memancang kota di sana di tempat Sawah Lagundi itu maka diparitnyalah rentang berkuliling aur pun ditanam berkuliling. Maka dengan takdir Allah subhanahu wa ta'ala negeri itu pun semakin lama semangkin ramai, Tuanku Bagonjong pun masyurlah khabarnya ka negeri asing-asing dubalangnya sekata, menterinya satu hukum, ra'yatnya banyak berkuliling rajanya gagah bukan kepalang. Demikianlah halnya Tuanku Bagonjong di kampung Barus."

[147]Ibid. "Maka lamalah antaranya Allah subhanahu wa ta'ala mentakdirkan Tuanku Bagonjong pun menyuruh memanggil kakandanya Tuanku Sultan ka kampung Simugari maksud henda' sepakat satu negeri."

create a united settlement (*sebuah kota*).[148] According to the chronicle, the population of Sawah Lagundi were joyful, ". . . because the Rajas were agreed—the younger and older brothers."[149] Once again, here, the Hilir text depicts an association between consensus (*pakat*) and pleasure (*suka*) which appears in a direct relationship to the creation of one, united, settlement (*sebuah kota*). As we saw in the previous episode, the association of these ideas in the text creates a paradigm or model of good government in which duality becomes coherent and acceptable. According to the text, after some time the Hulu Raja died. His subjects then moved downstream to the Hilir kampung which became very populous. At that time the dual government of the two Hilir brothers was confirmed,

> By the decree of God, may He be praised and exalted, the younger and older brothers were confirmed in the government of Barus.[150]

The establishment, here, by the two Hilir brothers of a further united and dual government in Sawah Lagundi (now called Barus) represents yet another example of the way in which dual government might successfully be established.

In this episode of the chronicle, therefore, a pattern of authority is presented in which duality in government is conventionalized. Examples of dual arrangements are offered which add to the feasibility of a world in which two rulers may coexist as one. Bagonjong leaves Barus under the dual authority of his brother and the Hulu Raja. He travels to Limbong, where he establishes authority under two local rulers and where he reminds them of the dual situation existing in Barus. He then returns to Barus, where he defeats the Acehnese aggressors and, despite an opportunity to take control of the *negeri*, he reestablishes dual authority. When he leaves and creates another settlement he does not rule alone; rather, he calls his brother and they establish *yet another dual situation*, using the pattern of consensus which is adopted in other parts of the text. Nothing of note happens, therefore, in Episode Five of the Hilir text which departs from the convention of dual government established in Episode Four. The text presents a series of vignettes which illustrate the appropriateness of dual government. In the narrative the obvious interests of the Hilir family are ignored in favor of the perpetuation of duality. It is with this theoretical concern that Episode Five of the Hilir chronicle is principally occupied.

*   *   *

In the Hulu version of Episode Five, we saw that, while a challenge to Hulu supremacy was acknowledged briefly to exist in the person of Sultan Bagonjong, the episode concludes with a very firm statement of the single Raja premise.

The differences of perspective which emerge from comparing these two chronicles reveal more than a competitive approach to the divergent political interests of

---

[148]Ibid. "Maka dengan takdir Allah subhanahu wa ta'ala kiranya Tuanku Sultan pun datang ka kampung Barus dengan anak bininya serta dengan segala hamba ra'yatnya di sanalah dianya sebuah kota."

[149]Ibid. "Maka suka ramailah sekalian hamba ra'yatnya karena raja sudah sepakat adik berkakak."

[150]Ibid. "Dengan takdir Allah subhanahu wa ta'ala tetaplah tuanku adik beradik jadi keraja'an di dalam kampung Barus itu."

the Barus royal families. Within the constraints of the Bagonjong story, which forms the thread linking the two texts, each chronicle works to present a coherent philosophy of its own. In so doing, both make creative and essentially local use of language and symbols which are conventionally associated with the Malay *kerajaan* model.

In perpetuating its concern with twos and illustrating examples of dual government, the Hilir text constructs a world in which it is possible for a conventionally impossible situation to exist—for two kings to rule as one. Within this world view emphasis is given to consensus and to the making and keeping of agreements which make duality possible. Simultaneously the conventional language of Malay court literature is employed, in this as in other episodes, to convey the aura and prestige of the Hilir princes. The Hilir presentation of political authority, which is framed here in a way which departs radically from traditional Malay ideas on government, is nonetheless expressed and acted out in the ceremonial terms which are conventionally used in Malay texts to depict relations between ruler and subject.

The message in this episode of the Hulu text is by no means so unconventional in Malay terms as that in the Hilir chronicle, but it too addresses itself to the issue of royal authority. In so doing, the chronicle illustrates the way in which the language and symbols of Malay kingship are used, once again, for a local purpose and in a local fashion. Whereas, in the Hilir text, ritual and ceremonial are depicted as part of the ruler's role, in the Hulu chronicle they are presented as appendages of political power. In the Hulu chronicle, these aspects of the *kerajaan* system are not incorporated in the text's presentation of the life of the kingdom. The Hulu text, we have seen, puts emphasis not on the ceremonial aspects of royal authority and the feelings of group loyalty that these can engender; rather, ceremony is used in this text as a means of signifying power and control, which is the key to political authority.

7

CRISIS AND DENOUEMENT:
EPISODES SIX AND SEVEN

In Episode Six the divergent approaches to political authority which are embodied in the two chronicles are even more apparent. As the narrative moves towards the crisis in relations between the royal families, which takes place in Episode Seven, the differences in approach and bias between the two texts are intensified and the narrative pace of the story also appears to quicken. Each text presents a genealogical account which conforms to its own viewpoint on the question of dual versus single rule, and, in so doing, both develop their different approaches to the issue of authority itself. Two distinct "casts of mind" become more apparent, each of which gives ideological context to the assertions made in the texts concerning the manner in which royal authority was held in Barus.

ASAL

The reign of Sultan Bongsu is a significant one in the Hulu chronicle. In Episode Five it served to emphasize the weight of Hulu authority, and the exclusive rights of the Hulu family to royal status in Barus. At the end of Episode Five we saw that the Hilir family was confined to the inferior position of *Bendahara* and the subservience of these officials is made plain in the text. In Episode Six the Hulu chronicle defines the position of the *Bendahara*, after Sultan Bongsu's death and again presents the Hulu case both in narrative sequence and by means of lists.

The Episode commences in narrative form and states that, when Tuanku Maharaja Bongsu died he left a son called Raja Kecil, who became Raja. But Raja Kecil was not yet of an age to hold office, so the Hilir *Bendahara*, Marah Sutan, was made regent and held the position of Raja as a temporary ruler or viceroy (*pemangku*) in place of Raja Kecil.[1] This marks the beginning of a prolonged period in which, according to the Hulu chronicle, a Hilir *Bendahara* acted as regent for the young princes of the Hulu house. As on other occasions, when this text acknowledges an involvement in government by the Hilir family, the chronicle depicts a marriage relationship between the two houses. Marah Sutan had married Raja Kecil's sister, and they had a son whose name was Sutan Marah Sihat.[2] Marriage relations between the

---

[1] *Asal*, pp. 28(31)–29(30). "Adapun Tuanku Maharaja Bongsu tatkala Tuanku Bergonjong /di Padang/ itu Maharaja Bongsu mati di Barus tinggal anaknya yang menjadi raja bernama Raja Kecil tetapi itu Raja Kecil balun sampai umur akan boleh memegang perkerja'an raja dari itu maka diambilnya Marah Sutan akan wakilnya memegang pekerja'an raja jadi pemangku dari Raja Kecil."

[2] Ibid., p. 29(30).

two families are, we have seen, frequently mentioned in the Hulu text, but only rarely in the Hilir chronicle.

When Raja Kecil came of age, the office of Raja is said to have returned to him and Marah Sutan held the office of *Bendahara*.[3] But after the Bendahara's death the chronicle states that his son, Marah Sihat, slandered (*difitnahkan*) Raja Kecil, by telling Daulat that Raja Kecil was ignorant of religion and had altered the regulations which had been fixed in the past. The text mentions no grounds for this accusation and Daulat is simply said to have murdered Raja Kecil.[4] The spare style of the narrative allows for no exploration of this incident, or for any indication of the repercussions caused in Barus by the ruler's death. It is simply stated that Raja Kecil's son, Sultan Marah Tulang, was too young to rule and so Marah Sihat acted as his regent.[5]

This series of events sounds suspiciously like a coup by the Hilir house, but that is not how it is portrayed. Marah Sihat is subsequently shown to be a loyal servant of the Hulu house and, despite holding the position of regent and *Bendahara*, Neither he nor any other member of the Hilir family challenges the right of the Hulu line to the position of Raja.

According to the chronicle, once Marah Tulang was old enough, the position of Raja became his.[6] The succession passed in time to his son, Sultan Menawar Syah, and to his grandson, Sultan Marah Pangkat.[7] During the period covered by these three reigns Sultan Marah Sihat, the Hilir Bendahara, still held the position of *pemangku* Raja.[8] Although this appears to be very like an example of dual government in the Hulu text, it is presented as an exceptional situation. Marah Sihat's continued involvement in government, according to the chronicle, was because of his age and experience in the position, and also because he had an aunt on Tuanku Sutan Marah Tulang's side.[9] Moreover, the text states, he had become *wakil* and had held the position of ruler jointly in the time of Sultan Marah Tulang and the position had not been changed since then.

The text, therefore, explains the circumstances which led to Sultan Marah Sihat's continued role in government, and the variety of reasons which are presented to jus-

---

[3]Ibid. "Adapun tatkala Raja Kecil suda gadang maka kembalilah pekerja'an raja kepadanya memegang jabatan. Tuanku Bendahara bergelar Marah Sutan jadi tuha dalam negeri pun boleh juga kuasa sedikit dari perkara memutuskan bicara."

[4]Ibid. "Lamalah pula antaranya maka itu Raja Kecil mati dibunuh Daulat di Kubu Penagin karena difitnahkan Sutan Marah Sihat kepada Daulat katanya itu Raja Kecil sangat jahil dan serta suda mungkir atas segala perjanjian tentangannya daripada aturan yang telah suda ditentukan itu sekarang suda diubahinya, itu sebab maka Daulat bunuh Raja Kecil."

[5]Ibid. "Tatkala suda mati Raja Kecil tinggal anaknya jadi raja bernama Sutan Marah Tulang tetapi sebab itu Sutan Marah Tulang lagi kecil maka diambil wakil itu Sutan Marah Sihat akan pemangkunya kembali bergelar Tuanku Bendahara. Tatkala Sutan Marah Tulang suda gadang kembali itu pekerja'an kepada Sutan Marah Tulang."

[6]Ibid.

[7]Ibid., p. 30.

[8]Ibid.

[9]Ibid., pp.29(30)–30(29). "Setelah mati Sutan Marah Tulang Sutan Menawar Syah menjadi raja dan beranak pula Sutan Menawar Syah bernama Sutan Marah Pangkat menjadi raja tetapi Sutan Marah Sihat dia balun mati dan dia ada tinggal juga ia memegang pekerja'an raja karena dia suda tuha labih banyak tahu dari pekerja'an dan lagi dia punya ma' ada dari sebelah Tuanku Sutan Marah Tulang juga, itu sebab dia orang sangka dan lagi dia pun suda jadi wakil juga sama-sama memegang perkerja'an tatkala dari Sutan Marah Tulang itu sebab orang balun berobah pekerja'annya."

tify the situation may suggest that it was a very unusual one. Special circumstances are responsible for the arrangement, and the situation does not apply to other members of his family. This is demonstrated in the text by Marah Sihat's own denial that he or any of his family had rights to the position of Raja.

As his death approached, Marah Sihat explained the situation in the kingdom to the Dutch. He entrusted the Company with what was, in effect, his last will and testament (*amanat*). It was essential, he said, that, on his death, the Hulu prince, Marah Pangkat, who was his son-in-law, should become the sole ruler (*dia sendiri yang menjadi raja*). This was because he was in possession of the *pusaka* to become Raja. His own position, Marah Sihat attested, had been merely that of *pemangku*, as Sultan Marah Tulang was still young when his father had died. He made this statement, he declared, in order that his own son would not dispute the succession after his death.[10]

The chronicle thus depicts the Hilir Bendahara renouncing any claim to royal authority for himself and his son. The Hulu prince alone, he declares, is the one to possess the *pusaka* to become Raja.

Having thus given his story to the Company, Sutan Marah Sihat died. Sutan Marah Pangkat duly became Raja on his own (*menjadi raja sendiri*) and, according to the chronicle, he received the *pusaka* of his ancestors and was raised to become Raja with many honors, not specifically described in the text.[11]

The Hilir family are thus excluded from office, and the text states that Marah Sihat's son, Sutan Larangan, was disappointed because his father had not granted him any position of authority. As a result he left Barus and moved to Sorkam, where he called himself Tuanku Bendahara. But he is said to have been Tuanku Bendahara only in name (*cuma nama saja*), since he did not govern there (*tidak memerintah*).[12]

---

[10]Ibid., p. 29. "Adapun Sutan Marah Sihat itu ada beranak laki-laki dan perempuan, yang laki-laki bernama Sutan Larangan yang perempuan bernama Putri Sari Gemalah. Adapun Putri Sari Gemalah itu dikawinkan dangan Sutan Marah Pangkat. Adapun Sutan Marah Sihat pada satu hari dia bicara kasi tahu kepada Kompeni Olanda katanya, 'Sekarang aku kasi tahu kepada tuan yang kami punya sahabat yang akan menolong membari selamat atas anak cucu kami dari awal sampai pada hari kemudian. Adapun sekarang saya suda tuha barangkali bareso' lusa aku mati melainkan tuan tolong kepada menantuku itu bergelar Sutan Marah Pangkat melainkan dia sendiri yang menjadi raja jikalau aku suda mati sebab dia punya itu pusaka jadi raja. Ada pun saya cuma jadi pemangku sahaja dahulu tatkala dahulu sebab Sultan Merah Tulang lagi kecil tatkala bapanya mati dan sudah berapa kali raja berganti aku juga jadi pemangkunya karena aku dia punya nenek dan bapa lagi sudah tahu sekarang pun sebab aku kasi tahu begitu kerena anakku ada laki laki supaya jangan nanti di belakangku sudah mati itu anak berselisih supaya tuan-tuan tal.u begitu kata Sultan Marsifat kepada kompeni tatkala itu.'"

[11]Ibid. p.31(28). "Alkisah adapun Sutan Marah Sihat tatkala dia suda membari amanat kepada Kompeni suda itu maka Sutan Marah Sihat mati. Adapun tatkala Sutan Marah Sihat suda mati maka mudi' Kompeni menerangkan kepada sekalian mereka itu bahawa Sutan Marah Pangkat sekarang menjadi raja sendirinya menarima pusaka nenek moyangnya dan serta diangkatnya pula pada masa itu dangan segala hormat Sutan Marah Pangkat menjadi raja."

[12]Ibid. "Adapun anak Sutan Marah Sihat yang bernama Sutan Larangan sebab bapa'nya tidak kasi masu' dianya di dalam itu pekerja'an lantas kasi kembali saja kepada Sutan Marah Pangkat dari sebab maka dia berkecil hati. Dalam pada itu maka dia berjalan dari Barus pergi ka Sorkam berdagang membawa' dirinya sampai dia di sana dia bikin dia punya gelar Tuanku Bendahara dangan angkatan sendirinya saja. Akan tetapi cuma nama saja dia Tuanku Bendahara dan dia tidak memerintah di sana sampai mati itu Sutan Larangan di Sorkam dibunuh anak Daulat yang bergelar Yang Dipertuan."

This sentence reveals much about the Hulu approach towards political authority and the extent to which this text is concerned with a conception of Rajaship which is different, not only from that of the Hilir chronicle, but from that of other court-based Malay texts. The importance of titles and names (*nama*) in Malay culture has long been realized, and it has recently been suggested that the quest to achieve and enhance *nama* was a dynamic force in traditional Malay society in which men were "characterised by their rank or title".[13] According to this model of the Malay *kerajaan*, *nama* was all important, and the ruler's most vital role was the "stewardship" of men's public selves, of their *nama*, which was acted out on the stage of ceremony, dress, and proper behavior.[14] In this context, the statement that Larangan's *nama* was empty, because he did not govern effectively, implies a set of political values which put less store on the ceremonial role of the ruler and more on "effective political power."

We have already seen on numerous occasions that the words *perintah* and *kuasa*, which imply power and control, are central to the political thinking of this chronicle. Later in this episode, the text details some of the areas over which, in the Hulu view, control was important.

In the narrative quoted above, the Hilir Bendahara was a mouthpiece for a firm statement of Hulu supremacy. Marah Sihat's speech to the Dutch, which is a long one by the standards of the chronicle, makes the involvement in government of a member of the Hilir family look exceptional. It appears, therefore, to be possible in the text for prominent members of the Hilir family, such as Sultan Bagonjong and Marah Sihat, to be acknowledged, providing that their presence in government is explained in terms of exceptional circumstances, such as Bagonjong's strength, Marah Sihat's loyalty to the Hulu family, or the inexperience of junior members of the Hulu house. Such explanations ensure that the premise of single rule, by the Hulu family remains unchallenged.

The Hulu account now changes in style from continuous narrative to a series of declaratory statements concerning the reigns of the next three Hulu Rajas. The presence of such stylistic breaks has already been noticed in both chronicles. They function as a means of emphasizing a significant event or statement. In the next pages of this episode, a list-like statement of reigns and what they achieved appears to perform just such an emphatic role. It also demonstrates the terms in which successful reigns are described in the Hulu chronicle, thereby adding dimension to the Hulu perception of political authority.

An account is first given of the reign of Sutan Marah Pangkat. This and the reign of his son and successor, Raja Adil, are described entirely in terms of the regulations which were instituted, agreements made, and definitions given concerning *bangsa* and land boundaries. First of all, the text states, Sutan Marah Pangkat instituted regulations (*aturan*) for the creation of wet rice lands (*sawah*). He distributed land to each *penghulu* and to all the people of good birth (*anak ba'ik-ba'ik*).[15]

---

[13]Milner, *Kerajaan*, p. 100. See also Bastin,"Problems of Personality," *passim*. On public selves Milner cites R. Sennet, *The Fall of Public Man* (Cambridge: Cambridge University Press, 1977).

[14]Milner, *Kerajaan*, p. 101.

[15]Asal, p. 32(27). "Alkisah maka tersebutlah perkata'an kepada Sutan Marah Pangkat tatkala suda menjadi raja dangan barapa lamanya pada masa itu dia bari aturan dalam negeri membikin sawah kepada setiap-tiap penghulu dibarinya tanah dan kepada segala anak ba'ik-ba'ik juga. Pada masa itu orang membikin rimbo jadi sawah kiri kanan babatang air. Segala mereka itu yang mengarjakan sawah ada yang dapat dari penghulu ada yang dapat dari anak ba'ik-

In that period the people created sawah out of the jungle (*rimbo*) on the left and right banks of the river. Everybody worked on that sawah which was aquired from the *penghulu* and from the *anak ba'ik-ba'ik* and the Raja.[16]

The *adat* (custom) concerning land inheritance is then mentioned and, in particular, the text states that only land which was received from the Raja could be treated as *pusaka* and inherited by future generations. Land which was obtained from the *penghulu* and *anak baik-baik* must return to the owner at the death of the person who worked it.[17] Only land which was received from the Raja could become *pusaka* in perpetuity.[18]

Control over land in the *negeri* was, therefore, firmly in the hands of the Raja, who distributed it to the *anak baik-baik* and to the *penghulu*, and who controlled the extent to which it might be inherited. Such an emphasis on the control of land is, we have observed, unusual in traditional Malay society, where the loyalty of population groups was generally considered to be more important. The Hulu chronicle continues to emphasize land as a concern in the list which follows of the areas which constituted the geographical perimeter of the kingdom. The list begins with the statement that "The area of land which is subject (*ta'lu'* or *takluk*) to *negeri* Barus is as follows. . . ."[19] Not all of the names in this part of the text are legible but they include areas such as Singkel and Sorkam which are said to be ". . . inside the area of Barus's command" (*masuk ke dalam perintah Barus*).[20]

Perintah, to command or govern, is also used in relation to the various population groups which came within the government of Barus (*di dalam perintah Barus*).[21] They were "one people" (*satulah bangsa*).[22]

The people who live here are Malays, Acehnese, Rawa, Korincis, Bataks from Mandailing and Angkola, Bugis, Javanese, and people from Timur. All of these people have mixed together (*suda bercampur*) as have their customs and clothing. There are also Hindus, Keling and people from Nias.[23]

---

ba'ik ada pula dari raja. Tetapi 'adatnya jikalau siapa dapat tanah dari penghulu atau dari anak ba'ik-ba'ik mengarjakan boleh dipakai selama umur hidupnya saja dan tidak boleh turun kepada anak yang mengarjakan itu melainkan jikalau suda mati yang mengarjakan itu tanah kembali kepada yang punya tetapi jikalau dapat daripada raja itu boleh jadi pusaka selama-lamanya turun-temurun kepada nan mengarjakannya ba'ik apa juga yang dibari raja demikian juga atau adat atau kebesaran demikian juga."

[16]Ibid.

[17]Ibid.

[18]Ibid.

[19]Ibid. "Adapun lingkaran tanah yang ta'lu' kepada negeri Barus."

[20]Ibid.

[21]Ibid.

[22]Ibid.

[23]Ibid. "Adapun di dalam perintah Barus itu satulah bangsa orang ada tinggal Melayu, Aceh, Rawa, Korinci, Batak Mandahailing, Angkola, Bugis, Jawa, Orang Timur itu orang semuhanya suda bercampur bagitu juga 'adatnya dan pakaian, ada juga Hindu, Keling dan Nias."

No mention is made here of the Bataks from the immediate hinterland of Barus, such as the Dairi, Toba, Pasaribu and Silindung Bataks. Like the list of land boundaries cited above, what is offered here appears to be a coastal definition of Barus. The statement that the population of Barus, though diverse, was nevertheless one people (*satu bangsa*) is repeated elsewhere in this text, as is the assertion that Barus *adat* was a blend from different sources.

Having defined the borders of Barus and listed the peoples contained within these borders, the chronicle also lists the names of all the settlements which were within the borders of Barus (*adapun nama-nama tanah di Barus*).[24] This list includes some forty place-names in Sorkam, Korlang, and Tapus, as well as in Barus itself. Not all of these are legible. The border of Tapus, between Barus and Singkel, is said to stretch inland only to the place where the camphor trees begin (*sehingganya ada tumbuh kayu kapur*).[25]

Dates are the next item listed. The dates for Sutan Marah Pangkat's reign (AD 1756–1798) are given, as well as those of his son, Sutan Baginda, whose title, we are told, was Raja Adil, and who became Raja in the year of his father's death. According to the text, the Dutch Company first came to Barus in 1644 and left in 1780.[26]

This description of Sutan Marah Pangkat's reign is concerned, then, with a definition of Barus. The borders of the kingdom are given, and the lands and people within it are listed. A sense of order is apparent in this part of the chronicle, as the components of Barus are classified and brought under control. Not only are people and places controlled in this way, but the presence of dates here, as in other parts of this text, also indicates concern with fixing events and thereby ordering the past.

The text turns to what is considered to be outside the borders of the kingdom, and again people and places are defined.

During Raja Adil's reign, agreements with the Bataks were made and consolidated.

> Concerning Sutan Baginda, who was entitled Raja Adil. When he became Raja he made agreements with the Bataks. These were in accordance with previous agreements from the very beginnings of *negeri* Barus which are mentioned in the *adat* which applies today.[27]

These agreements concern the assistance which should be given in times of trouble. Although the text mentions that the assistance should be both given and received (*tolong-menolong*),[28] the actual provisions mentioned here stress the duties of the Bataks and their subservience to the Raja of Barus, rather than the mutual responsibilities of both parties. The Bataks were expected to comply with the views of Raja Barus (*menurut segala pikiran Raja Barus*) and to offer marks of their respect (*tanda hormat*) to him. These differed according to the size of the Batak state. Large ones

---

[24]Ibid., p. 33(26).

[25]Ibid.

[26]Ibid. These dates are given according to the Muslim calendar. In sequence they are 1170 H, 1213 H, 1054 H and 1194 H.

[27]Ibid. "Adapun Sutan Baginda bergelar Raja 'Adil suda menjadi raja tatkala itu ada membikin perjanjian dangan orang Batak dan menurut perjanjian yang dahulu juga tatkala dari awal negeri Barus bagaimana ada tersebut di dalam 'adat yang di pegang sampai sekarang."

[28]Ibid.

were expected to send a horse, buffalo, or cow each year. Annual tribute was not expected from smaller states, but, according to the chronicle, if the Raja of Barus was uneasy, then the Batak Rajas must bring a buffalo in tribute (*persembahan kerbau*).[29] The states which were expected to bring annual tribute were Silindung, Limbung, Mentigi, Balige, and Bakara. According to the chronicle, Batak states which renounced these treaties or fell short in their obligations (*yang mungkir*) would be attacked (*maka diperang negerinya*), and other Batak states would be called upon to help.[30]

This statement of relations between Barus and the Batak states on her borders is very different in character from similar agreements mentioned in the Hilir text, which emphasizes mutuality and states not only that the Bataks would help the Malays to fight off their enemies, but that the Malays would help the Bataks. In that text, agreements with the Bataks are described in terms of consent and pleasure, *pakat* and *suka*, and there is no mention of making war on groups who did not submit. Indeed the language of submission and control is peculiar to the Hulu text and is consistent, as we have seen, with the command-oriented pattern of political thinking which it displays.

The description of treaties between Barus and the surrounding Batak states concludes the Hulu chronicle's account of Raja Adil's reign. Adil died in AD 1825[31] and was succeeded by his son, Sutan Sailan, who features in Episode Seven.

* * *

In Episode Six of the Hulu text, the premise of Hulu authority is maintained despite the presence of a prestigious Hilir figure, Sultan Marah Sihat. Statements made in this episode also reinforce the power-oriented character of Hulu ideas about government. This is true of the organizational details listed at the end of the episode as well as in the narrative itself. The concern demonstrated in this episode with land borders, population, chronology, and neighbors, indicates the important areas of control in this world view. The lists of arrangements made during the three Hulu reigns provides a sketch of the kingdom which is uncomplicated and tightly ordered. The style of presentation used is simple and straightforward and, as in previous episodes, it differs from the more subtle and involved explanations of the Hilir text.

SEJARAH

In the Hulu version of Episode Six, we have found that the first part consisted of a narrative account of genealogical information, and the second contained a list of regulations presented in declarative style. In the Hilir account of this episode, a similar break in style and content exists. Up until the point where the Hilir prince, Sultan Larangan, leaves for Sorkam, the text is principally concerned with an account of Hilir genealogy in Barus and the organization of government there. After Larangan's

---

[29]Ibid. "Adapun yang di dalam perjanjian itu, bermula tidak boleh menayai-nayai kalau kesukaran tolong-menolong dan lagi manurut segala pikiran Raja Barus itu sekalian Batak di atas nan keba'ikan dan serta membari tanda hormat Batak kepada raja-raja Barus bagaimana yang suda ditentukan, di atas negeri yang besar kuda atau kerbau atau jawi setiap tahun di atasnya negeri yang kecil tidak setiap tahun."

[30]Ibid., p. 34(25).

[31]Ibid. Hijrah 1241.

departure, the narrative concentrates on his position in Sorkam and the many agreements which he and his family made with the Bataks there. While this latter part of the Hilir version of Episode Six is not list-like, and continues in narrative form, it is highly repetitive and may have an emphatic function in the text similar to that of the regulations detailed in the latter part of the Hulu account. The chronicle acknowledges the exile of Sultan Larangan mentioned in the Hulu account, and the difficulties experienced by the Hilir family during this period of Barus's past lead in the text to an emphasis on their basis of support in Sorkam and on the nature and potency of Hilir authority among these people.

The first part of the episode consists of a genealogical account, which differs from that presented in the *Asal* and which emphasizes the establishment and maintenance of dual authority in Barus. The chronicle presents a complex account of Hilir genealogy and of relations between the families during this period. In the *Asal*, the period leading up to Sultan Larangan's exile was portrayed as one in which the Hilir *Bendahara* acted as regent for under-age Hulu Rajas. Here, in the Hilir chronicle, a series of dual governments are depicted.

Episode Five in the *Sejarah* chronicle concluded with the two Hilir brothers, Marah Sutan and Sultan Bagonjong, established in a united settlement at Sawah Lagundi. The next event mentioned in the text is the death of the Hulu Raja, Raja Bongsu, who was murdered by an unnamed person. According to the chronicle, Bongsu's son, Marah Pangkat, moved to join the Hilir *kampung*.[32] There is, in this part of the text's description, a sense of additional unease in relations between the two families. The Hilir text also uses the word *perintah* to indicate government or command in this passage. Marah Pangkat is said to have "followed the orders of Tuanku Bagonjong because he lived in his *kampung*."[33] A marriage relationship between the families is described for the first time in the *Sejarah*, when it is said that Marah Pangkat married (*semando*) Puteri Udam, the daughter of Bagonjong's brother, Marah Sutan. Marah Sutan himself died shortly afterwards. According to the text, this left Sultan Bagonjong in command (*pegang perintah*) of *kampung* Barus, where he ruled alone for a long time, holding the position of Tuanku Raja Barus.[34] Then he was called upon by the VOC (*kompeni*) in Padang to help them fight a war in which they were engaged. Bagonjong, therefore, traveled to Padang and left his brother's son-in-law, Marah Pangkat, acting as his representative (*wakil*) in Barus. Bagonjong is said to have been anxious to return quickly to Barus because he lacked confidence in the situation he had left behind.[35] However he failed to return and take over the throne because he died on his way back from Padang. His body, we are told, was buried in Barus with all the ceremony befitting a ruler. The burial ceremonies, which are

---

[32] *Sejarah*, p. 41.

[33] Ibid. "Alkisah maka tersebutlah perkata'an Tuanku Raja Bongsu maninggalkan anak seorang laki-laki bergelar Marah Pangkat berpindah lalu ka kampung Barus menurut perintah Tuanku Bagonjong karena tinggal di kampung halamannya demikianlah halnya tatkala itu."

[34] Ibid., p. 42. "Allah subhanahu wa ta'ala mentakdirkan Tuanku Sultan pun berpulang ka rahmat Allah maka tinggallah anaknya laki-laki perempuan dan saudaranya Tuanku Sultan Marah Laut tinggal pegang perintah di dalam kampung Barus dan beberapa lamanya seri paduka Tuanku Bagonjong memegang keraja'an dalam negeri Barus seorang-seorangnya jadi Tuanku Raja Barus."

[35] Ibid., p.43. "Maka dengan takdir Allah subhanahu wa ta'ala tuanku pun tercinta henda pulang ka negeri Barus sebab tida' ada yang tempat kepercayaannya ditinggalkannya di Barus maka seri paduka tuanku pun meminta memohon pulang ka negeri Barus kepada kompeni."

described in detail, resemble those used when Ibrahim's head was buried. After Bagonjong had been buried, Tuanku Marah Pangkat succeeded his father-in-law as Raja.[36] His son, Baginda Sultan, then succeeded him and afterwards his grandson, Tuanku Panjang Jirat. It sounds here as if the Hulu family took over Barus at this point, but they were not the sole rulers. It is then related that, in addition to his daughter Puteri Udam, Tuanku Sultan had two sons, one of whom was called Tuanku Sultan Perhimpunan and the other Tuanku Raja Kecil. Tuanku Sultan Perhimpunan is said to have assumed government in *kampung* Barus together with Baginda Sultan [the Hulu Raja].[37]

What is depicted here is a further instance of dual government. Hilir leadership passed from Tuanku Bagonjong to the eldest of his nephews, who ruled in Barus together with the Hulu prince, Baginda Sultan. But for once the Hilir text does not depict duality as producing pleasure and harmony.

> The populace were divided during this period; some put themselves under the authority of Tuanku Sultan Perhimpunan and others entered Baginda Sultan's sphere of authority.[38]

Difficulties continue in the next generation. When Sultan Perhimpunan died, the text records that the inhabitants of the *negeri* and all the Rajas of Pasaribu wanted to appoint his son, Sultan Larangan, in his place, but the Hulu Raja would not allow it. He declared that

> "Sultan Larangan may not assume government here as long as I am alive. The reason for this is that I am now Raja in this *negeri*. If he is obstinate towards me then this *negeri* will be split. A half will be his and a half will be mine."[39]

In the face of this determination to rule alone Sultan Larangan decided to leave Barus. He was dispirited, the text says, because he had few followers (*anak buah* and *hulubalang*). His aim was to become Raja in Sorkam (*hendak jadi Raja di dalam negeri Sorkam*).[40] Before describing Sultan Larangan's fate in Sorkam, the chronicle shifts

---

[36]Ibid., p. 45. "Syahadan maka tersebutlah perkata'an Tuanku Marah Pangkat maka tatkala dianya jadi keraja'an di kampung Barus karena mertuanya raja di dalam negeri itu sudah mati maka dianyalah jadi raja di sana." It is not explained in the text why it was Marah Pangkat who acted as Sultan Bagonjong's *wakil* and not one of his brothers-in-law. However, Marah Pangkat's position as a *semando*, or in-marrying, husband, might help to justify his role and balance the authority of the Hulu family in this episode of the *Sejarah*. On *semando* marriage see p. 94, n. 34 above.

[37]Ibid. "Alkisah maka tersebutlah perkata'an anak cucu Tuanku Sultan. Adapun seri paduka tuanku maharaja Tuanku Sultan beranak dua orang laki-laki seorang bergelar tuanku Sultan Perhimpunan yang kedua tuanku Raja Kecil. Adapun yang bergelar Tuanku Sultan Perhimpunan tatkala hayatnya ada dianya jadi keraja'an di dalam kampung Barus berdua dengan Baginda Sutan. Maka seketika itu ra'yat pun pecahlah di dalam negeri itu ada yang masuk dalam perintah Tuanku Sultan Perhimpunan ada yang masuk dalam perintah Tuanku Sutan Baginda. Demikianlah halnya tatkala itu."

[38]Ibid.

[39]Ibid. "Tida' boleh Sultan Larangan jadi keraja'an di dalam negeri selama ada hidup hamba karena hamba sekarang raja di dalam negeri ini dianya keras daripada hamba melainkan kita belah dua negeri ini separuh pulang kepadanya separuh pulang kepada hamba."

[40]Ibid.

briefly to describe the situation of the rest of the Hilir family in Barus. Larangan's uncle, Raja Kecil, stayed on to rule in Larangan's place (*jadi kerajaan menghukum segala hamba rakyatnya*).[41] The chronicle offers no explanation as to why Raja Kecil should succeed in ruling where Larangan failed. On Kecil's death his son, Sultan Emas, attempted to succeed him, but he was opposed in this by the Raja di Hulu. Sultan Emas, the text states, was forced to live sadly (*dengan duka percintaan*) in his kampung with his two *penghulu*.[42]

Both chronicles describe some form of united settlement and a special relationship between Marah Sutan and the son and successor of Raja Bongsu. Both also indicate that Sultan Larangan was excluded from a position of royal authority in Barus. There are, however, numerous discrepancies between the two accounts in this episode. Most obviously, names are confused and, whereas in other episodes there is general agreement concerning who followed whom in the two genealogies, here the succession of rulers in the two texts is quite different. The Hulu rulers, Kecil, Marah Tulang, and Menawar Syah, are not mentioned in the *Sejarah*, and in the *Asal* Sultan Perhimpunan and Raja Kecil do not appear. The Hulu chronicle explains the relationship between the two houses during this period in terms of the regentships of Marah Sutan and Marah Sihat. According to this view, kingship passed through the Hulu line and the Hilir family held a secondary position.

It is difficult to keep track of events in this episode of the *Sejarah*. In a text which employs frequent causal statements, there is little sense in this episode of how and why events follow each other. This is true, for instance, of Raja Bongsu's unexplained murder, the sudden reappearance of a strand of the Hilir family after the text has announced that all the Rajas in the negeri were dead, and Raja Kecil's ability to rule when his nephew, Larangan, had been opposed by the Raja di Hulu. These events and characters appear in the text without explanation, and they jar, to some extent, with the style of the chronicle which usually takes pains to explain the internal logic of the events it describes.

Both chronicles, in fact, present what read as particularly contrived versions of genealogy and royal succession in this episode. Potentially dual situations are presented in the *Asal* as regentships by Hilir princes, and a Hilir *Bendahara* is even portrayed explaining the situation in terms of Hulu supremacy.

What follows in the *Sejarah* chronicle concerns Sultan Larangan and his family in Sorkam. The chronicle acknowledges Larangan's exile and also the Hulu Raja's denial of the royal status of the remaining members of the family in Barus. In the pages which follow, the Hilir family is presented as consolidating its position in Sorkam, prior to an attempt to recover royal authority in Barus which takes place in Episode Seven of the text. The chronicle's account here of the Hilir family responding to adversity reveals much about the Hilir perception of political authority. Faced with a denial of their existence as rulers, the Hilir princes and their relations affirm their royal authority in a particularly Hilir fashion. They act as rulers by seeking to engender group loyalty.

During this period of adversity for the Hilir family, Sultan Ibrahim's descendants were pushed back to the group from which they appear to have derived their most persistent support. In Sorkam, Larangan and his family reaffirmed their bonds with the Bataks of Pasaribu and the surrounding hills. Agreements and oaths of loyalty

---

[41]Ibid., p. 46.

[42]Ibid.

were renewed and put to the test. A base of support was re-established which applied both to the Sorkam and Barus branches of the family.

Sultan Larangan is said to have left Barus sadly with his family and all his possessions. In Sorkam he joined the Raja Muda of Kampung Sebarang to whom he was related. Larangan's first act was to send envoys inland to inform the Batak Rajas of Pasaribu and Nai Pos Pos as to what had happened.[43] Meanwhile, Larangan made an agreement (*berpakat*) with the Raja Muda and all the elders of Kampung Sebarang that he should be appointed as ruler there (*jadi keraja'an*), and should establish his own *negeri*. He was given the title Tuanku Bendaharo.[44] When all the Batak Rajas arrived, therefore, a feast (*perjamuan*) was held. Then the Bataks and the people of the settlement raised Larangan to become their ruler. Everybody was extremely happy (*bersuka-sukaan*), and further festivities lasted for three months. When these were completed, Sultan Larangan made an agreement with the Bataks. According to the *adat* of the time, they would be given ammunition. And, it was declared, if the Bataks became involved in a disagreement, then help would be reciprocated.[45] This agreement, like others in the *Sejarah*, was sealed with a proverb: "If a white fowl flies downstream then it is white; if a white fowl flies towards the Bataks then it is also white."[46] The proverb, which implies the mutual nature of the undertakings made, appears to be a version of Malay legal expressions which employ a white fowl metaphor.[47] It was also promised that the agreement would not be broken by either side (*tiada jadi rusak-merusakkan*).

This agreement and its wording echo other agreements which occur throughout the *Sejarah*, resembling, in particular, the one made between Sultan Ibrahim and the Raja-Raja Pasaribu when Barus was founded. There it was promised that the *anak Melayu* would oppose seaborne enemies, and the *anak Batak* would resist those from the interior. Mutual protection was assured (*musoh sama dilawan*), and the armaments and wherewithal which would be necessary for a battle were mentioned. Larangan's new agreement with the Pasaribu is also reminiscent of the oath of loyalty (*bersumpah bersatia*) sworn between Ibrahim and the Raja di Hulu when Barus was founded. In that agreement, as in this, a proverb was used to seal the bond. Ibrahim and the Raja di Hulu expressed their common interest by pledging that they would be equally wet when in water and equally dry when out of it. The implication here, that the interests of the two parties were one, corresponds to that in the white fowl proverb, in which the suggestion seems to be that what happened to the Bataks also happened to the

---

[43]Nai Pos Pos is a *bius* grouping in the Silindung area, see Ypes, *Bijdrage*, pp. 53 and 545.

[44]*Sejarah*, p. 46. "Selama dianya menyuruh ka negeri Batak maka Sultan Larangan pun berpakat dengan Raja Muda dan segala yang tuha-tuha dan segala hamba ra'yatnya dalam negeri itu mengangkat Sultan Larangan jadi keraja'an ka Sebarang serta menusuk negeri dianya di sana." According to van der Toorn, *menyusuk* conveys "making a beginning of something." He gives the example of *basoesoea' kajo*—to establish a kingdom, *Minangkabausch-Maleisch-Nederlansch Woordenboek*, p. 227 .

[45]*Sejarah*, pp. 46–47.

[46]Ibid. "Jikalau tumbuh kepada anak Batak silang selesih pun sedemikian juga dan umpamanya jikalau ayam putih terbang ka hilir melainkan putih juga jikalau ayam putih terbang ka Batak putih juga dan tiada jadi rusak-maruskkan.' Demikianlah hal perjanjian tatkala masa itu."

[47]See, for instance, Wilkinson, *Malay-English Dictionary*, p. 55; and Pamuntjak et al. *Peribahasa*, for several other examples of "Ayam putih terbang" proverbs. M. A. Jaspan cites an example among the Rejang in "From Patriliny to Matriliny," p. 34.

Malays. These proverbs serve to encapsulate the sentiments of mutuality which the agreements were to forge, and their use of metaphor intensifies this message. Sultan Larangan's new agreement with the Pasaribu Bataks reinforced an intrinsic feature of his family's claim to authority in Barus, namely the substance bestowed upon those claims by Ibrahim's acceptance in the interior. This bond was evoked in the language of consensus and mutuality central to Hilir presentations of inter-group relations.

Sultan Larangan next presented symbols of friendship to the Batak Rajas (*membari tanda persahabatan akan tanda raja kepada raja Batak*). This was so that they should take the agreement seriously. The presents he gave and the Raja to whom they were presented are listed in the text. The gifts included items such as swords, gold objects, umbrellas, and head-dresses.[48] In Malay court literature the ideal sovereign is frequently depicted distributing just such gifts among his loyal subjects and chieftains. The presentation of gifts and robes of honor has been identified as an essential feature of the role of the ceremonial Malay Raja.[49] Hitherto in both Barus chronicles, royal gift giving is rarely mentioned, except in relation to the items which the ruler of Aceh granted to Sultan Ibrahim's head. This is true even of the Hilir chronicle which, we have seen, incorporates much more detailed descriptions of royal ceremonial than does the Hulu text. It is noteworthy, then, that in the *Sejarah* royal gifts are said to be given to the Pasaribu and Nai Pospos Bataks at a stage in the narrative when the sovereignty of the Hilir family was under attack. Larangan's distribution of gifts recalls the occasion in the Hilir origin story when Sultan Ibrahim was shown presenting an umbrella base to the Pasaribu as a sign of *kerajaan*, of being subject to a Malay Raja. The Bataks, it will be remembered, responded to Ibrahim with the words and phrases usually used by Malay subjects to honor their Raja. In this instance, as in Larangan's distribution of gifts, the text presents the Hilir family and the Pasaribu Bataks acting out this relationship between Malay ruler and subject.

The sovereignty of the Hilir family is thus reaffirmed in the *Sejarah*, despite the difficulties experienced by them in Barus. These passages also provide a further indication of the ceremonial style in which the Hilir text presents Hilir royal authority: it is in ceremonial terms that the Hilir family is seen to interact with and to attract the inland Bataks.

There follows in the Hilir text an account of Larangan's successors in Sorkam, and of the numerous agreements which they made and renewed with the Bataks of the interior. There is a repetitive quality about these passages, as the Bataks are several times called down from the interior to reaffirm the existing agreement and pledge their loyalty to the Hilir family. In the course of these events the strength of the Hilir family's position in Sorkam is established in the text.

Ritual and an emphasis on the sanctity of the Hilir family play a part in the text's description of these events. After Sultan Larangan's agreement with the Bataks, and after he is said to have been confirmed in the government of *negeri* Sorkam, Larangan and the Bataks burned benzoin incense and called on Allah and the Prophet and the ancestors of both groups to ensure that the agreement would not be broken.[50] After some time had passed, Daulat, who had also moved to Sorkam, wanted Sultan

---

[48]*Sejarah*, pp.47–48.

[49]This is usually known as *kurnia*, or royal bounty, although the word *kurnia* is not used in either of the texts considered here. On royal gift giving, see, for instance, Milner, *Kerajaan*, pp. 44–45.

[50]*Sejarah*, p. 48.

Larangan to marry his sister. Because Larangan refused, Daulat murdered him. Larangan, like Sultan Ibrahim, is said to have died without sinning (*tiada dengan dosa*), and, like Ibrahim and Sultan Bagonjong, his corpse showed no sign of physical death and was like a *cempaka* flower. Sultan Larangan's blood is also said to have been white like coconut milk.[51]

The people were distressed by Larangan's death, and they called his grandmother, Puteri Ma'anikam, from Korlang. Puteri Manikam set out to avenge Larangan's death. She traveled into the interior and told the Pasaribu and Nai Pos Pos Bataks what had happened, reminding them of their agreement with Larangan. The Bataks affirmed their commitment and declared that they would follow Puteri Ma'anikam.[52] After they had eaten together, the local people, the *anak Melayu*, and the *anak Batak* attacked Daulat's *kampung* and drove him away. Puteri Manikam became Raja.[53]

The Bataks then returned home, but Puteri Manikam meanwhile decided to appoint *penghulu* to govern the *negeri* in the event of her death. The Bataks were thus called once more to the coast. A feast was held, and not only were *penghulu* appointed but individuals were rewarded for their contribution in the war against Daulat.

Puteri Manikam spoke to the assembled Malays and Bataks in a gentle voice and asked them to ensure that, if any of her family came from Barus and wished to rule in Sorkam, the position of Raja there would be open to them.[54] She also specified the *angkatan* to be used in Sorkam and by the *penghulu*. The *penghulu* and the assembled gathering are said to have been happy to receive her instructions.

After Puteri Manikam had been Raja there for some time, Raja Kecil arrived from Barus. Raja Kecil summoned the Pasaribu and Nai Pos Pos Bataks to the coast once more and made a renewed agreement with them. They feasted on buffalo "as was proper" (*seperti patut*), and made an agreement "Bataks with Malays" that was not to be broken (*rusak-merusakkan*). Like other agreements between the Hilir family and the Bataks, they undertook to help each other against enemies and head-dresses were given to the Batak Rajas of the four *suku*. Incense was burned again and God, the Prophet, and the spirits of the ancestors of each side were appealed to as the parties solemnized their oath.[55]

The involvement of Raja Kecil from Barus in this further agreement of mutual loyalty may be intended to demonstrate that the loyalty of the Bataks applied to the Barus, and not merely to the Sorkam, branch of the Hilir family. This link with Barus

---

[51]Ibid., pp. 49–50.

[52]Ibid., p. 51. "Syahadan maka lalu menjawab pertuha di dalam negeri itu serta sembahnya demikian buninya, 'Ya nenekhanda adapun seperti kata nenekhanda itu dengan insya Allah subhanahu ta'ala kami jujunglah atas batu kepala kami hanya kami menurut perintah nenekhanda. Pabila kata nenekhanda berangkat perang di sanalah kami menurut dan tiada kami salahi khabar nenek handa hanya tentangan daripada sekalian raja-raja Batak inilah nenekhanda tentukan supaya dianya boleh tahu.'"

[53]Ibid., p. 52.

[54]Ibid., pp. 53–54. "Dan jikalau hamba mati kini hari jikalau datang anak cucu hamba dari negeri Barus dan jikalau dia berkehenda' jadi keraja'an di sini manggantikan hamba melainkan jangan tuan-tuan gagahi. Dan jikalau tuan-tuan gagahi eso' harinya melainkan aku sumpah seberat bumi dan langkit sebab dari anak cucu saudaraku ada banyak tinggal di Barus."

[55]Ibid., pp. 55–56.

is emphasized when Raja Kecil plants a piece of durian. Before returning to Barus, he instructs the inhabitants of Sorkam to tend the plant; and to call it Durian Barus because he, a man of Barus, planted it when the agreement was made.[56]

These events, and particularly the agreements made with the Bataks, are described at length in the text. The language is repetitive and, in the discussions which take place, the parties speak to each other in the formulaic phrases commonly used in *hikayat* to characterize intercourse between rulers and subjects. The way in which agreements are made here, acted upon, and renewed, is reminiscent of Episode Four in the *Sejarah*, where the people of the Hilir go upstream, back downstream, and then upstream again. Here, the Bataks are called to the coast on four occasions, and their loyalty to the Hilir family is plainly demonstrated.

After Raja Kecil returned to Barus, the narrative moves once more to the Barus strand of the family. The text mentions again that on Raja Kecil's death his son, Sultan Emas, was prevented from ruling by the Raja di Hulu.[57] The successors of Sultan Emas are the subjects of Episode Seven.

*   *   *

Two approaches to political authority become more apparent in Episode Six of the chronicles. Throughout the *Asal*, we have seen royal authority presented in terms of power and control. This approach to authority is consistent with the chronicle's presentation of a single pre-eminent ruler. In this episode these strands of Hulu thought are placed in the context of a kingdom which is itself tightly organized and under control. The Hulu depiction of Barus is of a kingdom with well-defined borders. The areas and people inside and outside those borders are clearly specified and distinct from each other. Just as there is one Raja, the inhabitants of Barus are said to be "one people" (*satu bangsa*). Ambiguity and variation in the ordering of political life is not admitted in the Hulu chronicle, and the total picture presented of the character of government in the kingdom assists the text's argument on behalf of the existence of a single, Hulu, Raja who governed through control.

By contrast, ambiguity and complexity are essential features of the *Sejarah*'s view of political authority. Here words such as *perintah* and *kuasa* are rarely mentioned. Just as the existence of duality depends on consensus and harmony, the exercise of authority itself appears to depend here upon group loyalty and acknowledgement. *Sumpah* and *perjanjian* do not apply simply to relations between two rulers, but authority itself is based upon consent. This consent is aquired and demonstrated in ceremonial terms. Here, instead of a tightly defined and self-contained political entity, a network of relationships is depicted. Political life, in the *Sejarah*, is expansive and dynamic. It involves the forging and constant maintenance of bonds of loyalty, which rest upon *pakat* and *suka* and which are given affirmation in feasts, celebration, and other ceremonial occasions.

In this episode, then, both texts in their own styles emphasize the royal authority of their ruling family. In this way, both appear to affirm the force of their arguments

---

[56]Ibid., p. 56. "Aku bertanam sebuah biji durian dan tuan-tuan usahakan baik-baik supaya dia hidup dan jikalau dia hidup eso' harinya tuan-tuan namakan Durian Barus sebab hamba yang bertanam orang Barus pada masa membuat perjanjian ini."

[57]Ibid.

and of their own family's position prior to the crisis in their relations which takes place in Episode Seven.

EPISODE SEVEN

In Episode Seven, the final episode in both texts, the crisis in relations between the families in Episode Six erupts in a war between them and a final resolution of their dispute. As might be expected, the character of this resolution is portrayed differently in each chronicle.

Episode Seven presents the culmination of arguments which advanced in earlier episodes of each text. In both chronicles these early events are incorporated in the final episode in a way which reinforces their respective Hulu and Hilir presentations of the past. Both narratives refer to their own versions of past events to support their final conclusions. This internal consistency adds weight to the rhetorical coherence of the chronicles.

ASAL

In Episode Six the *Asal* advanced a forceful argument on behalf of undisputed Hulu authority. The Hilir prince, Sutan Larangan, was denied royal status in Barus and went to Sorkam, where his position was described as being held "in name only." The chronicle then recorded the names and achievements of the next three Hulu rulers. Here the firm, control-oriented style of Hulu political authority was displayed.

Episode Seven takes up the story with the reign of the next Hulu ruler, Sultan Sailan, who came to the throne in AD 1825. In previous episodes of the text, royal ceremonial attributes, such as the possession of *pusaka* and the use of *kebesaran*, serve as a means of identifying those who possessed legitimate authority and those who did not. In contrast to the Hilir chronicle, where royal authority appears to be characterized by ceremonial, here the ritual or ceremonial aspects of rulership are used as a language by which royal authority is signified. This same language is used effectively in Episode Seven of the *Asal*, where the Hilir family are excluded once more by the Raja di Hulu from any position of royal authority in Barus.

During the reign of Sultan Sailan, the text records, Sutan Kesyari, who was Sutan Larangan's brother, complained to the Pasaribu Bataks because he was denied authority (*kuasa*) in Barus and was not allowed to employ *kebesaran*.[58] He was obliged to live as an ordinary person and had lost the *nama* of Tuanku Bendahara.[59] In response to this, the Pasaribu Bataks made Sutan Kesyari the Raja Bukit of Kota Tengah. That position did not help Sutan Kesyari in Barus, however.

> He returned to Barus but nobody paid any heed to him even though he had been given the title Raja Bukit by the Pasaribu Bataks.[60]

---

[58] *Asal*, p. 34(25). "Adapun Sutan Kesyari itu saudara Sutan Larangan yang mati di Sorkam itu yang mengadu karena dia tidak boleh kuasa Sutan juga di dalam negeri Barus dan tidak boleh memakai kebesaran satu apa juga melainkan ada tinggal seperti orang kebanyakan saja selama suda hilang nama Tuanku Bendahara. Di dalam pada itu maka Batak Pasaribu angkat dia di Kota Tengah jadi Raja Bukit namanya. Suda itu maka dia kembali ka Barus pun tidak juga orang peduli kepada itu Sutan Kesyari meskipun dia suda diangkat Batak Pasaribu menjadi Raja Bukit gelarnya melainkan tinggal bagaimana selamanya juga."

[59] Ibid.

[60] Ibid.

Once again a title achieved by the Hilir family outside Barus is disregarded in the Hulu text, and both Sutan Kesyari and the Pasaribu Bataks thereby appear to be denigrated there. Similar treatment is given to Kesyari's son, Sutan Main Alam. When Sutan Main Alam wished to marry, the Raja Barus, the title now used in the Hulu text to refer to Hulu Rajas, "forbade the use of ceremonial dress."[61] Denial by the Hulu Raja Barus, of any Hilir claims to royal authority is couched, therefore, in the same language of insignia and ceremonial privileges that was used in previous episodes to emphasize the Hulu claims to authority.

In the face of this opposition from the Raja Barus, Sutan Main Alam complained to a group from Meulaboh who were living in Kota Kuala Gedang. He asked them to make him Tuanku Bendahara if the Raja Barus would allow it.[62] The Meulaboh agreed to Main Alam's request, but added:

> "It is not necessary to ask for permission from the Raja Barus. We can make the appointment. Should the Raja Barus forbid this then we will oppose him."[63]

According to the text, the Meulaboh and Acehnese in Kota Kuala Gedang were numerous and rich, which was why they dared to oppose the Raja Barus.[64] They went ahead, therefore, and appointed Sutan Main Alam as Tuanku Bendahara in Kota Kuala Gedang. Main Alam, however, was more intimidated by the Raja Barus than were his patrons. He is said to have sent a letter to the Raja Barus in which he asked for pardon and requested the Raja's consent for his new position. The Raja Barus replied to this with anger. He asked why Sutan Main Alam had acted without consulting him, and told him not to return. Main Alam was frightened to hear the words of the Raja, and he sent a further letter asking him if he might go and make obeisance to the Raja Barus (*dia mahu datang menyembah kepada Raja Barus*). Raja Barus replied that he would not receive him. "If you come here I shall certainly kill you," he told Main Alam.[65]

---

[61]Ibid. "Adapun tatkala Sutan Main 'Alam berkawin maka Raja Barus larang memakai pakaian kebesaran dan serta dilarangnya juga memakai damping mahara marapulai." Wilkinson, *Malay-English Dictionary*, gives *marapulai* as a Minangkabau form for "bride or bridegroom." *Mahar* refers to the settlement made by a bridegroom.

[62]*Asal*, p. 34(25)–35(24). "Dalam pada itu maka Sutan Main 'Alam mengadu kepada Orang Melaboh di Kota Kuala Gadang minta dibikin dia jadi Tuanku Bendahara di Kota Kuala Gadang tetapi minta dangan izin Tuanku Raja Barus juga hendaknya tetapi Orang Melaboh itu dia minta tolong membicarakannya. Dalam pada itu maka mengaku Orang Melaboh, 'Jikalau Sutan Kesyari mahu kami bikin jadi Tuanku Bendahara di sini tara usah lagi minta izin kepada Raja Barus kami saja boleh angkat kiranya kalau Raja Barus melarang kami boleh melawan melainkan Sutan diam-diam saja,' kata Orang Melaboh pada masa itu kepada Sutan Main 'Alam. Sebab Orang Melaboh dangan Orang Aceh telalu suka sekali maangkat Sutan Main 'Alam jadi Tuanku sebab tatkala itu Orang Melaboh dangan Orang Aceh ada banyak dan kaya-kaya dia barani juga melawan kepada Raja Barus sentiasa dia mendugang juga pada masa itu sebab maka dia orang sekalian suka menjadikan Sutan Main 'Alam jadi Tuanku Bendahara di sana." In the *jawi* MS. Meulaboh is spelt m-l-a-b-w-h, and has been romanized in the Malay text as Melaboh.

[63]Ibid., p. 35(24).

[64]Ibid.

[65]Ibid. "Apabila kamu datang kemari niscaya aku bunuh kamu."

The Hilir family is thus portrayed behaving and being treated in a humiliating fashion. Their claims to sovereignty are squashed, and Main Alam is denied even the opportunity to make obeisance to the Raja of Barus. This is a presentation of Barus's past which is entirely consistent with the perspective of the Hulu chronicle.

The chronicle continues with a description of the war which broke out. The Meulaboh are said to have been angry with the Raja because of the way he spoke to Main Alam and because he refused to receive him. Their response was to block the roadway and to let nobody from the *kampung* upstream pass by. A war broke out, in which many on both sides were killed and which lasted, it is said, for two years. Much was expended in the fighting, we are told, "because it was the intention of the *orang Meulaboh* to take over the whole of *negeri Barus*."[66] Here, as in earlier sections of the Hulu chronicle, any challenge to pre-eminent Hulu authority is depicted in terms of the ruin of the state.

Eventually the Meulaboh are said to have grown tired of fighting, and they asked for help from Toku Raja Uda, an Acehnese who lived in Tapus. Toku Raja Uda set about negotiating a peace, and the terms in which he did this are consistent with the position set out so far in the Hulu chronicle. Toku Raja Uda made reference to events which are recorded in earlier episodes of the chronicle.

Toku Raja Uda asked the Raja to forgive Sutan Main Alam. He admitted that the Hilir prince was at fault for not asking the Raja's permission before he became *Bendahara*. Now, however, he suggested that, if Main Alam were pardoned, then his position should be confirmed.[67] The regulations in the *negeri* had not been changed, he said, and there was no reason to quarrel. According to Toku Raja Uda, things which seemed to have changed were in fact unaltered in their essence.[68] From early times, he suggested, there had been a Tuanku Bendahara who had used that *nama* in the region from Simugari to Lobo Dalam. From the time that the head of Sultan Ibrahim had been returned from Aceh, the Tuanku Raja Barus had received his rank and had used the title Sultan in the Hulu Kampung. Now little had changed, he suggested, because Sutan Main Alam was living in another place, remaining Tuanku Bendahara and not attempting to become Tuanku Raja Barus.[69]

---

[66]Ibid., p. 36(23). "Maksud orang Melaboh mahu mengambil negeri Barus semuanya."

[67]Ibid., pp. 36(23)–37(22). "Dari itu saya minta kepada Raja Barus bagaimana boleh hendaknya diampunkan kepadanya supaya kita boleh bikin habis itu perkara parang. Tetapi daripada kesalahan boleh ditimbang bagaimana patut tetapi kami harap tentangan daripada Sutan Main 'Alam dia suda salah sebab dia menjadi Tuanku Bendahara tidak dangan izin daripada Raja Barus. Tetapi sekarang kalau salahnya suda diampunkan melainkan kami minta hendaknya ditetapkan jua dangan angkatannya itu bukan lagi dipakai angkatan dahulu melainkan Tuanku Raja sendiri diterimanya. Sekarang tentangan daripada aturan daripada 'adat pusaka atau aturan negeri atau aturan kebesaran bagaimana ada tersebut dahulu juga bagitu sekarang tinggal terpakai selama-lamanya dan jangan berselisih pada hari kemudian lagi."

[68]Ibid., p. 37(22). "Tetapi ada pula yang berobah rupanya pada penglihatan tetapi pada rasanya tidak juga berobah; ialah seperti dari awal mula dari dahulu-dahulunya juga Tuanku Bendahara menjadi saja dari Simugari sampai ka Lobo Dalam dapat nama Tuanku Bendahara. Tatkala suda kembali kepala Sutan Ibrahim dari Aceh dan pada masa itu juga Tuanku Raja Barus beroleh pangkat memakai gelar Sultan sampai pula ka kampung Lagundi yaitu kampung Ulu melainkan tinggal di dalam satu kampung juga. Sekarang pun sebab kami katakan ada sedikit nan berubah karena Sutan Main 'Alam suda lain tempatnya di Kuala Gadang di kota tetapi meskipun dia lain tempat diam dianya ada tinggal jadi Tuanku Bendahara juga dan tidak dia jadi Tuanku Raja Barus."

[69]Ibid.

Toku Raja Uda is thus portrayed as advancing an argument on behalf of Sutan Main Alam and the Hilir family in general. He couches this appeal for Main Alam retaining his position as *Bendahara* in terms of the earlier history of the kingdom, but he phrases this according to the precepts of the Hulu chronicle. In referring to the preeminent position of Tuanku Raja Barus and to the time when Sultan Ibrahim's head was returned from Aceh to Barus, he articulates the Hulu view of the world as it has been presented in this text. The same, of course, is also true of Main Alam's snivelling behavior, when he requests permission for his new rank from the Raja and seeks to make obeisance to him. This premise of monocracy is never accepted in the Hilir text, despite the rare occasions in that version when one person ruled.

Toku Raja Uda does, however, advance one claim on behalf of the Hilir family, which appears to be inconsistent with a Hulu view. He suggests that, "as it was in the past," there should be two settlements; the *Bendahara*'s position should be confirmed; and there should be a definition of the *kebesaran* which might be used by each family.[70] Although this Acehnese mediator appears to have argued Main Alam's case in terms of a Hulu view of Barus (i.e., the right of the Hulu Raja Barus to rule alone in Barus, affirmed in the regulations made after the return of Ibrahim's severed head), the chronicle would, nevertheless, appear to contradict itself by presenting an argument for two settlements being allowed. We have seen that the *Asal* presents, up to this point, a case for single rule of an absolute kind.

Both princes, however, Hulu and Hilir, reject Toku Raja Uda's suggestion. It is as though the arguments which might be advanced to undermine the Hulu Raja's position have been presented in the chronicle in order then to discount them. The text states that Sultan Sailan's response to these suggestions was to agree with all that Toku Raja Uda said, except with regard to the territory within which the Tuanku Bendahara might rule.

> "I don't want that because in *negeri* Barus there has always been only one Raja. It is true that there has been a Tuanku Bendahara, but the Tuanku Bendahara was a support (*pohonnya*) to the Tuanku Raja Barus. Now, if the borders of the land are divided or fixed, it will be as if there are two Rajas in *negeri* Barus. This is why I object."[71]

Sultan Sailan thus restates the Hulu view, namely that the Hulu family alone was entitled to maintain the position of a single Raja Barus.

Sutan Main Alam then had his say. He also refused the suggestion, and declared that he did not want a division of the land because that would not be in keeping with the past. On the contrary, the two of them were one, he said. That was the situation when they moved to Simugari, to Lobo Dalam and to Sawah Lagundi. Also, in order

---

[70]Ibid., p. 22.

[71]Ibid., p. 38(21). "Tuanku Raja Barus yang bergelar Sutan Sailan menjawab perminta'an itu katanya, 'Tentangan dari itu perminta'an Toku Raja Uda saya perlakukan semuanya tetapi itu perminta'an satu ialah dari bari tanah hingganya yang di perintah Tuanku Bendahara saya tidak mahu sebab di dalam negeri Barus cuma satu Raja selama-lamanya. Batul ada Tuanku Bendahara tetapi itu Tuanku Bendahara pohonnya Tuanku Raja Barus. Sekarang jikalau suda dibahagi atau ditentu hingganya tanah melainkan suda tentu itu seperti suda keterangannya itu bahawasa raja suda dua di dalam negeri Barus. Itu sebab saya tidak mahu.'"

not to divide the land they had taken turns.[72] This speech of Sutan Main Alam's is important not only because it rejects the suggestion of a divided kingdom, and thus would seem to reject the "Hilir" position as Toku Raja Uda had described it, but also because it suggests something about the ordering of government which is also reflected in the external sources. The Dutch, it will be remembered, also reported that Rajaship rotated, and a system of rotating rule, as we have noticed, may have been disguised in the chronicle's account of the period when the Hilir *Bendahara* acted as regent for the Hulu Rajas. Of course, in another sense a two-in-one arrangement, such as is implied by Sutan Main Alam's statement, is very much the "Hilir" position, as identified in the *Sejarah*. It must be admitted that it is odd to find such a statement occurring in a text which, it is argued here, is primarily concerned to assert the predominant and indivisible authority of the Hulu Rajas. Main Alam's statement, however, is not unambiguous, and it is unclear whether the "two" refers to two Rajas or a Raja and *Bendahara*. The chronicle does not amplify or explain the remark, and a peace between the parties is concluded without further ado and without a clear statement of the terms reached.[73]

According to the chronicle, Toku Raja Uda's request was then accepted by the Raja Barus and put into effect. The war ended and all was well.[74] There is no mention of the parts of the proposal to which both Rajas objected, and no firm statement is made concerning the position of the *Bendahara*. Nevertheless, from here on the chronicle refers to the representatives of the two families as Raja and *Bendahara*, respectively. Tuanku Bendahara acts for the Raja, seemingly as his assistant and ally, and no longer offers any opposition. According to the *Asal*, the Hilir family were, apparently, fighting for the right to the secondary position of *Bendahara* and not to the position of Raja or co-ruler.

The Raja and *Bendahara* now act in concert in the chronicle. Sultan Sailan died and his son, Sultan Limbok Tua, succeeded him. Together, he and the *Bendahara* opposed a group of Acehnese who were established in Batu Gerigis, the settlement at the mouth of the Batu Gerigis river, which represents the main *kota* of Barus today. Having driven the Acehnese away, the Sultan ordered his brother to guard Batu Gerigis, but the Acehnese returned with reinforcements from Tapus and Ujung Batu. The kingdom was in such uproar as a result of the trouble caused by these attackers that the Sultan sent his brother to ask the Dutch for help. He was sent to Pulau Putjan, and the Dutch responded, six months later, by sending soldiers to Batu Gerigis and driving away the interlopers, with the assistance of the Raja and the *Bendahara*.

The text explains that, once the Dutch returned to Barus, they formalized the situation and provided salaries for those in authority. This part of the chronicle then

---

[72]Ibid. "Pada masa itu maka menyahut pula Sutan Main 'Alam katanya, 'Tentangan dari membahagi ini tanah itu saya juga pun tidak mahu karena tidak bagitu saja dari dahulu-dahulu melainkan kami ada jadi satu saja keduanya tatkala suda berpindah ka Simugari sampai ka Lobo Dalam dari sana sampai kepada Sawah Lagundi bagitu juga lagi kami suda semendo-menyemendo saja' dari dahulu-dahulu juga berganti-ganti sebab itu maka tiada jadi dibagi tanah.'"

[73]Ibid., p. 21.

[74]Ibid. "Adapun perminta'an Toku Raja Uda dan serta lain-lain orang tuha-tuha dan orang halim-halim ialah Tuanku nan Batuah telah diterimanya oleh Sultan Sailan Tuanku Raja Barus dan serta dilakukan orang tatkala itu bagaimana patutnya sampai suda habis itu perkara parang tatkala itu suda ba'ik sekalian mereka itu."

closes with a detailed list of the Rajas of the Hulu line who had ruled since the acceptance of Islam.[75] It is emphasized that the succession was held within the grasp of one family, that of the Raja Barus.

> These are the seventeen people who successively inherited the position of Raja, it was only inherited by children or brothers children [of the Raja] and passed within one *suku*, the *suku* of the Raja Barus, that is to say Tuka.[76]

The Hulu chronicle, therefore, deals firmly with the whole question of competing royal claims. It argues that the Hilir family held the position of *Bendahara*. This was the case at the time of Raja Bongsu's reign, and from that point in the history of Barus, it is argued, there was no question but that the Hulu family held the position of Raja. Indeed, in the latter part of the manuscript, discussed here in Episodes Four and Five, the text presents any conflict between the families as a question of whether or not the Hilir princes were to hold the position of *Bendahara*. It is not seriously considered that they might make claims to royal status. When Sutan Larangan left Barus, for instance, he called himself Tuanku Bendahara, and similarly Sutan Main Alam took the title *Bendahara* in Kota Kuala Gedang. The argument of the Hilir princes for the right to call themselves *Bendahara*, and to use the appropriate insignia, may of course be a euphemism in the text for Raja di Hilir status, but the later part of the Hulu text never admits that their claim is to any other than the inferior position of *Bendahara*. It is within these terms that the conflict is discussed, and not in terms of accepting or rejecting any claim to royal status. The genealogy of the Hulu Rajas listed in the text, and the pronouncement that the office of Raja was kept within their unbroken family line, confirms this.

Any doubt there might be about this firm message in the final part of the text is dispelled by the next eleven pages. Here the chronicle turns to an account of the origins of the Bendahara family. (*Alkisah maka tersebutlah perkata'an kepada Tuanku Bendahara dari mula asal keturunnya datang ka Barus*).[77] What is, in fact, presented here is a revised version of the Hilir narrative, a version in which the Hilir family's history and genealogy is fitted into the Hulu version of Barus's past as presented in the preceding pages. The account opens with the swordfish attack on Tarusan, and Sultan Ibrahim's departure from his homeland. This episode and the story of Ibrahim's journey through the Batak lands, is, in substance, the same as that recorded in the Hilir text; although it is abbreviated (he does not visit Silindung) and there no effusion over his many qualities as a sovereign, such as is found in the Hilir chronicle. Ibrahim's establishment of a Hilir *kampung* at Barus and the meeting with an Hulu Raja is also mentioned, but after that the story departs from the Hilir narrative.[78] On page eight the account mentions that another Raja killed Sultan Ibrahim by cutting off his head. There is no reference to Aceh, or to the honor with which the Raja of Aceh subsequently treated the head and its return to Barus. The text simply states that, after Ibrahim's death, all the populace, including Ibrahim's son Sutan Usuf,

---

[75]Ibid., pp. 42(17)–44(15).

[76]Ibid., p. 45(15). "Itu tujuh belas orang menjadi raja turun-temurun di dalam walinya dan tidak lapas dari walinya melainkan kepada anak dan kepada anak saudara bagitu saja dan di dalam satu suku juga adapun suku Raja Barus itu Tuka."

[77]Ibid.

[78]Ibid., pp. 45(15)–51(8).

moved to Simugari under Tuanku Marah Sifat (the Hulu Raja). At that time, we are told, Sutan Usuf lost the *pusaka* of Sultan Ibrahim.[79] The remainder of this short history of the *Bendahara* family consists of a single page list of Sultan Ibrahim's descendants and the positions they held. It opens with a statement that what follows is an explanation of the positions held by Sultan Ibrahim's descendants: those who held office and those who did not.[80] Briefly it states the following: Sutan Usuf did not hold office, but he acted as the deputy (*pemangku*) of Maharaja Bongsu; Sutan Usuf's child, Sutan Alam Shah, did not hold office; Sutan Alam Shah had two sons, Marah Sutan and Bagonjong; Marah Sutan was made *Bendahara* by the Dutch Company; Marah Sutan's son, Sutan Marah Sihat, acted as deputy to Sutan Marah Pangkat, the son of Tuanku Raja Barus; Sutan Marah Sihat's son was called Sutan Larangan, but after Marah Sihat's death the family no longer held the office of regent (*wakil*) to the Raja Barus or of Tuanku Bendahara. Sutan Larangan, therefore, held no position of state; Larangan's son, Sutan Emas, also held no position, but his son, Sutan Main Alam, held office anew as Tuanku Bendahara in Kota Kuala Gedang; his son, Sutan Marhimpun, held the same post.[81] The genealogy closes with an exposition of all the ways in which the Tuanku Bendahara was obliged to show public respect for the Raja: where, for instance, he should stand and sit in relation to the Raja on ceremonial occasions, and what *kebesaran* he was entitled to use.[82] All of these provisions indicate the subordinate position of the Bendahara and his limited authority.

This brief and authoritative statement of the positions held by Sultan Ibrahim's descendants is consistent with the role attributed to the Hilir family throughout the Hulu chronicle. Only Sultan Ibrahim held the position of Raja; after his death the Hilir family was reduced to a subordinate position within the Barus polity. This message differs markedly from the account of events offered in the Hilir chronicle, but it conforms with the "single raja" view of royal authority presented in this text. The Hulu chronicle closes with this definition of Hilir inferiority. By means of listing all the Hulu rulers who held the position of Raja Barus, and then detailing the subservient role of all the Hilir princes during that period, the text effectively encapsulates its argument of single, Hulu, rule. In ceremonial terms as well as in relation to the possession of *kuasa*, the Hilir family are excluded in this chronicle from a position of royal authority in Barus. Single, undivided, rule is thus maintained in the text.

SEJARAH

The *Sejarah* deals more briefly with this episode than does the *Asal*, but here, as in that version, the events of the past are invoked to justify the way in which conflict between the two families was resolved. Here, as in the Hulu account, the arguments presented in earlier episodes culminate in a final statement of Hilir principles concerning the issue of royal authority in Barus. As might be expected, the Hilir presentation of the events of Episode Seven is very different from that encountered in the *Asal*.

---

[79]Ibid., p. 52(7).

[80]Ibid. "Adapun keturunan Sultan Ibrahim ba'ik yang memegang pekerja'an ba'ik yang jadi Raja ba'ik yang jadi wakil ba'ik yang tidak memegang pekerja'an satu juga pun di bawah ini kenyata'annya."

[81]Ibid.

[82]Ibid., p. 54(6).

As we have seen, the *Sejarah* in Episode Six acknowledged the difficulties experienced by the Hilir family in Barus. The Hilir family responded to Hulu opposition, it was suggested, by reaffirming their base of support in Sorkam and among the Bataks of the interior. The use of successive treaties and solemn oaths of loyalty to ensure support is typical of the Hilir political style. This affirmation of Hilir authority and the recognition of Hilir sovereignty by the inhabitants of Sorkam and by the Pasaribu and Nai Pos Pos Bataks are linked in the text to the situation in Barus, as in Raja Kecil's planting of the Durian Barus in Sorkam. This revitalization and avowal of Hilir sovereignty is relevant for Episode Seven, where the Hilir family once more put forward their claims in Barus and, according to this version of events, succeeded in reestablishing dual authority there.

Raja Kecil's son, Sultan Emas, we saw, was prevented from becoming ruler by the Raja di Hulu. He had two sons, Sultan Kesyari and Sultan Pesisir. After Sultan Emas died, Sultan Kesyari himself had two children, Puteri Perhentian and Sultan Main Alam. Sultan Kesyari, in this version as in the Hulu text, is said to have been appointed by the Pasaribu Bataks to the position of Raja in Kampung Kota Tengah, and he went to *negeri* Pasaribu to take up his position.[83] His son, Sultan Main Alam, remained in Barus. Friction developed there, the text records, because:

> Sultan Main Alam adopted the courtly insignia of a Raja. Then by the decree of God, may He be praised and exalted, the Raja di Hulu forbade Sultan Main Alam to use symbols of Rajaship.[84]

Sultan Main Alam was unhappy about this restriction and thought to himself: "I am within somebody else's government. Where may I go so that I can hold office in safety?"[85]

Main Alam decided to attempt to make an agreement (*pakat*) with the merchants in Muara Gedang who were already involved in a disagreement with the Raja. He

---

[83]*Sejarah*, p. 57.

[84]Ibid. "ALKISAH maka tersebutlah perkata'an Sultan Main 'Alam anak Sultan Kasyari tinggal di dalam negeri Barus kampung Barus. Maka dengan takdir Allah subhanahu wa ta'ala tumbuhlah silang dan selisih. Adapun sebab maka tumbuh selisih itu nikah Sultan Main 'Alam jadi Sultan Main 'Alam membawa' angkatan keraja'an Raja. Maka dengan takdir Allah subhanahu wa ta'ala maka dilarang oleh raja di hulu Sultan Main 'Alam memakai keraja'an raja. Maka dengan takdir Allah subhanahu wa ta'ala kiranya terhentilah Sultan memakai angkatan keraja'an raja tatkala nikahnya itu."

[85]Ibid. "Maka sungutlah hati Sultan Main 'Alam serta pikir di dalam hatinya, 'Aku ini sekarang di dalam perintah orang. Mana perintah aku turut asal selamat perkerja'anku ini.' Maka dengan takdir Allah subhanahu wa ta'ala kiranya perkerja'an itu pun habis semuanya maka sekali persatua Sultan Main 'Alam pun berpikir di dalam hatinya, 'Adapun negeri ini ada berselisih dalam hati dagang segala anak dagang di Kuala Gadang dan jikalau dimudah-mudahan kiranya hati sekalian anak dagang boleh aku sebuah pakat dengan dianya. Baiklah aku pergi bicara kepada pertuha orang dagang di sana.' Maka Sultan Main 'Alam pun mahampirkan dirinya kepada segala anak dagang maka lama berkelama'an anak dagang pun kasih kepadanya. Maka dapatlah pertuah orang dagang kepadanya maka dengan takdir Allah subhanahu wa ta'ala kiranya sebuah pakatlah dianya dengan pertuha orang dagang di sana. Setelah pakat pun sudah hasil tatkala itu Sultan Main 'Alam pun sepakatlah dengan segala saudaranya jauh dan hampir mengatakan kata yang demimikian buninya, 'Adapun selama ini dari nenek moyang saya jadi keraja'an di dalam negeri ini sekarang kini tiada saya jadi keraja'an lagi dan sekarang pun demikianlah yang aku katakan kepada satu saudaraku. Apa pikiran tuan-tuan dan hamba ini sekarang?'"

duly made an agreement (*sebuah pakatlah*) with the chief among the merchants. Then Main Alam conferred (*sepakatlah*) with his relatives:

"Since the time of my ancestors we have held authority in this negeri. Now I no longer hold authority and that is why I am asking you for your views."[86]

Main Alam's relatives assured him his intention was proper (*patut*).[87] Main Alam was happy (*suka*) to hear this, because he was in agreement (*sebab sudah sepakat*) with all his relatives.

"Very well. I shall move from this *kampung* in the hulu downstream to Muara Gedang since my intention is to assume authority there. I do not want to assume government here because of the troubled atmosphere in this *kampung*."[88]

Sultan Main Alam therefore departed with his wife and all of his property, and he was received by the merchants in Muara Gedang. The next day Main Alam was elevated to "... become Raja in *negeri* Barus, succeeding his forebears."[89] He appointed the traditional four *penghulu*, who are named in the text.

Sultan Adil is said to have taken the title Tuanku Bendahara, although there is no doubt in the text that it was as Raja that he was appointed. According to the text, this was because he took the *nama* of his grandfather in Sorkam who was entitled Tuanku Bendahara. Main Alam's position is then said to have been confirmed (*tetaplah*) in the government of *negeri* Barus.[90]

When the Raja di Hulu heard what Sultan Main Alam had done he was very angry. He sent an envoy downstream to Sultan Main Alam with this message

"Why have you established a government (*kerajaan*) here? It is entirely improper and if you do not renounce this position then tomorrow morning we will make war on everybody here."[91]

Main Alam replied to the envoy,

---

[86]Ibid. "Adapun selama ini dari nenek moyang saya jadi keraja'an di dalam negeri ini sekarang kini tiada saya jadi keraja'an lagi dan sekarang pun demikianlah yang aku katakan kepada satu saudaraku. Apa pikiran tuan-tuan dan hamba ini sekarang?"

[87]Ibid., p. 58.

[88]Ibid. "Jikalau demikian kata tuan-tuan sekaliannya baiklah aku berpindah dari kampung ini di hulu hilir ka Muara Gadang karena di sana maksud saya aku jadi keraja'an. Tiada mahu aku di sini jadi keraja'an karena terlalu sukar rasanya di dalam kampung ini maka mana hanya akan sebuah umanatku kepada tuan sekalian saudara."

[89]Ibid. "Maka dengan takdir Allah subhanahu wa ta'ala diangkat oranglah pada ketika itu Sultan Main 'Alam jadi raja di dalam negeri Barus menggantikan neneknya jadi keraja'an."

[90]Ibid., p. 59. "Serta dinamakan Sultan Main 'Alam jadi bergelar Tuanku Bandaharo sebab menurut nama neneknya di Sorkam bergelar Tuanku Bendaharo. Demikianlah halnya tatkala itu tetaplah Tuanku Bendaharo mehukum jadi keraja'an di dalam negeri Barus tinggal di Kuala Gadang."

[91]Ibid. "'Kami ini disuruh raja di hulu mengatakan kata yang demikian. "Mengapa orang jadi keraja'an di sini? Tiada patut sekali-kali dan kiranya jikalau tiada mahu mahentikan pekerja'an itu melainkan nanti kami hari bareso' pagi kami perangi sekalian tuan-tuan yang ada di sini."' Demikianlah kata utusan itu kepada tuanku dan segala penghulu empat."

"Why should we renounce the positions we hold here? I have not taken the position of anyone else. Neither am I ruling over anybody else's territory or over the subjects of another. I am ruling over my own subjects, I live in my own territory and I employ my own government (*kerajaan*). Why should I be forbidden? If that is your intention, however, we will not oppose you because we have not seized the *kebesaran* [Min. *kegadangan*] of anyone else."[92]

This speech is not unlike that made by Sultan Ibrahim in Episode One of this text, where he asked the Raja di Hulu why he should want to fight since Ibrahim owned the land which he had settled.

The envoy returned home, and the next day the Hulu people came downstream to attack Muara Gadang. War broke out and many were killed and injured. Sultan Main Alam traveled to Pasaribu in order to enact the agreement which his ancestors had made with the Bataks there. When he reached the *negeri*, a feast was held and the old agreement was renewed. Sultan Main Alam returned home, accompanied by all the Batak Rajas who were going to help his side in the war. They feasted once more when they arrived in Muara Gadang, and then the Bataks entered the fighting with Sultan Main Alam "because of the agreements of the past."[93] Many more people died before an Acehnese, entitled Raja Uda, arrived [Toku Raja Uda].

As in the *Asal*, Raja Uda acted as a mediator in the dispute and he made a judgment:

"This issue can be settled if the Raja di Hilir is confirmed as Raja and the Raja di Hulu as Raja. This is because, from the beginning, there have been two Raja in this *negeri*."[94]

The Hilir chronicle, then, also refers to an earlier period of the kingdom's history, but here it is in order to affirm the principle of dual government and the rightful existence of two rulers. In his judgment, Raja Uda proposed that the *negeri* should be once more divided into two settlements. Tuanku Hilir should govern on the side of the rising sun, and Tuanku Mudik on the side of the setting sun.[95]

The word *perintah* is used to indicate government here in the Hilir text. Raja Uda's solution to the dispute only lasted for a month, however, after which, with no explanation, the war recommenced. After two more years of war, the Tuanku Bendahara died. He left behind him three sons, the oldest of whom was called Sultan

---

[92]Ibid. "Maka setelah mendengar kata yang demikian buninya lalu dijawab kata utusan tadi serta kata yang demikian buninya, 'Mengapa kami mahentikan pekerja'an kami yang telah lalu. Adapun saya bukan merampas kegadangan orang dan bukan mahukum atas tanah orang dan bukan mahukum atas anak buah orang. Aku ini mehukum atas anak buahku dan duduk atas tanahku memakai keraja'anku mengapa aku mahu dilarang orang? Dan jikalau apa maksud orang bukan kami lawan karena kami bukan marampas orang punya kegadangan.'"

[93]Ibid. "Maka setelah selesai daripada itu maka sekalian Batak pun menolong tuanku perang karena asal perjanjian tatkala dahulu sudah begitu sekarang baharu mendapati."

[94]Ibid., p. 60. "Tentangan daripada orang ini melainkan habislah sehingga ini, hanya tentangan dari raja di hilir tetaplah dianya jadi raja dan raja di hulu tetaplah dianya jadi raja karena asal dari mulanya dua juga raja di dalam negeri ini."

[95]Ibid. "Tentangan dari perbatasan tanah melainkan dibelah dua sebelah matahari hidub tuanku hilir punya perintah, sebelah matahari mati tuanku mudik punya perintah. Perbatasan tanah sehingga Lubu' Sekitar Emas menurut bandar Aceh lalu ka Muara, demikianlah perbatasan tuan yang kedua belah."

Perhimpunan. According to the text, the war ended because the Tuanku had died and Sultan Perhimpunan was raised by the people to assume government in place of his father. No mention is made here of further hostility from the Raja di Hulu. Sultan Perhimpunan is said to have assumed the title of Sultan Ibrahim "because he received the *pusaka* of his ancestor Tuanku Sultan Ibrahim."[96] The new Sultan then "assumed government in *negeri* Barus in kampung Hilir and the position of Raja passed to his descendants."[97]

This marks the close of the Hilir text, and only a date, the colophon which was mentioned in Chapter Three, and a genealogical chart remain in the manuscript.

* * *

Here then, both the Hulu and Hilir texts conclude their expositions with two different accounts of the nineteenth century war which broke out between them, and of its conclusion. Themes which were identified in earlier episodes recur here, as the Hulu text defines authority in terms of *kuasa* and denigrates the support and royal titles bestowed on the Hilir family by the Pasaribu Bataks, while the Hilir text mentions *pakat* frequently, the importance of *patut* behavior, and the support of the Pasaribu Bataks and the agreements made with them in the past.

The important point to make about this final episode is the consistency it reveals in the arguments set forth within each chronicle. According to the *Asal*, except for the brief period of Sultan Ibrahim's reign, there were not, and never had been, two rulers in Barus. The *Sejarah*, on the contrary, argues that two rulers was the norm. The essence of their disagreement about the resolution of the conflict between them concerns the legitimate existence of a second settlement, just as it did in Episode One when Sultan Ibrahim first arrived in Barus and was challenged by the Raja di Hulu.

In the Hilir account of Episode Seven, Main Alam declared that he was not impinging upon the rightful authority of anyone else by ruling in the Hilir *kampung*. He had his own *kebesaran*, subjects, and territory, and no contradiction is seen to exist here in the presence within the same *negeri* of another Raja. In the Hulu text, on the other hand, here as in other episodes, the existence of two settlements is equated with disaster. The Hilir family were acknowledged to exist but, as in Episode Five, they were entitled only to the position of *Bendahara* and that *Bendahara* lived within the settlement of the Raja Barus. If the land were split, the text indicates, it would be as if there were two rulers and this was never the case. Consistently the *Sejarah* texts makes a distinction between Barus's two parts, the Hulu and the Hilir. This is apparent in statements such as that already cited in which the chronicle distinguishes between circumstances in the Hulu and in the Hilir, and between the Rajas of each. It is also implicit in Sultan Main Alam's assumption that, by moving to Muara Gadang in Hilir Barus, he was outside the Hulu Raja's sphere of authority. The Hulu chronicle, on the other hand, defines Barus as one, geographically undivided, kingdom. This is demonstrated in the geographical descriptions of the kingdom which occur in

---

[96]Ibid. "Maka dengan takdir Allah subhanahu wa ta'ala Sultan Perhimpunan pun diangkat oranglah jadi keraja'an menggantikan ayahnya serta dinamakan akan gelarnya Tuanku Sultan Ibrahim karena mengambil pusaka nenek moyangnya Tuanku Sultan Ibrahim. Maka demikianlah halnya Tuanku Sultan Ibrahim jadi keraja'an di dalam negeri Barus di kampung hilir turun-tumurun kepada anak cucunya, tetaplah jadi keraja'an selama-lamanya."

[97]Ibid.

the Hulu chronicle, and in statements, such as those cited above, that Barus was composed of one people, whatever their origins.

These two arguments for one ruler, one settlement, versus two rulers and the possibility of two settlements within one state, are each couched in this final episode in terms of what happened in Barus in the past. A certain self-consciousness and a coherent view of the relevance of previous episodes to the principal issues involved appears, therefore, to exist in both texts. According to the Hulu chronicle, "there was always only one Raja" since the time when Ibrahim's head had been returned from Aceh; whereas in the Hilir text, it is said, "from the very beginning there were two Raja in Barus." We have seen from our reading of the two texts how that past is explained in each, and how it is possible for these two very different cases to be built on the basis of what superficially appears in the texts as a common past. What these statements clearly reveal in Episode Seven is the degree of internal coherence which each of the texts displays and the consistency of the position each adopts with regard to the question of dual or single Rajaship.

*   *   *

It was suggested earlier that, viewed side by side, these two chronicles present a discussion of political authority in Barus. As the previous seven episodes indicate, a systematic comparison of the two texts indeed reveals what might be called a "debate" concerning the issue of dual authority in Barus.

The question of how political authority was distributed and organized in Barus is the central concern of each text. From the origin stories, in which the foundation of each family's claims to authority are set out, to the end of Episode Seven, both texts are principally concerned with establishing their own family's royal status and defining this in relation to the other royal house. Little occurs in either chronicle that does not bear on this issue. Outsiders, and the presence of a larger, external, world, only impinge on the narrative when they are relevant to this main theme. Each episode, we have seen, has a point to make about the character of relations between the two families.

From beginning to end, then, the chronicles are preoccupied with one issue, and each presents this in a coherent fashion. Two distinct approaches to the central question of royal authority have been identified. Each text offers a consistent and structured argument in favor of one of two very different points of view. This structure is common to the two texts. Both present their argument by means of an origin story (Chapter Three); a meeting and accommodation between the Hulu and Hilir families (Episode One); the emergence of friction and competition between them (Episodes Two and Three), a statement of the political philosophy by which each explains the co-existence of the families (Episodes Four and Five); a crisis in their relations (Episode Six); and a denouement (Episode Seven). By means of this structure each chronicle consistently builds a case to reinforce its own position.

To this end, a variety of literary and rhetorical devices are employed which contribute to the force of the chronicles' arguments. Examples of these have been identified in the presence of significant dialogue concerning difficult and important issues, the reiteration of key words and phrases, a consistent and specific relationship between such words and phrases, changes in style, particularly from continuous narrative to list form or dialogue, the use of metaphor, symbolic representation in the use of ceremony, and the presence of stylized models of excellence and prowess.

Such devices, it has been suggested, occur in both texts in a way which emphasizes the rhetorical force of each.

Underlying and underpinning these two arguments, the texts, we have discovered, view authority differently. The language, style, and rhetoric in each contributes to a definition of authority and a political approach into which the claims of the two families are fitted. These distinct casts of mind, or political perspectives, are evident from the commencement of the narrative. In Chapter Four we saw that the way in which the chronicles established the claims of their ruling line was very different. In the Hulu text, the Pohan clan acquired territory, fought with other clans, and achieved dominance over a large area of upper Barus. The borders of this territory are defined, and the family's ownership of land, and of Barus itself, is asserted. The style of the Hulu text here, as in the subsequent seven episodes, is bald and assertive and displays an emphasis on control-based authority concepts. In the Hilir text, by contrast, Sultan Ibrahim traveled through the hinterland, inspiring loyalty and devotion. He made alliances and swore oaths with Batak groups and, in particular, with the all-important Pasaribu Bataks, who are depicted as supporting the Hilir family throughout this chronicle. The language used to describe Ibrahim's interaction with the Bataks and his attraction for them is highly ritualistic and emphasizes the qualities of the ceremonial Malay ruler.

This distinction in the way each text talks about authority is perpetuated and developed in the seven episodes examined above. The single Raja argument of the Hulu chronicle is encapsulated in a world view which perceives rulership in terms of control, of firm and apparently confident statements about land, boundaries, and people. Authority here is *kuasa*, which implies power, and *perintah*, to control or govern. These ideas are reflected in the language of the Hulu text. Doubt may exist here, and may even be disguised in the authoritative language of the text, but it is never explored, and the chronicle moves from point to point quickly in a spare and firm style. In contrast, the Hilir chronicle couches its arguments in a language of authority which is preoccupied with consensus and compromise, with *pakat* and *sumpah*. These are the means of ensuring loyalty which forms the basis of authority in the Hilir view. The world presented in the Hilir chronicle depicts a network of reassuring ties and relationships which reflect the harmony necessary for the existence of the two families in the Hilir presentation of duality. This view of political authority, with its emphasis on the ceremonial and ritual functions of a ruler, is reflected in the language of the text. It is tentative, causal, repetitive, and full of dialogue which conveys the subtlety, and indeed the creativity, of the Hilir argument.

Each of the texts can be read in the context of Malay *hikayat* from a wider tradition. As we have seen, they both employ many of the conventions of classical Malay literature; but use these conventions for their own ends. In Chapter Three it was remarked that these two Barus texts lack the elaborate and descriptive style of other examples of their genre. The basic and somewhat practical nature of their contents have turned out to be an advantage, however, because of the insights they provide into the issues which were important in the chronicles. Each of the texts departs in an individual fashion from the model of the Malay government which is illustrated in other, more conventional, court-based *hikayat*. Not only do the texts differ from each other, but in their creative use of categories from a wider cultural tradition they expand our understanding of the range of possibilities which can be incorporated within a "Malay world view."

8

CONCLUSION: UNITY AND DUALITY

In the previous chapters we have read several texts on Barus, all of which have emphasized the issues of duality and coastal-hinterland relations. These sources are not all contemporary with one another, and they issue from different perspectives, that of the seventeenth-century servants of the Dutch East India Company; eighteenth-century servants of the English East India Company; nineteenth-century officers in the Netherlands Indies Army; nineteenth-century Barus Malays from two families; and nineteenth-century Dutch ethnographers. None of these sources allows us to know exactly "what happened" in Barus, or provides us with a particularly privileged or "correct" view of the past. Yet, read together, they extend each other and offer a chance to understand the experience of duality in Barus.

A close textual reading of the two royal chronicles of Barus has been the most important analytical tool for this inquiry, but material from other sources has also been used as a means of introducing the chronicles and considering the context in which they were produced. The first chapter considered Barus as a frontier in the Malay world. Dual government was highlighted as a political issue, as were coastal-hinterland relations and the meeting between Batak and Minangkabau/Malay culture in Barus. Chapter Two looked more closely at European perceptions of political life in Barus. We saw that European observers offered their own insights into the relationship between the Hulu and Hilir families in Barus, and between Bataks and Malays there. We then turned to the two Malay chronicles.

In reading the Malay chronicles, the purpose was neither to use them as a means of entry into the history of Barus in the sense of discovering the facts of that history, nor to use them merely to confirm chronological conclusions derived from Dutch sources. Rather, an attempt has been made in the previous three chapters to view the texts in their own terms. They have been considered as a whole in order to discern the structures, oppositions, and categories which inform them. A detailed comparison of this type is a lengthy business. Such a treatment, however, offers a means of identifying local statements in the texts. Taking these superficially modest and unsophisticated chronicles seriously has led to the discovery of what appears to be a dialogue between them. A. Teeuw has referred to a "relation of opposition" between the *Hikayat Raja-Raja Pasai* and the *Sejarah Melayu*.[1] Such a relationship can certainly be discerned between the *Asal Keturunan Raja Barus* and the *Sejarah Tuanku Batu Badan*, where two divergent political philosophies are apparent in their descriptions of a common past. Having defined these two approaches through a close study of the

---

[1]A. Teeuw, "*Hikayat Raja-Raja Pasai* and *Sejarah Melayu*," in *Malayan and Indonesian Studies*, ed. John Bastin and R. Roolvink (Oxford: The Clarendon Press, 1964), p. 231.

texts, we may now turn to consider these conclusions in the context of the Sumatran frontier world discussed in Chapters One and Two.

The passage between text and "history" is not an entirely straightforward one in this instance. We do not, for instance, know enough about the immediate circumstances in which the Barus chronicles were composed to be able to relate their world view, with any certainty, to the precise political circumstances in Barus in the mid-nineteenth century. Indeed a deficiency here is the lack of external information about the Barus royal families in this period.[2] We can, however, now think in terms of a dialogue, or debate, in nineteenth-century Barus and may relate the terms of this debate to what we know about its context.

Read side by side, the Malay chronicles deepen our understanding of a past which is described in Dutch sources and reveal how those inside Barus thought about political issues of which Dutch observers were only superficially aware. An instance where the Malay texts can be fruitfully read alongside VOC sources is in the way hinterland relationships are described. Company records indicate that special relationships, which have been described here as lines of loyalty, bound the Hulu and Hilir families to particular groups in the interior in the seventeenth and eighteenth centuries. Dutch servants used terms such as obedience and loyalty to describe the link between the Dairi Bataks and the Hulu family, and between the Bataks of Sorkam, Pasaribu, and Silindung and the Hilir family; but an appreciation of the local meaning of these relationships is not possible just on the basis of VOC records. In the Malay texts, we find that links with the interior were central to each family's remembered perception of its own right to royal authority in Barus, and these are presented, in one chronicle at least, as an integral aspect of that authority.

As might be expected from the very different approaches to authority displayed in the chronicles, their views of the character of these special relations also differ. Although VOC sources refer to the influence of Hulu Rajas, such as Menawar Syah, with the Dairi Bataks, the *Asal* mentions no specific relationship between that family and the Dairi. It is, rather, the areas through which the Dairi had to pass on the way to the coast that are mentioned in the chronicle. Hulu authority in Rambe and Tukka is expressed in terms of the development of the Pohan *marga* in these regions, its dominance over rival clans, and its control over key pathways and intersections. Although the vocabulary in which these developments are described is Malay, the nineteenth-century descendants of the Hulu royal house evoked their Batak ancestry in order to establish their claims to authority in Barus, and to convey the nature of their influence inland. The *marga* relationships in upper Barus described in the chronicle correspond with those which European observers recorded when they first entered the interior in the nineteenth and twentieth centuries. We know from VOC sources, and from the evidence of modern ethnographers, that the creation of upland posts to block and control pathways and the establishment of inland markets (*onan*) were important aspects of trade and hinterland relations in Barus. What the *Asal* text reveals is the extent to which these features of Batak society in the interior of Barus were important to a Hulu perception of inland ties, a perception which appears to have been linked to the Batak origins of the Hulu line.

---

[2]It was not, unfortunately, possible to gain access to the nineteenth century records held in the Arsip Daerah collection in Jakarta during the period in which this study was produced. It is not clear, however, whether these records would provide any more detailed information about the Hulu and Hilir families after 1840 than other sources consulted here, such as the Department van Koloniën records held in the Algemeene Rijksarchief in the Hague.

In the *Sejarah*, relations with the interior are based on ties of loyalty rather than on Batak *marga* relationships. Although we know that the Hilir Rajas procured resin supplies from Pasaribu and Silindung, and brief mention is made in the Hilir origin story of future trade relations between Sultan Ibrahim and the Pasaribu, the substance of Hilir relations with the Bataks of Sorkam, Pasaribu, and Silindung, as they are presented in the Hilir chronicle, are concerned with *mupakat*. The important theme of loyalty and consensus in inter-group relations is illustrated in the Hilir family's contacts with the two areas of Sorkam and Pasaribu.

Support for the Hilir family from the people of Sorkam is a theme which appears in both external and internal sources. In VOC records, the Hilir family is said to have had great influence in Sorkam. One Hilir Raja died in Sorkam, and the population, who considered him to be "nearly holy," refused to give up his corpse. What the chronicle offers, in addition to a confirmation of the importance of this support in local perceptions, is an insight into the way the Hilir family itself viewed that relationship. For them Sorkam was a source of authority. It was the place to which they went to reestablish their support. There they were made rulers without hesitation, and the people promised continued loyalty to the descendants of the Hilir line. In Sorkam the ceremonial role of the Hilir Rajas is emphasized, as *pakat* are made and renewed, and numerous feasts are held in which all parties rejoice in their mutual consensus and agreement—their *mupakat*.

The same theme is developed in the Hilir family's relationship with the Bataks of the interior. The great loyalty shown to the Hilir line by the Pasaribu Bataks is frequently mentioned and we have seen from VOC sources that special bonds existed between the Hilir family and the Bataks of Pasaribu and Silindung in the seventeenth and eighteenth centuries. In the text a Batak acknowledgement of Ibrahim's sovereignty in the interior is portrayed as underpinning his successful establishment of authority in Barus, and this relationship is perpetuated by his descendants. Although it encompasses strong elements of mutuality and consent, the bond between the Hilir house and these Batak groups is depicted in terms of the ceremonial royal role of the Hilir kings and Batak pleasure in acknowledging this. It was among the people of Sorkam and the Bataks in the interior that the Hilir family enacted their kingly role in the text.

Discussing Batak/Malay relations in east Sumatra, Anthony Reid has commented on the advantages of Malay port culture, first its "mediating role with the outside world," and second the "exalted but flexible notion of kingship which enabled it to preside loosely over the conflicts of the Bataks, intervening only where necessary to draw some advantage."[3] One of the benefits to be derived from close study of the Barus texts has been the detailed insight it allows into the precise nature of this notion of kingship in one local situation. We have seen, not only that "notions of kingship" differed in Barus, but that Batak acknowledgment of, and participation in, that sovereignty was an essential aspect of it. Our sources are evidence of coastal perceptions only, but they reveal how Malay sovereignty is portrayed as incorporating Batak priorities in one instance. Examples of this are found in the Hilir chronicle, in the adaptation of Batak versions of the story of Si Singa Mangaraja's birth and in the appeals made both to God and to the Batak ancestors when oaths were solemnized. Although the ceremonial role of the Hilir kings is presented as a vital ingredi-

---

[3] Anthony Reid, *The Blood of the People: Revolution and the End of Traditional Rule in Northern Sumatra* (Kuala Lumpur: Oxford University Press, 1979), p. 2.

ent of their appeal to the Bataks, these Malay rulers are not portrayed as simply be-dazzling the Bataks with their sophisticated ways. Instead, the coastal rulers became involved in a reciprocal and consensual interaction with the Bataks where, as in the relationship between a Malay Raja and his subjects, each side participated in mutu-ally rewarding rituals and affirmations.

VOC sources have been used here a means of providing a context for the Malay material. It is possible, however, that VOC and Malay sources from Barus can be read against each other in other ways, despite their lack of contemporaneity. One won-ders, for instance, to what extent the Company's promotion of monarchy versus du-ality as an issue in Barus affairs influenced the local debate. The position of Raja Barus, which was instituted by the Company in 1694, is, we have seen, invoked in the *Asal*, at the point where the Hilir *pemangku*, Sutan Marah Sihat, gave instructions to the Company that Sultan Marah Pangkat was the one who possessed the appropriate *pusaka* to become Raja. From this point in the chronicle, Marah Pangkat is given the title Raja Barus. In 1709 the ruling Raja Barus, a Raja di Hilir, wrote to the Dutch complaining that Barus was no longer like a monarchical state, and that it was as if there were once again two rulers of Barus. To what extent the existence of two royal families was a problem before the VOC arrived is hard to tell, but it may be that the friction that VOC officials detected between the two families had been complemen-tary in nature before the Dutch introduced single rule, and that the terms of the later debate were influenced by a hundred-and-fifty years of Dutch imposed monocracy.[4] In the *Asal* the VOC are certainly associated with consolidation of the kingdom under one ruler as in the time of Sultan Maharaja Bongsu and Sultan Marah Pangkat. It is hard to say, however, whether the reason the VOC figure in these instances is be-cause this was the sequence of events, because the VOC is associated with monocratic rule, or simply because they represent a powerful external arbiter.

In both texts, sections of the narrative can be equated with the chronological record laid out in the external sources. This is clearly true of Episode Seven which describes the nineteenth century conflict between the families, and it may also be the case with Episode Six. We saw that in both chronicles the narrative in Episode Six appeared to falter and become strained. A possible reason for this is that the Episode reflects the complex period in the eighteenth century when the royal families appear to have shared power through a process of rotation. The names of rulers mentioned in the VOC sources correspond with those in the chronicles. The names Ibrahim and Bongsu used by the Hilir and Hulu families respectively are very common in the chronicles, and in the external record too. It is therefore difficult to identify individu-als, particularly in VOC sources. But Sultan Menawar Syah, Sultan Marah Pangkat, and a Sultan Bongsu are all mentioned in VOC letters between 1714 and 1760 and in Episode Six of the *Asal*. What appears as rotation in VOC records is depicted in the *Asal* as a period when the Hilir family, in the person of Sutan Marah Sihat, acted as *wakil*. In the *Sejarah*, too, Marah Pangkat is described as Sutan Bagonjong's *wakil*

---

[4]James Fox describes how, on Roti, the VOC imposed titles which perpetuated their initial misunderstanding of the political structure. "The Dutch East India Company's policy of for-mally recognizing a regent (Manek) and a Second Regent (Fetor) created, in effect, a dual sovereignty in each domain. But this formal division , whatever its status at the time of Dutch contact, did not represent the primary diarchy within the nusak. The primary opposition to which the oral histories and genealogies of each domain attest is that between the ritual authority of the Dae Langgak and the political power of the Manek." Fox, "Obligation and Alliance," p. 107.

when he went to fight for the Company in Padang, although here the Hilir chronicle depicts dual settlements. Rotation is not discussed or sanctioned in either chronicle, except in necessary situations of regency where a ruler was too young to hold office. It may be then that, in both the Malay texts, the strained quality of the narrative in this episode is related to the difficulty of explaining this period—a confusing one in Dutch sources—within the precepts of Hulu and Hilir views of the past.

Other personae in the Malay narratives are certainly identifiable in European sources. For instance, the occasion mentioned in Episode Six of the *Sejarah*, when Sultan Larangan's grandmother called upon the Bataks to defeat Daulat and avenge Larangan's death, may be reflected in an account by Marsden in the late eighteenth century. According to Marsden:

> Inland of a place called *Sokum*, great respect was paid to a female chief or *uti*, . . . whose jurisdiction comprehended many tribes. Her grandson, who was the reigning prince, had lately been murdered by an invader, and she had assembled an army of two or three thousand men, to take revenge.[5]

Sultan Baginda, too, is mentioned in VOC sources as well as those of the English Company, and in both the *Asal* and *Sejarah*. In 1814 Sultan Baginda told Canning that he had been undisputed sovereign of Barus for many years, and that his ancestors had also ruled in Barus. There is no indication that Canning was then aware of the existence of the Hilir family, yet, less than ten years later, Barus was once again embroiled in conflict between the two families. To Canning Sultan Baginda expressed his sense of oppression at Acehnese encroachment down the west coast, and this constant harassment, which is mentioned in all the European sources, may in part help to explain the popularity of the Sultan Ibrahim story in Barus, even among those of the Hulu house. The two Hilir heroes in the Hulu chronicle, Sultan Ibrahim and Sutan Bagonjong, are both princes who resisted attack from Aceh. Ibrahim stands, in both chronicles, as a metaphor for the royal status of Barus and of independence from Aceh, and it is, therefore, no surprise that his story is incorporated in the *Asal* and skillfully employed to attest the royal independence and sovereignty of the next Hulu ruler.

The possibilities for future readings of the *Asal* and *Sejarah* chronicles are not confined to considering them in the light of European sources. The *Sejarah Sultan Fansuri*, which was referred to in Chapter Three, mentions eighteenth and nineteenth century rulers such as Sultan Marah Pangkat and Sultan Baginda. The text details numerous *perjanjian*, among which are agreements with the English Company and the one, mentioned in the *Asal*, between Sultan Marah Pangkat and the Batak regions surrounding Barus. In its emphasis on *perjanjian*, the *Sejarah Sultan Fansuri* displays some of the preoccupations of the *Sejarah Tuanku Batu Badan*. Although many of the rulers who figure in the agreements come from the Hulu family, the approach taken towards duality in Barus appears to be more relaxed in this text than that of the *Asal*. We may deepen our understanding of differing approaches to the past in Barus by attempting to read the *Sejarah Sultan Fansuri* in its own terms, and considering how those terms intersect with the "Hulu" and "Hilir" paradigms identified here.

In a study which examined concepts of Malay ethos in indigenous writing, Virginia Matheson noted that, over and above the shared themes which were present

---

[5]Marsden, *History of Sumatra*, p. 375.

in the texts she examined, each work, "had its own particular and specific interests, not reflected in the other texts."[6] The Barus chronicles, too, have their own specific interests. They clearly respond to a particular situation, and it is within this context that they must be viewed. On the subject of dual government, VOC servants mention the existence of tension between the royal families and notice the enduring nature of the rivalry between them. But Dutch observers cannot take us beyond the surface of events, and it is the local sources that take us more deeply into the nature of the tension.

On one level competition between two rulers may seem natural and require no explanation, but in the light of *hikayat* from the *kerajaan* tradition, which in many ways these texts resemble, competition between two rulers is a radical prospect. What is of interest here is how, in view of the way in which the indivisibility of kingship is presented in Malay literature and in much of the theoretical discussion, these works present duality. What we have discovered in the chronicles are two very different responses to the problem. These two responses may, in some degree, reflect the respective positions of the two families. It may have been that the Hulu family was more often "on top" in Barus affairs, while the position of the Hilir family was more precarious and demanded greater agility and compromise. A close reading of the Barus texts has allowed us to say something of the way in which they formulate their respective approaches to the nature of royal authority itself. In the Hulu chronicle we have seen that the terms *kuasa* and *perintah* appear frequently, and a pattern of authority is developed in which ideas of control and ownership are crucial. In the Hilir text, by contrast, consensus, mutual loyalty, and group acclamation based on the ceremonial role of the king are central to the text's presentation of authority. To what extent are these two patterns representative of the "model" which informs our present understanding of a "Malay world view"? Further, can these conclusions contribute to an understanding of Sumatran political life in particular? In this study, the Barus chronicles have been read in the context of court-based Malay *hikayat*. The language and literary conventions employed in the chronicles certainly indicate that the *hikayat* is one genre in which they can be considered. It may also, however, be possible to read these texts in the context of more specifically Sumatran concerns and texts, although this is an area where less scholarly work has been undertaken.

It is, of course, very difficult to speak of "Sumatran patterns." Merely in the limited context of this study we may contrast the references made in Chapter One above to the *Hikayat Aceh*, which presents dual kingship as an impossibly shameful occurrence, with the apparently institutionalized presence of three rulers in the highlands of Minangkabau. Each text and each *negeri* must be considered in its specific context. We may, nevertheless, find that certain themes are particularly prominent in Sumatran texts, and specifically in coastal or frontier situations. The Inderapura Sultanate, for instance, is an example of a Sumatran coastal region where the meeting between two rival political traditions is thought to have led to a lengthy struggle within the kingdom. J. Kathirithamby-Wells has described the conflict in Inderapura between what she characterizes as "the egalitarian character of Minangkabau political organization" and "centralized autocratic rule by an independent monarch."[7] Jaspan considered that, among the Rejang, the office of "*radjo*," "Appears to have been an attempt by Minangkabau *rantau* emigrants to establish hegemony over

---

[6]Matheson, "Concepts of Malay Ethos in Indigenous Malay Writings," p. 357.

[7]Kathirithamby-Wells, "Inderapura Sultanate," p. 84 and passim.

Redjang society."[8] A treaty is said to have been concluded between four remaining clans and four migratory clans, which echoes the language of treaties made for mutual defense between the Hilir family in Barus and the inland Bataks.[9] Further north, John Bowen's work on the Gayo and his identification of siblingship as a "Code for a discourse about kinds of authority and legitimacy," may echo the local statements identified in the two Barus texts. Elder brother authority, Bowen finds, is "jural," or pertaining to rights, while younger brother authority "comes from inner, spiritual power."[10] This opposition is not unlike the two approaches to authority revealed in the Barus chronicles.

The words *kuasa* and *perintah*, which typify the Hulu presentation of royal authority, are by no means unusual in traditional Malay court writing, where they form a conventional part of the vocabulary of government. What is striking in the Hulu chronicle, however, is the frequency with which these appear, especially in comparison with the Hilir presentation. We have also noticed a preoccupation, in this text, with the organizational aspects of government, and this was evident in the lists of *aturan* concerning both the practical and ceremonial aspects of government. A distinction was noted between the way in which ceremony was dealt with in the two chronicles, and it was suggested that, in contrast to the Hilir text, even the ceremonial aspects of kingship were presented, in the Hulu view, as a means of control and dominance rather than as a means of engendering loyalty. Lists of regalia, royal privileges, and prohibitions also occur in other Malay texts, and details concerning land tenure and other organizational aspects appear in Malay legal digests. It is, however, the combination of, and concentration upon, these aspects of political life which, in the context of the chronicle's argument about kingship, appear to be noteworthy.

Land ownership is another important theme in the Hulu chronicle. The first settlement of Barus by the Pohan clan, for instance, is presented in terms of their possession of the area. Land rights formed the basis of the Hulu challenge to Ibrahim's right to settle in Barus, and Hulu definitions of the kingdom involve concepts of territoriality. Land, however, is an issue which is rarely emphasized in Malay texts. Land ownership is not generally considered to have been an important aspect of Malay political and legal thinking.[11] Land was abundant and, as Gullick points out, in the Malay states, "political power, even though it is exercised in respect of a defined territorial area, was based on control of people."[12] According to Marsden in Sumatra, "Land is so abundant in proportion to the population that they scarcely consider it as a subject of right any more than the elements of air and water."[13] The exact boundaries of

---

[8]Jaspan, *From Patriliny to Matriliny*, p. 48.

[9]Ibid.

[10]Bowen, *History and Structure of Gayo Society*, p. 466. See also pp. 160–61, where Bowen argues that the leaders of two rival lineages were seen to derive their authority from different sources: one form of authority, characterized as "inner power" was recognized by the Sultan of Aceh; and the other came from a line which was often traced to Minangkabau or to the Prophet and which drew "powers and renown from foreign sources."

[11]According to Winstedt, "Land was hardly as valuable as slaves in medieval Malaya. And the law relating to land was so familiar to Malays that it occupies little space in the digests." R. O. Winstedt, *The Malays, A Cultural History* (London: Routledge and Kegan Paul, 1961), pp. 109–10.

[12]Gullick, *Indigenous Political Systems*, p. 113.

[13]Marsden, *History of Sumatra*, p. 244.

Malay states were often unknown, and it has been said that "the actual location of the Malay state . . . appears to have been a matter of relatively little importance."[14]

In Barus, however, the Hulu royal line appears to have proclaimed its authority partly in terms of control over land and, in Episode Seven, where the conflict between the two families is played out for the last time, the Hulu belief that the land should not be divided is made plain. Maintenance of the principle of single rule in the Hulu chronicle appears to have led to an unusual emphasis on ownership of a defined area. A further area in which the Hulu text departs from our expectations of a Malay text is in the treatment of relations between ruler and subjects. Here again, while the terminology employed is Malay, the manner in which the ruler's role is presented differs from the model of Malay political behavior which has been constructed on the basis of other texts. Generations of Malay scholars have commented on the importance for Malays of the ceremonial aspects of rulership, and recent attempts to analyze this role have concentrated on what the ceremonial ruler did for his subjects. By creating and advancing men's *nama* through titles and ceremonies, the ruler, it has been suggested, confirmed the social and spiritual identity of his subjects. Royal authority, according to this formulation of the "*kerajaan* system," was based on this reciprocal relationship in which, just as a Raja needed subjects to reflect his *nama*, subjects required a Raja to protect their own.[15] In the Hulu chronicle, however, ruler and subject are not presented in this way. In so far as subjects are considered at all, they are under the authority of the ruler, without participating in rituals which confirm his position. As we have seen, ceremony in this text is used, not as a means of elaborating the consent and acknowledgement of the ruled, but seemingly as a means to enhance the ruler's prestige and contribute to the force of the "single rule" argument.

In the *Asal*, a variety of means are employed to deemphasize the sovereign status of the Hilir family. Intermarriage is one these. Marriage relations between the families are mentioned much more frequently in the *Asal* than in the *Sejarah*, and this relationship is often used as a way of explaining the inclusion of members of the Hilir family in government. Interaction between different ethnic groups, and between new settlers and original inhabitants in Sumatran settlements, has received attention in anthropological literature.[16] A feature which is sometimes emphasized in these studies is a change in, or variation between, different forms of marriage arrangement such as *semando*, which is, broadly speaking, defined as matrilocal, and *jujur* marriage which represents a patrilocal pattern of marriage settlement.[17] Both of these terms are used in the Barus chronicles, although they do not appear in either text in a consistent pattern.[18] The *semando* form, which is commonly associated with Minangkabau culture, is used principally on two occasions in the *Asal* to define the subordinate status of the Hilir family. The term *semando* is used, for instance, in reference to Sultan Ibrahim's marriage into the family of Sultan Marah Pangkat, whose

---

[14]Milner, *Kerajaan*, p. 8.

[15]Ibid., Chapter 6 and passim.

[16]See, for instance, Jaspan, *Structural Change;* Wuisman, *Social Verandering in Bengkulu;* and Bowen, *History and Structure of Gayo Society.*

[17]According to Bowen, "The key point of ambiguity in Gayo social structure is in the relationship between virilocal and uxorilocal modes of marriage." *History and Structure of Gayo Society,* p. xv.

[18]The commonly used Malay terms *kawin* and *nikah* are also used frequently in both texts.

son-in-law (*menantu*) he becomes. The term *mamak* (uncle or mother's brother), which is commonly used in Minangkabau kinship relations, occurs several times in the text, and is applied to the relationship of the Hulu Raja, Marah Sifat, with Sultan Ibrahim's son, Sutan Usuf. Again, Sutan Marah Sihat's *pemangku* status in Episode Six of the Hulu chronicle is explained in terms of his possessing a mak' or mama' (aunt or uncle) on the Hulu side.[19] By implying that the Hilir family had intermarried into the Hulu line (*semando*), the text may be alluding to the incorporation of Si Purbah's line in the origin story of the *Asal* and may even be invoking the Batak notion of a *boru* or in-dwelling *marga*.[20]

In the *Sejarah,* the *semando* form of marriage is distinguished from *jujur* on the occasion of Sultan Larangan's refusal to marry *semando* into Daulat's family, on the grounds that a) he was already married to a princess from Bengkulu; and b) he was to receive a bride by *jujur* marriage from Korlang. Earlier in the same text the Hulu prince, Marah Pangkat, is depicted marrying-in by *semando* to the Hilir family, where he becomes the *menantu* or son-in-law of Marah Sutan. In both chronicles, therefore, marriage alliances appear to be used as a device for portraying the junior status of the other family, but in neither is a marriage relationship between the families elaborated in a consistent pattern.

Both the *Bendahara* position and the use of *wakil*-ship might be considered as another means of explaining the role of the Hilir family in the *Asal*, without admitting the possibility of two rulers.[21] Such a reading has been explored above, although we do not find here a pattern of alliance between the *Bendahara* family and the ruling dynasty, as in the *Sejarah Melayu* for example.[22] In the *Sejarah,* the title Tuanku Bendaharo was used by Sutan Larangan when he moved to Sorkam and governed there; it was also used by Sultan Main Alam, who is clearly presented as a ruler, but whose adoption of the title Tuanku Bandaharo is explained in the text by the statement that he was following the *nama* of his grandfather in Sorkam.[23] The title *Bendahara* or *Bandara* was used, we saw, in Barus in the nineteenth century, and the *cap* which appears to have been used by members of the Hilir family also carries an ambiguous inscription, which seems to suggest that members of the Hilir family used the title *Bendahara* and perhaps also the appellation *wakil*.[24] There is insufficient evidence to come to a firm conclusion concerning these uses of the title *Bendahara*, but the indications are that the title was more than simply a textual device employed in the Hulu chronicle, and that the position of *Bendahara* may have been a means by which potential conflict between the two royal families in Barus was diffused.

The presentation of royal authority found in the *Asal* confirms many of the conventional expectations of a *kerajaan* text, yet its aggressive style also dispenses with

---

[19]When Marah Sihat's daughter married the incumbent Hulu Raja, however, the relationship is not described as *semando* but simply as *kawin*.

[20]See Chapter 5 above and Vergouwen, *Customary Law*, p. 51.

[21]According to Wilkinson, *wakil* was sometimes used as a title of rank as, for instance, in Perak where the "*Raja Muda* and *Raja Bendahara* are *wakil al-Sultan*," *Malay-English Dictionary*, p. 1277.

[22]See Bowen, "Cultural Models," passim.

[23]*Sejarah*, p. 59. "Serta dinamakan Sultan Main 'Alam jadi bergelar Tuanku Bandaharo sebab menurut nama neneknya di Sorkam bergelar Tuanku Bendaharo. Demikianlah halnya tatkala itu tetaplah Tuanku Bendaharo mehukum jadi keraja'an di dalam negeri Barus tinggal di Kuala Gadang."

[24]See p. 45, n. 113 above.

many of the elaborate, ceremonial conventions usually found in *Kerajaan* texts. This is not true of the Hilir chronicle, where the relationship between ruler and subject, and the loyal support given to the Hilir family, are emphasized. Indeed the picture of authority presented in that text echoes the distinction made between the rulers by Melman over a hundred and fifty years earlier, that the Hulu Raja had more influence in "government," while the Hilir family commanded much support among the "citizenry." In the *Sejarah* the presence of two rulers is treated as an acceptable and harmonious feature of government. Here Malay concepts of kingship are adapted to incorporate the notion of duality, although the language and style of kingship is couched in the familiar terms of the *kerajaan* model.

The Hilir equation of authority depended not only on the ruler's ability to create satisfaction and contentment amongst his people, but also upon consensus and agreement between rulers. The importance of *mupakat* in Malay thought is generally accepted. According to Barbara Andaya, government in Perak "functioned by consensus (*mupakat*)," and this was a traditional aspect of Malay *adat*.[25] Snouck Hurgronje, who defined *mupakat* as, "decision by palaver" noted that "The Acehnese are great lovers of mufakat, in form at least if not in actuality."[26] Among the Rejang of south Sumatra, Jaspan has written, "Harmony among men, peace and security are the most prized values of . . . society."[27]

The exceptional emphasis on consensus in the Hilir chronicle is probably most directly attributable, however, to the Minangkabau origins of the Hilir family, and to the role of Minangkabau culture in the western *rantau*. Both chronicles are written in language which employs aphorisms, spelling forms, and specific vocabulary from Minangkabau. Minangkabau *adat* is stated to be an important component of Barus *adat* in both the Hulu and Hilir chronicles, and the ruler of Minangkabau is invoked in the royal seals at the beginning of the *Sejarah*. The importance of consensus in Minangkabau thought is well recognized. *Mupakat*, as Taufik Abdullah puts it, is a means of balancing the "intrinsic dualism of adat."[28] This dualism is expressed in the two *adat* traditions or *laras* of Minangkabau which, according to de Josselin de Jong, exhibit characteristics which are typical of a phratry relationship: "frequent sharp rivalry, with nevertheless an underlying sense of unity, as one cannot exist without the other and the cooperation of both is needed to make up the total community."[29] From this division extends what observers describe as the pervasive "dualism" of Minangkabau society. The harmonious mutual antagonism, which de Josselin de Jong refers to in order to describe the relationship between Bodi Caniago and Koto Piliang in Minangkabau, is certainly reminiscent of the insistent "two in one," "distinct but joined" perspective of the *Sejarah*. There can be little doubt that the ideas represented in this chronicle owe much to Minangkabau thought, although they are expressed in a language of sovereignty which is familiar from more conventional *kerajaan* texts. A text from the southerly part of the west coast *rantau*, a *Tambo Radja dan Loewaq Menangkabau*, uses language which is similar to that of the *Sejarah* to

---

[25]B. W. Andaya, *Perak*, p. 28. The role of *mupakat* in Malay customary law is discussed in Hooker, *Adat Laws*, pp. 35 and 39.

[26]Snouck Hurgronje, *Acehnese*, 1: 76.

[27]Jaspan, *From Patriliny to Matriliny*, p. 82.

[28]Taufik Abdullah, "Modernization in the Minangkabau World," p. 190.

[29]De Josselin de Jong, *Minangkabau and Negeri Sembilan*, p. 73.

describe *adat* rivalry in Minangkabau.[30] The text is a history of *rantau* settlement and is particularly concerned with the regions of Tarusan, Bayang, and Padang. Migrants from different parts of the interior settled in these places, and adherents of the different *laras* were obliged to find an accommodation with each other. Since this is the very area from which Malay migrants are said to have first traveled to Barus, it does not seem strained to postulate a relationship between this conceptual approach to *adat* rivalry and the dual sovereignty argument embodied in the *Sejarah*.

It is important to note, however, that in the special emphasis it places on the idea of consensus, the Hilir chronicle appears to be drawing on an element of a still wider cultural matrix. Ricklefs, for instance, stresses the importance of consensus in the government of eighteenth-century Java, and recent commentators have noticed the role of ideas of consensus, contract, and confederation in the political history of south Sulawesi.[31] Just as *mupakat* was clearly important for Malays and others outside Barus, so too the creation of agreements and the making of oaths (*perjanjian* and *sumpah*) are aspects of Malay and Sumatran political thought which appear in other sources. In the eighteenth century Marsden commented on the importance of the oath in Sumatran law, and on the role of ceremonies such as the burning of incense, drinking specially prepared liquids, and the uttering of imprecations, all of which often accompanied the making of oaths.[32] Snouck Hurgronje also mentions the significance of various types of oath-taking ceremonies among the Acehnese,[33] and, according to Vergouwen, oaths and *janji* friendship alliances, also had a place in Batak society.[34]

Among the earliest pieces of evidence available to us of Malay societies are the inscriptions of Srivijaya, in which curses or oaths are prominent and where frightful imprecations list the disasters which would result if the oaths were broken.[35] We have already noticed the view of Miksic that the presence of oath stones in the Pasemah region in the interior of Palembang may be evidence of the character of intercourse between the ruler and inland inhabitants of a region in early times. The importance of oaths and agreements as a medium of interaction between rulers and Bataks in the Hilir text, and as a means of engendering mutuality, may be not unrelated to such early patterns of Sumatran political organization.[36] At the same time, the character of the relations revealed in the Barus texts may throw light on the nature of the "social bonds" of which such inscriptions are evidence.

To what extent can the different approaches to authority in the Barus texts be explained by reference to the ethnic background of the royal families? In a Dutch de-

---

[30]*Tambo Radja dan Loewaq Menangkabau serta Tambo Solok dengan Pasisir Rantau Padang Bujang Tarusan*, V. E. Korn Collection Ms. no. 363.

[31]Ricklefs, *Jogjakarta under Sultan Mangkubumi*, p. 19 and passim. Also H. Sutherland, "Power and Politics in South Sulawesi 1860–1880," *RIMA* 17 (1983): 164; and L. Andaya, "Treaty Conceptions and Misconceptions: A Case Study from South Sulawesi," *BKI* 134 (1978: 275–95.

[32]Marsden, *History of Sumatra*, p. 242–43 also p. 386 on Batak oath-taking ceremonies.

[33]Snouck Hurgronje, *Achehnese*, 2:94–95, and 302–3.

[34]Vergouwen, *Customary Law*, pp. 126 and 142–43.

[35]J. G. de Casparis, *Prasasti Indonesia: Selected Inscriptions from the 7th to the 9th Century A.D.*, vol. 2 (Bandung: Masa Baru, 1956), pp. 1–36.

[36]See Wolters' comments on the indications such oaths provide of neighborhood relations and shared "spiritual values" which may have linked the ruler with those living further inland in "Studying Srivijaya," p. 18.

scription of Barus which appears to have been compiled at the beginning of the twentieth century, the anonymous author describes Barus in terms of a mixture of a republican Minangkabau form of government, based upon *"moepakat,"* and a Batak approach, which he terms auto/democratic, in which the raja acts the part of an auto-cratic ruler, but is not obeyed unless it suits his people.[37] This hasty sketch of Barus politics is not substantiated in the manuscript, but it does reflect some of the impor-tant differences between the "Hulu" and "Hilir" definitions of authority in Barus which have been detected here. To categorize these simply as a "Batak" and "Minangkabau" approach is to ignore many of the similarities in the chronicles and the Malay terms in which they are communicated. Although the Batak origins of the Hulu kings are by no means disguised in their royal chronicle, and although it may be that the importance of tribal land in Batak society[38] contributed in some degree to the Hulu view, it is not possible to say, on the basis of the evidence considered here, that the Hulu family were better, or worse, or different, Malays *because* of their Batak origins. Neither can the forthright and plain character of the *Asal* necessarily be de-scribed simply in terms of its Batak connections. A west Sumatran *Tambo Padang* which, like the *Tambo Radja dan Loewaq Menangkabau* mentioned above, describes the settlement of west coast *rantau* areas by Minangkabau migrants from the *darat*, dis-plays some of the same concerns and motifs as the Hulu chronicle. These include family quarrels, the opening of new land, territorial definitions, and a concern with borders between neighboring states.[39]

In these Barus chronicles the whole issue of ethnicity is flexible and confused. *Bangsa* (people, race) is often associated with concepts of Malay identity, yet in both chronicles *bangsa* is used in a variety of contexts which defy a strict definition of the term. In the Hilir chronicle, the people of the interior and of east Sumatra are referred to as *bangsa berlainan*, yet no such distinction is used when referring to the Hulu fam-ily. In both texts the Hilir prince, Sultan Bagonjong, is praised in terms of his *bangsa*, yet the Hulu chronicle also defines the people of Barus who were drawn from differ-ent races, as one people, *satu bangsa*. In the *Asal*, the word Batak is used when Alang Pardoksi's name is said to have been the greatest of all the rajas in *"negeri Batak."* "Batak" is applied to the people of the Dairi region, and is used several times in the Hulu text in reference to the form of mixed *adat* and the mixed *bangsa* of Barus. The terms Batak and Malay occur in these instances, along with Aceh, Minangkabau, Hindu, Ceti, and Islam. In the *Asal*, neither royal family is referred to specifically as being Batak or Malay, and the emphasis on the mixed origins of the people of Barus in this text suggests that the issue may have been a sensitive one in which unquali-fied use of these two terms was to be avoided. In Episode Two of the *Sejarah*, the name Raja Batak, used in reference to the existing royal family in Barus is, at one point, altered. The word "Batak" is crossed out and replaced in the MS with the term "Hulu." At no other point, however, are members of the Hulu family referred to as "Batak" in this chronicle, and the term is only applied to people of the interior. Such references, we saw, apply the terms "Batak" and "Melayu" freely in a relationship of opposition which reinforces the establishment of harmony between two distinct groups. The incoming Tarusan family are clearly defined as Malays in their story of origin and throughout the Hilir text.

---

[37]"Onze Vestiging te Baroes," pp. 38–39.

[38]Vergouwen, *Customary Law*, Ch.3 especially pp. 106–8.

[39]*Tambo Negeri Padang*, V. E. Korn Collection MS. no. 343.

Islamic faith is presented as a feature which distinguished Malays and Bataks in the *Sejarah*, but not, apparently, the Hulu and Hilir families. The significance of Islam in these texts is a large question in itself. Insofar as it is possible to distinguish between the chronicles in this area, however, the *Sejarah* appears to exibit a more tentative attitude, in which God's will and support are frequently invoked. References of this kind are particularly common in places where the text is describing a meeting or accommodation, as in relations with the Bataks and, in Episode Four, where the establishment of dual kingship is explored. Conventionalized appeals to *takdir*, the will or decree of God, do also appear in the *Asal*, but not with the same frequency. In the Hulu chronicle, references to Islam, we have seen, appear in the context of the regulations which were instituted by the Hulu family in Barus, and to the ordering of Barus as an Islamic State. Differences between the texts concerning their treatment of Islam would appear to reflect their overall authoritative versus consensual orientations. In neither text does Islam or Islamic Malay identity appear as an issue which divided the Hulu and Hilir families.

In his work on Mandailing immigrants in west Malaysia, Tugby has commented on the difficulty of establishing a measurable standard of "real" Malay culture.[40] What appears to be significant about the ethnic background of the two Barus families is that, because two different sources of royal authority existed within the one kingdom, it became necessary to adapt Malay categories in order to explain the co-existence. The rulers of Barus were obliged to be creative, and each family in its own way employed the cultural tools at its disposal to fashion an explanation of political authority which made its position coherent. In eighteenth century Java, the courts of Surakarta and Yogyakarta faced unprecedented theoretical problems in legitimizing the existence of two kings and the permanent division of the realm. As Ricklefs has shown, that dilemma was resolved through literature.[41] In their own way, these modest Malays of Barus, on the edge of the Malay world, were faced with a similar problem, and they, too, attempted to reconcile it in literature. The importance of the two Barus chronicles lies in the creative and individual use each makes of the cultural matrix. Barus informs us of the possibilities for variation which exist in the "Malay world."

O. W. Wolters has suggested that we may learn more about the individual characteristics of local Southeast Asian cultures by examining their interaction with foreign cultures and beliefs. He goes on to argue that this process, which he terms "localization," applies also to local cultures themselves in their contact with each other.[42] Barus provides an example of just that kind of interaction. A small kingdom on the frontier of the Malay cultural sphere, it offers an opportunity to examine Malay political assumptions in a frontier situation where they appear to have been subject to local redefinition.

In discussing the relationship between different cultures, James Boon observes of Hocart that, "Throughout his work Hocart emphasized: 'the pattern of behaviour between two moieties: mutual aid combined with playful hostility...'" Boon extends this to suggest that "Through inscription, all cultures may stand as moieties, each

---

[40]D. Tugby, *Cultural Change and Identity* (St. Lucia: University of Queensland Press, 1977), p. xiv.

[41]Ricklefs, *Jogjakarta under Sultan Mangkubumi*, p. 187.

[42]Wolters, *History, Culture and Religion*, pp. 52–55.

playing to the other the vis-a-vis."[43] Our reading of some of the sources from Barus has shown how strands of what, initially, may look like a homogeneous tradition known as the Malay World are, in juxtaposition, each exaggerated against the other, *pakat* and *kuasa*, Hulu and Hilir, Batak and Malay.

This study has commenced a reading of Barus texts. Directions for future research are suggested by the existence of other manuscripts from Barus, which may be read alongside the *Asal* and *Sejarah* chronicles and which will extend the terms of this reading. Future work on other west Sumatran manuscripts will provide a better understanding of this category of frontier literature, with its common themes of travel, settlement, coastal-hinterland relationships, and accommodation between rival groups. The *Tambo Radja dan Loewaq Menangkabau* mentioned above includes, in one chapter, the story of Sultan Ibrahim's journey to Barus, his meeting with Bataks, and his defiance of Aceh which, in this version, is stated in terms of his already being under the sovereignty of Minangkabau. The inclusion of the Ibrahim story and the meeting and accommodation of Bataks and Malays in Barus in a text from the Tarusan region, shows us that links were maintained between the Tarusan settlers in Barus and their original homeland. It also suggests the existence of a textual tradition on the west coast of Sumatra in which texts which were concerned with similar problems of migration, settlement, and cultural meetings drew upon one another for their conventions and shared motifs.

---

[43]Boon, *Other Tribes, Other Scribes*, p.26.

GENEALOGIES

HULU GENEALOGY FROM *ASAL* TEXT

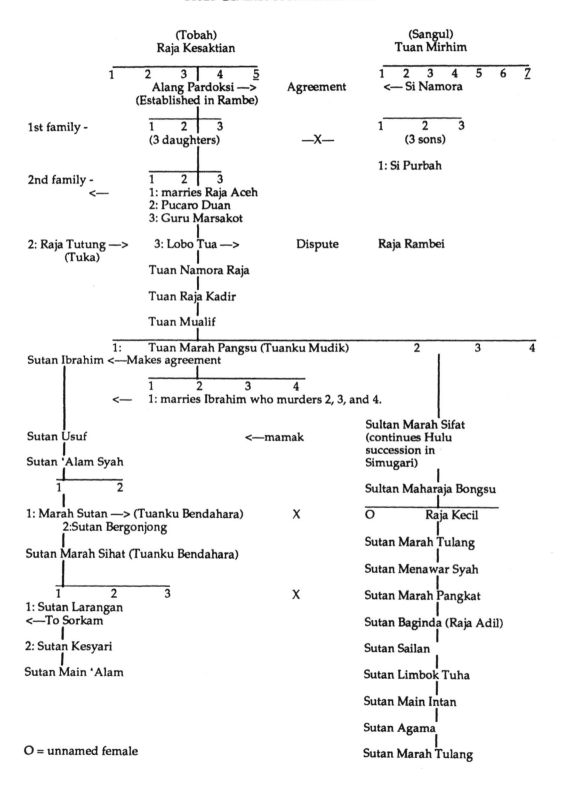

O = unnamed female

HILIR GENEALOGY FROM *SEJARAH* TEXT

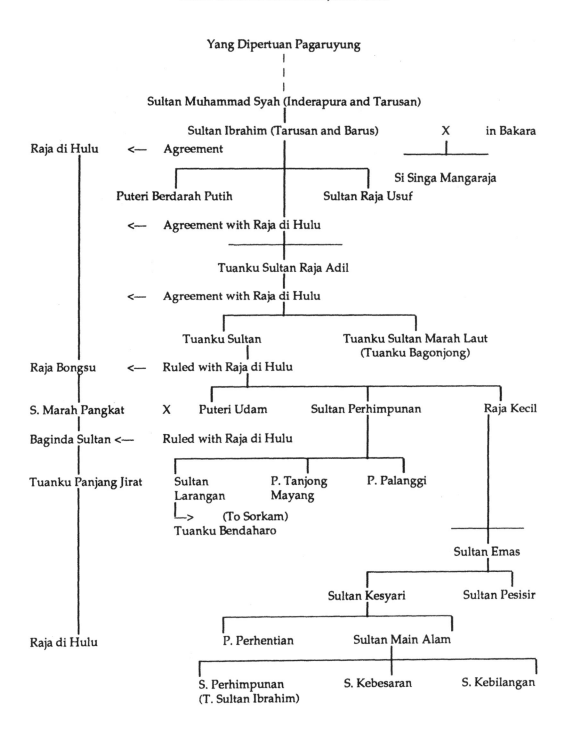

BIBLIOGRAPHY

MANUSCRIPT SOURCES

A) MALAY

Central to this study are two Malay texts from Barus. These are:

1. *Asal Keturunan Raja-Raja Barus.*

2. *Sejarah Tuanku Batu Badan.*

The *Asal* is held in the manuscripts section of the Museum Nasional in Jakarta, ML. 162. The *Sejarah* is in the possession of the descendants of the Raja di Hilir family in Barus. The texts are described in full in Chapter Three.

A Romanized and printed, though unpublished, version of the *Sejarah* has also been consulted. This is:

3. *Sejarah Kedatangan Tuanku Batu Badan ke Daerah Barus*, romanized by Azhar bin Marah Hasyim Gelar Namora Ladang—Barus, 1973. Printed privately.

4. Leiden University Library:

Cod. Or 3303

Cod. Or.3205 B

5. V. E. Korn Collection:

No. 436, *Tambo asal-oesoel ketoeroenan raja Taroesan datang kenegeri Baroes*, containing 3 MSS.

No. 343, *Tambo Negeri Padang.*

6. Instituut voor de Tropen, Amsterdam:

Hikajat Ketoeroenan Radja di Koeria Ilir,

Ijzeren Kastlijst G 58 -112.4 143 Sin 997=540

B) DUTCH

Dutch manuscript sources which have been consulted include:

1. Papers in the Algemeen Rijksarchief, The Hague. Relevant papers from:

Overgekomen Brieven en Papieren (Batavia's Inkomend Brievenboek), Sumatra's Westkust, Sillida and Tico, 1661–1735.

2. Papers in the Arsip Nasional, Jakarta.

SWK 8	*Memorie van F. van de Wall, 1760.*
SWK 10	*J. L.. van Bazel, De Radicaale Beschrijving van Sumatra's Westkust, 1761.*
SWK 20	*Contractbundel, Sumatra's Westkust—1660–1694.*

Memorie van Overgave en Politieke Verslagen:

Lith, P. C. A. *Memorie van overgave van het bestuur der onderafdeeling Baroes, Bataklanden en Tapanoeli, 1911.*

Gobee, E. *Memorie van overgave van het bestuur der onderafdeeling Baroes, Bataklanden en Tapanoeli, 1914.*

Instituut voor de Tropen, Amsterdam:

"Onze Vestiging te Baroes." Broch Onz. 93=542.

C) ENGLISH

Canning, Captain J. Report of the 24th November 1814, *Sumatra Factory Records*, vol. 27.

PUBLISHED SOURCES

MALAY TEXTS

Brakel, L. F., ed. *The Hikayat Muhammad Hanafiyyah* 2 vols. The Hague: Martinus Nijhoff, 1975.

Brown, C. C., trans. *Sejarah Melayu; or Malay Annals.* Kuala Lumpur: Oxford University Press, 1976.

Cense, A. A., ed. *De Kroniek van Bandjarmasin.* Santpoort: C. A. Mees, 1928.

Drewes, G.W., ed. *Hikajat Potjut Muhamat: An Acehnese Epic.* The Hague: Martinus Nijhoff, 1979.

Hadidjaja, Tardjan, ed. *'Adat Raja-Raja Melayu.* Kuala Lumpur: Pustaka Antara, 1964.

Hill, A. A., trans. "Hikayat Raja-Raja Pasai." *JMBRAS* 33, 2 (1960): 1–215.

Iskandar, Teuku, ed. *De Hikayat Aceh.* The Hague: Martinus Nijhoff, 1958.

Liaw Yock Fang, ed. *Undang-Undang Melaka.* The Hague: Martinus Nijhoff, 1976.

Low, J., trans. *Marong Mahawangsa: The Kedah Annals.* Bangkok: American Presbyterian Mission Press Bangkok, 1908.

Raja Ali Haji ibn Ahmad. *The Precious Gift—Tuhfat al-Nafis,* an annotated translation by Virginia Matheson and Barbara Watson Andaya. Kuala Lumpur: Oxford University Press, 1982.

Raja Chulan. *Misa Melayu.* Kuala Lumpur: Pustaka Antara, 1966.

Ras, J. J., ed. *Hikayat Bandjar: A Study in Malay Historiography.* The Hague: Martinus Nijhoff, 1968.

Teeuw, A. and Wyatt, D. K., eds. *Hikayat Patani: The Story of Patani.* The Hague: Martinus Nijhoff, 1970.

OTHER PUBLISHED SOURCES

Aardrijkskundig en Statistisch Woordenboek van Nederlandsch Indië. Amsterdam: van Kampen, 1861.

Abdullah, Taufik. "Adat and Islam: An Examination of Conflict in Minangkabau." *Indonesia* 2 (1966): 1–24.

———. "Some Notes on the Kaba Tjindua Mato: An Example of Minangkabau Traditional Literature." *Indonesia* 9 (1970): 1–23.

———. "Modernization in the Minangkabau World." In *Culture and Politics in Indonesia,* edited by C. Holt, pp. 179–246. Ithaca: Cornell University Press, 1972.

al-Attas, Syed M. Naguib. "New Light on the Life of Hamza Fansūrī." *JMBRAS* 40, 1 (1967): 42–51.

———. *The Mysticism of Hamza Fansuri.* Kuala Lumpur: University of Malaya Press, 1970.

———. *Rānīri and the Wujūdiyyah of 17th Century Aceh.* Kuala Lumpur: Malaysian Branch of the Royal Asiatic Society, 1966.

Alwi bin Sheikh Alhady. *Malay Customs and Traditions.* Singapore: Eastern Universities Press Ltd., 1962.

Andaya, B. W. "The Nature of the State in Eighteenth Century Perak." In *Pre-Colonial State Systems in Southeast Asia*, edited by A. Reid and L. Castles. Kuala Lumpur: Malaysian Branch of the Royal Asiatic Society, 1975.

————. *Perak: The Abode of Grace*. Kuala Lumpur: Oxford University Press, 1979.

Andaya, L. *The Kingdom of Johor, 1641–1728*. Kuala Lumpur: Oxford University Press, 1975.

————. "Treaty Conceptions and Misconceptions: A Case Study from South Sulawesi." *BKI* 134 (1978): 275–95.

Anon. "Verslag van een reis van den controleur van Baros naar de beoosten Baros gelegen onafhankelijke landschappen in het Jaar 1883." *TBB* 52 (1917): 195–205; 252–65.

————. "Battaksche Landschappen grenzende aan de Residente Tapanolie." *TNI* n.s. 1, 1 (1882): 32–40.

————. "Bijdrage tot de kennis van het Grondbezit op Sumatra." *TNI* 14, 2 (1852): 109–18.

Barbier, J. P. "The Megaliths of the Toba Batak Country." In *Cultures and Societies of North Sumatra*, edited by Rainer Carle. Berlin and Hamburg: Reimer, 1987.

Bartlett, H. H. "A Batak and Malay Chant on Rice Cultivation, with Introductory Notes on Bilingualism and Acculturation in Indonesia." *Proceedings of the American Philosophical Society* 96 (1952): 629–52.

Bastin, J. "Problems of Personality in the Reinterpretation of Modern Malaysian History." In *Malaysian and Indonesian Studies*, edited by J. Bastin and R. Roolvink, pp. 141–55. Oxford: Clarendon Press, 1964.

———— *The British in West Sumatra*. Kuala Lumpur: University of Malaya Press, 1965.

Bataksch Instituut, Leiden. *De Islam in de Bataklanden*. Leiden: S. C. van Doesburg, 1909.

Bazel, J. L. van "Begin en Voortgang van Onze Handel en Bezittingen op Sumatra's Westkust." *TNI* 9, 2 (1847): 1–95.

Beck, W. J. "De Bestuursreorganisatie in Tapanoeli." *TBB* 52 (1917): 283–91.

Boon, James A. *Other Tribes, Other Scribes. Symbolic Anthropology in the Comparative Study of Cultures, Histories, Religions, and Texts*. Cambridge: Cambridge University Press, 1982.

Bosch, F. D. K. "De Rijkssieraden van Pagar Roejoeng." *OV* (1930), pp. 202–15.

Bowen, John R. "Cultural Models for Historical Genealogies: The Case of the Melaka Sultanate." In *Melaka. The Transformation of a Malay Capital*, edited by Kernial Singh Sandhu and Paul Wheatley. Kuala Lumpur: Oxford University Press, 1983.

Brakel, L. F. "The Birth Place of Hamza Fansuri." *JMBRAS* 42, 2 (1969): 206–12.

————. "Hamza Pansuri. Notes on: Yoga Practices, Lahir dan Zahir, the 'Taxallos', Punning, A Difficult Passage in the Kitāb al Muntahī, Hamza's Likely Place of Birth, and Hamza's Imagery." *JMBRAS* 52, 1, (1979): 73–99.

————, trans. *Notes on the Structure of the Classical Malay Hikayat*, by A. Bausani, Clayton: Monash University Centre of Southeast Asian Studies, 1979.

Bronson, B. "Exchange at the Upstream and Downstream Ends: Notes Toward a Functional Model of the Coastal State in Southeast Asia." In *Economic Exchange and Social Interaction in Southeast Asia: Perspectives from Prehistory, History and Ethnography*, edited by K. L. Hutterer, pp. 39–52. Ann Arbor: University of Michigan, 1978.

Buchari. "Sri Maharaja Mapanji Garasakan." *Madjalah Ilmu-Ilmu Sastra Indonesia* 4, 1 and 2 (1968): 8–9.

Burkhill, I. H. *A Dictionary of the Economic Products of the Malay Peninsula*. 2 vols. Kuala Lumpur: Governments of Malaysia and Singapore, 1966; first published London, 1935.

Burton and Ward, "Report of a Journey into the Batak Country in the Interior of Sumatra in the Year 1824." *Transactions of the Royal Asiatic Society* 1 (1827): 485–513.

Casparis, J. G. de. *Prasasti Indonesia. Selected Inscriptions from the 7th to the 9th Centuries*. Bandung: Masa Baru, 1956.

Castles, L. "Statelessness and Stateforming Tendencies among the Batak before Colonial Rule." In *Pre-Colonial State Systems in Southeast Asia*, edited by A. Reid and L. Castles, pp. 67–76. Kuala Lumpur: Malaysian Branch of the Royal Asiatic Society, 1975.

Chijs, J. A. van der. *Inventaris van 's Lands Archief te Batavia 1602–1816*. Batavia: Landsdrukkerij, 1882.

Cortesão, A., trans. *The Suma Oriental of Tomé Pires*. 2 vols. London: Haklyut Society, 1944.

Coolhaas, W. Ph. *Generale Missiven van Gouverneurs-Generaal en Raden aan Heren XVII Der Verenigde Oostindische Compagnie*. 7 vols. The Hague: Martinus Nijhoff, 1960–1985.

Couperus, F. E. *Het rechtswezen op Sumatra's Westkust*. Leiden: P. Somerwil, 1882.

Couperus, P. Th. "De Residentie Tapanoeli (Sumatra's westkust) in 1852." *TBG* 4 (1855): 216–56.

Cunningham, C. E. "Order and Change in an Antoni Diarchy." *Southwestern Journal of Anthropology* 21 (1965): 359–81.

Dagh-Register, Gehouden int Casteel Batavia vant passerende daer ter plaetse als over geheel Nederlandts-India. 31 vols. The Hague: M. Nijhoff, 1887–1931.

Dept. Pendidikan dan Kebudayaan. *Katalogus Koleksi Naskah Melayu Museum Pusat*. Jakarta: DP&K, 1972.

Deutz, G. J. J. "Baros." *TBG* 22 (1874): 156–63.

Dijk, P. A. L. E. "Eenige Aanteekeningen omtrent de van Verschillende Stammen (Margas) en de Stamverdeeling bij de Bataks. Het Priesterhoofd Si Singa Mangaradja, zijn Ontstaan en zijne Afkomst. Het Eten van Menschenvleesch bij de Battaks." *TBG* 38 (1895): 296–315.

Djajadiningrat, R. H. "Critische overzicht van de in Maleishe werken vervatte gegevens over de geschiedenis van he Soeltanaat van Atjeh." *BKI* 65 (1911): 135–265.

Dobbin, C. *Islamic Revivalism in a Changing Peasant Economy—Central Sumatra, 1784–1847*. Copenhagen: Scandinavian Institute of Asian Studies, 1983.

Drakard, Jane "Upland-Downland Relationships in Barus: A Northwest Sumatran Case Study." In *The Malay-Islamic World of Sumatra*, edited by J. Maxwell, pp. 74–95. Clayton: Monash University Centre of Southeast Asian Studies, 1982.

——— "Ideological Adaptation on a Malay Frontier." *JSEAS* 17, 1 (March, 1986): 39–58.

——— "An Indian Ocean Port: Sources for the Earlier History of Barus." *Archipel* 37 (1989): 53–83.

———, ed. *Sejarah Raja-Raja Barus. Dua Naskah dari Barus*. Jakarta, Bandung: Ecole Française D'Extreme-Orient, 1988.

Dunn, F. G. *Rain Forest Collectors and Traders: A Study of Resource Utilization in Modern and Ancient Malaya*. Kuala Lumpur: Malaysian Branch of the Royal Asiatic Society, 1975.

Edwards McKinnon, E. "A Note on the Discovery of Spur-marked Yueh-type Sherds at Bukit Seguntang, Palembang." *JMBRAS* 52, 2 (1979): 41–46.

Ekadjati, S. E. *Penyebaran Agama Islam di Pulau Sumatera*. Jakarta: P. T. Sanggabuwana, 1975.

Emerson, R. *Malaysia*. Kuala Lumpur: University of Malaya Press, 1964.

Encylopaedia van Nederlansch-Indië. 9 vols. The Hague: Martinus Nijhoff and E. J. Brill, 1917.

Endert, F. H. "Boschbouwkundige Aanteekeningen over een Reis in Atjeh, Sumatra's Oostkust, Tapanoeli en Sumatra's Westkust." *Tectona*, no. 18 (1925): 1–16.

Errington, S. "Some Comments on Style in the Meanings of the Past." *JAS* 38, 2 (1979): 231–44.

Fatimi, S. Q. "In Quest of Kalah." *JSEAH* 1, 2 (1960): 65–109.

Ferrand, G. *Relations de voyages et textes géographiques arabs, persans et turks relatifs a l'Extrême-Orient du VIIIe au XVII siècles*. 2 vols. Paris, 1913–1914.

——— "Le K'ouen-louen et les anciennes navigations interoceaniques dans les mers du sud." *JA* (July–August, 1919): 5–68.

Forster, E. M. *The Hill of Devi*. London: Harmondsworth, 1965.

Fox, James J. "Obligation and Alliance: State Structure and Moiety Organization in Thie, Roti." In *The Flow of Life*, edited by James J. Fox. Cambridge, Mass: Harvard University Press, 1980.

————. "Models and Metaphors: Comparative Research in Eastern Indonesia." In *The Flow of Life*, edited by James J. Fox, pp. 327–33.

————, ed. *To Speak in Pairs: Essays on the Ritual Languages of Eastern Indonesia*. Cambridge, Mass: Cambridge University Press, 1988.

Francis, E. "Korte Beschrijving van het Nederlansche Grondgebeid ter Westkust van Sumatra in 1839." *TNI* 2, no. 1 (1839): 28–45; no. 2, pp. 90–112; no. 4, pp. 203–21.

————. "De Vestiging der Nederlanders ter Westkust van Sumatra." *TBG* 5 (n.s. 2), 1–2 (1856): 8–121.

Freeman-Grenville, G. S. P. *The Muslim and Christian Calendars*. London: Oxford University Press, 1963.

Geertz, C. *Negara: The Theatre State in Nineteenth Century Bali*. Princeton: Princeton University Press, 1980.

Gent, H. C., trans. *The Voyages and Adventures of Fernand Mendez Pinto*. London: Printed by J. Macock for Henry Cripps and Lodowick Lloyd, 1653.

Gobee, E. "Dr. Neubronner van der Tuuk's Bezoek aan Si Singa Mangaradja in 1853 van Bataksche zijde Toegelicht." *TAG* 34 (1917): 366–69.

Goldsworthy, D. "Honey Collecting Ceremonies on the East Coast of North Sumatra." In *Studies in Indonesian Music*, edited by M. J. Kartomi. Clayton: Monash University Centre of Southeast Asian Studies, 1978.

Goudie, D. "Syair Perang Siak: An Example of a Misunderstood but Rewarding Eighteenth Century Malay Text." *Archipel*, no. 20 (1980): 233–55.

Gullick, J. M. *Indigenous Political Systems of Western Malaya*. London: The Athlone Press, 1958.

Graves, E. E. *The Minangkabau Response to Dutch Colonial Rule in the Nineteenth Century*. Ithaca: Cornell Modern Indonesia Project, 1981.

Hadidjaja, Tardjan, ed. '*Adat Raja-Raja Melayu*. Kuala Lumpur: Pustaka Antara, 1964.

Hall, K.R. "The Coming of Islam to the Archipelago: A Reassessment." in K.L. Hutterer (ed.), Economic Exchange and Social Interaction in Southeast Asia, Ann Arbor: University of Michigan,1978, pp.213–33.

Heeres, J. E. and Stapel, F. W., eds. *Corpus Diplomaticum Neerlando-Indicum*. Vols. I–V. *BKI* (The Hague: Martinus Nijhoff), vol. 57 (1907); vol. 87 (1931); vol. 91 (1934); vol. 93 (1935); vol. 96 (1938).

Heine-Geldern, R. "Le Pays de P'i-k'ien, Le Roi au Grand Cou et Le Singa Mangaradja." *BEFEO* 49 (1959): 361–404.

Hellwig, C. M. S. and Robson, S. O. *A Man of Indonesian Letters. Essays in Honour of Professor A. Teeuw*. Dordrecht, Holland/Cinnaminson, N.J.: Foris, 1986.

Hooker, M. B. *Adat Laws in Modern Malaya*. Kuala Lumpur: Oxford University Press, 1972.

Ijzerman, J. W. *Dwars door Sumatra, Tocht van Padang naar Siak*. Haarlem: F. Bohn, 1895.

Iskandar, T. *Kamus Dewan*. Kuala Lumpur: Dewan Bahasa dan Pustaka, 1970.

James, K. A. "De Geboorte van Singa Maharadja en het ontstaan van de Koeria (District) Ilir in de Onderafdeeling Baros." *TBG* 45 (1902): 134–45.

Johns, A. H. "The Turning Image: Myth and Reality in Malay Perceptions of the Past." In *Perceptions of the Past in Southeast Asia*, edited by A. Reid and D. Marr, pp. 43–67. Singapore: Published for the Asian Studies Association of Australia by Heinemann Educational Books (Asia) Ltd., 1979.

Josselin De Jong, P. E. de *Minangkabau and Negeri Sembilan*. The Hague: Martinus Nijhoff, 1952.

————. "The Character of the Malay Annals." In *Malayan and Indonesian Studies*, edited by J. Bastin and R. Roolvink, pp. 235–42. Oxford: Clarendon Press, 1964.

Joustra, M. *Batakspiegel*. Vol. 1. Leiden: S. C. van Doesburgh, 1910.

————. *Van Medan naar Padang en Terug.* Leiden: S.C. van Doesburg, 1915.

————. *Minangkabau. Overzicht van land, geschiedenis en volk.* Leiden: Minangkabau Instituut, 1920.

Juynboll, H. H. *Catalogus van de Maleische en Sundaneesche handschriften der Leidsche Universiteits-Bibliotheek.* Leiden: E. J. Brill, 1899.

Kartomi, M. "Minangkabau Musical Culture." In *What Is Modern Indonesian Culture?* edited by G. Davis. Athens, Ohio: Ohio University, Center for International Studies, 1979.

————. "Kapri: A Synthesis of Malay and Portuguese Music on the West Coast of Sumatra." In *Cultures and Societies of North Sumatra,* edited by Rainer Carle. Berlin and Hamburg: Dietrich Reimer Verlag, 1987.

Kathirithamby-Wells, J. "Acehnese Control over West Sumatra up to the Treaty of Painan, 1663." *JSEAH* 10, 3 (1969): 453–70.

————. "The Inderapura Sultanate: The Foundations of Its Rise and Decline from the Sixteenth to Eighteenth Centuries." *Indonesia* 21 (1976): 65–85.

————. *The British West Sumatra Presidency (1760–85): Problems of Early Colonial Enterprise.* Kuala Lumpur: Universiti Malaya, 1977.

Kato, Tsuyoshi. *Matriliny and Migration. Evolving Minangkabau Traditions in Indonesia.* Ithaca: Cornell University Press, 1982.

————. "Rantau Pariaman: The World of Minangkabau Coastal Merchants in the Nineteenth Century." *JAS* 39 (1980): 729–52.

Kemp, P. H. van der. "Eene Bijdrage tot E.B. Kielstra's Opstellen over Sumatra's Westkust." *BKI* 44 (1894): 257–320; 525–615.

Kempe, J.E. and Winstedt, R.O., eds. "A Malay Legal Digest." *JMBRAS* 21, 2 (1948): 1–67.

Kern, H. *Verspreide Geschriften Onder Zijn Toezicht Verzameld.* Vol. 6. The Hague: Martinus Nijhoff, 1913–1928.

Kielstra, E. B. "Onze Kennis van Sumatra's Westkust, omstreeks de helfd der Achttiende Eeuw." *BKI* 36, (1887): 499–559.

————. "Sumatra's Westkust van 1826–32." *BKI* 36, (1887): 8–163.

————. "Sumatra's Westkust van 1826–32." *BKI* 37 (1888): 216–380.

————. "Sumatra's Westkust van 1833–1835." *BKI* 38 (1889): 161–249; 313–79; 467–514.

————. "Sumatra's Westkust van 1836–40." *BKI* 39 (1890): 127–221; 263–348.

————. "Sumatra's Westkust van 1841–49." *BKI* 40 (1891): 106–47; 385–462; 531–611.

————. "Sumatra's Westkust Sedert 1850." *BKI* 41 (1892): 254–330; 42 (1892): 622–706.

Klerck, E. S. de *De Atjèh Oorlog.* 2 vols. The Hague: Martinus Nijhoff, 1912.

Kreemer, J. "De Winning van Kamferhout, Kamferolie en kamfer in het Singkelsche." *TAG* 33 (1916): 880–87.

Kroeskamp, H. *De Westkust en Minangkabau 1665–1668.* Utrecht: Academisch Proefschrift University of Leiden, printed by Schotanus and Jens, 1931.

Krom, N. J. *Hindoe-Javaansche Gescheidenis.* The Hague: Martinus Nijhoff, 1930.

Lange, H. M. *Het Nederlandsch Oost-Indische Leger ter Westkust van Sumatra (1819–1845).* 's-Hertogenbosch: Gebroeders Muller, 1854.

Leeuw, W. J. A. de. *Het Painainsche Contract.* Amsterdam: H. J. Paris, 1926.

Ligny, J. de. "Legendarische Herkomst der Kamfer Baroes." *TBG* 63 (1923): 549–55.

Lith, P. A. van. *Nederlandsche Oost-Indië.* Doesborgh: J. C. van der Schenk Brill, 1877.

Lijst van de Voornaamste Aardrijkskundige Namen in de Nederlandsch Indischen Archipel. Westevreden: Landsdrukkerij, 1923.

Lombard, D. *Le Sultanat D'Atjeh au temps D'Iskandar Muda, 1607–1636.* Paris: Ecole Français D'Extrême Orient, 1967.

Loos, H. "Iets over Benzoe in Tapanoelie." *Teysmannia,* no. 32 (1921): 398–408.

Low, Hugh. "Selesilah (Book of Descent) of the Rajas of Bruni." *JMBRAS* 5 (1880): 1–35.

Lukman Nurhakim. "La Ville de Barus: Etude archéologique préliminaire." *Archipel* 37 (1989): 43–53.

Macknight, C. C. "The Rise of Agriculture in South Sulawesi before 1600." *RIMA* 17 (1983): 92–116.

Macleod, N. "De Oost-Indische Compagnie op Sumatra in de 17e eeuw." *Indische Gids* 1 (1904): 620–638; 2 (1904): 795–805; 1 (1905): 470–568; 2 (1905): 127–42; 1 (1906): 777–808; 2 (1906): 1420–49.

Maier, Hendrik M. J. *In the Center of Authority: The Malay Hikayat Merong Mahawangsa*. Ithaca: Cornell Southeast Asia Program Studies on Southeast Asia, 1988.

Majolelo, Yunus St. *Kamus Kecil Bahasa Minangkabau*. Jakarta: Mutuara, 1983.

Manguin, P.-Y. "Shipshape Societies: Boat Symbolism and Early Political Systems in the Malay World." In *Southeast Asia in the 9th to 14th Centuries*, edited by David G. Marr and A. C. Milner. Singapore: Institute of Southeast Asian Studies, 1986.

Marsden, W. The History of Sumatra. London, 1811. Reprinted Kuala Lumpur: Oxford University Press, 1975.

———. *A Dictionary and Grammar of the Malayan Language*. London: Printed for the author by Cox and Baylis, 1812. Reprinted Singapore: Oxford University Press, 1984 with an Introduction by Russel Jones, 2 vols.

———. *Memoirs of a Malayan Family*. London: Oriental Translation Fund, 1830.

Matheson, V. "Concepts of State in the Tuhfat al Nafis." In *Pre-Colonial State Systems in Southeast Asia*, edited by A Reid and L. Castles, pp. 12–22. Kuala Lumpur: Malaysian Branch of the Royal Asiatic Society, 1975.

———. "Concepts of Malay Ethos in Indigenous Malay Writings." JSEAS 10, 2 (1979): 351–71.

———. "Sovereigns and Scribes: Life as Reflected in Some of the Literature of the Malays." In *Australian Perspectives*, vol. 1, edited by J. J. Fox et al., pp. 183–97. Canberra: Research School of Pacific Studies, Australian National University, 1980.

———. "Strategies of Survival: The Malay Royal Line of Lingga-Riau." JSEAS 17, 1 (March 1986): 5–39.

Matheson, V. and Hooker, M. B. "Slavery in the Malay Texts: Categories of Dependency and Compensation." In *Slavery, Bondage and Dependency in Southeast Asia*, by A. Reid, pp. 182–209. St. Lucia: University of Queensland Press, 1983.

Matheson, V. and Milner, A. C. *Perceptions of the Haj: Five Malay Texts*. Singapore: Institute of Southeast Asian Studies, 1984.

Maxwell, W. E. "Notes on Two Perak Manuscripts." *JSBRAS* 2 (1878): 183–93.

Meerwaldt, J. H. *Handleiding tot de Beoefening der Bataksche Taal*. Leiden: E. J. Brill, 1904.

Meilink-Roelofsz, M. A. P. *Asian Trade and European Influence in the Indonesian Archipelago between 1500 and about 1630*. The Hague: Martinus Nijhoff, 1962.

Mennes, H. M. M. "Eenige Aanteekeningen Omtrent Djambi." *Kolonial Tijdschrift* (1932): 26–36.

Meurexa, Dada. *Sejarah Masuknya Islam ke Bandar Barus Sumatera Utara*. Medan: Sasterawan, 1963.

Miksic, J. "Classical Archaeology in Sumatra." *Indonesia* 30 (1980): 43–66.

Miles, D. *Cutlass and Crescent Moon: A Case Study in Social and Political Change in Outer Indonesia*. Sydney: Centre for Asian Studies, University of Sydney, 1976.

Milner, A. C. "Islam and Malay Kingship." *JRAS* 1 (1981): 46–70.

———. *Kerajaan: Malay Political Culture on the Eve of Colonial Rule*. Tucson: The University of Arizona Press, 1982.

Milner, A. C., McKinnon, E. Edwards and Tengku Luckman Sinar S.H. "Aru and Kota Cina." *Indonesia* 26 (1978): 1–42.

Moor, J. H. *Notices of the Indian Archipelago and Adjacent Countries*. London, 1837. Reprinted London: Cass, 1968.

Mulia, R. *Nias: The Only Older Megalithic Tradition in Indonesia.* Jakarta: Bulletin of the Research Centre of Archaeology of Indonesia, No. 16, 1981.

Naim, Asma M. and Mochtar, eds. *Bibliografi Minangkabau.* Singapore: Singapore University Press, 1975.

Naim, Mochtar. "Merantau: Minangkabau Voluntary Migration" Ph.D. thesis, University of Singapore, 1973. Published in Indonesian as *Merantau: Pola Migrasi Suku Minangkabau.* Yogyakarta: Gadjah Mada University Press, 1979.

————, ed. *Menggali Hukum Tanah dan Hukum Waris.* Padang: Centre for Minangkabau Studies, 1968.

Netscher, E. "Togtjes in het gebied van Riouw en Onderhoorigheden." *TBG* 14 (1864): 340–51.

Newbold, T. J. *British Settlements in the Straits of Malacca.* 2 vols. London, 1839. Reprinted Kuala Lumpur: Oxford University Press, 1971.

Nihom, Max. "Ruler and Realm: The Division of Airlangga's Kingdom in the Fourteenth Century." *Indonesia* 42 (1986): 78–101.

Pamoentjak St. M. Thaib. *Kamoes Bahasa Minangkabau-Bahasa Melajoe-Riau.* Batavia: Balai Poestaka, 1935.

Pamuntjak K. St. et al. *Peribahasa.* Jakarta: Balai Pustaka, 1983.

Pelliot, P. "Deux itinéraires de Chine en Inde à la fin du VIIIe siècle." *BEFEO* 4 (1904): 131–413.

Pigeaud, T. G. *Java in the Fourteenth Century: A Study in Cultural History.* Vol. 4. The Hague: Martinus Nijhoff, 1960.

Pleyte, C. M. "De Verkenning der Bataklanden." *TAG* 12 (1895): 71–96 and 727–740.

————. "Herinneringen Uit Oost Indië–Soematra's Westkust." *TAG* 17 (1900): 1–48.

Poerbatjaraka, R. M. Ng., Voorhoeve, P., and Hooykaas, C. *Indonesische Handschriften.* Bandung: A. C. Nix and Co., 1950.

Pusat Penelitian Purbakala. *Pra Seminar Penelitian Sriwijaya.* Jakarta: Proyek Penelitian Purbakala Jakarta, Departmen P & K, 1979.

Raet, J.A.M. van Cats Baron De. "Reize in de Battaklanden in December 1886 en Januarij 1867." *TBG* 22 (1875):164–219.

Rainer, Carle, ed. *Cultures and Societies of North Sumatra.* Berlin/Hamburg: Reimer, 1987.

Reid, A. *The Contest for North Sumatra: Aceh, the Netherlands and Britain, 1858–1898.* Kuala Lumpur: Oxford University Press, 1969.

————. *The Blood of the People: Revolution and the End of Traditional Rule in Northern Sumatra.* Kuala Lumpur: Oxford University Press, 1979.

————. "A Great Seventeenth Century Indonesian Family: Matoaya and Pattingalloang of Makassar." *Masyarakat Indonesia* 8, 1 (1981): 1–28.

————. "The Rise of Makassar." *RIMA* 17 (1983): 117–60.

Ricklefs, M. C. *Jogjakarta under Sultan Mangkubumi 1749–1792.* London: Oxford University Press, 1974.

————. *A History of Modern Indonesia.* London: Macmillan, 1981.

Risala Seminar Sedjarah Masuknya Islam ke Indonesia. Medan: Panitia Seminar Sedjarah Masuknja Islam ke Indonesia, 1963.

Ritter, W. L. "Korte Aanteekeningen over het Rijk van Atjin." *TNI* 1, 2 (1838): 454–76; 2, 1 (1839): 1–27; 2, 2 (1839): 67–90.

Ronkel, Ph. S. "Catalogus der Maleische Handschriften in het van Museum van het Bataviaasch Genootschap van Kunsten en Wetenschappen." *VBG* 57 (1909): 475–509.

————. *Supplement-Catalogus der Maleische en Minangkabausche Handschriften in de Leidsche Universiteit-s-Bibliotheek.* Leiden: E. J. Brill, 1921.

————. "Nadere gegevens omtrent het Hasan-Hoesain feest." *TBG* 56 (1914): 334–45.

Rosenberg, H. van. "Beschrijving van het District Singkel." *TBG* 3 (1855): 394–476.

Sastri, K. A. Nilakanta. "A Tamil Merchant Guild in Sumatra." *TBG* 72 (1932): 314–27.

Sauvaget, J. *Aḥ bār aṣ-Ṣīn wa'l-Hind: Relation de la Chine et de l'Inde, rédigée en 851.* Paris: Belles Lettres, 1948.

Schnepper, W. C. R. "Benzoë Cultuur en Volkswelvaart in Tapanoeli (Sumatra)." Tectona, no. 16 (1923): 264–75.

Schrieke, B. *Indonesian Sociological Studies.* 2 vols. The Hague and Bandung: W. van Hoeve, 1957.

Sejarah Gereja Katolik Indonesia. Vol. 1. Flores: Bagian Dokumentasi Penerangan Kantor Waligereja Indonesia, 1974.

Sheppard, Mubin. *Taman Indera. A Royal Pleasure Garden: Malay Decorative Arts and Pastimes.* Kuala Lumpur: Oxford University Press, 1972.

Siagian, Toenggoel P. "Bibliography of the Batak Peoples." *Indonesia* 2 (1966): 161–84.

Sidjabat, W. B. *Ahu Si Singamangaraja.* Jakarta: Sinar Harapan, 1982.

Siegel, J. "Awareness of the Past in the Poetjoet Moehamat." In *Southeast Asian History and Historiography,* edited by C. D. Cowan and O. W. Wolters, pp. 321–31. Ithaca: Cornell University Press, 1976.

————. *Shadow and Sound: The Historical Thought of a Sumatran People.* Chicago: University of Chicago Press, 1979.

Skeat, W. W. and Blagden, C. O. *Malay Magic.* London: Macmillan and Co. Ltd., 1900.

————. *Pagan Races of the Malay Peninsula.* 2 vols. London: Frank Cass & Co., First Published 1906, New Impression 1966.

Skinner, C. "The Influence of Arabic upon Modern Malay." *Intisari,* no. 2, 1 (n.d.): 34–47.

Snouck Hurgronje. *The Acehnese.* 2 vols. Translated by A. W. S. O'Sullivan. Leiden/London: E. J. Brill, 1906.

Stapel, F. W. "Een Verhandeling over het ontstaan van het Minangkabausche rijk en zijn Adat." *BKI* 92 (1935): 459–70.

Stemfoort, J. W. and Siethoff, J. J. *Atlas van Nederlandsch Oost-Indië.* Batavia: Department van Kolonien, 1897–1904.

Sutherland, H. "Power and Politics in South Sulawesi 1860–1880." *RIMA* 17 (1983): 161–207.

Sweeney, A. "Silsilah Raja-Raja Berunai." *JMBRAS* 41, 2 (1968): 1–82.

————. *Authors and Audiences in Traditional Malay Literature.* Berkeley: Center for South and Southeast Asian Studies, University of California, 1980.

————. "The 'Literary' Study of Malay-Indonesian Literature: Some Observations." *JMBRAS* 56, 1 (1983): 33–47.

————. *A Full Hearing. Orality and Literacy in the Malay World.* Berkeley: University of California Press, 1987.

Teeuw, A. "Hikayat Raja-Raja Pasai" and "Sejarah Melayu." In *Malayan and Indonesian Studies,* edited by J. Bastin and R. Roolvink, pp. 222–35. Oxford: Clarendon Press, 1964.

————. "Some Remarks on the Study of So-called Historical Texts in Indonesian Languages." In *Profiles of Malay Culture,* edited by Sartono Kartodirdjo. Jakarta: Ministry of Education and Culture, Directorate General of Culture, 1976.

Tibbetts, G. R. "Pre-Islamic Arabia and South-East Asia." *JMBRAS* 29, 3 (1956): 182–208.

————. "Early Muslim Traders in Southeast Asia." *JMBRAS* 30, 1 (1957): 1–45.

————. *Arab Navigation in the Indian Ocean before the Coming of the Portuguese.* London: Royal Asiatic Society, 1971.

————. *A Study of the Arabic Texts Containing Material on Southeast Asia.* Leiden and London: E. J. Brill for the Royal Asiatic Society, 1979.

Tideman, J. *Hindoe Invloed in de Noordelijke Bataklanden.* Amsterdam: Bataksche Instituut, 1936.

Tideman, J. and Sigar, Ph. F. L. *Jambi.* Amsterdam: Druk de Bussy, 1938.

Tiele, P. A. "De Europeërs in de Maleischen Archipel, 1509–1623." *BKI* 25 (1877): 321–420; 27 (1879): 1–69; 36 (1887): 199–307.

Tugby, D. *Cultural Change and Identity: Mandailing Immigrants in West Malaysia*. Queensland: University of Queensland Press, 1977.

Tuuk, H. N. van der. *Bataksch-Nederduitsch Woordenboek*. Amsterdam: F. Muller, 1861.

_____. *De Pen in Gal Gedoopt, Letters of H. Neubronner van der Tuuk*, edited by R. Nieuwenhuys, Amsterdam: van Oorschot, 1962.

Valentijn, F. *Oud en Nieuw Oost Indien*. Vol. 5, Pt. 2. Dordrecht: J. van Braam, 1724–1726.

Vergouwen, J. C. *The Social Organization and Customary Law of the Toba Bataks of Northern Sumatra*. Translated by Jeune Scott-Kembal. The Hague: Martinus Nijhoff, 1964.

Veth, P. J., ed. *De Vestiging en Uitbreiding der Nederlanders ter Westkust van Sumatra door Generaal-Majoor H. J. J. L. Ridder de Steurs*. Amsterdam: P. N van Kampen, 1849.

Vollenhoven, C. van. *Het Adatrecht van Nederlandsch Indië*. Leiden: E. J. Brill, 1918.

Volz, W. *Nord-Sumatra*. Vol. 1, *Die Bataklander*. Berlin: D. Reimer (E. Vohsen), 1909–1912.

Voorhoeve, P. "Geschiedenis van Baroes." *TBG* 70 (1930): 91–92.

_____. *Critical Survey of Studies on the Languages of Sumatra*. The Hague: Martinus Nijhoff, 1955.

_____. *Codices Batacici*. Leiden: Universitaire Pers, 1977.

Vriese, W. H. de. *De Kamferboom van Sumatra*. Leiden: H. R. de Breuk, 1851.

Vuuren, L. van. "De Handel van Baroes, als oudste haven op Sumatra's Westkust, verklaard; en voor de Toekomst Beschouwd." *TAG* 25, 6 (1908): 1389–1402.

Wake, C. H. "Melaka in the Fifteenth Century: Malay Historical Traditions and the Politics of Islamization." In *Melaka. The Transformation of a Malay Capital*, edited by Kernial Singh Sandhu and Paul Wheatley. Kuala Lumpur: Oxford University Press, 1983.

Westenenk, L. C. "Opstellen over Minangkabau." *TBG* 55 (1913): 234–51.

_____. *De Minangkabausche Nagari*. Weltevreden: Visser, 1918.

Willinck, G. D. *Het Rechtsleven bij de Minangkabausche Maleiers*. Leiden: E. J. Brill, 1909

Wilkinson, R. J. *A Classic Jawi-Malay-English Dictionary*. Singapore: Kelly and Walsh Ltd, 1903.

_____. *Malay-English Dictionary (Romanised)*. 2 vols. London: Macmillan, 1959.

Winstedt, R. O. "Kedah Laws." *JMBRAS* 6, 2 (1928): 1–44.

_____. *Malay Grammar*. 2nd ed. rev. Oxford: Clarendon Press, 1939.

_____. "Kingship and Enthronement in Malaya." *JMBRAS* 20, 1 (1947): 129–40.

_____. *An Unabridged Malay-English Dictionary*. Kuala Lumpur: Marican and Sons, 1967.

_____. "An Old Malay Legal Digest from Perak." *JMBRAS* 26, 1 (1953): 1–13.

_____. *The Malays. A Cultural History*. London and Boston: Routledge & Kegan Paul, 1961.

Wolters, O. W. *Early Indonesian Commerce*. Ithaca: Cornell University Press, 1967.

_____. "Studying Srivijaya." *JMBRAS* 52, 2 (1979): 1–33.

_____. *History, Culture and Region in Southeast Asian Perspective*. Singapore: Institute of Southeast Asian Studies, 1982.

_____. "Possibilities for a Reading of the 1293–1357 Period in the Vietnamese Annals." In *Southeast Asia in the 9th to 14th Centuries*, edited by David G. Marr and A. C. Milner. Singapore: Institute of Southeast Asian Studies, 1986.

Wuisman, J. J. J. M. *Sociale Verandering in Bengkulu. Een Cultuur- sociologische analyse*. Dordrecht, Holland/Cinnaminson, N.J.: Foris Publications, 1985.

Ypes, W. H. K. "Nota Omtrent Singkel en de Pak-Pak Landen." *TBG* 49 (1907): 355–642.

_____. *Bijdrage tot de Kennis van de stamverwantschap, de inheemsche rechts–gemeenschappen en het grondenrecht der Toba en Dairibataks*. Leiden: Uitgegeven door de Adatrechtstichting te Leiden, 1932.

Yule, H. and Cordier, H., trans. *The Book of Ser Marco Polo the Venetian, concerning the Kingdoms and Marvels of the East*. 2 vols. 3rd ed. St. Helier: Armorica, 1975.

Yule, H. and Burnell, A. C., eds. *Hobson-Jobson. A Glossary of Colloquial Anglo-Indian Words and Phrases*. London and New York: Routledge and Kegan Paul, 1968. Originally published 1886.

Zon, P. van. "Korte Mededeeling omtrent den Kamferboom (Dryobalanops aromatica)." *Tectona* 8 (1915): 220–24.

UNPUBLISHED SOURCES

Bowen, J. R. "The History and Structure of Gayo Society: Variation and Change in the Highlands of Aceh." Ph.D. Thesis, The University of Chicago, 1984.

Castles, L. "The Political Life of a Sumatran Residency." Ph.D. Thesis, Yale University, 1972.

Daulay, Z. "Minangkabau: A Preliminary Study of the Culture and People." M.A. Thesis, Cornell University, 1960.

Drakard, J. "A Malay Frontier: The Adaptation of Malay Political Culture in Barus." M.A. Thesis, Monash University, 1984.

Fansuri. "Pembangunan Khusus Kecamatan Barus/Sorkam dan Sekitarnya." Roneod booklet, Jakarta, 1980.

Jaspan, M. A. "From Patriliny to Matriliny. Structural Change among the Redjang of Southwest Sumatra." Ph.D. Thesis, Australian National University, 1964.

Lukman Nurhakim. "Makam Kuno di Daerah Barus. Sumbangan Data Arkeologi Islam." M.A. Thesis, Facultas Sastra, Universitas Indonesia, 1979.

Matheson, V. "Tuhfat Al-Nafis (The Precious Gift), A Nineteenth Century Malay History Critically Examined." Ph.D. Thesis, Department of Indonesian and Malay, Monash University, 1973.

Naim, Mochtar. "Merantau: Minangkabau Voluntary Migration" Ph.D. Thesis, University of Singapore, 1984.

Nurhadi. "Laporan Penelitian Arkeologi Barus." Report of the Pusat Penelitian Arkeologi Nasional, Jakarta 1985.

Reber, Anne Lindsey. "The Private Trade of the British in West Sumatra 1735–1770." Ph.D. Thesis, University of Hull, 1977.

Sinar, Tengku Luckman. "Sibolga dan Pantai Barat Sumatera Utara Dalam Lintasan Sejarah." Unpublished paper, Medan, 1980.

Young, R. L. "The English East India Company and Trade on the West Coast of Sumatra, 1730–1760." Ph.D. Thesis, University of Pennsylvania, 1970.

Wee, Vivienne. "Melayu: Hierarchies of Being in Riau." Ph.D. Thesis, Australian National University, 1985.

ABBREVIATIONS

JOURNALS

BEFEO	*Bulletin de l'Ecole Français d'Extrême-Orient*
BKI	*Bijdragen tot de Taal-, Land- en Volkenkunde van Nederlandsch-Indië.* Koninklijk Instituut voor Taal-, Land- en Volkenkunde van Nederlandsch-Indie
JA	*Journal Asiatique*
JAS	*Journal of Asian Studies*
JMBRAS	*Journal of the Malaysian Branch of the Royal Asiatic Society*
JRAS	*Journal of the Royal Asiatic Society of Great Britain and Ireland*
JSBRAS	*Journal of the Straits Branch of the Royal Asiatic Society*
JSEAH	*Journal of Southeast Asian History*
JSEAS	*Journal of Southeast Asian Studies*
OV	*Oudheidkundige Verslag*
RIMA	*Review of Indonesian and Malayan Studies*
TAG	*Tijdschrift van het Koninklijk Nederlandsch Aardijskundig Genootschap*
TBB	*Tijdschrift voor het Binnenlandsch Bestuur*
TBG	*Tijdschrift voor Indische Taal-, Land- en Volkenkunde* Bataviaasch Genootschap van Kunsten en Wetenschappen
Tectona	*Boschbouwkundig Tijdschrift*
TNI	*Tijdschrift voor Nederlandsch-Indië*
VBG	*Verhandelingen van het Bataviaasch Genootschap van Kunsten en Wetenschappen*

OTHER ABBREVIATIONS

Asal	*Asal Keturunan Raja-Raja Barus*
ENI	*Encyclopaedie van Nederlandsch-Indië*
fol.	folio
MS/MSS	Manuscript/Manuscripts
r.	recto
Sejarah	*Sejarah Tuanku Batu Badan*
SWK	Sumatra's Westkust
v.	verso
VOC	Vereenigde Oostindische Compagnie

INDEX

The majority of proper names and titles used in the Malay Chronicles from Barus are given by chapter rather than page numbers in this index.

SOUTHEAST ASIA PROGRAM PUBLICATIONS

Cornell University

Studies on Southeast Asia

Number 37   *Sumatran Sultanate and Colonial State: Jambi and the Rise of Dutch Imperialism, 1830-1907*, Elsbeth Locher-Scholten, trans. Beverley Jackson. 2003. 332 pp. ISBN 0-87727-736-2.

Number 36   *Southeast Asia over Three Generations: Essays Presented to Benedict R. O'G. Anderson*, ed. James T. Siegel and Audrey R. Kahin. 2003. 398 pp. ISBN 0-87727-735-4.

Number 35   *Nationalism and Revolution in Indonesia*, George McTurnan Kahin, intro. Benedict R. O'G. Anderson (reprinted from 1952 edition, Cornell University Press, with permission). 2003. 530 pp. ISBN 0-87727-734-6.

Number 34   *Golddiggers, Farmers, and Traders in the "Chinese Districts" of West Kalimantan, Indonesia*, Mary Somers Heidhues. 2003. 316 pp. ISBN 0-87727-733-8.

Number 33   *Opusculum de Sectis apud Sinenses et Tunkinenses (A Small Treatise on the Sects among the Chinese and Tonkinese): A Study of Religion in China and North Vietnam in the Eighteenth Century*, Father Adriano de St. Thecla, trans. Olga Dror, with Mariya Berezovska. 2002. 363 pp. ISBN 0-87727-732-X.

Number 32   *Fear and Sanctuary: Burmese Refugees in Thailand*, Hazel J. Lang. 2002. 204 pp. ISBN 0-87727-731-1.

Number 31   *Modern Dreams: An Inquiry into Power, Cultural Production, and the Cityscape in Contemporary Urban Penang, Malaysia*, Beng-Lan Goh. 2002. 225 pp. ISBN 0-87727-730-3.

Number 30   *Violence and the State in Suharto's Indonesia*, ed. Benedict R. O'G. Anderson. 2001. Second printing, 2002. 247 pp. ISBN 0-87727-729-X.

Number 29   *Studies in Southeast Asian Art: Essays in Honor of Stanley J. O'Connor*, ed. Nora A. Taylor. 2000. 243 pp. Illustrations. ISBN 0-87727-728-1.

Number 28   *The Hadrami Awakening: Community and Identity in the Netherlands East Indies, 1900-1942*, Natalie Mobini-Kesheh. 1999. 174 pp. ISBN 0-87727-727-3.

Number 27   *Tales from Djakarta: Caricatures of Circumstances and their Human Beings*, Pramoedya Ananta Toer. 1999. 145 pp. ISBN 0-87727-726-5.

Number 26   *History, Culture, and Region in Southeast Asian Perspectives*, rev. ed., O. W. Wolters. 1999. 275 pp. ISBN 0-87727-725-7.

Number 25   *Figures of Criminality in Indonesia, the Philippines, and Colonial Vietnam*, ed. Vicente L. Rafael. 1999. 259 pp. ISBN 0-87727-724-9.

Number 24   *Paths to Conflagration: Fifty Years of Diplomacy and Warfare in Laos, Thailand, and Vietnam, 1778-1828*, Mayoury Ngaosyvathn and Pheuiphanh Ngaosyvathn. 1998. 268 pp. ISBN 0-87727-723-0.

Number 23   *Nguyễn Cochinchina: Southern Vietnam in the Seventeenth and Eighteenth Centuries*, Li Tana. 1998. Second printing, 2002. 194 pp. ISBN 0-87727-722-2.

Number 22   *Young Heroes: The Indonesian Family in Politics*, Saya S. Shiraishi. 1997. 183 pp. ISBN 0-87727-721-4.

Number 21 *Interpreting Development: Capitalism, Democracy, and the Middle Class in Thailand*, John Girling. 1996. 95 pp. ISBN 0-87727-720-6.

Number 20 *Making Indonesia*, ed. Daniel S. Lev, Ruth McVey. 1996. 201 pp. ISBN 0-87727-719-2.

Number 19 *Essays into Vietnamese Pasts*, ed. K. W. Taylor, John K. Whitmore. 1995. 288 pp. ISBN 0-87727-718-4.

Number 18 *In the Land of Lady White Blood: Southern Thailand and the Meaning of History*, Lorraine M. Gesick. 1995. 106 pp. ISBN 0-87727-717-6.

Number 17 *The Vernacular Press and the Emergence of Modern Indonesian Consciousness*, Ahmat Adam. 1995. 220 pp. ISBN 0-87727-716-8.

Number 16 *The Nan Chronicle*, trans., ed. David K. Wyatt. 1994. 158 pp. ISBN 0-87727-715-X.

Number 15 *Selective Judicial Competence: The Cirebon-Priangan Legal Administration, 1680–1792*, Mason C. Hoadley. 1994. 185 pp. ISBN 0-87727-714-1.

Number 14 *Sjahrir: Politics and Exile in Indonesia*, Rudolf Mrázek. 1994. 536 pp. ISBN 0-87727-713-3.

Number 13 *Fair Land Sarawak: Some Recollections of an Expatriate Officer*, Alastair Morrison. 1993. 196 pp. ISBN 0-87727-712-5.

Number 12 *Fields from the Sea: Chinese Junk Trade with Siam during the Late Eighteenth and Early Nineteenth Centuries*, Jennifer Cushman. 1993. 206 pp. ISBN 0-87727-711-7.

Number 11 *Money, Markets, and Trade in Early Southeast Asia: The Development of Indigenous Monetary Systems to AD 1400*, Robert S. Wicks. 1992. 2nd printing 1996. 354 pp., 78 tables, illus., maps. ISBN 0-87727-710-9.

Number 10 *Tai Ahoms and the Stars: Three Ritual Texts to Ward Off Danger*, trans., ed. B. J. Terwiel, Ranoo Wichasin. 1992. 170 pp. ISBN 0-87727-709-5.

Number 9 *Southeast Asian Capitalists*, ed. Ruth McVey. 1992. 2nd printing 1993. 220 pp. ISBN 0-87727-708-7.

Number 8 *The Politics of Colonial Exploitation: Java, the Dutch, and the Cultivation System*, Cornelis Fasseur, ed. R. E. Elson, trans. R. E. Elson, Ary Kraal. 1992. 2nd printing 1994. 266 pp. ISBN 0-87727-707-9.

Number 7 *A Malay Frontier: Unity and Duality in a Sumatran Kingdom*, Jane Drakard. 1990. 2nd printing 2003. 215 pp. ISBN 0-87727-706-0.

Number 6 *Trends in Khmer Art*, Jean Boisselier, ed. Natasha Eilenberg, trans. Natasha Eilenberg, Melvin Elliott. 1989. 124 pp., 24 plates. ISBN 0-87727-705-2.

Number 5 *Southeast Asian Ephemeris: Solar and Planetary Positions, A.D. 638–2000*, J. C. Eade. 1989. 175 pp. ISBN 0-87727-704-4.

Number 3 *Thai Radical Discourse: The Real Face of Thai Feudalism Today*, Craig J. Reynolds. 1987. 2nd printing 1994. 186 pp. ISBN 0-87727-702-8.

Number 1 *The Symbolism of the Stupa*, Adrian Snodgrass. 1985. Revised with index, 1988. 3rd printing 1998. 469 pp. ISBN 0-87727-700-1.

SEAP Series

Number 20   *Southern Vietnam under the Reign of Minh Mạng (1820-1841): Central Policies and Local Response*, Choi Byung Wook. 2004. 226pp. ISBN 0-87727-138-0.

Number 19   *Gender, Household, State: Đổi Mới in Việt Nam*, ed. Jayne Werner and Danièle Bélanger. 2002. 151 pp. ISBN 0-87727-137-2.

Number 18   *Culture and Power in Traditional Siamese Government*, Neil A. Englehart. 2001. 130 pp. ISBN 0-87727-135-6.

Number 17   *Gangsters, Democracy, and the State*, ed. Carl A. Trocki. 1998. Second printing, 2002. 94 pp. ISBN 0-87727-134-8.

Number 16   *Cutting across the Lands: An Annotated Bibliography on Natural Resource Management and Community Development in Indonesia, the Philippines, and Malaysia*, ed. Eveline Ferretti. 1997. 329 pp. ISBN 0-87727-133-X.

Number 15   *The Revolution Falters: The Left in Philippine Politics after 1986*, ed. Patricio N. Abinales. 1996. Second printing, 2002. 182 pp. ISBN 0-87727-132-1.

Number 14   *Being Kammu: My Village, My Life*, Damrong Tayanin. 1994. 138 pp., 22 tables, illus., maps. ISBN 0-87727-130-5.

Number 13   *The American War in Vietnam*, ed. Jayne Werner, David Hunt. 1993. 132 pp. ISBN 0-87727-131-3.

Number 12   *The Voice of Young Burma*, Aye Kyaw. 1993. 92 pp. ISBN 0-87727-129-1.

Number 11   *The Political Legacy of Aung San*, ed. Josef Silverstein. Revised edition 1993. 169 pp. ISBN 0-87727-128-3.

Number 10   *Studies on Vietnamese Language and Literature: A Preliminary Bibliography*, Nguyen Dinh Tham. 1992. 227 pp. ISBN 0-87727-127-5.

Number 8   *From PKI to the Comintern, 1924–1941: The Apprenticeship of the Malayan Communist Party*, Cheah Boon Kheng. 1992. 147 pp. ISBN 0-87727-125-9.

Number 7   *Intellectual Property and US Relations with Indonesia, Malaysia, Singapore, and Thailand*, Elisabeth Uphoff. 1991. 67 pp. ISBN 0-87727-124-0.

Number 6   *The Rise and Fall of the Communist Party of Burma (CPB)*, Bertil Lintner. 1990. 124 pp. 26 illus., 14 maps. ISBN 0-87727-123-2.

Number 5   *Japanese Relations with Vietnam: 1951–1987*, Masaya Shiraishi. 1990. 174 pp. ISBN 0-87727-122-4.

Number 3   *Postwar Vietnam: Dilemmas in Socialist Development*, ed. Christine White, David Marr. 1988. 2nd printing 1993. 260 pp. ISBN 0-87727-120-8.

Number 2   *The Dobama Movement in Burma (1930–1938)*, Khin Yi. 1988. 160 pp. ISBN 0-87727-118-6.

Cornell Modern Indonesia Project Publications

Number 75   *A Tour of Duty: Changing Patterns of Military Politics in Indonesia in the 1990s*. Douglas Kammen and Siddharth Chandra. 1999. 99 pp. ISBN 0-87763-049-6.

Number 74   *The Roots of Acehnese Rebellion 1989–1992*, Tim Kell. 1995. 103 pp. ISBN 0-87763-040-2.

Number 73   *"White Book" on the 1992 General Election in Indonesia,* trans. Dwight King. 1994. 72 pp. ISBN 0-87763-039-9.

Number 72   *Popular Indonesian Literature of the Qur'an,* Howard M. Federspiel. 1994. 170 pp. ISBN 0-87763-038-0.

Number 71   *A Javanese Memoir of Sumatra, 1945–1946: Love and Hatred in the Liberation War,* Takao Fusayama. 1993. 150 pp. ISBN 0-87763-037-2.

Number 70   *East Kalimantan: The Decline of a Commercial Aristocracy,* Burhan Magenda. 1991. 120 pp. ISBN 0-87763-036-4.

Number 69   *The Road to Madiun: The Indonesian Communist Uprising of 1948,* Elizabeth Ann Swift. 1989. 120 pp. ISBN 0-87763-035-6.

Number 68   *Intellectuals and Nationalism in Indonesia: A Study of the Following Recruited by Sutan Sjahrir in Occupation Jakarta,* J. D. Legge. 1988. 159 pp. ISBN 0-87763-034-8.

Number 67   *Indonesia Free: A Biography of Mohammad Hatta,* Mavis Rose. 1987. 252 pp. ISBN 0-87763-033-X.

Number 66   *Prisoners at Kota Cane,* Leon Salim, trans. Audrey Kahin. 1986. 112 pp. ISBN 0-87763-032-1.

Number 65   *The Kenpeitai in Java and Sumatra,* trans. Barbara G. Shimer, Guy Hobbs, intro. Theodore Friend. 1986. 80 pp. ISBN 0-87763-031-3.

Number 64   *Suharto and His Generals: Indonesia's Military Politics, 1975–1983,* David Jenkins. 1984. 4th printing 1997. 300 pp. ISBN 0-87763-030-5.

Number 62   *Interpreting Indonesian Politics: Thirteen Contributions to the Debate, 1964–1981,* ed. Benedict Anderson, Audrey Kahin, intro. Daniel S. Lev. 1982. 3rd printing 1991. 172 pp. ISBN 0-87763-028-3.

Number 60   *The Minangkabau Response to Dutch Colonial Rule in the Nineteenth Century,* Elizabeth E. Graves. 1981. 157 pp. ISBN 0-87763-000-3.

Number 59   *Breaking the Chains of Oppression of the Indonesian People: Defense Statement at His Trial on Charges of Insulting the Head of State, Bandung, June 7–10, 1979,* Heri Akhmadi. 1981. 201 pp. ISBN 0-87763-001-1.

Number 57   *Permesta: Half a Rebellion,* Barbara S. Harvey. 1977. 174 pp. ISBN 0-87763-003-8.

Number 55   *Report from Banaran: The Story of the Experiences of a Soldier during the War of Independence,* Maj. Gen. T. B. Simatupang. 1972. 186 pp. ISBN 0-87763-005-4.

Number 52   *A Preliminary Analysis of the October 1 1965, Coup in Indonesia (Prepared in January 1966),* Benedict R. Anderson, Ruth T. McVey, assist. Frederick P. Bunnell. 1971. 3rd printing 1990. 174 pp. ISBN 0-87763-008-9.

Number 51   *The Putera Reports: Problems in Indonesian-Japanese War-Time Cooperation,* Mohammad Hatta, trans., intro. William H. Frederick. 1971. 114 pp. ISBN 0-87763-009-7.

Number 50   *Schools and Politics: The Kaum Muda Movement in West Sumatra (1927–1933),* Taufik Abdullah. 1971. 257 pp. ISBN 0-87763-010-0.

Number 49   *The Foundation of the Partai Muslimin Indonesia,* K. E. Ward. 1970. 75 pp. ISBN 0-87763-011-9.

Number 48   *Nationalism, Islam and Marxism*, Soekarno, intro. Ruth T. McVey. 1970. 2nd printing 1984. 62 pp. ISBN 0-87763-012-7.

Number 43   *State and Statecraft in Old Java: A Study of the Later Mataram Period, 16th to 19th Century*, Soemarsaid Moertono. Revised edition 1981. 180 pp. ISBN 0-87763-017-8.

Number 39   Preliminary Checklist of Indonesian Imprints (1945-1949), John M. Echols. 186 pp. ISBN 0-87763-025-9.

Number 37   *Mythology and the Tolerance of the Javanese*, Benedict R. O'G. Anderson. 2nd edition, 1996. Reprinted 2004. 104 pp., 65 illus. ISBN 0-87763-041-0.

Number 25   *The Communist Uprisings of 1926–1927 in Indonesia: Key Documents*, ed., intro. Harry J. Benda, Ruth T. McVey. 1960. 2nd printing 1969. 177 pp. ISBN 0-87763-024-0.

Number 7   *The Soviet View of the Indonesian Revolution*, Ruth T. McVey. 1957. 3rd printing 1969. 90 pp. ISBN 0-87763-018-6.

Number 6   *The Indonesian Elections of 1955*, Herbert Feith. 1957. 2nd printing 1971. 91 pp. ISBN 0-87763-020-8.

Translation Series

Volume 4   *Approaching Suharto's Indonesia from the Margins*, ed. Takashi Shiraishi. 1994. 153 pp. ISBN 0-87727-403-7.

Volume 3   *The Japanese in Colonial Southeast Asia*, ed. Saya Shiraishi, Takashi Shiraishi. 1993. 172 pp. ISBN 0-87727-402-9.

Volume 2   *Indochina in the 1940s and 1950s*, ed. Takashi Shiraishi, Motoo Furuta. 1992. 196 pp. ISBN 0-87727-401-0.

Volume 1   *Reading Southeast Asia*, ed. Takashi Shiraishi. 1990. 188 pp.

ISBN 0-87727-400-2.

Language Texts

INDONESIAN

Beginning Indonesian through Self-Instruction, John U. Wolff, Dédé Oetomo, Daniel Fietkiewicz. 3rd revised edition 1992. Vol. 1. 115 pp. ISBN 0-87727-529-7. Vol. 2. 434 pp. ISBN 0-87727-530-0. Vol. 3. 473 pp. ISBN 0-87727-531-9.

Indonesian Readings, John U. Wolff. 1978. 4th printing 1992. 480 pp. ISBN 0-87727-517-3

Indonesian Conversations, John U. Wolff. 1978. 3rd printing 1991. 297 pp. ISBN 0-87727-516-5

Formal Indonesian, John U. Wolff. 2nd revised edition 1986. 446 pp. ISBN 0-87727-515-7

TAGALOG

Pilipino through Self-Instruction, John U. Wolff, Maria Theresa C. Centeno, Der-Hwa V. Rau. 1991. Vol. 1. 342 pp. ISBN 0-87727—525-4. Vol. 2. 378 pp. ISBN 0-87727-526-2. Vol 3. 431 pp. ISBN 0-87727-527-0. Vol. 4. 306 pp. ISBN 0-87727-528-9.

THAI

A. U. A. Language Center Thai Course, J. Marvin Brown. Originally published by the American University Alumni Association Language Center, 1974. Reissued by Cornell Southeast Asia Program, 1991, 1992. Book 1. 267 pp. ISBN 0-87727-506-8. Book 2. 288 pp. ISBN 0-87727-507-6. Book 3. 247 pp. ISBN 0-87727-508-4.

A. U. A. Language Center Thai Course, Reading and Writing Text (mostly reading), 1979. Reissued 1997. 164 pp. ISBN 0-87727-511-4.

A. U. A. Language Center Thai Course, Reading and Writing Workbook (mostly writing), 1979. Reissued 1997. 99 pp. ISBN 0-87727-512-2.

KHMER

Cambodian System of Writing and Beginning Reader, Franklin E. Huffman. Originally published by Yale University Press, 1970. Reissued by Cornell Southeast Asia Program, 4th printing 2002. 365 pp. ISBN 0-300-01314-0.

Modern Spoken Cambodian, Franklin E. Huffman, assist. Charan Promchan, Chhom-Rak Thong Lambert. Originally published by Yale University Press, 1970. Reissued by Cornell Southeast Asia Program, 3rd printing 1991. 451 pp. ISBN 0-300-01316-7.

Intermediate Cambodian Reader, ed. Franklin E. Huffman, assist. Im Proum. Originally published by Yale University Press, 1972. Reissued by Cornell Southeast Asia Program, 1988. 499 pp. ISBN 0-300-01552-6.

Cambodian Literary Reader and Glossary, Franklin E. Huffman, Im Proum. Originally published by Yale University Press, 1977. Reissued by Cornell Southeast Asia Program, 1988. 494 pp. ISBN 0-300-02069-4.

HMONG

White Hmong-English Dictionary, Ernest E. Heimbach. 1969. 8th printing, 2002. 523 pp. ISBN 0-87727-075-9.

VIETNAMESE

Intermediate Spoken Vietnamese, Franklin E. Huffman, Tran Trong Hai. 1980. 3rd printing 1994. ISBN 0-87727-500-9.

* * *

Southeast Asian Studies: Reorientations. Craig J. Reynolds and Ruth McVey. Frank H. Golay Lectures 2 & 3. 70 pp. ISBN 0-87727-301-4.

Javanese Literature in Surakarta Manuscripts, Nancy K. Florida. Vol. 1, *Introduction and Manuscripts of the Karaton Surakarta*. 1993. 410 pp. Frontispiece, illustrations. Hard cover, ISBN 0-87727-602-1, Paperback, ISBN 0-87727-603-X. Vol. 2, *Manuscripts of the Mangkunagaran Palace.* 2000. 576 pp. Frontispiece, illustrations. Paperback, ISBN 0-87727-604-8.

Sbek Thom: Khmer Shadow Theater. Pech Tum Kravel, trans. Sos Kem, ed. Thavro Phim, Sos Kem, Martin Hatch. 1996. 363 pp., 153 photographs. ISBN 0-87727-620-X.

In the Mirror: Literature and Politics in Siam in the American Era, ed. Benedict R. O'G. Anderson, trans. Benedict R. O'G. Anderson, Ruchira Mendiones. 1985. 2nd printing 1991. 303 pp. Paperback. ISBN 974-210-380-1.

To order, please contact:

Cornell University
Southeast Asia Program Publications
95 Brown Road
Box 1004
Ithaca NY 14850

Online: http://www.einaudi.cornell.edu/southeastasia/publications/
Tel: 1-877-865-2432 (Toll free – U.S.)
Fax: (607) 255-7534

E-mail: SEAP-Pubs@cornell.edu
Orders must be prepaid by check or credit card (VISA, MasterCard, Discover).